UNDERSTANDING OPTIONS

UNDERSTANDING OPTIONS

Robert Kolb

John Wiley & Sons, Inc.

New York • Chichester • Brisbane • Toronto • Singapore

Portions of this book have been previously published under the titles *Understanding Swaps,* South-Western, 1989, and *The Swaps Market, Second Edition,* Kolb Publishing, 1993.

Library of Congress Cataloging-in-Publication Data:

Kolb, Robert W.
    Understanding options / Robert Kolb.
       p.   cm. — (Wiley marketplace book series)
    Includes bibliographical references and index.
    ISBN 0-471-08554-5
    1. Options (Finance) I. Title. II. Series.
  HG6024.A3K653   1995
  332.63'228—dc20
                                                    94-34050

To Lori
upon whom I exercised
the call option I held on her
before she exercised
the put option she held on me

Preface

In *Understanding Options*, we build our knowledge from the simple to the more complex. Chapter 1 introduces the essential institutional features of the U.S. options market. Chapter 2 begins the analytical portion of the book by exploring popular trading strategies and their payoffs at expiration. When an option is at expiration, there is no difference between an American and European option. (An American option can be exercised at any time; a European option can be exercised only at expiration.) Also, it is easy to specify what the price of an option must be when it is about to expire. Chapter 3 uses no-arbitrage arguments to place rational bounds on options prices. We assume that traders in options markets are moneyhungry and not foolish. Such traders will exploit any trading opportunity that offers a sure profit with no risk and no investment. By assuming that no such profit opportunities exist, we learn much about what options prices can rationally prevail. The bounds developed in Chapter 3 follow solely on our assumptions of greed and the absence of stupidity. These boundaries do not provide exact options prices, but they specify the range in which the exact price must lie.

To specify the exact price that an option should have requires a model of how stock prices can move. Chapter 4 develops formal pricing models for European options. The price of an option depends on the characteristics of the underlying instrument, notably upon the way in which the price of the underlying instrument can vary. We consider the Binomial Model and eventually elaborate this model into the Black–Scholes Model. Chapter 4 also explores the Merton Model. Thus, in Chapter 4 we begin by assuming that the stock price can change only once before the option expires and that the stock price can rise or fall only by a certain percentage. Next, we allow slightly more realism by allowing the stock price to change more frequently before the option expires. Finally, we allow the stock price to change continuously. Under each circumstance, we can say precisely what the option price should be. By following this building block approach, we come to understand the factors that affect options prices. In addition, we can understand the principles of options pricing without suffering mathematical fatigue. At the end of Chapter 4, we are able to specify prices for options that conform very closely to the prices we observe in the marketplace. Chapter 5 is a companion to Chapter 4 in that it explores the options sensitivities of the Black–Scholes and Merton models. These sensitivities (DELTA, THETA, VEGA, GAMMA, and RHO) are extremely important in using options to hedge or in controlling the risk of speculative strategies.

Chapter 6 develops an extensive treatment of American options. It includes coverage of American puts, the exact American call option pricing formula, the analytic approximation approach to pricing American options, and the binomial model as it applies to options with and without dividends. The coverage of the binomial model for American options with dividends includes continuous dividend yields, episodic dividend yields, and cash dividends.

Chapter 7 explores stock index options, foreign currency options, and options on futures. In doing so, it covers both European and American options. The chapter begins by focusing on European options and the application of the Black–Scholes and Merton models to these options. Soon the discussion shifts to American options, and the chapter applies the analytic approximation technique, the exact American call option pricing model, and the binomial model to pricing American options with and without dividends.

Chapter 8 shows that the principles of options pricing can be extended to analyze corporate securities. The chapter considers the options features of common stock, straight bonds, convertible bonds, callable bonds, and warrants. One of the most useful features of this chapter is that it illustrates the power of the options approach to the world of finance.

Acknowledgments

The preparation of this book has benefitted from the assistance of a number of people. Andrea Coens provided timely editing and many useful suggestions about the book. Phil Rizika and Adam Carlin reviewed the manuscript and software, and Evelyn Gosnell prepared the graphical illustrations.

The students in my futures and options classes in Fall 1993 studied from the pageproofs of this book, giving me a chance to test it in the classroom before publication. A large number of scholars around the country contributed their time and effort to help improve the book. The following individuals commented on the book and made numerous suggestions for improvement. My profound thanks to them all:

Peter Alonzi
Chicago Board of Trade

Fernando Alvarez
Babson College

Michael Auster
University of Nevada

Ron Best
University of South Alabama

Laurence E. Blose
University of North Carolina

Gerald Buetow
James Madison University

Joe Brocato
Tarleton State University

Anthony Byrd
Tulane University

Alyce Rita Campbell
University of Oregon

Chao Chen
California State University

Ren-Raw Chen
Rutgers University

Ray Chiang
University of Miami

Jin Wook Choi
*Chicago Institute of
Futures and Options*

Kewn Victor Chow
West Virginia University

Andreas Christofi
Azusa Pacific University

Dennis Debrecht
Carroll College

Karen Craft Denning
West Virginia University

David Ding
*Nanyang Technological
University–Singapore*

Richard J. Dowen
Northern Illinois University

Don Fehrs
University of Notre Dame

James H. Filkins
University of St. Thomas

Hung Gay Fung
University of Baltimore

Dean Furbush
Economists Incorporated

Gerry Gay
Georgia State University

Nicolas Gressis
Wright State University

G. D'Anne Hancock
University of Missouri

T. Harikumar
University of Alaska

Delvin Hawley
University of Mississippi

Shantaram Hegde
University of Connecticut

Anthony Herbst
University of Texas

Joanne Hill
Goldman Sachs

Marcus Ingram
Clark Atlanta University

Ameeta Jaiswal
University of St. Thomas

Kurt R. Jesswein
Laredo State University

Joan Junkus
DePaul University

Kandice Kahl
Clemson University

Dongcheol Kim
Rutgers University

Dorothy Koehl
University of Puget Sound

Gary Koppenhaver
Iowa State University

William Kracaw
Pennsylvania State University

Paul Laux
University of Texas—Austin

C. Jevons Lee
Tulane University

Chun Lee
Southern Illinois University

Jae Ha Lee
University of Oklahoma

Jay Marchand
Westminster College

Michael B. Madaris
University of Southern Mississippi

A.G. Malliaris
Loyola University of Chicago

David Martin
Davidson College

Robert Mooradian
University of Florida

R. Charles Moyer
Wake Forest University

Dec Mullarkey
Boston College

Richard Osbourne
American University

Jayendu Patel
Harvard University

Ramon Rabinovitch
University of Houston

Sailesh Ramamurtie
Georgia State University

Cyrus Ramezani
University of Wisconsin

Dick Rendleman
University of North Carolina

Bruce Resnick
Indiana University

Tom Schneeweis
University of Massachusetts

Robert Schweitzer
University of Delaware

R. Stephen Sears
Texas Tech University

Bipin Shah
University of Nebraska

Kuldeep Shastri
University of Pittsburgh

Bruce Sherrick
University of Illinois

Sandeep Singh
State University of New York

William E. Stein
Texas A & M University

Hans R. Stoll
Vanderbilt University

Steve Swidler
University of Texas

Alex Tabarrok
George Mason University

Russ Taussig
University of Hawaii

Kashi Nath Tiwari
Kennesaw State College

Alex Triantis
University of Wisconsin

George Tsetskos
Drexel University

Anne Fremault Vila
Boston University

Joseph Vu
DePaul University

James Wansley
University of Tennessee

Brian Webb
Indiana University

Paul Weller
University of Iowa

Tony R. Wingler
University of North Carolina

John Yeoman
University of Georgia

Jin Zhenhu
University of Houston

Contents

6 American Options Pricing   235

7 Options on Stock Indexes, Foreign Currency, and Futures   271

1
The Options Market

INTRODUCTION

Everyone has options. When buying a car we can add more equipment to the automobile that is "optional at extra cost." In this sense, an option is a choice. This book examines options in financial markets. This is a very specific type of option—an option created through a financial contract. This chapter defines the options created by these financial contracts, and shows how participants in financial markets can use these special options contracts.

Options have played a role in security markets for many years, although no one can be certain how long. Initially, options were created by individualized contracts between two parties. However, until recently there was no organized exchange for trading options. The development of options exchanges stimulated greater interest and more active trading of options. In many respects, the recent history of options trading can be regarded as an options revolution. This chapter considers the options exchanges and the well-defined options contracts that trade on these exchanges.

In modern options trading, an individual can contact a broker and trade an option on an exchange in a matter of moments. This chapter explains how orders flow from an individual to the exchange, and how the order is executed and confirmed for the trader. At first, the options exchanges only traded options on stocks. Now exchanges trade options on a wide variety of underlying goods, such as bonds, futures contracts, and foreign currencies. The chapter concludes with a brief consideration of these diverse types of options.

The importance of options goes well beyond the profit-motivated trading that is most visible to the public. Today, sophisticated institutional traders use options to execute extremely complex strategies. For instance, large pension funds and investment banking firms trade options in conjunction with stock and bond portfolios to control risk and capture additional profits. Corporations use options to execute their financing strategies and to hedge unwanted risks that they could not avoid in any other way. Options research has advanced in step with the exploding options market. Scholars have found that there is an options way of thinking that allows many financial decisions to be analyzed using an options framework. Together, these developments constitute an options revolution.

WHAT IS AN OPTION?

Every exchange-traded option is either a **call option** or a **put option**.[1] The owner of a call option has the right to purchase the underlying good at a specific price, and this right lasts until a specific date. The owner of a put option has the right to sell the underlying good at a specific price, and this right lasts until a specific date. In short, the owner of a call option can call the underlying good away from someone else. Likewise, the owner of a put option can put the good to someone else by making the opposite party buy the good. To acquire these rights, owners of options buy them from other traders by paying the price, or premium, to a seller.

Options are created only by buying and selling. Therefore, for every owner of an option there is a seller. The seller of an option is also known as an **option writer**. The seller receives payment for an option from the purchaser. In exchange for the payment received, the seller confers rights to the option owner. The seller of a call option receives payment and, in exchange, gives the owner of a call option the right to purchase the underlying good at a specific price with this right lasting for a specific time. The seller of a put option receives payment from the purchaser and promises to buy the underlying good at a specific price for a specific time, if the owner of the put option so chooses.

In these agreements, all rights lie with the owner of the option. In purchasing an option, the buyer makes payments and receives rights to buy or sell the underlying good on specific terms. In selling an option, the seller receives payment and promises to sell or purchase the underlying good on specific terms—at the discretion of the option owner. With put and call options and buyers and sellers, four basic positions are possible. Notice that the owner of an option has all the rights. After all, that is what the owner purchases. The seller of an option has all the obligations, because the seller undertakes obligations in exchange for payment.

Every option has an underlying good. Through most of this book, we will speak of a share of stock as the underlying good. However, all the principles that we will develop apply to options on different underlying goods. The call writer gives the purchaser the right to demand the underlying good from the writer. However, the writer of a call need not own the underlying good when he or she writes the option. If a seller writes a call and does not own the underlying good, the call is a **naked call**. If the writer owns the underlying good, he has sold a **covered call**. When a trader writes a naked call, he undertakes the obligation of immediately securing the underlying good and delivering it if the purchaser of the call chooses to exercise the call.

AN OPTION EXAMPLE

Consider an option with a share of XYZ stock as the underlying good. Assume that today is March 1 and that XYZ shares trade at $110. The market, we assume, trades a call option to buy a share of XYZ at $100 with this right lasting until August 15 and the price of this option being $15. In this example, the owner of a call must pay $100 to acquire the stock. This $100 price is called the **exercise price** or the **striking price**. The price of the option, or the **option premium**, is $15. The option expires in 5.5 months, which gives 168 days until expiration.

If a trader buys the call option, he pays $15 and receives the right to purchase a share of XYZ stock by paying an additional $100, if he so chooses, by August 15. The seller of the option receives $15, and she promises to sell a share of XYZ for $100 if the owner of the call chooses to buy before August 15. Notice that the price of the option, the option premium, is paid when the option trades. The premium the seller receives is hers to keep whether or not the owner of the call decides to exercise the option. If the owner of the call exercises his option, he will pay $100 no matter what the current price of XYZ stock may be. If the owner of the option exercises his option, the seller of the option will receive the $100 exercise price when she delivers the stock as she promised.

At the same time, puts will trade on XYZ. Consider a put with a striking price of $100 trading on March 1 that also expires on August 15. Assume that the price of the put is $5. If a trader purchases a put, he pays $5. In exchange, he receives the right to sell a share of XYZ for $100 at any time until August 15. The seller of the put receives $5, and she promises to buy the share of XYZ for $100 if the owner of the put option chooses to sell before August 15.

In both the put and call examples, the payment by the purchaser is gone forever at the time the option trades. The seller of the option receives the payment and keeps it, whatever the owner of the option decides to do. If the owner of the call exercises his option, then he pays the exercise price as an additional amount and receives a share. Likewise, if the owner of the put exercises his option, then he surrenders the share and receives the exercise price as an additional amount. The owner of the option may choose never to exercise. In that case, the option will expire on August 15. The payment the seller receives is hers to keep whether or not the owner exercises. If the owner chooses not to exercise, the seller has a profit equal to the premium received and does not have to perform under the terms of the option contract. Table 1.1 shows the disposition of stock options in 1992. It is a good guide to the frequency with which options are disposed of by exercise, by sale, or by expiring worthless. Approximately half are sold and another third expire worthless. A relatively small percentage of options are exercised.

MONEYNESS

"Moneyness" is an option concept that is as important as the word is awkward. It refers to the potential profit or loss from the immediate exercise of an option. An option may be **in-the-money, out-of-the-money**, or **at-the-money**.

A call option is in-the-money if the stock price exceeds the exercise price. For example, a call option with an exercise price of $100 on a stock trading at $110 is $10 in-the-money. A call option is out-of-the-money if the stock price is less than the exercise price. For example, if the stock is at $110 and the exercise price on a call is $115, the call is $5 out-of-the-money. A call option is at-the-money if the stock price equals (or is very near to) the exercise price.

Table 1.1   Disposition of Equity Options, 1992

Disposition	Percentage Disposition	
	Calls	Puts
Exercise	8.4	12.6
Sale	57.0	49.8
Long expired worthless	34.7	37.6

Source: Chicago Board Options Exchange, *Market Statistics,* 1992.

A put option is in-the-money if the stock price is below the exercise price. As an example, consider a put option with an exercise price of $70 on a stock that is worth $60. The put is $10 in-the-money, because the immediate exercise of the put would give a $10 cash inflow. Similarly, if the put on the same stock had an exercise price of $55, the put would be $5 out-of-the-money. If the put had an exercise price equal to the stock price, the put would be at-the-money. Puts and calls can also be **deep-in-the-money** or **deep-out-of-the-money**, if the cash flows from an immediate exercise would be large in the speaker's judgment.

AMERICAN AND EUROPEAN OPTIONS

There are two fundamental kinds of options: the American option and the European option. An **American option** permits the owner to exercise at any time before or at expiration. The owner of a **European option** can exercise only at expiration. Thus, the two kinds of options differ because the American option permits early exercise. To this point, we have considered option values only at expiration. If the option is at expiration, American and European options will have the same value. Both can be exercised immediately or be allowed to expire worthless. Prior to expiration, we will see that the two options are conceptually distinct. Further, they may have different values under certain circumstances. In this chapter, and through the remainder of the book, we will need to distinguish the principles that apply to each kind of option.

Consider any two options that are just alike, except one is an American option and the other is a European option. By saying that the two options are just alike, we mean that they have the same underlying stock, the same exercise price, and the same time remaining until expiration. The American option gives its owner all the rights and privileges that the owner of the European option possesses. However, the owner of the American option also has the right to exercise the option before expiration if he desires. From these considerations, we can see that the American option must be worth at least as much as the European option.

The owner of an American option can treat the option as a European option just by deciding not to exercise until expiration. Therefore, the American option cannot be worth less than the European option. However, the American option can be worth more. The American option will be worth more if it is desirable to exercise earlier. Under certain circumstances, which we explore later, the right to exercise before expiration can be valuable. In this case, the American option will be worth more than the otherwise identical European option.

In some cases, the right to exercise before expiration will be worthless. For these situations, the American option will have the same value as the European option. In general, the European option is simpler and easier to analyze. However, in actual markets, most options are American options. This is true both in the United States and throughout the world. We should not associate the names "American" and "European" with geographic locations. In the present context, the names simply refer to the time at which holders can exercise these options.

WHY TRADE OPTIONS?

Options trading today is more popular than ever before. For the investor, options serve a number of important roles. First, many investors trade options to speculate on the price movements of the underlying stock. However, investors could merely trade the stock itself. As we will see, trading the option instead of the underlying stock can offer a number of advantages. Call options are always cheaper than the underlying stock, so it takes less money to trade calls. Generally, but not universally, put options are also cheaper than the underlying goods. In relative terms, the option price is more volatile than the price of the underlying stock, so investors can get more price action per dollar of investment by investing in options instead of investing in the stock itself.

Options are extremely popular among sophisticated investors who hold large stock portfolios. Accordingly, institutional investors, such as mutual funds and pension funds, are prime users of the options market. By trading options in conjunction with their stock portfolios, investors can carefully adjust the risk and return characteristics of their entire investment. As we will see, a sophisticated trader can use options to increase or decrease the risk of an existing stock portfolio. For example, it is possible to combine a risky stock and a risky option to form a riskless combined position that performs like a risk-free bond.[2]

Many investors prefer to trade options rather than stocks in order to save transaction costs, avoid tax exposure, and avoid stock market restrictions.[3] We already mentioned that some investors trade options to achieve the same risk exposure with less capital. In many instances, traders can use options to take a particular risk position and pay lower transaction costs than stocks would require. Likewise, specific provisions of the tax code may favor options trading over trading the underlying stock. If different traders face different tax schedules, one may find advantage in buying options and another may find advantage in selling options, relative to trading stocks. Finally, the stock and options markets have their own institutional rules. Differences in these rules may stimulate options trading. For example, selling stock short is highly restricted.[4] By trading in the options market, it is possible to replicate a short sale of stock and avoid some stock market restrictions.[5]

THE OPTIONS CONTRACT

One of the major reasons for the success of options exchanges is that they offer standardized contracts. In a financial market, traders want to be able to trade a good quickly and at a fair price. They can do this if the market is **liquid**. A liquid market provides an efficient and cost-effective trading mechanism with a high volume of trading. Standardizing the options contract has helped promote liquidity. The standardized contract has a specific size and expiration date. Trading on the exchange occurs at certain well-publicized times, so traders know when they will be able to find other traders in the marketplace. The exchange standardizes the exercise prices at which options will trade. With fewer exercise prices, there will be more trading available at a given exercise price. This too promotes liquidity.

Each options contract is for 100 shares of the underlying stock. Exercise prices are specified at intervals of $10, $5, or $2.50, depending on the share price. For example, XYZ trades in the $100 range, and XYZ options have exercise prices spaced at $5 intervals. Every option has a specified expiration month. The option expires on the Saturday after the third Friday in the exercise month. Trading in the option ceases on the third Friday, but the owner may exercise the option on the final Saturday.

THE OPTIONS MARKET

In this section, we consider the most important facets of the options market in the United States. We begin by considering the exchanges where options trade. We then consider an extended example to see how to read option prices as they appear in the *Wall Street Journal*. We conclude this section by analyzing the market activity in the different types of options that are traded on the various exchanges.

Reading Options Prices

Table 1.2 shows typical price quotations for options on a common stock from a U.S. newspaper. Prices are for January 26 for trading options on the stock of XYZ corporation. On that day, XYZ closed at 96 7/8 per share. The table shows listings for XYZ options with striking prices of $90, 95, 100, and 105. It would not be unusual for other striking prices

Table 1.2 Options Price Quotations

XYZ		Calls			Puts		
96 7/8		FEB	MAR	APR	FEB	MAR	APR
	90	6 5/8	s	9 1/8	5/8	s	1 3/8
	95	2 7/8	4 3/8	5 1/2	1 5/8	2 5/8	3 1/8
	100	7/8	1 7/8	3 1/8	4 5/8	r	6 1/4
	105	1/4	13/16	1 5/8	9 1/2	r	11

to be represented as well. Options expire in February, March, and April of the same year, and the table shows option prices for both puts and calls. An "r" indicates that the option was not traded on the day for which prices are reported, while an "s" shows that the specific option is not listed for trading.[6]

As an example, consider the call option with a striking price of $100 that expires in March. This option has a price of $1 7/8 or $1.875. This is the price of the call for a single share. However, each options contract is written for 100 shares. Therefore, to purchase this option, the buyer would pay $187.50 for one contract. Owning this call option would give the buyer the right to purchase 100 shares of XYZ at $100 per share until the option expires in March.

We can learn much from a careful consideration of the price relation-ships revealed in the table. First, notice that option prices are generally higher the longer the time until the option expires. This is true for both calls and puts. Other things being equal, the longer one has the option to buy or sell, the better. Thus, we expect options with longer terms to expiration to be worth more. Second, for a call, the lower the striking price, the more the call option is worth. For a call, the striking price is the amount the call holder must pay to secure the stock. The lower the amount one must pay, the better; therefore, the lower the exercise price, the more the call is worth. Third, for a put option, the higher the striking price, the more the put is worth. For a put, the striking price is the value the put holder receives when he exercises his option to sell the put. Therefore, the more the put entitles its owner to receive, the greater the value of the put. A moment's reflection shows that these simple rela-tionships make sense. Later chapters explore these and similar relation-ships in detail.

Options Exchanges

Trading options undoubtedly grew up with the development of financial markets. In the nineteenth century, investors traded options in an informal market; however, the market was subject to considerable corruption. For example, some sellers of options would refuse to perform as obligated. In the twentieth century, the United States developed a more orderly market called the Put and Call Broker and Dealers Association. Member firms acted to bring buyers and sellers of options together. However, this was an over-the-counter market. The market had no central exchange floor, and standardization of options contract terms was not complete. The lack of an exchange and imperfect standardization of the contracts kept this options market from flourishing.

In 1973, the Chicago Board of Trade, a large futures exchange, created the Chicago Board Options Exchange (CBOE). The CBOE is an organized options exchange that trades highly standardized options contracts. It opened on April 26, 1973, to trade calls; put trading began in 1977. Since 1973, other exchanges have begun to trade options, with annual trading of about 300,000,000 options.

Trading of options on organized exchanges in the United States embraces a number of different underlying instruments. First among these is the stock option—an option on an individual share of common stock issued by a corporation. While we focus most closely on this type of option for the majority of this book, there are other important classes of options with very different underlying instruments. Options trade on various financial indexes. These indexes can measure the performance of groups of stocks, or precious metals, or any other good for which an index can be constructed as a measure of value. Options also trade on foreign currencies. For these foreign currency options, the underlying good is a unit of a foreign currency, such as a Japanese yen, and traders buy and sell call and put options on the yen, as well as other currencies. Another major type of underlying good is a futures contract. For an option on futures, also known as futures options, the underlying good is a position in a futures contract. As we will see, this is an important class of options. Futures contracts are written on a wide variety of goods, such as agricultural products, precious metals, petroleum products, stock indexes, foreign currency, and debt instruments. Therefore, futures options by themselves embrace a tremendous diversity of goods.

Table 1.3 lists the principal options exchanges in the United States, and it shows the kinds of options traded on each exchange. The 15 exchanges in Table 1.3 may be classified into three groups depending on whether the primary business of the exchange is the trading of options, stocks, or futures. The Chicago Board Options Exchange (CBOE) deals exclusively in options, and as the leading options exchange in the United States, it trades a wide variety of options. The Philadelphia Stock Exchange (PHLX), the American Stock Exchange (AMEX), the Pacific Stock

Table 1.3 Principal Options Exchanges in the United States

Chicago Board Options Exchange (CBOE)	Options on individual stocks, options on stock indexes, and options on Treasury securities
Philadelphia Stock Exchange (PHLX)	Stocks, futures, and options on individual stocks, currencies, and stock indexes
American Stock Exchange (AMEX)	Stocks, options on individual stocks, and options on stock indexes
Pacific Stock Exchange (PSE)	Options on individual stocks and a stock index
New York Stock Exchange (NYSE)	Stocks and options on individual stocks and a stock index
Chicago Board of Trade (CBOT)	Futures, options on futures for agricultural goods, precious metals, stock indexes, and debt instruments
Chicago Mercantile Exchange (CME)	Futures, options on futures for agricultural goods, stock indexes, debt instruments, and currencies
Coffee, Sugar and Cocoa Exchange (CSCE)	Futures and options on agricultural futures
Commodity Exchange (COMEX)	Futures and options on futures for metals
Kansas City Board of Trade (KCBT)	Futures and options on agricultural futures
MidAmerica Commodity Exchange (MIDAM)	Futures and options on futures for agricultural goods and precious metals
Minneapolis Grain Exchange (MGE)	Futures and options on agricultural futures
New York Cotton Exchange (NYCE)	Futures and options on agricultural, currency, and debt instrument futures
New York Futures Exchange (NYFE)	Futures and options on stock indexes
New York Mercantile Exchange (NYME)	Futures and options on energy futures

Exchange (PSE), and the New York Stock Exchange (NYSE) are principally stock markets that also trade options. The underlying instruments for the options at these exchanges go far beyond stocks, as we will see. The third group consists of futures exchanges, such as the Chicago Board of Trade (CBOT), the Chicago Mercantile Exchange (CME), the Coffee, Sugar and Cocoa Exchange (CSCE), the Kansas City Board of Trade (KCBT), the MidAmerica Exchange (MIDAM), the New York Cotton

Exchange (NYCE), the New York Futures Exchange (NYFE), and the New York Mercantile Exchange (NYME). These futures exchanges trade options on futures exclusively, and they tend to trade options on the futures contracts in which they specialize.

Exchange Diversity and Market Statistics

In this section, we consider the options market in more detail. Table 1.4 shows the volume of all exchange-traded options in the United States in 1992 by the type of option—stock, index, foreign currency, and options on futures. Stock options continue to lead in terms of volume, but they are closely followed by index options. Options on futures are also widely traded, but foreign currency options account for only about 4 percent of all options traded.[7]

Stock Options. Options on individual stocks trade on the Chicago Board Options Exchange and four exchanges that principally trade stocks themselves. These same five exchanges trade all options in the United States, except options on futures, which trade on futures exchanges.

Table 1.5 shows the relative importance of these five exchanges (CBOE, AMEX, PHLX, PSE, and NYSE) in options trading. The CBOE clearly dominates with 60 percent of all trading volume. Together, these exchanges traded more than 200 million options contracts in 1992. Regarding these 200 million options, we have already seen that options on stocks are the most prevalent. Table 1.6 shows the distribution of trading volume in stock options among the five exchanges. Again, the CBOE

Table 1.4 Options Volume in the United States by Type of Option

Type of Option	1992 Volume	
	Contracts	Percentage
Stock Options	106,484,452	39.42
Index Options	83,247,081	30.82
Foreign Currency Options	10,826,068	4.01
Options on Futures	69,590,346	25.76
Total	270,147,947	100.00

Source: Chicago Board Options Exchange, *Market Statistics*, 1992; Commodity Futures Trading Commission, *Annual Report*, 1992. Date for options on futures are for the fiscal year ending September 30, 1992.

Table 1.5 Total Options Volume by Exchange, 1992

Exchange	Contract Volume	Percentage
Chicago Board Options Exchange	121,467,604	60.14
American Stock Exchange	42,314,942	20.95
Philadelphia Stock Exchange	22,947,867	11.36
Pacific Stock Exchange	13,066,618	6.47
New York Stock Exchange	2,177,041	1.08
Total	201,974,072	100.00

Source: Chicago Board Options Exchange, *Market Statistics*, 1992.

Table 1.6 Equity Options Volume by Exchange, 1992

Exchange	1992 Volume	Percentage
Chicago Board Options Exchange	44,968,235	42.23
American Stock Exchange	36,067,822	33.87
Philadelphia Stock Exchange	10,408,628	9.77
Pacific Stock Exchange	12,996,923	12.21
New York Stock Exchange	2,042,844	1.92
Total	106,484,452	100.00

Source: Chicago Board Options Exchange, *Market Statistics*, 1992.

dominates with more than 40 percent of the volume, but the American Stock Exchange (AMEX) is also a strong contender.

Figure 1.1 shows a sample of the price quotations for options on individual stocks that appear each day in the *Wall Street Journal*. The first column lists the identifier for the stock and shows the closing stock price for the shares immediately beneath the identifier. The next two columns of data show the exercise price and the month the option expires. The option will expire on a specific date in the expiration month. For the call and the put separately, the quotations show the volume and the final price for the option. Options trade on hundreds of individual stocks.

Index Options. Table 1.7 shows the distribution of trading in index options by exchange. The lead of the CBOE is overwhelming. Most index options are based on various stock indexes. The most successful single index contract is based on the S&P 100 and trades at the CBOE. In 1992, the CBOE traded more than 60 million S&P 100 option contracts. While

MOST ACTIVE CONTRACTS

Option/Strike	Vol	Exch	Last	Net Chg	a-Close	Open Int
ParaCm Oct 80	14,143	CB	2⅜	...	78	...
ParaCm Oct 75	9,709	CB	5¾ +	½	78	12,025
ParaCm Oct 70	8,939	CB	9¾ +	¾	78	13,821
ParaCm Oct 85	7,157	CB	1¹/₁₆	...	78	...
Chase Dec 30	p 5,203	AM	⅜ +	¹/₁₆	36½	2,328
ParaCm Oct 65	5,046	CB	14 +	1	78	18,531
ParaCm Oct 65	p 4,251	CB	⅝ −	⅛	78	5,642
Cisco Oct 40	4,203	XC	⁷/₁₆ −	⁹/₁₆	47¼	4,887
Merck Oct 35	3,826	CB	⁵/₁₆ +	¹/₁₆	31½	23,637
USWst Jan 45	3,750	AM	3⅞ +	⅛	48¼	7,196
USWst Oct 45	3,619	AM	3⅜ +	⅜	48¼	8,505
GenDyn Oct 93	3,512	CB	3⅞	...	90¼	...
ParaCm Oct 70	p 3,494	CB	1⁵/₁₆ −	²/₁₆	78	4,783
ParaCm Oct 75	p 3,274	CB	2⅜ −	¼	78	1,087
ParaCm Nov 75	3,169	CB	6¼ +	¾	78	1,675
Nthrop Nov 30	3,000	CB	5½ −	1⅞	35⅜	...
Intel Oct 65	2,979	AM	3¾ +	1	67¼	8,743
ParaCm Nov 85	2,866	CB	2⅛	...	78	...
Intel Oct 70	2,712	AM	1⅜ +	⁷/₁₆	67¼	5,711
G M Oct 40	p 2,610	CB	¼	...	45⅝	421
ParaCm Nov 80	2,390	CB	4	...	78	...
Amgen Oct 40	2,264	AM	1⁵/₁₆ +	⁹/₁₆	39⅛	8,521
Chryslr Oct 45	2,253	CB	2 +	⁷/₁₆	46¼	11,859
ConAgr Nov 25	2,148	AM	⅞	...	25¼	...
ParaCm Dec 75	2,065	CB	7½ +	1⅛	78	6,766
Deere Oct 70	2,040	AM	1⁹/₁₆ +	⁵/₁₆	68½	2,677
3Com Jan 25	p 2,033	PC	1½ −	³/₁₆	31⅜	450
Carmrk Nov 17½	p 2,010	XC	1½ +	⁷/₁₆	17⅜	10
USWst Jan 45	p 2,000	AM	1⁵/₁₆ −	⅛	21⅛	1,118
Infrmx Nov 15	1,993	XC	6⅛ +	1⅝	21⅛	2,000
Motrla Oct 95	1,980	AM	3⅛ +	⅞	94¾	4,938
Disney Oct 35	p 1,965	XC	⁷/₁₆ +	¹/₁₆	38⅝	3,659
Cisco Oct 50	1,941	XC	1³/₁₆ +	⅜	47¼	6,440
SnapBv Oct 40	p 1,940	XC	1¼ +	⅝	46	1,564
AT&T Jan 55	p 1,789	CB	1⁵/₁₆ −	¹/₁₆	58¾	1,790
I B M Oct 45	1,764	CB	⅜	...	42	16,560
Travel Feb 35	1,735	PC	3 +	¾	36⅜	1,872
Motrla Oct 100	1,705	AM	1¼ +	⁵/₁₆	94¾	3,552
Cisco Oct 45	1,653	XC	3⅞ +	1⅛	47¼	2,934
Keycp Nov 35	p 1,635	XC	1³/₁₆ +	³/₁₆	37⅝	163

Option/Strike	Exp.	-Call- Vol.	Last	-Put- Vol.	Last
A M D 20	Oct	...	...	50	¹/₁₆
29⅞ 22½	Oct	...	...	160	⅛
29⅞ 25	Oct	730	5¼	49	⁵/₁₆
29⅞ 25	Jan	1	6½	130	1½
29⅞ 25	Apr	150	7⅞	...	...
29⅞ 30	Oct	898	1½	403	1½
29⅞ 30	Nov	119	2⅜	...	...
29⅞ 30	Jan	66	3½	55	3⅝
29⅞ 35	Oct	132	¼	...	...
29⅞ 35	Nov	166	¾	...	...
29⅞ 35	Jan	55	1¾	10	6½
A M P 65	Oct	90	1½	...	...
A M R 60	Oct	20	4	35	¾
63 60	Nov	...	...	77	1¹³/₁₆
63 65	Oct	48	1	29	2⅞
63 65	Nov	68	2¼	7	3⅝
63 70	Oct	60	⅛	20	7
63 70	Nov	71	¾	...	...
A S A 35	Oct	40	6⅞	40	⅛
42¼ 35	Nov	60	7⅛	...	...
Allste 30	Jan	60	3⅛	...	...
32 35	Oct	45	¹/₁₆	...	...
Altera 30	Oct	55	1⅜	...	...
Alza 22½	Oct	30	1⁵/₁₆	25	¾
Am Cya 55	Oct	31	1¹/₁₆	...	...
Am Exp 25	Jan	25	9⅛	...	...
34⅜ 30	Jan	...	...	50	1
34⅜ 35	Oct	487	½	...	...
34⅜ 35	Jan	25	1¾	...	...
34⅜ 35	Apr	201	2⅜	...	...
Am Hom 55	Oct	...	...	30	⅛
62 60	Oct	10	2½	25	⅞
62 65	Oct	62	⁵/₁₆	10	3⅛
AmBrnd 30	Dec	20	2⅜	27	⅝
32½ 35	Dec	164	¼	140	3½
AmStrs 45	Nov	41	1¼	...	...
Amax 20	Oct	70	3	...	...
22⅛ 22½	Oct	105	¾	...	...
22⅛ 22½	Dec	50	1¼	...	...
22⅛ 25	Dec	270	½	...	...
52⅜ 55	Oct	145	⅝	...	...
BanySy 20	Nov	25	1½	...	...
Bard 25	Oct	53	⅜	...	...
22⅝ 25	Jan	29	1¼	...	...
Barnet 40	Nov	10	4⅞	1505	1
43⅞ 45	Oct	15	⅞	62	2½
BattlM 7½	Oct	69	1	30	¼
8⅜ 7½	Oct	130	1⅜	...	...
8⅜ 10	Oct	784	¼	...	...
8⅜ 10	Nov	43	¼	...	...
8⅜ 10	Jan	334	½	...	...
Baxter 20	Oct	258	1⅜	15	⅜
21 20	Nov	342	1⅞	476	1
21 22½	Oct	91	¼	...	...
21 22½	Nov	110	⅜	20	2¹/₁₆
21 22½	Feb	144	1¼	5	2⅜
21 25	Feb	35	⁹/₁₆	2	4½
Baybks 50	Oct	1000	¼	...	...
BearSt 25	Jan	50	1½	...	...
BedBth 25	Oct	37	3¾	21	⁹/₁₆

FIGURE 1.1 Price Quotations for Stock Options from the *Wall Street Journal*

Table 1.7 Index Options Contract Volume by Exchange, 1992

Exchange	Total Volume	Percentage
Chicago Board Options Exchange	76,442,064	91.83
American Stock Exchange	6,247,120	7.50
Philadelphia Stock Exchange	354,005	0.43
Pacific Stock Exchange	69,695	0.08
New York Stock Exchange	134,197	0.16
Total	83,247,081	100.00

Source: Chicago Board Options Exchange, *Market Statistics*, 1992.

the S&P 100 index captures the price movements of the largest stocks in the market, many index options are based on more narrow stock market indexes. For example, the AMEX trades index options based on biotech stocks. Figure 1.2 shows a sample of the quotations for index options from the *Wall Street Journal*. It also indicates the wide variety of indexes that underlie various options. Notice that these include stock indexes for foreign stock markets. The quotations show the expiration month, the exercise price, whether the option is a call or a put, the volume, the closing price, the change since the previous day's close, and the open interest.

Foreign Currency Options.   Options trading on individual foreign currencies is concentrated at the Philadelphia Stock Exchange (PHLX).[8] Table 1.8 details some of the essential features of the market. Each options contract is written for a specific number of units of the foreign currency. For example, a contract is for 62,500 German marks, 31,250 British pounds, or 6,250,000 Japanese yen. These different amounts of the foreign currencies place the U.S. dollar value of each contract in the range of $25,000 to $75,000. Prices for the options are quoted in U.S. dollars and the exercise prices are stated in U.S. dollars as well. As Table 1.8 indicates, the dominant currency is the German mark, with the Japanese yen being a distant second.[9]

Figure 1.3 shows price quotations for these options from the *Wall Street Journal*, and the quotations are organized in the same fashion as the others we have already considered. The PHLX trades American- and European-style options, and it also trades some options with expirations at the end of selected months. However, the American-style options continue to be the dominant market.

Options on Futures.   In the United States, options on futures trade only on futures exchanges, and futures exchanges trade only options on futures. In general, each futures exchange trades options on its own active futures contracts. Therefore, the variety of options on futures is almost as diverse as futures contracts themselves.

Because the futures market is dominated by two large exchanges, the Chicago Board of Trade (CBOT) and the Chicago Mercantile Exchange (CME), these two exchanges have the largest share of trading of options on futures. Table 1.9 shows the relative volume of trading in options on futures by exchange. Together the CBOT and CME have about 80 percent of all volume. Both of these exchanges trade options on agricultural commodities and financial instruments. The New York Mercantile Exchange is the third largest exchange for trading options on futures, largely because

INDEX OPTIONS TRADING

Wednesday, September 22, 1993

Volume, close, net change and open interest for all contracts. Volume figures are unofficial. Open interest reflects previous trading day. p–Put c–Call

Strike	Vol.	Last	Net Chg.	Open Int.

CHICAGO

FINTIMES-SE100(FSX)

	Strike	Vol.	Last	Net Chg.	Open Int.
Oct	290 p	16	1	...	...
Oct	300 p	1	3¾ −	⅜	25
Oct	305 p	7	6⅝ −	⅝	12

Call vol. ....0 Open Int............553
Put vol..............24 Open Int............659

RUSSELL 2000(RUT)

	Strike	Vol.	Last	Net Chg.	Open Int.
Oct	240 c	275	7 +	⅛	225
Oct	240 p	555	1¹¹⁄₁₆ −	1³⁄₁₆	814
Oct	245 c	42	3⅜ +	¾	232
Oct	245 p	130	2½ −	2¾	947
Nov	245 c	50	4¾ −	1⅝	380
Dec	245 p	100	6⅛ −	1¾	40
Oct	250 c	7	1⅜ −	³⁄₁₆	110
Nov	250 c	100	3¼	...	...
Dec	250 c	9	5¼ +	⅝	150
Oct	255 c	25	⁵⁄₁₆ −	³⁄₁₆	110

Call vol. ....508 Open Int........9,320
Put vol. ....785 Open Int........15,380

S & P 100 INDEX(OEX)

	Strike	Vol.	Last	Net Chg.	Open Int.
Oct	375 p	3,008	¼ −	⁷⁄₁₆	10,237
Jan	380 p	110	3⅛ −	1⅛	175
Oct	380 p	1,649	⅜ −	½	8,956
Nov	380 p	659	1¼ −	¾	7,643
Dec	380 p	1,306	1¹⁵⁄₁₆ −	1⁹⁄₁₆	4,455
Oct	385 p	918	½ −	⁹⁄₁₆	12,760
Nov	385 p	306	1¾ −	1⅝	1,228
Dec	385 p	115	2½ −	¾	190
Jan	390 p	210	4¾ +	¼	69
Oct	390 p	1,259	⁷⁄₁₆ −	¹¹⁄₁₆	26,570
Nov	390 p	789	1¹³⁄₁₆ −	1³⁄₁₆	6,747
Dec	390 p	218	2⅝ −	1⅝	3,048
Oct	395 p	3,665	¾ −	⅞	31,355
Nov	395 p	849	2¼ +	1¼	7,645
Dec	395 p	118	3⅞ +	1	38
Jan	400 p	714	6⅝ −	⅞	733
Oct	400 c	31	22 +	3¼	799
Oct	400 p	6,364	1 −	1	35,639
Nov	400 p	3,056	2¾ −	1⅜	9,071
Dec	400 p	636	4½ −	1¼	3,521
Oct	405 c	30	18 +	1½	1,360
Oct	405 p	7,867	1¾ −	1¼	29,224
Nov	405 c	33	19⅝ +	1	312
Nov	405 p	2,017	3½ −	1½	4,006
Dec	405 c	11	22⅛ +	1⅜	2
Dec	405 p	42	5½ −	3	90
Jan	410 p	126	8¼ −	1¾	1,024
Oct	410 c	572	14 +	2	6,087
Oct	410 p	15,395	1⅞ −	1⅝	34,573
Nov	410 c	10	15½ +	1⅝	1,969
Nov	410 p	1,558	4⅝ −	2⅛	13,197
Dec	410 p	81	7⅛ −	1⅛	7,114
Oct	415 c	5,034	9¼ +	1⅛	12,351
Oct	415 p	19,051	2¾ −	1⅞	30,349
Nov	415 c	725	12¼ +	1¾	1,260
Nov	415 p	2,292	5¾ −	1⅞	6,226
Dec	415 c	1	13¾ +	⅞	...
Dec	415 p	26	8 −	2¾	122
Jan	420 c	70	12½ +	¾	366
Jan	420 p	168	12⅜ +	1⅝	36
Oct	420 c	33,155	5⅞ +	¾	46,743

RANGES FOR UNDERLYING INDEXES

Wednesday, September 22, 1993

	High	Low	Close	Net Chg.	From Dec. 31	% Chg.
S&P 100 (OEX)..........	421.83	418.18	421.08	+ 2.90	+ 24.44	+ 6.2
S&P 500 -A.M.(SPX)...	456.92	452.94	456.19	+ 3.23	+ 20.48	+ 4.7
S&P 500 -P.M.(NSX)...	456.92	452.94	456.19	+ 3.23	+ 20.48	+ 4.7
FT-SE 100 (FSX)......	300.75	300.11	300.75	+ 0.59	+ 16.10	+ 5.7
Russell 2000 (RUT)...	246.48	243.67	246.48	+ 2.81	+ 25.48	+ 11.5
Lps S&P 100 (OEX)..	42.18	41.82	42.11	+ 0.29	+ 2.45	+ 6.2
Lps S&P 500 (SPX)...	45.69	45.29	45.62	+ 0.32	+ 2.05	+ 4.7
S&P Midcap (MID)...	172.14	170.35	172.14	+ 1.79	+ 11.59	+ 7.2
Major Mkt (XMI)....	361.51	358.37	359.78	+ 0.45	+ 12.98	+ 3.7
Leaps MMkt (XLT)..	36.15	35.84	35.98	+ 0.04	+ 1.30	+ 3.7
Institut'l -A.M.(XII)..	452.62	448.84	451.76	+ 2.92	+ 8.06	+ 1.8
Institut'l -P.M.(PXP).	452.62	448.84	451.76	+ 2.92	+ 8.06	+ 1.8
Eurotop 100 (EUR)...	109.06	108.44	108.86	− 0.36	+ 21.30	+ 24.3
Japan (JPN)...........			204.55	− 2.94	+ 33.32	+ 19.5
Pharma (DRG).........	166.38	163.86	164.83	+ 0.12	− 33.01	− 16.7
Biotech (BTK)........	105.34	102.37	105.00	+ 1.03	− 65.64	− 38.5
NYSE (NYA)............	253.41	251.59	253.27	+ 1.68	+ 13.06	+ 5.4
Wilshire S-C (WSX)..	320.53	316.87	320.53	+ 3.66	+ 30.22	+ 10.4
Gold/Silver (XAU)...	107.12	103.44	106.40	− 2.91	+ 35.10	+ 49.2
Value Line (VLE)...	431.61	427.98	431.61	+ 3.68	+ 45.53	+ 11.8
OTC (XOC)...............	563.86	550.28	562.58	+11.91	+ 31.83	+ 6.0
Bank (BKX).............	278.67	276.36	278.31	+ 3.07	+ 24.85	+ 9.8

Strike	Vol.	Last	Net Chg.	Open Int.

AMERICAN

BIO TECH(BTK)

	Strike	Vol.	Last	Net Chg.	Open Int.
Oct	95 p	4	⅝ −	³⁄₁₆	28
Oct	100 p	100	¾ −	⁷⁄₁₆	232
Oct	105 c	41	2¾ +	³⁄₁₆	30
Dec	105 c	1	5⅞	...	...

Call vol. ....52 Open Int............593
Put vol. ....104 Open Int............859

EUROTOP (EUR)

Call vol. ....0 Open Int............488
Put vol. ....0 Open Int............431

INSTITUTIONAL-AM(XII)

	Strike	Vol.	Last	Net Chg.	Open Int.
Oct	440 c	50	14⅜ +	1⅞	50
Oct	445 c	25	9⅛ +	1⅛	225
Oct	450 c	100	5¼ −	2⅞	75
Nov	450 p	25	8¼	...	...
Oct	460 p	125	10¾ +	½	50
Oct	465 c	50	½ −	1⅝	27
Oct	465 p	125	14	...	...
Nov	475 c	100	1³⁄₁₆ −	¹⁄₁₆	5

Call vol. ....325 Open Int........25,947
Put vol. ....275 Open Int........23,096

INSTITUTIONAL - P.M. (PXP)

	Strike	Vol.	Last	Net Chg.	Open Int.
Oct	90 p	10	½ +	⅛	380
Dec	90 p	10	1¹³⁄₁₆ −	⅝	58
Oct	95 c	4	10⅞ −	1⅝	48
Oct	95 p	15	1¹¹⁄₁₆ +	⅝	195
Dec	95 p	3	3¼ −	⅝	29
Oct	100 c	37	7⅞ −	2¼	296
Oct	100 p	34	1¹⁵⁄₁₆ +	⁹⁄₁₆	249
Dec	100 p	15	9¾ −	2¾	75
Oct	100 p	25	5⅛ −	2⅛	27
Oct	105 c	251	4⅝ −	2⅜	623
Oct	105 p	346	3¾ +	1	226
Nov	105 c	55	5⅝ −	2⅝	108
Oct	105 c	10	7½ −	3¼	62
Oct	110 c	204	3 −	1¼	549
Oct	110 p	145	7⅜ +	2⅜	133
Nov	110 p	17	4⅝ −	2⅝	59
Nov	110 p	2	9¼ −	5¾	6
Dec	110 c	10	5⅛ −	2¼	166
Oct	115 c	1,080	1 −	1¹¹⁄₁₆	389
Oct	115 p	14	11⅜ −	¾	28
Nov	115 c	1	3 −	1½	49
Oct	120 c	69	½ −	⅝	680
Nov	120 c	9	2 −	1⅜	28
Dec	120 c	30	3¼ −	¾	265
Oct	125 c	195	¼ −	¼	279
Oct	130 c	4	⅛ −	⅛	216
Nov	130 c	4	⁹⁄₁₆ −	⁹⁄₁₆	89
Dec	135 c	8	⅝ +	⅛	117

Call vol. ....2,040 Open Int...........5,920
Put vol. ....610 Open Int...........1,944

FIGURE 1.2 Price Quotations for Index Options from the *Wall Street Journal*

Table 1.8   Foreign Currency Options at the Philadelphia Stock Exchange

Currency	Units of Foreign Currency per Contract	1992 Market Statistics	
		1992 Volume	Year-End Open Interest
German Mark	62,500	7,966,240	556,470
Japanese Yen	6,250,000	1,305,042	61,756
British Pound	31,250	788,769	42,514
Swiss Franc	62,500	434,432	23,217
Canadian Dollar	50,000	188,860	20,730
Australian Dollar	50,000	142,725	9,871
Total		10,826,068	714,558

Source: *Futures and Options World*, February 1993.

of its successful oil-related products. The other exchanges have only minor volume.

Table 1.10 shows the volume of trading in futures options by the type of the underlying futures. Financial instruments account for the majority of futures options and include options on stock index futures and interest rate futures. Options on foreign exchange futures, traded principally at the CME, come next. Options on energy and wood product futures constitute the third largest category, and this volume stems mainly from options on oil-related futures traded primarily at the New York Mercantile Exchange (NYME). Options on traditional agricultural futures are much less important than options on financial instruments, currencies, and energy products. Figure 1.4 shows a sample of the quotations for options on futures.

OPTIONS TRADING PROCEDURES

Every options trader needs to be familiar with the basic features of the market. This section explores the action that takes place on the market floor and the ways in which traders away from the exchange can have their orders executed on the exchange. From its image in the popular press and television, one gets the impression that the exchange floor is the scene of wild and chaotic action. While the action may become wild, it is never chaotic. Understanding the role of the different participants on the floor helps dispel the illusion of chaos. Essentially, there are three types of people on the exchange floor: traders, clerical personnel asso-

CURRENCY TRADING

OPTIONS
PHILADELPHIA EXCHANGE

	Calls Vol.	Calls Last	Puts Vol.	Puts Last
FFranc				**176.27**
250,000 French Franc EOM-European style.				
17½ Sep	...	...	300	0.60
SFranc				**70.38**
62,500 Swiss Francs-European style.				
70 Sep	...	...	10	0.33
Australian Dollar				**65.58**
50,000 Australian Dollars-cents per unit.				
65 Dec	...	...	1	1.23
67 Oct	...	...	300	1.75
67 Dec	12	0.67	...	...
73 Dec	3	0.07	...	...
British Pound				**151.74**
31,250 British Pound EOM-cents per unit.				
147½ Sep	...	...	20	0.04
152½ Oct	...	...	110	3.45
155 Sep	20	0.12	...	...
31,250 British Pounds-European Style.				
150 Oct	...	...	1	1.62
155 Oct	32	0.96	...	...
31,250 British Pounds-European units.				
145 Oct	...	...	1	0.36
31,250 British Pounds-cents per unit.				
147½ Oct	...	...	10	0.63
147½ Nov	...	...	90	1.57
147½ Dec	...	...	196	2.53
150 Oct	...	...	478	1.50
150 Nov	...	...	60	2.49
150 Dec	...	...	2	3.25
152½ Oct	114	1.83	4	2.63
152½ Dec	...	...	2	4.57
155 Oct	408	0.95	...	...
155 Nov	160	1.72	...	...
155 Dec	1	2.10	...	...
157½ Nov	100	1.03	...	...
160 Dec	200	1.05	...	...
British Pound-GMark				**247.34**
31,250 British Pound-German Mark cross.				
246 Oct	...	...	57	1.46
250 Oct	57	1.20	...	...
31,250 British Pound-German mark EOM.				
252 Oct	4	0.94	...	...
Canadian Dollar				**75.82**
50,000 Canadian Dollars-European Style.				
76 Oct	...	...	20	0.41
50,000 Canadian Dollars-cents per unit.				
76 Oct	100	0.38	...	...
76½ Oct	20	0.20	...	...
77 Nov	100	0.28	1	1.64
ECU				**117.57**
62,500 European Currency Units-cents per unit.				
118 Oct	18	1.11	...	...
French Franc				**176.27**
250,000 French Franc EOM-10ths of a unit per unit.				
17½ Oct	8	2.75	8	3.15
250,000 French Francs-10ths of a cent per unit.				
16½ Oct	...	...	27	0.14
17 Oct	...	...	27	0.56
17½ Oct	...	...	54	2.12
17¾ Oct	27	1.62	...	...
18 Oct	47	0.84	...	...
250,000 French Francs-European Style.				
16 Nov	400	14.66	...	...
16¾ Nov	...	...	30	0.86
17½ Oct	...	...	300	1.90
GMark-JYen				**65.11**
62,500 German Mark-Japanese Yen cross.				
66 Oct	...	...	80	0.70

	Calls Vol.	Calls Last	Puts Vol.	Puts Last
67 Oct	160	0.39	...	...
German Mark				**61.36**
62,500 German Marks EOM-cents per unit.				
58 Oct	...	...	2000	0.22
60 Sep	...	...	100	0.06
60½ Sep	60	0.87	300	0.07
61 Sep	120	0.54	475	0.20
61½ Sep	542	0.35	105	0.67
61½ Oct	380	0.93	...	...
62 Sep	300	0.16	...	...
62½ Sep	40	0.08	...	...
63 Sep	200	0.03	...	...
64 Oct	2000	0.18	...	...
62,500 German Marks-European Style.				
56 Oct	...	...	20	0.02
58½ Oct	...	...	200	0.12
59 Nov	...	...	20	0.53
59 Dec	...	...	65	0.80
60 Oct	10	1.54	...	...
60 Nov	...	...	50	0.75
60½ Oct	200	1.12	200	0.63
60½ Nov	...	...	48	1.00
61 Nov	...	...	93	1.18
61 Oct	38	1.45	...	...
61½ Oct	60	0.59	60	1.25
61½ Nov	...	...	26	1.45
62½ Oct	50	0.39	...	...
63 Dec	500	0.71	50	2.92
64 Nov	68	0.32	...	...
64 Dec	500	0.44	...	...
62,500 German Marks-cents per unit.				
55 Dec	...	...	100	0.12
56 Oct	30	5.39	60	0.17
57 Oct	...	...	102	0.03
58 Dec	...	...	851	0.45
59 Oct	...	...	1775	0.18
59 Nov	...	...	46	0.44
59 Dec	...	...	116	0.71
59½ Oct	...	...	1070	0.29
60 Oct	...	...	2272	0.40
60 Nov	5	1.85	320	0.74
60 Dec	20	1.91	97	1.09
60½ Oct	...	...	1305	0.56
60½ Nov	...	...	270	0.93
61 Oct	724	0.93	391	0.75
61 Nov	10	1.31	194	1.17
61 Dec	265	1.46	278	1.51
61½ Oct	1558	0.80	745	0.98
61½ Nov	3	1.03	635	1.44
61½ Dec	...	...	188	1.83
62 Oct	1614	0.50	1504	1.33
62 Nov	15	0.78	...	...
62 Dec	21	0.96	77	2.06
62½ Oct	405	0.40	...	...
62½ Nov	20	0.64	...	...
62½ Dec	100	0.83	...	...
63 Oct	246	0.24	2100	1.99
63 Dec	20	0.64	...	...
63½ Oct	100	0.18	...	...
64 Dec	260	0.45	...	...
66 Dec	10	1.97	...	...
Japanese Yen				**94.20**
6,250,000 Japanese Yen EOM-100ths of a cent per unit.				
92 Oct	...	...	18	0.81
94 Sep	...	...	30	0.48

	Calls Vol.	Calls Last	Puts Vol.	Puts Last
95 Sep	...	...	6	1.09
6,250,000 Japanese Yen EOM.				
92½ Sep	...	...	40	0.12
93½ Sep	...	...	140	0.34
95½ Sep	50	0.18	...	...
6,250,000 Japanese Yen-100ths of a cent per unit.				
86 Dec	...	...	10	0.24
89 Dec	...	...	1	0.60
90 Dec	...	...	6	0.79
91 Oct	...	...	40	0.36
91 Nov	...	...	14	0.78
91 Dec	...	...	15	1.13
91½ Oct	...	...	10	0.42
92 Oct	...	...	1310	0.57
92 Nov	...	...	142	1.16
93 Nov	...	...	1	1.39
93 Dec	...	...	25	1.87
93½ Nov	...	...	1	1.61
94 Oct	10	1.46	311	1.30
94 Oct	...	...	54	2.23
95 Oct	...	...	39	1.88
95 Nov	...	...	1	2.40
95 Dec	...	...	1	2.77
95½ Oct	30	0.83	...	...
96 Oct	50	0.70	...	...
96 Dec	...	...	20	3.31
97 Oct	10	0.40	...	...
98 Oct	10	0.30	...	...
99 Oct	52	0.19	...	...
99 Nov	15	0.48	...	...
99 Dec	10	0.77	...	...
102 Oct	10	0.04	...	...
Swiss Franc				**70.38**
62,500 Swiss Franc EOM-cents per unit.				
68 Sep	...	...	200	0.u..
70 Sep	...	...	5	0.31
72 Sep	100	0.06	...	...
62,500 Swiss Francs EOM.				
70½ Sep	15	0.36	...	...
62,500 Swiss Francs-European Style.				
63½ Dec	...	...	40	0.04
65 Dec	...	...	40	0.24
65½ Nov	...	...	40	0.15
67 Dec	...	...	40	0.58
69 Oct	...	...	6	0.44
69 Nov	40	2.22	...	...
69 Dec	40	2.44	...	...
69½ Oct	...	...	80	1.12
70 Nov	...	...	80	1.32
70½ Oct	...	...	10	1.11
71½ Oct	50	0.62	...	...
71½ Nov	45	1.02	...	...
73 Nov	80	0.58	...	...
74 Nov	125	0.37	...	...
62,500 Swiss Francs-cents per unit.				
65 Dec	...	...	15	0.30
68 Oct	...	...	10	0.26
68 Dec	...	...	25	0.86
69 Dec	...	...	7	1.26
70 Dec	3	1.84	8	1.75
70½ Oct	40	0.98	...	...
71½ Dec	100	1.37	...	...
72 Oct	4	0.49	...	...
72 Dec	25	1.12	...	...
73 Nov	1	0.57	...	...
74 Dec	10	0.60	...	...
78 Dec	5	0.16	...	...

Call Vol 19,503   Open Int ... 548,904
Put Vol 55,165   Open Int ... 540,617

FIGURE 1.3 Price Quotations for Foreign Currency Options from the *Wall Street Journal*

Table 1.9 Futures Options Volume, by Exchange, 1992

	Contracts Traded	
Exchange	Contracts	Percentage
Chicago Board of Trade	29,353,388	42.18
Chicago Mercantile Exchange	29,959,843	37.30
New York Mercantile Exchange	8,808,028	12.65
Commodity Exchange	2,189,131	3.15
Coffee, Sugar & Cocoa Exchange	1,863,287	2.68
New York Cotton Exchange & Association	1,224,471	1.76
Kansas City Board of Trade	97,245	0.14
New York Futures Exchange	43,528	0.06
MidAmerica Commodity Exchange	36,098	0.05
Minneapolis Grain Exchange	15,327	0.02
Total	69,590,346	100.00

Source: *Annual Report,* Commodity Futures Trading Commission (CFTC), 1992. Data are for the fiscal year of the CFTC ending September 30, 1992.

Table 1.10 Futures Options Open Interest and Volume, 1992

Type of Underlying Good	Average Open Interest		Contracts Traded	
	Contracts	Percentage	Contracts	Percentage
Financial Instruments	1,585,846	51.33	39,928,140	57.38
Currencies	479,223	15.51	9.975,773	14.33
Energy/Wood Products	409,491	13.25	8,776,175	12.61
Grains	24,160	0.78	3,216,275	4.62
Other Agricultural	199,069	6.44	2,358,160	3.393
Metals	193,638	6.27	2,238,322	.22
Oilseeds	129,115	4.18	2,217,621	3.19
Livestock	69,002	2.23	879,880	1.26
Total	3,089,544	100.00	69,590,346	100.00

Source: *Annual Report,* Commodity Futures Trading Commission (CFTC), 1992. Data are for the fiscal year of the CFTC ending September 30, 1992.

ciated with the traders, and exchange officials. First we describe the system that the CBOE uses. Later, we note some differences among exchanges.

Types of Traders

There are three different kinds of traders on the floor of the exchange: market makers, floor brokers, and order book officials. A trader who

FUTURES OPTIONS PRICES

Wednesday, September 22, 1993.

AGRICULTURAL

CORN (CBT)
5,000 bu.; cents per bu.

Strike	Calls–Settle			Puts–Settle		
Price	Dec	Mar	May	Dec	Mar	May
230	17¼	24¾	29	1¼	1¼	1½
240	10¼	17	21½	4⅜	3¾	3½
250	6⅛	11½	15	10	8	7
260	3¼	7⅝	10¾	17½	14	13
270	1⅜	4¾	7½	25¾	....	....
280	⅝	3	4⅞	34¾	....	....

Est vol 15,000 Tues 7,102 calls 2,162 puts
Op int Tues 117,467 calls 59,148 puts

SOYBEANS (CBT)
5,000 bu.; cents per bu.

Strike	Calls–Settle			Puts–Settle		
Price	Nov	Jan	Mar	Nov	Jan	Mar
600	39½	47½	54¾	1¼	2¾	4
625	19½	30	36¾	6⅜	10¼	11¼
650	8⅝	19	26½	20½	23¾	24½
675	4¼	11½	17½	41½	42	41¼
700	2	7¾	12½	83¾	62½	61¼
725	1	5½	9¼	87¾	85	82¼

Est vol 13,000 Tues 9,948 calls 3,176 puts
Op int Tues 144,496 calls 53,773 puts

SOYBEAN MEAL (CBT)
100 tons; $ per ton

Strike	Calls–Settle			Puts–Settle		
Price	Dec	Jan	Mar	Dec	Jan	Mar
190	8.50	9.40	....	1.20	1.40	....
195	5.50	6.10	8.60	2.85	3.25	....
200	3.25	4.10	6.00	5.75	6.00	5.60
210	1.35	2.25	3.25	13.80	13.85	12.75
220	.70	1.30	2.20	23.00	22.90	21.40
230	.30	.90	1.55	32.70	....	....

Est vol 200 667s calls 459 puts
Op int Tues 14,023 calls 14,066 puts

SOYBEAN OIL (CBT)
60,000 lbs.; cents per lb.

Strike	Calls–Settle			Puts–Settle		
Price	Dec	Jan	Mar	Dec	Jan	Mar
170	1.60	3.85	5.15	6.10	7.10	7.15
175	.50	2.25	3.20	10.00	10.50	10.20
180	.15	1.35	2.20	14.55	14.60	14.20

Est vol 324 Tues 515 calls 572 puts
Op int Tues 10,158 calls 10,982 puts

LIVESTOCK

CATTLE-FEEDER (CME)
55,000 lbs.; cents per lb.

Strike	Calls–Settle			Puts–Settle		
Price	Sep	Oct	Nov	Sep	Oct	Nov
82	4.55	3.60	....	0.00	0.05	0.17
84	2.57	1.85	....	0.02	0.25	0.45
86	0.67	0.65	0.82	0.12	1.10	1.10
88	0.02	0.12	0.30	1.47	....	2.45
90	0.00	0.02	0.10	....	....	4.37
92	0.00	0.02	0.02	....	....	....

Est vol 57 Tues 90 calls 77 puts
Op int Tues 2,110 calls 6,080 puts

CATTLE-LIVE (CME)
40,000 lbs.; cents per lb.

Strike	Calls–Settle			Puts–Settle		
Price	Oct	Dec	Feb	Oct	Dec	Feb
70	....	....	....	0.02	0.35	0.45
72	1.47	2.60	....	0.15	0.77	0.80
74	0.30	1.37	2.57	0.97	1.52	1.42
76	0.02	0.60	1.55	2.70	2.72	2.35
78	0.00	0.22	0.80	4.67	4.35	3.57
80	0.00	0.05	0.35	....	....	5.12

Est vol 3,028 Tues 635 calls 1,142 puts
Op int Tues 14,587 calls 25,515 puts

HOGS-LIVE (CME)
40,000 lbs.; cents per lb.

Strike	Calls–Settle			Puts–Settle		
Price	Oct	Dec	Feb	Oct	Dec	Feb
44	4.37	4.30	3.67	0.00	0.35	0.77
46	2.47	2.67	2.40	0.10	0.72	1.50
48	0.87	1.57	1.42	0.50	1.60	2.52
50	0.17	0.82	0.85	1.80	2.82	3.90
52	0.05	0.42	....	....	....	5.50
54	....	0.20	....	....	....	....

Est vol 129 Tues 44 calls 120 puts
Op int Tues 2,321 calls 3,327 puts

DEUTSCHEMARK (CME)
125,000 marks; cents per mark

Strike	Calls–Settle			Puts–Settle		
Price	Oct	Nov	Dec	Oct	Nov	Dec
6000	1.28	1.62	1.90	0.37	0.72	1.00
6050	0.96	1.34	1.60	0.55	0.93	1.19
6100	0.70	1.06	1.35	0.79	1.17	1.44
6150	0.49	0.84	1.14	1.08	1.43	1.72
6200	0.33	0.67	0.93	1.42	1.75	2.01
6250	0.21	0.52	0.77	1.80	....	2.34

Est vol 20,567 Tues 19,318 calls 28,-879 puts
Op int Tues 140,852 calls 126,828 puts

CANADIAN DOLLAR (CME)
100,000 Can.$, cents per Can.$

Strike	Calls–Settle			Puts–Settle		
Price	Oct	Nov	Dec	Oct	Nov	Dec
7450	1.13	....	1.52	0.11	0.35	0.51
7500	0.74	1.04	1.21	0.22	0.52	0.69
7550	0.44	0.75	0.94	0.42	0.73	0.92
7600	0.23	0.53	0.72	0.71	1.01	1.20
7650	0.11	0.36	0.53	1.09	1.33	1.50
7700	0.05	0.23	0.38	1.53	....	1.85

Est vol 480 Tues 186 calls 304 puts
Op int Tues 5,445 calls 4,896 puts

BRITISH POUND (CME)
62,500 pounds; cents per pound

Strike	Calls–Settle			Puts–Settle		
Price	Oct	Nov	Dec	Oct	Nov	Dec
1450	5.98	....	7.16	0.24	0.90	1.44
1475	3.88	....	5.48	0.62	1.56	2.24
1500	2.22	3.30	4.06	1.46	2.54	3.30
1525	1.10	2.16	2.90	2.84	3.90	4.62
1550	0.46	1.34	2.00	4.70	....	6.20
1575	0.18	0.78	1.34	6.90	....	....

Est vol 1,059 Tues 809 calls 571 puts
Op int Tues 11,193 calls 8,343 puts

SWISS FRANC (CME)
125,000 francs; cents per franc

Strike	Calls–Settle			Puts–Settle		
Price	Oct	Nov	Dec	Oct	Nov	Dec
6900	1.60	2.02	2.36	0.44	0.87	1.21
6950	1.26	....	....	0.60	1.06	1.42
7000	0.98	1.45	1.81	0.82	1.29	1.65

FIGURE 1.4 Price Quotations for Options on Futures from the *Wall Street Journal*

trades for his own account is a market maker. A trader who executes orders for another is a floor broker. The order book official is an employee of the exchange who makes certain kinds of option trades and keeps the book of orders awaiting execution at specified prices.

The Market Maker. The typical market maker owns or leases a seat on the options exchange and trades for his or her own account to make a profit. However, as the name implies, the market maker has an obligation to make a market for the public by standing ready to buy or sell options. Typically, a market maker will concentrate on the options of just a few stocks. Focusing on a few issues allows the market maker to become quite knowledgeable about the other traders who deal in options on those stocks.

Market makers follow different trading strategies, and they switch freely from one strategy to another. Some market makers are scalpers. The scalper follows the psychology of the trading crowd and tries to anticipate the direction of the market in the next few minutes. The scalper tries to buy if the price is about to rise and tries to sell just before it falls. Generally, the scalper holds a position for just a few minutes, trying to make a profit on moment to moment fluctuations in the option's price. By contrast, a position trader buys or sells options and holds a position for a longer period. This commitment typically rests on views about the underlying worth of the stock or movements in the economy. Both scalpers and position traders often trade options combinations. For example, they might buy a call at a striking price of 90 and sell a call with a striking price of 95. Such a combination is called a **spread**. A spread is any options position in two or more related options. In all such combination trades, the trader seeks to profit from a change in the price of one option relative to another.

The Floor Broker.   Many options traders are located away from the trading floor. When an off-the-floor trader enters an order to buy or sell an option, the floor broker has the job of executing the order. Floor brokers typically represent brokerage firms, such as Merrill Lynch or Prudential Bache. They work for a salary or receive commissions, and their job is to obtain the best price on an order while executing it rapidly. Almost all brokers have support personnel that assist in completing trades. For example, major brokerage firms will have clerical staff that receive orders from beyond the trading floor. These individuals deal with all of the record keeping necessary to execute an order and assist in transmitting information to and from the floor brokers. In addition, many brokerage firms engage in proprietary trading—trading for their own account. Therefore, they have a number of trained people on the floor of the exchange to seek trading opportunities and to execute transactions through a floor broker.

The Order Book Official.   The order book official is an employee of the exchange who can also trade. However, the official cannot trade for his or her own account. Instead, the order book official primarily helps to facilitate the flow of orders. The order book is the listing of orders that are awaiting execution at a specific price. The order book official discloses the best limit orders (highest bid and lowest ask) awaiting execution. In essence, the order book official performs many of the functions of a specialist on a stock exchange. The order book official also has support personnel to help keep track of the order book and to log new orders into the book as they come in.

Exchange Officials.   Exchange officials comprise the third group of floor participants. We have already noted that the order book official and assistants are exchange employees. They serve the special function we described above. However, there are other exchange employees on the floor, such as price reporting officials and surveillance officials. After every trade, price reporting officials enter the order into the exchange's price reporting system. The details of the trade immediately go out over a financial reporting system so that traders all over the world can obtain the information reflected in the trade. This process takes just a few seconds. Then traders and other interested parties around the world will know the price and quantity of a particular option that just traded. In addition to personnel involved with price reporting, the exchange has personnel on the floor to monitor floor activity. The exchange has the responsibility of providing an honest marketplace, so it strives to maintain an orderly market and to ensure that brokers and market makers follow exchange rules.

Other Trading Systems

The alignment of personnel described here follows the practice at the CBOE and the Pacific Stock Exchange. Other exchanges, such as the American and Philadelphia Stock Exchanges, use a specialist instead of an order book official. In this system, the specialist keeps the limit order book but does not disclose the outstanding orders. Also, the specialist alone bears the responsibility of making a market, rather than relying on a group of market makers. In place of market makers, these exchanges have registered options traders who buy and sell for their own accounts or act as brokers for others.

One of the most important differences between the two systems is the role of the market makers and registered options traders. At the CBOE and the Pacific Stock Exchange, a market maker cannot act as a broker and trade for his or her account on the same day. The same individual can play different roles on different days, however. Restricting individuals from simultaneously acting as market makers and brokers helps avoid a conflict of interest between the role of market maker and that of broker. The system of allowing an individual simultaneously to trade for himself (as a market maker) and to execute orders for the public (a broker) is called dual trading. Many observers believe that dual trading involves inherent conflicts of interest between the role of broker and market maker. For example, consider a dual trader who holds an order to execute as a broker. If this dual trader suddenly confronts a very attractive trading opportunity, he may well decide to take it for his own profit, rather than execute the order for his customer.

Types of Orders

Every options trade falls into one of four categories. It can be an order to (1) open a position with a purchase; (2) open a position with a sale; (3) close a position with a purchase; or (4) close a position with a sale.

For example, a trader could open a position by buying a call and later close that position by selling the call. Alternatively, one could open a position by selling a put and close the position by buying a put. An order that closes an existing position is an **offsetting order**.

As in the stock market, there are numerous types of orders in the options market. The simplest order is a market order. A market order instructs the floor broker to transact at whatever price is currently available in the marketplace. For example, one might place an order to buy one call contract for a stock at the market. The floor broker will fill this order immediately at the best price currently available. As in the stock market, the alternative to a market order is a limit order. In a limit order, the trader instructs the broker to fill the order only if certain conditions are met. For example, assume an option trades for $5 1/8. In this situation, one might place a limit order to buy an option only if the price is $5 or less. In a limit order, the trader tells the broker how long to try to fill the order. If the limit order is a day order, the broker is to fill the order that day if it can be filled within the specified limit. If the order cannot be filled that day, the order expires. Alternatively, a trader can specify a limit order as being good-until-canceled. In this case, the order stays on the limit order book indefinitely.

Order Routing and Execution

To get a better idea of how an order is executed, let's trace an order from an individual trader. A college professor in Miami decides that today is the day to buy an option on XYZ. He calls his local broker and places a market order to buy a call. The broker takes the order and makes sure she has recorded the order correctly. The broker then transmits the order to the brokerage firm's representatives at the exchange. Usually this is done over a computerized system operated by the brokerage firm.

The brokerage firm's clerical staff on the floor of the exchange receives the order and gives it to a runner. The runner quickly moves to the trading area and finds the firm's floor broker who deals in XYZ options. The floor broker executes the order by trading with another floor broker, a market maker, or an order book official. Then the floor broker records the price obtained and information about the opposite trader. The runner takes this information from the floor broker back to the clerical staff on the exchange floor. The brokerage firm clerks confirm the order to the Miami broker, who tells the professor the result of the transaction. Normally, the entire process takes about two minutes and the professor can reasonably expect to receive confirmation of his order in the same phone call used to place the order.

THE CLEARINGHOUSE

In executing the trade just described, the buyer of a call has the right to purchase 100 shares of XYZ at the exercise price. However, it might seem that the buyer of the call is in a somewhat dangerous position, because the seller of the call may not want to fulfill his part of the bargain if the price of XYZ rises. For example, if XYZ sells for $120, the seller of the call may be unwilling to part with the share for $100. The purchaser of the call needs a mechanism to secure his position without having to force the seller to perform.

The clearinghouse, Options Clearing Corporation (OCC), performs this role. After the day's trading, the OCC first attempts to match all trades. For the college professor's transaction, there is an opposite trading party. When the broker recorded the purchase for the professor, she traded with someone else who also recorded the trade. The clearinghouse must match the paperwork from both sides of the transaction. If the two records agree, the trade is a matched trade. This process of matching trades and tracking payments is called **clearing**. Every options trade must be cleared. If records by the two sides of the trade disagree, the trade is an **outtrade** and the exchange works to resolve the disagreement.

Assuming the trade matches, the OCC guarantees both sides of the transaction. The OCC becomes the seller to every buyer and the buyer to every seller. In essence, the OCC interposes its own credibility for that of the individual traders. This has great advantages. The college professor did not even know the name of the seller of the option. Instead of being worried about the credibility of the seller, the professor need only be satisfied with the credibility of the OCC. But the OCC is well capitalized and anxious to keep a smoothly functioning market. Therefore, the college professor can be assured that the other side of his option transaction will be honored. If an options trader fails to perform as promised, the OCC absorbs the loss and proceeds against the defaulting trader. Because the OCC is a buyer to every seller and a seller to every buyer, it has a zero net position in the market. It holds the same number of short and long positions. Therefore, the OCC has very little risk exposure from fluctuating prices.

MARGINS

Besides having a zero net position, the clearinghouse further limits its risk by requiring margin payments from its clearing members. A clearing member is a securities firm having an account with the clearinghouse. All option trades must be channeled through a clearing member to the clearinghouse. Most major brokerage firms are clearing members. However, individual market makers are not clearing members, and they must clear their trades through a clearing member. In effect, the clearing member represents all of the parties that it clears to the clearinghouse. By demanding margin payments from its clearing members, the clearinghouse further ensures its own financial integrity. Each clearing member in turn demands margin payments from the traders it clears. The margin payments are immediate cash payments that show the financial integrity of the traders and help to limit the risk of the clearing member and the clearinghouse.

To understand margins, we recall that there are four basic positions: long a call or long a put and short a call or short a put. The margin rules differ with the type of position. First, options cannot be bought on credit. The buyer of an option pays the full price of the option by the morning of the next business day. For example, the college professor in Miami who buys a call or put must pay his broker in full for the purchase. We may think of long option positions as requiring 100 percent margin in all cases.

For options sellers, margin rules become very important. The Federal Reserve Board sets minimum margin requirements for options traders. However, each exchange may impose additional margin requirements. Also, each broker may require margin payments beyond those required by the Federal Reserve Board and the exchanges. A single broker may also impose different margin requirements on different customers. Further, options on different underlying instruments are subject to different margin requirements. Because these options requirements may differ so radically and because they are subject to frequent adjustment, this section illustrates the underlying principles of margin rules for options on stocks.[10]

The seller of a call option may be required to deliver the stock if the owner of a call exercises his option. Therefore, the maximum amount the seller can lose is the value of the share. If the seller keeps money on deposit with the broker equal to the share price, then the broker, clearing member, and clearinghouse are completely protected. This sets an upper bound on the reasonable amount of margin that could be required. Sometimes the seller of a call has the share itself on deposit with the broker. In this case, the seller has sold a **covered call**—the call is covered by the deposit of the shares with the broker. If the call is exercised against the seller of a covered call, the stock is immediately available to deliver. Therefore, there is no risk to the system in a covered call. Accordingly, the margin on a covered call is zero.

If the seller of a call does not have the underlying share on deposit with the broker, the seller has sold an **uncovered call** or a **naked call**. We have just seen that the maximum possible loss is the value of the share. For the writer of a put, the worst result is being forced to buy a worthless stock at the exercise price. This worst case gives a loss equal to the exercise price. Therefore, if the margin equaled the exercise price, the broker, clearing member, and clearinghouse would be fully protected. Instead of demanding complete protection, the seller of a call or put must deposit only a fraction of the potential loss as an **initial margin**.

For a seller of an option, the margin requirement depends on whether the option is in-the-money or out-of-the-money. If the option is in-the-money, the initial margin equals 100 percent of the proceeds from selling the option plus an amount equal to 20 percent of the value of the underlying stock. For example, assume a stock currently sells for $105 and a trader sells a call contract for 100 shares with a striking price of $100 on this stock for $6 per share. Ignoring brokerage fees, the proceeds from selling the call would be $600. To this we add 20 percent of the value of the underlying stock, or $2,100 for the 100 shares. Therefore, the initial margin requirement is $2,700.

If the option is out-of-the-money, the rule is slightly different. The initial margin equals the margin sale proceeds plus 20 percent of the value of the underlying stock minus the amount the option is out-of-the-money. However, this margin rule could result in a negative margin, so the initial margin must also equal 100 percent of the option proceeds plus 10 percent of the value of the underlying security. Consider a call that is out-of-the-money, with the stock trading at $15 per share and the option having an exercise price of $20 and trading for $1. Based on a 100-share contract and ignoring any brokerage commissions, the margin must be the proceeds from selling the option ($100), plus 20 percent of the value of the underlying stock (.20 × $15 × 100 = $300), less the amount the option is out-of-the-money ([\$20 − \$15] × 100 = \$500). This gives a margin requirement that is negative (\$100 + \$300 − \$500 = −\$100). Therefore, the second part of the rule comes into play. The minimum margin must equal the sale proceeds from the option (\$100) plus 10 percent of the value of the underlying stock (.10 × \$15 × 100 = \$150). Therefore, the margin for this trade will be \$250.

The margins we have been discussing are initial margin requirements. The trader must make these margin deposits when he or she first trades. If prices move against the trader, he or she will be required to make additional margin payments. As the stock price starts to rise and cause losses for the short trader, the broker requires additional margin payments, called maintenance margin. By requiring maintenance margin payments, the margin system protects the broker, clearing member, and clearinghouse from default by traders. This system also benefits traders, because they can be confident that payments due to them will be protected from default as well.

Many options traders trade options combinations. Margin rules apply to these transactions as well, but the margin requirements reflect the special risk characteristics of these positions. For many options combinations, the risk may be less than the risk of a single long or short position in a put or call.[11]

COMMISSIONS

As we have seen, the same brokerage system that trades stocks can execute options transactions. In stocks, commission charges depend on the number of shares and the dollar value of the transaction. A similar system applies for call options contracts. The following schedule shows a representative commission schedule from a discount broker. Full-service brokerage fees can be substantially higher.[12] In addition to these fees, each transaction can be subject to certain minimum and maximum fees. For instance, a broker might have a maximum fee per contract of \$40.

Representative Discount Brokerage Commissions

Dollar Value of Transaction	Commission
\$0–2,500	\$29 + 1.6% of principal amount
\$2,500–10,000	\$49 + 0.8% of principal amount
\$10,000 +	\$99 + 0.3% of principal amount

As an example of commissions with this fee schedule, assume that you buy five contracts with a quoted price of \$6.50. The cost of the option would be $650 per contract, for a total cost of $3,250. The commission would be: $49 + .008 × $3,250 = $75. For the same dollar value of a transaction in stocks, the commission tends to be lower. However, once the dollar amount of the transaction approaches $10,000, commissions on stocks and options tend to be similar.

Even though the commission per dollar of options traded may be higher than for stocks, there can be significant commission savings in trading options. In our example, the option price is $6.50 per share of stock. The share price might well be $100 or more. If it were $100, trading 500 shares would involve a transaction value of $50,000. Commissions on a stock transaction of $50,000 would be much higher than commissions on our option transaction. Trading the option on a stock and trading the stock itself can give positions with very similar price actions. Therefore, options trading can provide commission savings over stock trading. This principle holds, even though options commissions tend to be higher than stock commissions for a given dollar transaction.

Another way to see this principle is to realize that options inherently have more leverage than a share of stock. As an example, assume the stock price is $100 and the option on the stock trades for $6.50. If the stock price rises 3 percent to $103, the option price could easily rise 30 percent to $8.45. On a percentage basis, the option price moves more than the stock price. Unfortunately for option traders, this happens for price increases and decreases. With this greater leverage, the same dollar investment in an option will give a greater dollar price movement than investment in the stock.

TAXATION

Taxation of option transactions is no simple matter. We cannot hope to cover all of the nuances of the tax laws in this brief section. Further, the passage of the 1993 tax act further complicates matters in ways that have not been fully resolved at this writing. Therefore, this section attempts merely to illustrate the basic principles.

Disposition of an option, either through sale, exercise, or expiration gives rise to a profit or loss. Profits and losses on options trading are treated as capital gains and losses. Therefore, options profits and losses are subject to all the regular rules that pertain to all capital gains and losses. Capital gains may be classified as long-term or short-term capital gains. A capital gain is a long-term gain if the instrument generating the gain has been held longer than one year, otherwise the gain or loss is short-term. In general, long-term capital gains qualify for favorable tax treatment.

Capital losses offset capital gains and thereby reduce taxable income. However, capital losses are deductible only up to the amount of capital gains plus $3,000. Any excess capital loss cannot be deducted, but must be carried forward to offset capital gains in subsequent years. For example, assume that a trader has capital gains of $17,500 from securities trading. Unfortunately for the trader, he also has $25,000 in capital losses. Therefore, $17,500 of the losses completely offset the capital gains, freeing the trader from any taxes on those gains. This leaves $7,500 of capital losses to consider. The trader can then use $3,000 of this excess loss to offset other income, such as wages. In effect, this protects $3,000 of wages from taxation. The remaining $4,500 of losses must be carried forward to the next tax year, where it can be used to offset capital gains realized in that tax year.

Option transactions give rise to capital gains and losses, and the tax treatment differs for buyers and sellers of options. Further, the tax treatment becomes very complicated for combinations of options. Therefore, we consider only the four simplest stock option positions: long a call, short a call, long a put, or short a put.

Long a Call

If a call is exercised, the price of the option, the exercise price, and the brokerage commissions associated with purchasing and exercising the option are treated as the cost of the stock for tax purposes. The holding period for the stock begins on the day after the call is exercised, so the stock must be held for a year to qualify for treatment as a long-term capital gain. If the call expires worthless, it gives rise to a short-term or long-term capital loss equal to the purchase price of the option plus any associated brokerage fees incurred in purchasing the option. If the option is sold before expiration, the capital gain or loss is the sale price of the option minus the purchase price of the option minus any brokerage fees incurred.

Short a Call

When a trader sells a call, the premium that is received is not treated as immediate income. Instead, the treatment of this premium depends on the disposition of the short call. If the call expires without being exercised, the gain on the transaction equals the prices of the option less any brokerage fees, and this gain is always treated as a short-term gain, no matter how long the position was held. If the trader offsets the position before expiration, the capital gain or loss equals the sale price minus the purchase price minus any commissions, and this gain or loss is considered a short-term gain or loss without regard to how long the position is held. If the call is exercised against the trader, the strike price plus the premium received minus any commissions becomes the sale price of the stock for determining the capital gain or loss. The gain or loss will be short-term or long-term depending on how the stock that is delivered was acquired. For example, if the trader delivers stock that had been held for more than one year, the gain or loss would be a long-term gain or loss.

Long a Put

If a put is purchased and sold before expiration, the gain or loss equals the sale price minus the purchase price minus any brokerage commissions, and the gain or loss will be short-term or long-term depending on how long the put was held. If the put expires worthless, the loss equals the purchase price plus the brokerage commissions, and the loss can be either short-term or long-term. If the trader exercises the put, the cost of the put plus commission reduces the amount realized upon the sale of the stock delivered to satisfy the exercise. The resulting gain or loss can be either short-term or long-term depending on how long the delivered stock was held.

Short a Put

The premium received for selling a put is not classified as income until the obligation from the sale of the put is completed. If the trader offsets the short put before expiration, the capital gain or loss equals the sale price minus the purchase price minus the brokerage commissions, and the resulting gain or loss is always a short-term gain or loss. If the put expires worthless, the capital gain equals the sale price less the brokerage commissions, and the capital gain is a short-term gain. If the put is exercised against the trader, the basis of the stock acquired in the exercise equals the strike price plus the commission minus the premium received when the put was sold. The holding period for determining a capital gain or loss begins for the stock on the day following the exercise.

There are other special and more complicated rules for taxing options transactions, so the account here is not definitive. Additional complications arise for some options on stock indexes, for example. Also, there are special tax rules designed to prevent options trading merely to manipulate taxes.

THE ORGANIZATION OF THE TEXT

The remainder of this text is organized as follows. Chapter 2 explores the payoffs from a variety of option strategies. As we will see, options can be held as individual investment, or they can be combined to provide very specific investment opportunities that pay only in certain circumstances. This flexibility makes options an extremely useful and powerful risk management tool.

Chapter 2 considers payoffs only when options expire, because this special time is much easier to analyze than the value of options prior to expiration. Chapter 3 begins the analysis of options prior to expiration by using the idea of arbitrage. An **arbitrage opportunity** is a chance to make a riskless profit with no investment. Thus, arbitrage is akin to finding free money. Chapter 3 approaches options pricing by asking the question: "What option prices are consistent with the absence of arbitrage opportunities?" This key idea of no-arbitrage pricing turns out to be an extremely powerful analytical tool that we employ throughout the text.

Options pricing inescapably involves some rather complicated mathematics. The mathematics are much simpler for European options than for American options. Chapter 4 extends the no-arbitrage approach to analyze the pricing of European options and explains the famous Black-Scholes options pricing model. The Black-Scholes model expresses the price of an option as a function of the price of the underlying stock, the exercise price, the time until expiration, the risk-free rate of interest, and the volatility of the underlying stock. As we will see, it gives extremely accurate results. Chapter 5 explores in detail the exact way in which option prices respond to the various parameters in the Black-Scholes model. These sensitivities can be used to shape the risk-and-return characteristics of options positions with great precision.

While European options pricing is simpler than American options pricing, most options traded in the actual market are American options. Therefore, Chapter 6 explores the pricing of American options. The principles of European options pricing still hold, but American options pricing involves some special considerations.

Chapter 7 applies the conceptual apparatus developed in earlier chapters to three special instruments: options on indexes, options on foreign currencies, and options on futures. The pricing of these instruments requires applying the concepts already developed to the particular institutional features of these underlying goods.

Chapter 8 shows the power of options pricing and analysis in a very different application. The concepts of options pricing can be used to analyze corporate securities as having options characteristics. Therefore, the options approach to corporate securities yields a totally new and very powerful way of thinking about common stock, bonds, convertible debt, and other corporate securities.

SUMMARY

This chapter has introduced the options market. In the short time since options started trading on the Chicago Board Options Exchange, they have helped to revolutionize finance. They permeate the world of speculative investing and portfolio management. Corporations use them in their financing decisions to control risk. Beyond their uses as trading vehicles, options provide a new way to analyze many financial transactions.

The chapters that follow build an understanding of the options revolution on several levels. Foremost, we seek to build an understanding of options trading and speculating as a topic that is interesting in its own right. However, by following the argument of this book, the reader will develop skills in financial thinking that will apply to many problem areas. After completing the book, the careful reader should even be able to analyze many financial problems using an options framework. At that point, the reader has become part of the options revolution.

REVIEW QUESTIONS

1. State the difference between a call and a put option.
2. How does a trader initiate a long call position, and what rights and obligations does such a position involve?
3. Can buying an option, whether a put or a call, result in any obligations for the option owner? Explain.
4. Describe all of the benefits that are associated with taking a short position in an option.
5. What is the difference between a short call and a long put position? Which has rights associated with it, and which involves obligations? Explain.
6. Consider the following information. A trader buys a call option for $5 that gives the right to purchase a share of stock for $100. In this situation, identify: the exercise price, the premium, and the striking price.
7. Explain what happens to a short trader when the option he or she has sold expires worthless. What benefits and costs has the trader incurred?

8. Explain why an organized options exchange needs a clearing-house.

9. What is the difference between an American and a European option?

10. Assume a trader does not want to continue holding an options position. Explain how this trader can fulfill his or her obligations, yet close out the options position.

NOTES

1. There are also more complicated types of options that are not traded on exchanges. For example, an **exchange option** is an option to exchange one asset for another. As we will see when we discuss options on futures, there is a **delivery option** that gives a trader the right to choose which of several assets to surrender. There are still other types of options, but the most important market for options is the options exchange, where just put and call options trade.

2. Christopher K. Ma and Ramesh P. Rao, "Information Asymmetry and Options Trading," *The Financial Review*, 23:1, February 1988, 39–51, discuss the different roles that options can play for informed and uninformed traders. The informed trader is one with special knowledge about the underlying stock; the uninformed trader has no special knowledge. In their analysis, the informed trader tends to take an outright position in the option, while the uninformed trader is likely to use options to reduce the risk of an existing stock position. While these factors may benefit market participants, the same authors analyze the effect of a new listing of options on stock prices in "The Effect of Call-Option-Listing Announcement on Shareholder Wealth," *Journal of Business Research*, 15:5, October 1987, 449–465. Ma and Rao show that the listing of an option on a stock that never had options before leads to stock price declines and thus to a loss of shareholder wealth. Apparently, this drop in stock prices reflects the market's view that new options trading is likely to make the stock more volatile. However, Ma and Rao also find that stock prices rebound when the option actually begins to trade.

3. Consider an options position and a stock position designed to give the same profits and losses for a given movement in the stock price. If we consider a short-term investment horizon, the options strategy will almost always be cheaper and incur lower transaction costs. This is not necessarily true for a long-term investment horizon. All exchange-traded options are dated; that is, they expire within the next few months. Therefore, maintaining an options position in the long-term involves trading to replace expiring options. By contrast, taking the stock position requires only one transaction, and the stock can be held indefinitely. Therefore,

the repeated transaction costs incurred with the options strategy can involve greater transaction costs in the long-term than the stock strategy.

4. Selling stock short involves borrowing a share, selling it, repurchasing the share later, and returning it to its owner. The short seller hopes to profit from a price decline by selling before the decline and repurchasing after the price falls. Rules on the stock exchange restrict the timing of short selling and the use of short sale proceeds.

5. Stephen A. Ross, "Options and Efficiency," *Quarterly Journal of Economics*, 90, February 1976, 75–89, shows that options serve a useful economic role by completing markets. In a complete market, a trader can trade for any pattern of payoffs that he or she desires. The more nearly complete a market is, the greater is its likely efficiency. Thus, because options help to complete markets, they contribute to economic efficiency and thereby raise the welfare level of society as a whole.

6. The "r" and "s" have no specific meaning. However, this is the convention used by the *Wall Street Journal* for its option price reports.

7. However, some futures options are options on foreign currency futures, and these are traded on the CME.

8. The Chicago Mercantile Exchange trades foreign currency futures and options on those futures in a robust market. However, the CME trades no options on the foreign currencies themselves.

9. The table does not show statistics on very small market currencies, such as the French franc and the European Currency Unit (ECU).

10. George Sofianos, "Margin Requirements on Equity Instruments," *Federal Reserve Bank of New York Quarterly Review*, 13:2, Summer 1988, 47–60, explains margin rules in more detail. Stephen Figlewski, "Margins and Market Integrity: Margin Setting for Stock Index Futures and Options," *Journal of Futures Markets*, 4:3, Fall 1984, 385–416, argues that margins on stocks are set too high relative to margins on options and futures. According to his analysis, the margin requirements give different levels of protection for different instruments.

11. Margins can be devilishly complicated. Andrew Rudd and Mark Schroeder, "The Calculation of Minimum Margin," *Management Science*, 28, December 1982, 1368–1379, present a linear program to compute minimum margin under a variety of scenarios.

12. A discount broker executes unsolicited orders for its customers. It provides little or no research information but seeks to offer fully competitive order execution at reduced prices. Charles Schwab and Quick and Reilly are two leading discount brokerage firms. By contrast, full discount brokers typically have account executives that actively solicit orders from their customer base. The full discount broker also maintains a research department.

2

Options Payoffs and Options Strategies

INTRODUCTION

This chapter considers the factors that determine the value of an option at expiration and introduces the principal strategies used in options trading. When an option is about to expire, it is relatively easy to determine its value. Thus, we begin our analysis by considering options values at expiration. When we say that an option is at expiration, we mean that the owner has a simple choice: exercise the option immediately or allow it to expire as worthless. As we will see, the value of an option at expiration depends only on the stock price and the exercise price. We also give rules for whether an owner should exercise an option or allow it to expire.

With all assets, we consider either the value of the asset or the profit or loss incurred from trading the asset. The value of an asset equals its market price. As such, the value of an asset does not depend on the purchase price. However, the profit or loss on the purchase and sale of an asset depends critically on the purchase price. In considering options, we keep these two related ideas strictly distinct. We present graphs for both the value of options and the profits from trading options, but we want to be sure not to confuse the two. By graphing the value of options and the profits or losses from options at expiration, we develop our grasp of options pricing principles. To focus on the principles of pricing, we ignore commissions and other transaction costs in this chapter.

Options traders often trade options with other options and with other assets, particularly stocks and bonds. This chapter analyzes the payoffs from combining different options and from combining options with the underlying stock. Many of these combinations have colorful names such as spreads, straddles, and strangles. Beyond the terminology, these combinations interest us because they offer special profit and loss characteristics. We also explore the particular payoff patterns that traders can create by trading options in conjunction with stocks and bonds.

STOCKS AND BONDS

We begin our analysis with the two most familiar securities—common stock and a default-free bond. Figure 2.1 presents the graph of the value of a share of stock and the value of a bond at a certain date. At any time, the value of a risk-free pure discount bond is just the present value of the par value. The graph expresses the value of a share of stock and the value of a bond as functions of stock price. In other words, we graph the stock price, or stock value, against the stock price. In the graph, a line runs from the bottom-left to the upper-right corner. Also, the graph has a horizontal line that intersects the Y-axis at $100.

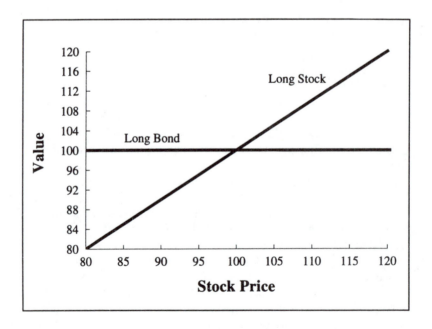

FIGURE 2.1 The Value of a Stock and a Bond

The diagonal line shows the value of a single share of the stock. When the stock price on the X-axis is $100, the value of the stock is $100. The horizontal line reflects the value of a $100 face value default-free bond at maturity. The value of the bond does not depend on the price of the stock. Because it is default-free, the bond pays $100 when it matures, no matter what happens to the stock price. For convenience, we assume that the bond matures in one year, and we graph the value of the stock and bond on that future date. Notice that the value of these instruments does not depend in any way on the purchase price of the instruments.

We now consider possible profits and losses from the share of stock and the risk-free bond. Let us assume that the stock was purchased for $100 at time t and that the pure discount (zero-coupon) risk-free bond was purchased one year before maturity at $90.91. This implies an interest rate of 10 percent on the bond. Figure 2.2 graphs the profit and losses from a long and short position in the stock. The solid line running from the bottom left to the top right of Figure 2.2 shows the profits and losses for a long position of one share in the stock, assuming a purchase price of $100. When the stock price is $100, our graph shows a zero profit. If the stock price is $105, there is a $5 profit, which equals the stock price of $105 minus the purchase price of $100.

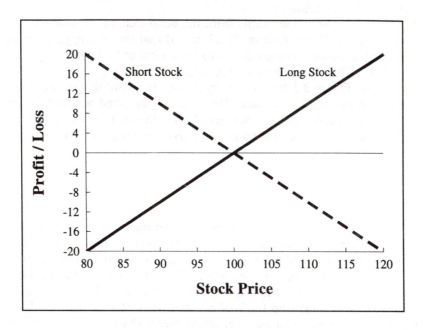

FIGURE 2.2 Profits and Losses from a Stock

The dotted line in Figure 2.2 runs from the upper-left corner to the bottom-right corner and shows the profits or losses from a short position of one share, assuming that the stock was sold at $100. Throughout this book, we used dotted lines to indicate short positions in value and profit and loss graphs. If the stock is worth $105, the short position shows a loss of $5. The short trader loses $5 because he sold the stock for $100. Now with the higher stock price, the short trader must pay $105 to buy the stock and close the short trade. As Figure 2.2 shows, the short trader bets that the stock price will fall. For example, if the trader sold the stock short at a price of $100 and the stock price falls to $93, the short trader can buy the stock and repay the person from whom he borrowed the share, earning a $7 profit (+$100 −$93).

As a final point on stock values and profits, consider the profit and loss profile for a combination of a position that is long one share and short one share. If the stock trades at $105, the long position has a profit of $5 and the short position has a loss of $5. Similarly, if the stock trades at $95, the long position has a loss of $5 and the short position has a profit of $5. No matter what stock price we consider, the profits and losses from the long and short positions cancel each other. The profit or loss is always zero. Thus, taking a long and short position in exactly the same good is a foolish exercise.

Figure 2.3 graphs the profits from the bond that we considered. The purchase price of the bond is $90.91, and it matures in one year paying $100 with certainty. The profit equals the payoff of $100 minus the cost of $90.91. Thus, the owner of the bond has a sure profit of $9.09 at expiration. Figure 2.3 shows this profit with the solid line in the upper portion of the graph. Similarly, the issuer of the bond will lose $9.09. The issuer receives $90.91, but pays $100. Presumably, the issuer has some productive use for the bond proceeds during the year that will yield more than $9.09.

ARBITRAGE

To explain the value of options, we rely throughout the book on the concept of **arbitrage**—trading to make a riskless profit with no investment. Consider the following example of arbitrage, in which we ignore transaction costs. Some stocks trade on both the New York and Pacific Stock Exchanges at the same time. Suppose that IBM sells for $100 on the New York Stock Exchange and for $102 on the Pacific Stock Exchange. With these prices a trader can simultaneously buy a share in New York and sell the same share on the Pacific Exchange for a $2 profit.

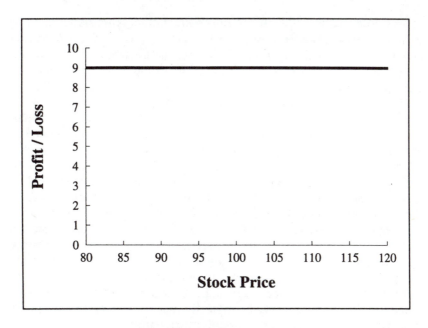

FIGURE 2.3   Profits from a Bond

This transaction provides an arbitrage profit. First, there is no investment, because the trader buys and sells the same good at the same time. Second, the profit is certain once the trader enters the two positions. Notice that we ignore transaction costs in this example. We also ignore other real-world problems, such as execution risk, the risk that we cannot execute both transactions simultaneously at the quoted prices. Nonetheless, the example shows a classic case of arbitrage, and the trader who engages in such transactions is called an **arbitrageur**.

Properly functioning financial markets allow no such arbitrage opportunities. If the two prices of our example prevailed, arbitrageurs would trade exactly as we described. They would buy the cheap share, and sell the expensive share. Of course, they would do this for as many shares as possible, not just the single share of our example. These transactions would generate a tremendous demand for IBM shares in New York and a tremendous supply of IBM shares on the Pacific Exchange. This high demand would raise the price of shares in New York, and the excess supply would cause prices on the Pacific Exchange to fall. The prices on the two exchanges would continue to adjust until they were equal, thus removing the arbitrage opportunity. If a financial market functions properly, there should be no such arbitrage opportunities in the market. In other words, in a smoothly functioning market, traders are alert and immediately compete away such opportunities as they arise. These reflections give rise to a **no-arbitrage principle**. Under the no-arbitrage pricing principle, we examine the prices of financial instruments under the assumption that the price of an instrument excludes any arbitrage possibility.

While we have assumed that there are no transaction costs, we can see their effect within the framework of our example. Assume that the transaction cost of monitoring the market and trading one share is $.10. In our example, a trader must trade two shares, buying a share in New York and selling it on the Pacific Exchange. Thus, the trader faces transaction costs of $.20 to exploit the strategy we have considered. Now assume that the price of a share is $100 in New York and $100.15 on the Pacific Exchange. The trader cannot trade profitably on such a small discrepancy. If he tries, he will pay $100 for the New York share and incur $.20 in transaction costs trying to exploit the apparent arbitrage opportunity in an effort to get a share worth $100.15. Thus, the arbitrage attempt loses $.05. This example shows that small differences in prices can persist if the difference is less than the cost of trading to exploit the difference. We know that such small discrepancies in prices can persist in actual markets; however, we ignore these differences for the sake of simplicity in our examples, and we continue to assume that transaction costs are zero.

OPTIONS NOTATION

We now introduce some notation for referring to options. As we will see, in analyzing options we are often interested in the option price as a function of the stock price, the time until expiration, and the exercise price. The options may be either calls or puts, and the options may be either European or American. Therefore, we adopt the following notation:

S_t = price of the underlying stock at time t

X = exercise price for the option

T = expiration date of the option

c_t = price of a European call at time t

C_t = price of an American call at time t

p_t = price of a European put at time t

P_t = price of an American put at time t

We will often write the value of an option in the following form:

$$c_t(S_t, X, T - t)$$

which means the price of a European call at time t given a stock price at t of S_t, for a call with an exercise price of X, which expires at time T, which is an amount of time $T - t$ from now (time t). For convenience, we sometimes omit the "t" subscript, as in:

$$p\ (S,\ X,\ T)$$

In such a case, the reader may assume that the current time is time $t = 0$, and that the option expires T periods from now. In this chapter, we focus principally on the value of options at expiration, so we will be concerned principally with values such as:

$$C_T(S_T,\ X,\ T)$$

which indicates the price of an American call option at expiration, when the stock price is S_T, the exercise price is X, and the option expires at time T, which happens to be immediately.

EUROPEAN AND AMERICAN OPTIONS VALUES AT EXPIRATION

In general, the difference between an American and a European option concerns only the exercise privileges associated with the option. An American option can be exercised at any time, while a European option can be exercised only at expiration. At expiration, both European and American options have exactly the same exercise rights. Therefore, European and American options at expiration have identical values, assuming the same underlying good and the same exercise price:

$$C_T(S_T,\ X,\ T)\ =\ c_T(S_T,\ X,\ T)\ \text{and}\ P_T(S_T,\ X,\ T)\ =\ p_T(S_T,\ X,\ T)$$

Throughout this chapter, we focus on options values and profits at expiration. Therefore, we use the notation for an American option throughout, but the results hold perfectly well for European options as well.

BUY OR SELL A CALL OPTION

We now consider the value of call options at expiration, along with the profits or losses that come from trading call options. At expiration, the owner of an option has an immediate choice: exercise the option or allow it to expire worthless. Therefore, the value of the option will either be zero or it will be the **exercise value** or the **intrinsic value**—the value of the option if it is exercised immediately. The value of a call at expiration (whether European or American) equals zero, or the stock price minus the exercise price, whichever is greater. At expiration, there is no question of early exercise, so the principles we explore pertain equally to both American and European calls. For our discussion of options values and profits at expiration, we use the notation for American options (C_T or P_T), but the principles apply identically to European options as well.

$$C_T = \text{MAX}\{0, S_T - X\} \qquad\qquad 2.1$$

To understand this principle, consider a call option with an exercise price of $100 and assume that the underlying stock trades at $95. At expiration, the call owner may either exercise the option or allow it to expire worthless. With the prices we just specified, the call owner must allow the option to expire. If the owner of the call exercises the option, he pays $100 and receives a stock that is worth $95. This gives a loss of $5 on the exercise, so it is foolish to exercise. Instead of exercising, the owner of the call can merely allow the option to expire. If the option expires, there is no additional loss involved with the exercise, because the owner of the call avoids exercising. In our example:

$$S_T - X = \$95 - \$100 = -\$5$$

The call owner need not exercise. By allowing the option to expire, the option owner acknowledges the call is worthless. With our example numbers at expiration:

$$C_T = \text{MAX}\{0, S_T - X\} =$$
$$\text{MAX}\{0, \$95 - \$100\} = \text{MAX}\{0, -\$5\} = 0$$

We can extend this example to any ending stock price we wish to consider. For any stock price less than the exercise price, the value of $S_T - X$ will be negative. Therefore, for any stock price less than the exercise price, the call will be worthless. If the stock price equals the exercise price, the value of $S_T - X$ equals zero, so the call will still be worthless. Therefore, for any stock price equal to or less than the exercise price at expiration, the call is worth zero.

If the stock price exceeds the exercise price, the call is worth the difference between the stock price and the exercise price. For example, assume that the stock price is $103 at expiration. The call option with an exercise price of $100 now allows the holder to exercise the option by paying the exercise price. Therefore, the owner of the call can acquire the stock worth $103 by paying $100. This gives an immediate payoff of $3 from exercising. Notice that this example conforms to our principle. Using these numbers we find:

$$C_T = \text{MAX}\{0, S_T - X\} =$$
$$\text{MAX}\{0, \$103 - \$100\} = \text{MAX}\{0, \$3\} = \$3$$

Figure 2.4 graphs the value of our example call at expiration. Here the value of the call equals the maximum of zero or the stock price minus the exercise price. As the graph shows, the value of the call is unlimited, at least in principle. If the stock price were $1,000 at expiration, the call would be worth $\text{MAX}\{0, S_T - X\} = \$900$. This graph shows the characteristic shape for a long position in a call option.

Figure 2.4 also shows the value of a short position in the same call option. The dotted line graphs the short position. (For stock prices between 0 and $100, both graphs lie on the same line.) Notice that the short position has a zero value for all stock prices equal to or less than the

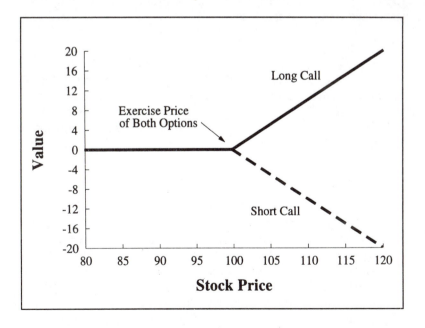

FIGURE 2.4 The Value of a Call at Expiration

exercise price. If the stock price exceeds the exercise price, the short position is costly. Using our notation, the value of a short call position at expiration is:

$$-C_T = - \text{MAX}\{0, S_T - X\}$$

Assume that the stock price is \$107 at expiration. In this case, the call owner will exercise the option. The seller of the call must then deliver a stock worth \$107 and receive the exercise price of \$100. This means that holding a short position in the call is worth $-\$7$. The short position never has a value greater than zero, and when the stock price exceeds the exercise price, the short position is worse than worthless. From this consideration, it appears that no one would ever willingly take a short position in a call option. However, this leaves out the payments made from the buyer to the seller when the option first trades.

Continuing with our same example of a call option at expiration with a striking price of \$100, we consider profit and loss results. We assume that the call option was purchased for \$5. To profit, the holder of a long position in the call needs a stock price that will cover the exercise price and the cost of acquiring the option. For a long position in a call acquired at time $t < T$ the cost of the call is C_t. The profit or loss on the long call position held until expiration is:

$$C_T - C_t = \text{MAX}\{0, S_T - X\} - C_t$$

The seller of a call receives payment when the option first trades. The seller continues to hope for a stock price at expiration that does not exceed the exercise price. However, even if the stock price exceeds the exercise price, there may still be some profit left for the seller. The profit or loss on the sale of a call, with the position being held until expiration is:

$$C_t - C_T = C_t - \text{MAX}\{0, S_T - X\}$$

Figure 2.5 graphs the profit and losses for the call option positions under the assumptions we have been considering. Graphically, bringing profits and losses into consideration shifts the long call graph down by the \$5 purchase price and shifts the short call graph up by the \$5 purchase price.

We can understand Figure 2.5 for both the long and short positions by considering a few key stock values. We begin with the long position. To acquire a long position in the call option, the trader paid \$5. If the stock price is \$100 or less, the value of the option is zero at expiration and the owner of the call lets it expire. Therefore, for any stock price

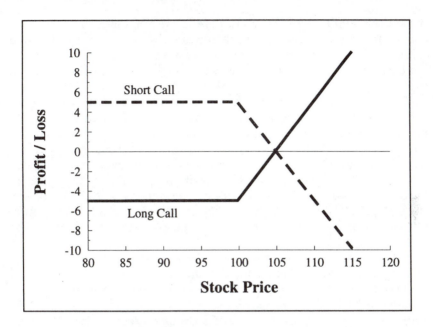

FIGURE 2.5   Profits and Losses from a Call at Expiration

equal to or less than the $100 exercise price, the call owner simply loses the entire purchase price of the option. If the stock price at expiration is above $100 but less than $105, the graph shows that the holder of the long call still loses, but loses less than the total $5 purchase price. For example, if the stock price at expiration is $103, the long call holder loses $2 in total. The call owner exercises, buying the $103 stock for $100, and makes $3 on the exercise. This $3 exercise value, coupled with the $5 paid for the option, gives a net loss of $2. As another example, if the stock price is $105 at expiration, the holder of the call makes $5 by exercising, a profit that exactly offsets the purchase price of the option, so there is no profit or loss. From this example, we see that the holder of a call makes a zero profit if the stock price equals the exercise price plus the price paid for the call. To profit, the call holder needs a stock price that exceeds the exercise price plus the price paid for the call.

Figure 2.5 shows several important points. First, for the call buyer, the worst that can happen is losing the entire purchase price of the option. Comparing Figure 2.5 with Figure 2.2, we can see that the potential dollar loss is much greater if we hold the stock rather than the call. However, a small drop in the stock price can cause a complete loss of the option price. Second, potential profits from a long position in a call option are theoretically unlimited. The profits depend only on the price of the stock at expiration. Third, our discussion and graph show that the holder of a call option will exercise any time the stock price at expiration exceeds the exercise price. The call holder will exercise to reduce a loss or to capture a profit.

We now consider profit and losses on a short position in a call option. When the long trader bought a call, he paid $5 to the seller. As we noted in Chapter 1, the premium paid by the purchaser at the time of the initial trade belongs to the seller no matter what happens from that point forward. As Figure 2.5 shows, the greatest profit the seller of the call can achieve is $5. The seller attains this maximum profit when the holder of the call cannot exercise. In our example, the seller's profit is $5 for any stock price of $100 or less, because the call owner will allow the option to expire worthless for any stock price at expiration at or below the exercise price.

If the call owner can exercise, the seller's profits will be lower and the seller may incur a loss. For example, if the stock price is $105, the owner of the call will exercise. In this event, the seller will be forced to surrender a share worth $105 in exchange for the $100 exercise price. This represents a loss for the seller in the exercise of $5, which exactly offsets the price the seller received for the option. So with a stock price of $105, the seller makes a zero profit, as does the call owner. If the stock price exceeds $105, the seller will incur a loss. For example, with a stock price of $115, the call owner will exercise. At the exercise, the seller of the call delivers a share worth $115 and receives the $100 exercise price. The seller thereby loses $15 on the exercise. Coupled with the $5 the seller received when the option traded, the seller now has a net loss of $10.

In summary, we can note two key points about the profits and losses from selling a call. First, the best thing that can happen to the seller of a call is never to hear any more about the transaction after collecting the initial premium. As Figure 2.5 shows, the best profit for the seller of the call is to keep the initial purchase price. Second, potential losses from selling a call are theoretically unlimited. As the stock price rises, the losses for the seller of a call continue to mount. For example, if the stock price went to $1,000 at expiration, the seller of the call would lose $895.

Figure 2.5 also provides a dramatic illustration of one of the most important and sobering points about options trading. The profits from the buyer and seller of the call together are always zero. The buyer's gains are the seller's losses and vice versa.

$$\text{Long call profits} + \text{Short call profits} =$$
$$(C_T - C_t) + (C_t - C_T) =$$
$$(\text{MAX}\{0, S_T - X\} - C_t) + (C_t - \text{MAX}\{0, S_T - X\}) = 0$$

Therefore, the options market is a **zero-sum game**; there are no net profits or losses in the market.[1] The trader who hopes to speculate successfully must be planning for someone else's losses to provide his profits. In other words, the options market is a very competitive arena, with profits coming only at the expense of another trader.

CALL OPTIONS AT EXPIRATION AND ARBITRAGE

What happens if options values stray from the relationships we analyzed in the preceding section? In this section, we use the no-arbitrage pricing principle to show that call options prices must obey the rules we just developed.[2] If prices stray from these relationships, arbitrage opportunities arise. In the preceding section, we considered an example of a call option with an exercise price of $100. At expiration, with the stock trading at $103, the price of a call option must be $3. In this section, we show that any other price for the call option will create an arbitrage opportunity. If the price is too high, say $4, there is one arbitrage opportunity. If the call is too cheap, say $2, there is another arbitrage opportunity. To see why the call must trade for at least $3, consider the arbitrage opportunity that arises if the call is only $2. In this case, the money-hungry arbitrageur would transact as follows.

Transaction	Cash Flow
Buy 1 call	−2
Exercise the call	−100
Sell the share	+103
Net Cash Flow	+$1

These transactions meet the conditions for arbitrage. First, there is no investment because all the transactions occur simultaneously. The only cash flow is a $1 cash inflow. Second, the profit is certain once the trader enters the transaction. Therefore, these transactions meet our conditions for arbitrage: They offer a riskless profit without investment. If the call were priced at $2, traders would follow our strategy mercilessly. They would madly buy options, exercise, and sell the share. These transactions would cause tremendous demand for the call and a tremendous supply of the share. These supply and demand forces would subside only after the call and share price adjust to prevent the arbitrage.

We now consider why the call cannot trade for more than $3 at expiration. If the call price exceeds $3, a different arbitrage opportunity arises. If the call were priced at $4, for example, arbitrageurs would simply sell the overpriced call. Then they would wait to see whether the purchaser of the call exercises. We consider transactions for both possibilities—the purchaser exercises or does not exercise.

If the purchaser exercises, the arbitrageur has already sold the call and received $4. Now to fulfill his exercise commitment, the seller acquires a share for $103 in the market and delivers the share. Upon delivery, the seller of the call receives the exercise price of $100. These three transactions yield a profit of $1. If the purchaser foolishly neglects to exercise, the situation is even better for the arbitrageur. The arbitrageur already sold the call and received $4. If the purchaser fails to exercise, the option expires and the arbitrageur makes a full $4 profit. The worst-case scenario still provides the arbitrageur with a profit of $1. Therefore, these transactions represent an arbitrage transaction. First, there is no investment. Second, the transactions ensure a profit.

With a $4 call price, an exercise price of $100, and a stock price at expiration of $103, traders would madly sell call options. The excess supply of options at the $4 price would drive down the price of the option. The process would stop only when the price relationships offer no more arbitrage opportunities. This happens when the price of the call and stock conform to the relationships we developed in the preceding section. In other words, prices in financial markets must conform to our no-arbitrage principle by adjusting to eliminate any arbitrage opportunity.

The Purchaser Exercises

Transaction	Cash Flow
Sell 1 call	+4
Buy 1 share	−103
Deliver share and collect exercise price	+100
Net Cash Flow	+$1

The Purchaser Does Not Exercise

Transaction	Cash Flow
Sell 1 call	+4
Net Cash Flow	+$4

BUY OR SELL A PUT OPTION

This section deals with the value of put options and the profits and losses from buying and selling puts when the put is at expiration. Again, we use the notation for an American put (P_T), but all of the conclusions hold identically for European puts. In most respects, we can analyze put options in the same way we analyzed call options. At expiration, the holder of a put has two choices—exercise or allow the option to expire worthless. If the holder exercises, he surrenders the stock and receives the exercise price. Therefore, the holder of a put will exercise only if the exercise price exceeds the stock price. The value of a put option at expiration equals zero, or the exercise price minus the stock price, whichever is higher:

$$P_T = MAX\{0, X - S_T\} \qquad\qquad 2.2$$

We can illustrate this principle with an example. Consider a put option with an exercise price of $100 and assume that the underlying stock trades at $102. At expiration, the holder of the put can either exercise or allow the put to expire worthless. With an exercise price of $100 and a stock price of $102, the holder cannot exercise profitably. To exercise the put, the trader would surrender the stock worth $102 and receive the exercise price of $100, thereby losing $2 on the exercise. Consequently, if the stock price is above the exercise price at expiration, the put is worthless. With our example numbers we have:

$$P_T = MAX\{0, X - S_T\} = MAX\{0, \$100 - \$102\} = MAX\{0, -\$2\} = 0$$

Now consider the same put option with the stock trading at $100. Exercising the put requires surrendering the stock worth $100 and receiving the exercise price of $100. There is no profit in exercising and the put is at expiration, so the put is still worthless. In general, if the stock price equals or exceeds the exercise price at expiration, the put is worthless.

When the stock price at expiration falls below the exercise price, the put has value. In this situation, the value of the put equals the exercise price minus the stock price. For example, assume the stock trades at $94 and consider the same put with an exercise price of $100. Now the put is worth $6 because it gives its owner the right to receive the $100 exercise price by surrendering a stock worth only $94. Using these numbers we find:

$$P_T = MAX\{0, X - S_T\} = MAX\{0, \$100 - \$94\} = MAX\{0, \$6\} = \$6$$

Figure 2.6 graphs the value of our example put option at expiration. The graph shows the value of a long position as the solid line and the

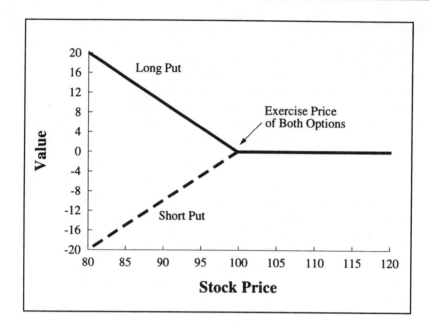

FIGURE 2.6   The Value of a Put at Expiration

value of a short position as the dotted line. For stock values equaling or exceeding the $100 exercise price, the put has a zero value. If the stock price is below the exercise price, however, the put is worth the exercise price minus the stock price. As our example showed, if the stock trades for $94, the put is worth $6. The graph reflects this valuation.

Figure 2.6 also shows the value of a short position in the put. For stock prices equaling or exceeding the exercise price, the put has a zero value. This zero value results from the fact that the holder of the long put will not exercise. However, when the stock price at expiration is less than the exercise price, a short position in the put has a negative value, which results from the opportunity that the long put holder has to exercise. For example, if the stock price is $94, the holder of a short position in the put must pay $100 for a stock worth only $94 when the long put holder exercises. In this situation, the short position in the put will be worth −$6.

Our analysis of put values parallels our results for call options in several ways. First, as we saw with the values of call options at expiration, the value of long and short positions in puts always sums to zero for any stock price. We noted in our discussion of call options that the option market is a zero-sum game. The same principle extends to put options with equal force. Second, we see for put options, as we noted for call options, that a short position can never have a positive value at expiration. The seller of a call or put hopes that nothing happens after the initial transaction when he collects the option price. The best outcome for the seller of either a put or a call is that there will be no exercise and that the option will expire worthless. Third, noting that a short put position has a zero value at best, we might wonder why anyone would accept a short position. As we saw with a call option, the rationality of selling a put requires us to consider the sale price. This leads to a consideration of put option profits and losses.

We continue with our example of a put option with an exercise price of $100. Now we assume that this option was purchased for a price of $4. We consider how profits and losses on long and short put positions depend on the stock price at expiration. As we did for calls, we consider a few key stock prices.

First, we analyze the profits and losses for a long position in the put, where the purchase price is $4 and the exercise price is $100. If the stock price at expiration exceeds $100, the holder of the put cannot exercise profitably and the option expires worthless. In this case, the put holder loses $4, the purchase price of the option. Likewise, if the stock price at expiration equals $100, there is no profitable exercise. Exercising in this situation would only involve surrendering a stock worth $100 and receiving the $100 exercise price. Again, the buyer of the put option loses the purchase price of $4. Therefore, if the stock price at expiration equals or exceeds the exercise price, the buyer of a put loses the full purchase price. Figure 2.7 shows the profits and losses for long and short positions in the put.

If the stock price at expiration is less than the exercise price, there will be a benefit to exercising. For example, assume the stock price is $99 at expiration. Then, the owner of the put will exercise, surrendering the $99 stock and receiving the $100 exercise price. In this case, the exercise value of the put is $1. With the $99 stock price, the holder of the put makes $1 on the exercise but has already paid $4 to acquire the put. Therefore, the total loss is $3. If the stock price is $96 at expiration, the buyer of the put makes a zero profit. The $4 exercise value exactly offsets the price of the put. When the stock price is less than $96, the put buyer makes a profit. For example, if the stock price is $90 at expiration, the owner of a put exercises. In exercising, he surrenders a stock worth $90 and receives the $100 exercise price. This gives a $6 profit after considering the $4 purchase price of the option.

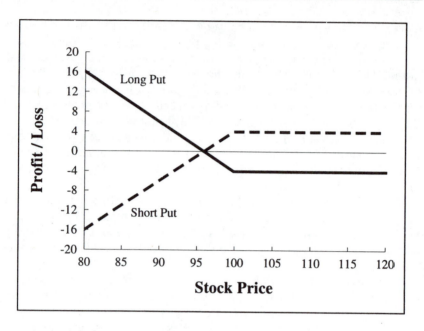

FIGURE 2.7   Profits and Losses from a Put at Expiration

MONEYNESS

In the preceding sections, we have explored the value of calls and puts at expiration. We noted that calls have a positive value at expiration if the stock price exceeds the exercise price, and puts have a positive value at expiration if the exercise price exceeds the stock price. We now introduce important terminology that applies to options both before and at expiration. Both calls and puts can be **in-the-money**, **at-the-money**, or **out-of-the-money**. The following table shows the conditions for puts and calls to meet these moneyness conditions for any time t.

	Calls	Puts
In-the-money	$S_t > X$	$S_t < X$
At-the-money	$S_t = X$	$S_t = X$
Out-of-the-money	$S_t < X$	$S_t > X$

In addition, options can be **near-the-money** if the stock price is close to the exercise price. Further, a call is **deep-in-the-money** if the stock price is considerably above the exercise price, and a put is deep-in-the-money if the stock price is considerably smaller than the exercise price.

OPTIONS COMBINATIONS

This section discusses some of the most important ways that traders can combine options. By trading options combinations, traders can shape the risk and return characteristics of their option positions, which allow more precise speculative strategies. For example, we will see how to use options combinations to profit when stock prices move a great deal or when they stagnate.

The Straddle

A **straddle** consists of a call and a put with the same exercise price and the same expiration. The buyer of a straddle buys the call and put, while the seller of a straddle sells the same two options.[3] Consider a call and put, both with $100 exercise prices. We assume the call costs $5 and the put trades for $4. Figure 2.8 shows the profits and losses from purchasing each of these options. The profit and losses for buying the straddle are just the combined profits and losses from buying both options. If we designate T as the expiration date of the option and let t be the present, then C_t is the current price of the option and C_T is the price of the option at expiration. Similarly, P_t is the present price of the put and P_T is the price of the put at expiration. Using this notation, the cost of the long straddle is:

$$C_t + P_t$$

and the value of the straddle at expiration will be:

$$C_T + P_T = \text{MAX}\{0, S_T - X\} + \text{MAX}\{0, X - S_T\} \qquad 2.3$$

Similarly, the short straddle position costs:

$$- C_t - P_t$$

so the short trader receives a payment for accepting the short straddle position. The value of the short straddle at expiration will be:

$$- C_T - P_T = - \text{MAX}\{0, S_T - X\} - \text{MAX}\{0, X - S_T\}$$

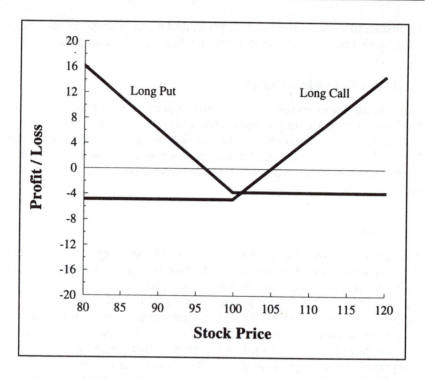

FIGURE 2.8   Profits and Losses at Expiration from the Options in a Straddle

Because the options market is always a zero-sum game, the short trad-er's profits and losses mirror those of the long position. Figure 2.9 shows the profits and losses from buying and selling the straddle. As the graph shows, the maximum loss for the straddle buyer is the cost of the two options. Potential profits are almost unlimited for the buyer if the stock price rises or falls enough. As Figure 2.9 also shows, the maximum profit for the short straddle trader occurs when the stock price at expiration equals the exercise price. If the stock price equals the exercise price, the straddle owner cannot exercise either the call or the put profitably. There-fore, both options expire worthless and the short straddle trader keeps both option premiums for a total profit of $9. However, if the stock price diverges from the exercise price, the long straddle holder will exercise either the call or the put. Any exercise decreases the short trader's profits and may even generate a loss. If the stock price exceeds the exercise price, the call owner will exercise, while if the stock price is less than the exercise price, the straddle owner will exercise the put.

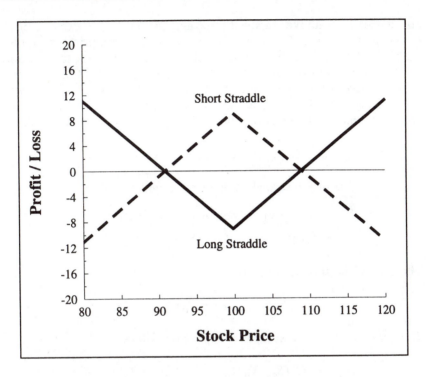

FIGURE 2.9   Profits and Losses at Expiration from a Straddle

Figure 2.9 shows that the short trader essentially bets that the stock price will not diverge too far from the exercise price, so the seller is betting that the stock price will not be too volatile. In making this bet, the straddle seller risks theoretically unlimited losses if the stock price goes too high. Likewise, the short trader's losses are almost unlimited if the stock price goes too low.[4] The short trader's cash inflows equal the sum of the two option prices. At expiration, the short trader's cash outflow equals the exercise result for the call and for the put. If the call is exercised against him at expiration, the short trader loses the difference between the stock price and the exercise price. If the put is exercised against him, the short trader loses the difference between the exercise price and the stock price.

The Strangle

Like a straddle, a **strangle** consists of a put and a call with the same expiration date and the same underlying good. In a strangle the call has an exercise price above the stock price and the put has an exercise price below the stock price. Let X_1 and X_2 be the two exercise prices, such that $X_1 > X_2$. Therefore, a strangle is similar to a straddle, but the put and call have different exercise prices. Let $C_{t,1}$ denote the cost of the call with exercise price X_1 at time t, and let $P_{t,2}$ indicate the cost of the put with exercise price X_2. The long strangle trader buys the put and call, while the short trader sells the two options. The cost of the long strangle is:

$$C_t(S_t, X_1, T) + P_t(S_t, X_2, T)$$

Then the value of the strangle at expiration will be:

$$C_T(S_T, X_1, T) + P_T(S_T, X_2, T) =$$
$$\text{MAX}\{0, S_T - X_1\} + \text{MAX}\{0, X_2 - S_T\} \qquad 2.4$$

The cost of the short strangle is:

$$- C_t(S_t, X_1, T) - P_t(S_t, X_2, T)$$

The value of the short strangle at expiration will be:

$$- C_T(S_T, X_1, T) - P_T(S_T, X_2, T) =$$
$$- \text{MAX}\{0, S_T - X_1\} - \text{MAX}\{0, X_2 - S_T\}$$

To illustrate the strangle, we use a call with an exercise price of $85 and a put with an exercise price of $80. The call price is $3 and the put price is $4. Figure 2.10 graphs the profits and losses for long positions in these two options. The call has a profit for any stock price above $88, and the put has a profit for any stock price below $76. However, for the owner of a strangle to profit, the price of the stock must fall below $76 or rise above $88. Figure 2.11 shows the profits and losses from buying and selling the strangle based on these two options. The total outlay for the two options is $7. To break even, either the call or the put must give an exercise profit of $7. The call makes an exercise profit of $7 when the stock price is $7 above the exercise price of the call. This price is $92. Similarly, the put has an exercise profit of $7 when the stock price is $73. Any stock price between $73 and $92 results in a loss on the strangle, while any stock price outside the $73–$92 range gives a profit on the strangle.

Figure 2.11 shows that buying a strangle is betting that the stock price will move significantly below the exercise price on the put or above the

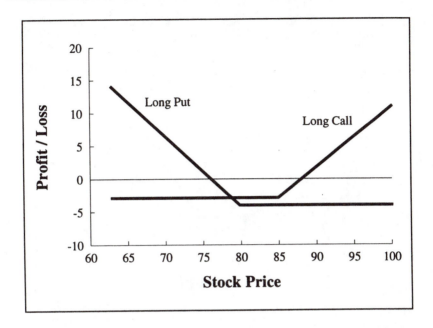

FIGURE 2.10 Profits and Losses at Expiration from the Options in a Strangle

exercise price on the call. The buyer of the strangle has the chance for very large profits if the stock price moves dramatically away from the exercise prices. Theoretically, the profit on a strangle is boundless. A stock price at expiration of $200, for example, gives a profit on the strangle of $108.

The profits on the short position are just the negative values of the profits for the long position. Figure 2.11 shows the profits and losses for the short strangle position as dotted lines. At any stock price from $80–$85, the short strangle has a $7 profit. Between these two prices, the long trader cannot profit by exercising either the put or the call, so the short trader keeps the full price of both options. For stock prices below $80, the straddle buyer exercises the put, and for stock prices above $85, the straddle buyer exercises the call. Any exercise costs the short trader, who still has some profit if the stock price stays within the $73–$92 range. However, for very low stock prices, the short strangle position gives large losses, as it does for very high stock prices. Therefore, the short strangle trader is betting that stock prices stay within a fairly wide band. In essence, the short strangle trader has a high probability of a small profit, but accepts the risk of a very large loss.

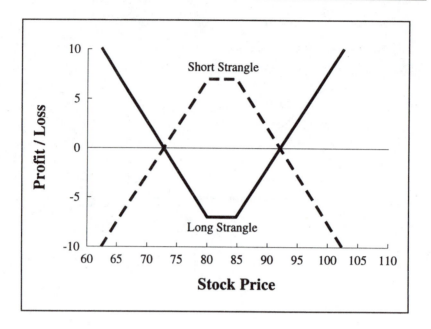

FIGURE 2.11 Profits and Losses at Expiration from a Strangle

Bull and Bear Spreads with Call Options

A **bull spread** in the options market is a combination of options designed to profit if the price of the underlying good rises.[5] A bull spread utilizing call options requires two calls with the same underlying stock and the same expiration date, but with different exercise prices. The buyer of a bull spread buys a call with an exercise price below the stock price and sells a call option with an exercise price above the stock price. The spread is a "bull" spread, because the trader hopes to profit from a price rise in the stock. The trade is a "spread," because it involves buying one option and selling a related option. Compared to buying the stock itself, the bull spread with call options limits the trader's risk, but the bull spread also limits the profit potential.

The cost of the bull spread is the cost of the option that is purchased, less the cost of the option that the trader sells. Letting $C_{t,1}$ be the cost of the first option that is purchased at time t with exercise price X_1, and letting $C_{t,2}$ be the cost of the second option with exercise price X_2, such that $X_1 < X_2$, the cost of the bull spread is:

$$C_t(S_t, X_1, T) - C_t(S_t, X_2, T)$$

At expiration, the value of the bull spread will be:

$$C_T(S_T, X_1, T) - C_T(S_T, X_2, T) =$$
$$\text{MAX}\{0, S_T - X_1\} - \text{MAX}\{0, S_T - X_2\} \qquad 2.5$$

To illustrate the bull spread, assume that the stock trades at $100. One call option has an exercise price of $95 and costs $7. The other call has an exercise price of $105 and costs $3. To buy the bull spread, the trader buys the call with the lower exercise price, and sells the call with the higher exercise price. In our example, the total outlay for the bull spread is $4. Figure 2.12 graphs the profits and losses for the two call positions individually. The long position profits if the stock price moves above $102. The short position profits if the stock price does not exceed $108. As the graph shows, low stock prices result in an overall loss for the bull spread, because the cost of buying the call with the lower exercise price

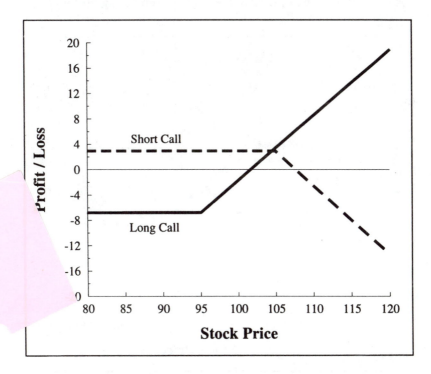

FIGURE 2.12   Profits and Losses at Expiration from the Options in a Bull Spread

exceeds the proceeds from selling the call with the higher exercise price. It is also interesting to consider prices at $105 and above. For every dollar by which the stock price exceeds $105, the long call portion of the spread generates an extra dollar of profit, but the short call component starts to lose money. Thus, for stock prices above $105, the additional gains on the long call exactly offset the losses on the short call. Therefore, no matter how high the stock price goes, the bull spread can never give a greater profit than it does for a stock price of $105.

Figure 2.13 graphs the bull spread as the solid line. For any stock price at expiration of $95 or below, the bull spread loses $4. This $4 is the difference between the cash inflow for selling one call and buying the other. The bull spread breaks even for a stock price of $99. The highest possible profit on the bull spread comes when the stock sells for $105. Then the bull spread gives a $6 profit. For any stock price above $105, the profit on the bull spread remains at $6. Therefore, the trader of a bull spread bets that the stock price goes up, but he hedges his bet. We can see that the bull spread protects the trader from losing any more than

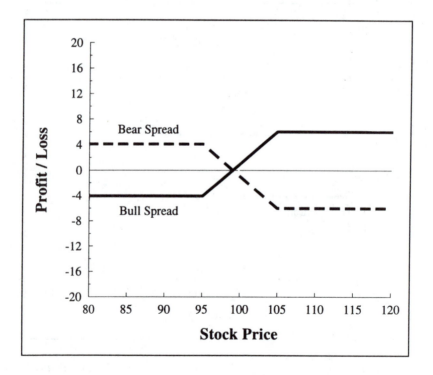

FIGURE 2.13   Profits and Losses at Expiration from a Bull Spread with Calls

$4. However, the trader cannot make more than a $6 profit. We can compare the bull spread with a position in the stock itself in Figure 2.2. Comparing the bull spread and the stock, we find that the stock offers the chance for bigger profits, but it also has greater risk of a serious loss.

A bear spread in the options market is an option combination designed to profit from falling stock prices. To execute a bear spread with call options requires two call options with the same underlying stock and the same expiration date. The two calls, however, have different exercise prices. To execute a bear spread with calls, a trader would sell the call with the lower exercise price and buy the call with the higher exercise price. In other words, the bear spread with calls is just the short position to the bull spread with calls.

The cost of a bear spread is:

$$- C_t(S_t, X_1, T) + C_t(S_t, X_2, T)$$

At expiration, the value of the bear spread will be:

$$- C_T(S_T, X_1, T) + C_T(S_T, X_2, T) =$$
$$- \text{MAX}\{0, S_T - X_1\} + \text{MAX}\{0, S_T - X_2\} \qquad 2.6$$

Figure 2.13 shows the profit and loss profile for a bear spread with the same options we have been considering. The dotted line shows how profit and losses vary if a trader sells the call with the $95 strike price and buys the call with the $105 strike price. In a bear spread, the trader bets that the stock price will fall. However, the bear spread also limits the profit opportunity and the risk of loss compared to a short position in the stock itself. We can compare the profit and loss profiles of the bear spread in Figure 2.13 with the short position in the stock shown as the dotted line in Figure 2.2.[6]

Bull and Bear Spreads with Put Options

It is also possible to execute bull and bear spreads with put options in a manner similar to the bull and bear spread with call options. The bull spread consists of buying a put with a lower exercise price and selling a put with a higher exercise price. The bear spread trader sells a put with a lower exercise price and buys a put with a higher exercise price. Consistent with our notation for call options, the cost of the bull spread with puts is:

$$P_t(S_t, X_1, T) - P_t(S_t, X_2, T)$$

with exercises prices X_1 and X_2, respectively, such that $X_1 < X_2$. The value of the bull spread at expiration will be:

$$P_T(S_T, X_1, T) - P_T(S_T, X_2, T) =$$
$$\text{MAX}\{0, X_1 - S_T\} - \text{MAX}\{0, X_2 - S_T\} \qquad 2.7$$

It is also possible to initiate a bear spread with puts. The bear spread is just the opposite of a bull spread. For a put bear spread, the trader uses two options on the same underlying good that have the same time until expiration. The trader sells the put with the lower exercise price and buys the put with the higher exercise price. The bear spread with puts is simply the complementary position to the bull spread, and costs:

$$- P_t(S_t, X_1, T) + P_t(S_t, X_2, T)$$

The value of the bear spread with puts at expiration is:

$$- P_T(S_T, X_1, T) + P_T(S_T, X_2, T) =$$
$$- \text{MAX}\{0, X_1 - S_T\} + \text{MAX}\{0, X_2 - S_T\}$$

To illustrate bull and bear spreads with put options, consider two puts with the same expiration date and the same underlying stock. Assume that one put has an exercise price of $90 and the other has an exercise price of $110. The put with an exercise price of $90 trades at $3, while the put with an exercise price of $110 trades at $9.

The bull trader would buy the put with $X = \$90$ and sell the put with $X = \$110$, for a total cash inflow of $6. Assume the stock price at expiration is $90. The bull trader cannot exercise the put option with $X = \$90$. However, the put option with $X = \$110$ that the trader sold will be exercised, giving our trader an exercise loss of $20. Thus, the total loss for the bull trader will be $14, the initial cash inflow of $6, minus the $20 exercise loss. For any terminal stock price lower than $90, the bull trader will lose an additional dollar on the short put position. However, if the stock price falls below $90, the bull trader can exercise the long put with a striking price of $90. Thus, the gain on the long put will offset any further losses on the short put for stock prices lower than $90. Therefore, the maximum loss on the bull spread of $14 occurs with a stock price of $90 or lower.

If the stock price at expiration is $110 or higher, the short put cannot be exercised against the bull trader of our example. Also, the long put cannot be exercised, because it cannot be exercised at any price of $90 or higher. With no exercises occurring, the bull trader merely keeps the initial cash inflow that occurred when the position was assumed, and the bull trader nets a profit of $6.

For prices between $90 and $110, the short put will be exercised against the bull trader and will reduce the trader's profits or generate a loss. For example, if the stock price is $100 at expiration, the bull trader will lose $10 on the exercise of the put with $X = \$110$. This loss, coupled with the initial cash inflow of $6, gives a total loss on the trade of $4. Figure 2.14 shows the profits and losses from this bull trade with puts as the solid line, and it shows the bear spread with puts as a dotted line. As Figure 2.14 shows, the bear trader takes the opposite position from the bull trader.

In terms of our example, the bear trader would buy the put with $X = \$110$ and sell the put with $X = \$90$, for a total outlay of $6. For any terminal stock price less than $110, the bear trader can exercise the put with $X = \$110$, and will break even for a terminal stock price of $104. For any stock price below $90, the bear trader's short call will be exercised against her as well, giving an exercise loss on that option. This exercise loss will offset any further profits on the long put with $X = \$110$. As a result, the bear trader cannot make more than $14. This $14 profit occurs

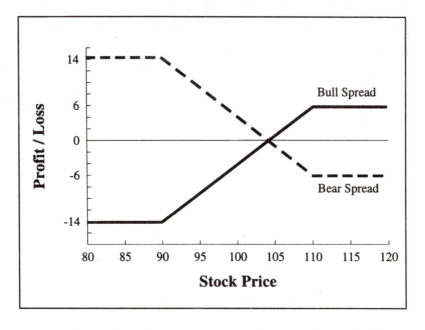

FIGURE 2.14   Profits and Losses at Expiration from a Bull Spread with Puts

for any stock price of $90 or less. For example, if the terminal stock price is $85, the bear trader has an exercise profit of $25 on the long put with $X = \$110$ and an exercise loss of $-\$5$ on the short put with $X = \$90$. This total exercise profit of $20 must be reduced by the $6 outlay required to assume the bear spread, for a net gain of $14. This gain of $14 when the stock price is $85 exactly equals the loss of $14 that the bull spread holder would incur.

The Box Spread

A box spread consists of a bull spread with calls plus a bear spread with puts, with the two spreads having the same pair of exercise prices. In terms of our notation, the box spread costs:

$$C_t(S_t, X_1, T) - C_t(S_t, X_2, T) + P_t(S_t, X_1, T) - P_t(S_t, X_2, T)$$

The value of the box spread at expiration is:

$$
\begin{aligned}
C_T(S_T, X_1, T) - C_T(S_T, X_2, T) - P_T(S_T, X_1, T) + P_T(S_T, X_2, T) = \\
\text{MAX}\{0, S_T - X_1\} - \text{MAX}\{0, S_T - X_2\} - \\
\text{MAX}\{0, X_1 - S_T\} + \text{MAX}\{0, X_2 - S_T\}
\end{aligned}
\qquad 2.8
$$

As an example, consider the following four transactions:

Transaction	Exercise Price
Long 1 call	$95
Short 1 call	105
Long 1 put	105
Short 1 put	95

The value of the box spread at expiration will be:

$$
\begin{aligned}
\text{MAX}\{0, S_T - \$95\} - \text{MAX}\{0, S_T - \$105\} + \\
\text{MAX}\{0, \$105 - S_T\} - \text{MAX}\{0, \$95 - S_T\}
\end{aligned}
$$

For a stock price of $102 at expiration, the payoff will be:

$$\$7 - \$0 + \$3 - \$0 = \$10$$

For a stock price of $80, the payoff at expiration will be:

$$\$0 - \$0 + \$25 - \$15 = \$10$$

In fact, for any terminal stock price, the box spread will pay the difference between the high and low exercise prices, $X_2 - X_1$, which is $10 in this example. Thus, the box spread is a riskless investment strategy. To avoid potential arbitrage opportunities, the price of the box spread must be the present value of the certain payoff. Therefore, the cost of the box spread purchased at time t must be:

$$\frac{X_2 - X_1}{(1 + r)^{(T - t)}}$$

Continuing with this example, let us assume that the options expire in one year and that the risk-free interest rate is 10 percent. Under these assumptions, the box spread must cost $9.09. Any other price would lead to arbitrage.

The Butterfly Spread with Calls

A butterfly spread can be executed by using three calls with the same expiration date on the same underlying stock. The long trader buys one call with a low exercise price, buys one call with a high exercise price, and sells two calls with an intermediate exercise price. Continuing to let X_i represent exercise prices such that $X_1 < X_2 < X_3$, the cost of the long butterfly spread is:

$$C_t(S_t, X_1, T) - 2\,C_t(S_t, X_2, T) + C_t(S_t, X_3, T)$$

The value of the butterfly spread at expiration is:

$$C_T(S_T, X_1, T) - 2\,C_T(S_T, X_2, T) + C_T(S_T, X_3, T) =$$
$$\text{MAX}\{0, S_T - X_1\} - 2\,\text{MAX}\{0, S_T - X_2\} + \text{MAX}\{0, S_T - X_3\} \quad 2.9$$

The short trader takes exactly the opposite position, selling one call with a low exercise price, selling one call with a high exercise price, and buying two calls with an intermediate exercise price. The cost of the short position is:

$$- C_t(S_t, X_1, T) + 2\,C_t(S_t, X_2, T) - C_t(S_t, X_3, T)$$

The value of the short butterfly spread at expiration is:

$$- C_T(S_T, X_1, T) + 2 C_T(S_T, X_2, T) - C_t(S_T, X_3, T) =$$
$$- \text{MAX}\{0, S_T - X_1\} + 2 \text{MAX}\{0, S_T - X_2\} - \text{MAX}\{0, S_T - X_3\}$$

For the long trader, the spread profits most when the stock price at expiration is at the intermediate exercise price. In essence, the butterfly spread gives a payoff pattern similar to a straddle. Compared to a straddle, however, a butterfly spread offers lower risk at the expense of reduced profit potential.

As an example of a butterfly spread, assume that a stock trades at $100 and a trader buys a butterfly spread by trading options with the prices shown in the following table. As the table shows, the buyer of a butterfly spread sells two calls with a striking price near the stock price and buys one each of the calls above and below the stock price.

	Exercise Price	Option Premium
Long 1 call	$105	$3
Short 2 calls	100	4
Long 1 call	95	7

Figure 2.15 graphs the profits and losses from each of these three options positions. To understand the profits and losses from the butterfly spread, we need to combine these profits and losses, remembering that the spread involves selling two options and buying two, a total of four options with three different exercise prices.

Let us consider a few critical stock prices to see how the butterfly spread profits respond. The critical stock prices always include the exercise prices for the options. First, if the stock price is $95, the call with an exercise price of $95 is worth zero and a long position in this call loses $7. The long call with the $105 exercise price also cannot be exercised, so it is worthless, giving a loss of the $3 purchase price. The short call position gives a profit of $4 per option and the spread sold two of these options, for an $8 profit. Adding these values gives a net loss on the spread of $2, if the stock price is $95. Second, if the stock price is $100, the long call with a striking price of $95 loses $2 (the $5 stock profit minus the $7 purchase price). The long call with an exercise price of $105 loses its full purchase price of $3. Together, the long calls lose $5. The short call still shows a profit of $4 per option, for a profit of $8 on the two options. This gives a net profit of $3 if the stock price is $100. Third,

FIGURE 2.15 Profits and Losses at Expiration for the Options in a Butterfly Spread

if the stock price is $105 at expiration, the long call with an exercise price of $95 has a profit of $3. The long call with an exercise price of $105 loses $3. Also, the short call position loses $1 per option for a loss on two positions of $2. This gives a net loss on the butterfly spread of $2. In summary we have: a $2 loss for a $95 stock price, a $3 profit for a $100 stock price, and a $2 loss for a $105 stock price.

Figure 2.16 shows the entire profit and loss graph for the butterfly spread. At a stock price of $100, we noted a profit of $3. This is the highest profit available from the spread. At stock prices of $95 and $105, the spread loses $2. For stock prices below $95 or above $105, the loss is still $2. As the graph shows, the butterfly spread has a zero profit for stock prices of $97 and $103. The buyer of the butterfly spread essentially bets that stock prices will hover near $100. Any large move away from $100 gives a loss on the butterfly spread. However, the loss can never exceed $2. Comparing the butterfly spread with the straddle in Figure 2.9, we see that the butterfly spread resembles a short position in the straddle. Compared to the straddle, the butterfly spread reduces the risk of a very large loss. However, the reduction in risk necessarily comes at the expense of a chance for a big profit.

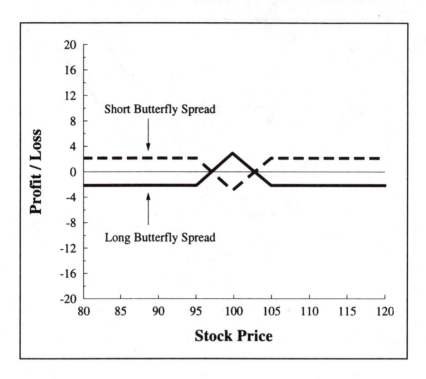

FIGURE 2.16 Profits and Losses at Expiration for a Butterfly Spread with Calls

The Butterfly Spread with Puts

The butterfly spread can also be initiated with a combination of put options. For a long position in a butterfly spread, the trader buys a put with a low exercise price, buys a put with a high exercise price, and sells two puts with an intermediate exercise price. The short trader sells a put with a low exercise price, sells a put with a high exercise price, and buys two puts with an intermediate exercise price.

For the long position in the butterfly spread with puts, the cost is:

$$P_t(S_t, X_1, T) - 2\,P_t(S_t, X_2, T) + P_t(S_t, X_3, T)$$

The value at expiration is:

$$P_T(S_T, X_1, T) - 2\,P_T(S_T, X_2, T) + P_T(S_T, X_3, T) =$$
$$\text{MAX}\{0, X_1 - S_T\} - 2\,\text{MAX}\{0, X_2 - S_T\} + \text{MAX}\{0, X_3 - S_T\} \quad 2.10$$

For the short trader, the cost of the short position is:

$$- P_t(S_t, X_1, T) + 2 P_t(S_t, X_2, T) - P_t(S_t, X_3, T)$$

The value at expiration for the short butterfly spread with puts is:

$$- P_T(S_T, X_1, T) + 2 P_T(S_T, X_2, T) - P_T(S_T, X_3, T) =$$
$$- \text{MAX}\{0, X_1 - S_T\} + 2 \text{MAX}\{0, X_2 - S_T\} -$$
$$\text{MAX}\{0, X_3 - S_T\}$$

The long and short butterfly trades with puts give a profit pattern just like the butterfly trade with calls, as illustrated in Figure 2.16.

To explore these transactions more fully, consider the following transactions for a long butterfly spread with puts.

	Exercise Price	Option Premium
Long 1 put	$95	$5
Short 2 puts	100	7
Long 1 put	105	10

The total cost of this position is $1. If the stock price at expiration is exactly $95, the put with $X = \$95$ cannot be exercised. However, both puts with $X = \$100$ will be exercised against the long trader, for an exercise loss of $10. The long trader will be able to exercise the put with $X = \$105$, for an exercise profit of $10, so the long butterfly trader will experience no net gain or loss on the exercise. The same is true for any stock price lower than $95. Lower stock prices will generate larger losses on the exercise of the puts with $X = \$100$, but these will be exactly offset by higher exercise gains on the two long puts that constitute the long butterfly spread. Thus, for any stock price of $95 or lower, there is no exercise gain or loss and the trader loses the $1 cost of the butterfly spread. At a terminal stock price of $105 or higher, no put can be exercised, so there is no exercise gain or loss and the purchaser of the butterfly spread loses the $1 cost of the position. Figure 2.17 shows these profits and losses as a solid line.

For a stock price at expiration between $95 and $105, the long trader has an exercise gain that will offset the $1 cost of the position and may even make the entire transaction profitable. For example, if the terminal stock price is $100, the puts with $X = \$95$ and $X = \$100$ cannot be

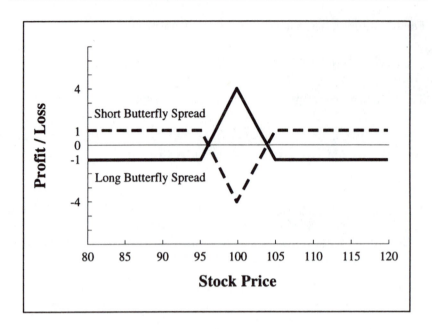

FIGURE 2.17 Profits and Losses at Expiration for a Butterfly Spread with Puts

exercised. In this situation, the trader can exercise the put with $X = \$105$ for a $5 exercise profit. This exercise profit, offset by the $1 cost of the position, gives a total gain on the trade of $4, and this is the maximum profit from the trade. For terminal stock prices between $95 and $100 or between $100 and $105, the gain will be less and may even be a loss. For a terminal stock price of $96, for example, the trader will exercise the put with $X = \$105$ for a $9 exercise profit. However, the two short puts with $X = \$100$ will be exercised against her, for an exercise loss of $-\$8$. The net exercise gain will be $1, which exactly offsets the $1 cost of the position. Thus, the trade has a zero gain/loss at a terminal stock price of $96. The same occurs if the terminal stock price is $104. For a terminal stock price between $96 and $104, there is some profit, with the maximum profit of $4 occurring when the stock price is $100.

As we noted at the beginning of this section, it is also possible to initiate a short butterfly position with puts. With the options of this example, the short butterfly transaction would require selling a put with $X = \$95$, selling a put with $X = \$105$, and buying two puts with $X = \$100$, for a total cash inflow of $1. This short butterfly position would have profits and losses that exactly mirror those of the long position. Figure 2.17

shows the profits and losses for this short butterfly position with puts as a dotted line.

The Condor with Calls

A condor is a specialized position that involves four options on the same underlying good and the same expiration date. The four options have different exercise prices. For a long condor entered with call options, a trader buys a call with a low exercise price, sells a call with a somewhat higher exercise price, sells a call with a yet higher exercise price, and buys a call with the highest exercise price. Notice that this is like a butterfly, in that the long trader buys two calls with extreme exercise prices, and sells two calls with intermediate exercise prices. In a butterfly, the intermediate exercise price is the same for the two calls, while a condor uses two different intermediate exercise prices. Thus, the cost of a long condor is:

$$C_t(S_t, X_1, T) - C_t(S_t, X_2, T) - C_t(S_t, X_3, T) + C_t(S_t, X_4, T)$$

The value of the long condor at expiration is:

$$\begin{aligned} C_T(S_T, X_1, T) - C_T(S_T, X_2, T) - C_T(S_T, X_3, T) + C_T(S_T, X_4, T) = \\ \mathrm{MAX}\{0, S_T - X_1\} - \mathrm{MAX}\{0, S_T - X_2\} - \\ \mathrm{MAX}\{0, S_T - X_3\} + \mathrm{MAX}\{0, S_T - X_4\} \end{aligned} \qquad 2.11$$

For the short condor position executed with calls, the cost of the position is:

$$- C_t(S_t, X_1, T) + C_t(S_t, X_2, T) + C_t(S_t, X_3, T) - C_t(S_t, X_4, T)$$

For the short condor, the value at expiration is:

$$\begin{aligned} - C_T(S_T, X_1, T) + C_T(S_T, X_2, T) + C_T(S_T, X_3, T) - C_T(S_T, X_4, T) = \\ - \mathrm{MAX}\{0, S_T - X_1\} + \mathrm{MAX}\{0, S_T - X_2\} + \\ \mathrm{MAX}\{0, S_T - X_3\} - \mathrm{MAX}\{0, S_T - X_4\} \end{aligned}$$

The following transactions illustrate a long condor position entered with call options.

	Exercise Price	Option Premium
Long 1 call	$90	$10
Short 1 call	95	7
Short 1 call	100	4
Long 1 call	105	2

The total cost of the condor is $1. If the terminal stock price is $90 or less, no call can be exercised and the position expires worthless for a total loss of $1. If the stock price at expiration is $95, for example, the long trader can exercise the call with $X = $ $90 for an exercise profit of $5. This gives a total profit on the position of $4. For any stock price above $95, the short call with $X = $ $95 will be exercised against the purchase of the condor, and for any stock price above $100, the short call with $X = $ $100 will also be exercised. For example, if the terminal stock price is $102, the transactions give the following result. The long call with $X = $ $90 will have a $12 exercise profit, the short call with $X = $ $95 will generate an exercise loss of $7, and the short call with $X = $ $100 will generate an exercise loss of $2. These exercise results, coupled with the $1 initial cost of the position, give a final profit of $4.

For higher terminal stock prices, those of $105 or higher, the exercise gains and losses are exactly offsetting. For example, if the terminal stock price is $107, the exercise gains and losses are: $17 for the call with $X = $ $90, $-$12 for the call with $X = $ $95, $- $7 for the call with $X = $ $100, and $2 for the call with $X = $ $105, for a net exercise result of zero. This leaves a loss of $1, which was the original cost to enter the position. Figure 2.18 shows the short condor position with the dotted line. As usual, the results for the short position are a mirror image of those for the long position. In a zero-sum game, the winner's gains exactly match the loser's losses.

The Condor with Puts

As with the other strategies we have considered, it is also possible to initiate a condor with puts as well as with calls. Again, all options have the same underlying stock and the same expiration date. For a long condor with puts, the trader buys a put with the lowest exercise price, sells a put with a higher exercise price, sells a put with a yet higher exercise price, and buys a put with the highest exercise price. The short condor trader takes the opposite side of the long position, selling a put with the lowest exercise price, buying a put with a higher exercise price, buying a put

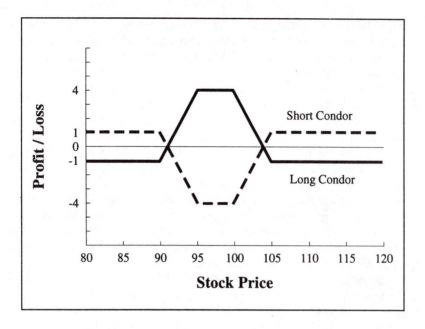

FIGURE 2.18 Profits and Losses at Expiration for a Condor with Calls

with a yet higher exercise price, and selling a put with the highest exercise price.

The cost of a long condor with puts is:

$$P_t(S_t, X_1, T) - P_t(S_t, X_2, T) - P_t(S_t, X_3, T) + P_t(S_t, X_4, T)$$

The value of the long condor with puts at expiration is given by:

$$
\begin{aligned}
P_T(S_T, X_1, T) - P_T(S_T, X_2, T) &- P_T(S_T, X_3, T) + P_T(S_T, X_4, T) = \\
&\text{MAX}\{0, X_1 - S_T\} - \text{MAX}\{0, X_2 - S_T\} - \qquad \text{2.12} \\
&\text{MAX}\{0, X_3 - S_T\} + \text{MAX}\{0, X_4 - S_T\}
\end{aligned}
$$

The following transactions illustrate a long condor initiated with puts.

	Exercise Price	Option Premium
Long 1 put	$90	$2
Short 1 put	95	5
Short 1 put	100	9
Long 1 put	105	13

With these prices, the long condor position costs $1. For a terminal stock price of $105 or higher, none of these puts can be exercised, so the total loss on the position is $1. For a stock price of $90, three puts will be exercised, but there will be no net gain or loss on the exercise. The long trader will exercise the put with $X = \$105$ for an exercise gain of $15, but two puts will be exercised against the trader for an exercise loss of $5 on the put with $X = \$95$ and a loss of $10 on the put with $X = \$100$. This gives a zero result from the exercise, and the long trader loses the $1 cost of the position. For any stock price less than $90, the long condor trader can exercise the put with $X = \$90$, so the exercise result is zero for any stock price of $90 or less.

As with the long condor executed with calls, the long condor with puts pays best when the terminal stock price is between the two intermediate exercise prices. In our example, this range extends from $95 to $100. For a terminal stock price of $100, for example, the long trader can exercise the put with $X = \$105$ for an exercise gain of $5. Given the $1 cost of the position, the total profit on the transaction would then be $4. This is the same for any terminal stock price in the range of $95 to $100, as Figure 2.19 shows.

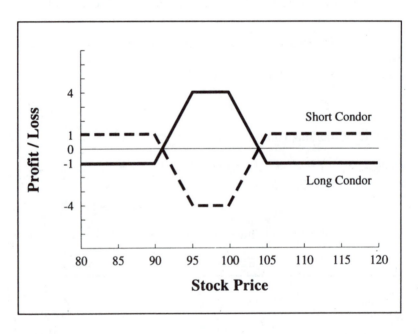

FIGURE 2.19   Profits and Losses at Expiration for a Condor with Puts

The short condor trader could use puts as well, again taking the mirror position of the long trader. Specifically, the short condor with puts requires selling the put with the lowest exercise price, buying a put with a higher exercise price, buying a put with a yet higher exercise price, and selling a put with the highest exercise price. Thus, the short condor executed with puts costs:

$$- P_t(S_t, X_1, T) + P_t(S_t, X_2, T) + P_t(S_T, X_3, T) - P_t(S_t, X_4, T)$$

The value of the short condor with puts at expiration is given by:

$$- P_T(S_T, X_1, T) + P_T(S_T, X_2, T) +$$
$$P_T(S_T, X_3, T) - P_T(S_T, X_4, T) =$$
$$- \text{MAX}\{0, X_1 - S_T\} + \text{MAX}\{0, X_2 - S_T\} +$$
$$\text{MAX}\{0, X_3 - S_T\} - \text{MAX}\{0, X_4 - S_T\}$$

With our example prices, that would involve selling a put with $X = \$90$, buying a put with $X = \$95$, buying a put with $X = \$100$, and selling a put with $X = \$105$. Figure 2.19 shows the profits and losses for the short condor position as a dotted line.

Ratio Spreads

A **ratio spread** is a spread transaction in which two or more related options are traded in a specified proportion. For example, a trader might buy a call with a lower exercise price and sell three calls with a higher exercise price. As the ratio of one instrument to the other can be varied without limit, there are infinitely many different possible ratio spreads. Consequently, we will consider just one fairly simple ratio spread as a guide to the variety of ratio spreads available.

In a ratio spread, the number of contracts bought differs from the number of contracts sold to form the spread. For example, buying two options and selling one gives a 2:1 ratio spread. The spread can be varied infinitely by changing the ratio between the options that are bought and sold. Thus, it is impossible to provide a complete catalog of ratio spreads. Consequently, we illustrate the idea behind ratio spreads by considering a 2:1 ratio spread.

Earlier we considered a bull spread using call options and illustrated this trade by considering two call options, one with an exercise price of $95 and costing $7, the other with an exercise price of $105 and costing $3. Figure 2.13 presented the profits and losses from that position. For comparison, consider a ratio spread in which a trader buys two calls with

$X = \$95$ and sells one call with $X = \$105$. (In this case, the trader has utilized a 2:1 ratio.) The total cost of the position is $11. For any terminal stock price of $95 or less, neither call can be exercised and the trader loses $11. If the stock price exceeds $95, the trader can exercise both of the purchased calls. For example, with a stock price of $105, the trader exercises both calls for an exercise profit of $20, giving a total gain on the trade of $9. For any stock price above $105, the trader will exercise the two calls purchased with $X = \$95$, but the call sold with $X = \$105$ will be exercised against her as well. This partially offsets the benefits derived from exercising the two calls with $X = \$95$. For example, a stock price of $110 gives an exercise profit on the two options with $X = \$95$ of $30. This gain is partially offset by the exercise against our trader of the option with $X = \$105$, for an exercise loss of $5. The net gain at exercise is $25, which more than compensates for the $11 cost of the position and gives a net profit of $14 on the trade.

Figure 2.20 shows the profits and losses for the bull spread with call options, repeating the information of Figure 2.13, and it shows profits

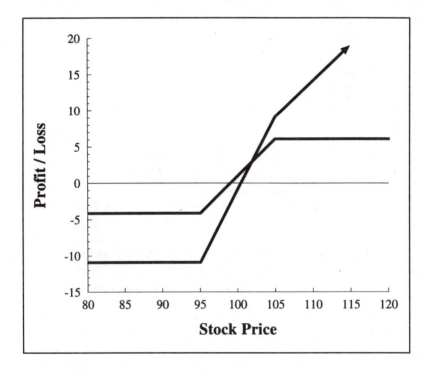

FIGURE 2.20   Profits and Losses at Expiration for a 2:1 Ratio Spread

and losses from the ratio spread we are considering. In comparing these two profit and loss patterns, we see that the ratio spread costs more to undertake, but that it also offers higher profits if the stock price rises sufficiently.

As we observed, the profit on the ratio spread is $9 for a terminal stock price of $105. For higher stock prices, the ratio call profits increase dramatically. By contrast, the bull spread we have been considering reaches its maximum profitability of $4 at a terminal stock price of $105. By varying the ratio between the options in a spread, it is possible to create a wide variety of payoff patterns.

Summary

In this section, we have considered the wide variety of options combinations available when all of the options have a common expiration date. As the variety of combinations shows, it is possible to construct a wide range of profit and loss profiles by choosing the correct combination of options. Table 2.1 summarizes the variety of positions we have considered and tabulates the cost to undertake the position, along with the value of the position at expiration. In addition, the table shows the condition that would make such a trade reasonable.

It is also possible to create an options combination with options that have different expiration dates. When an options combination has more than one expiration date represented in the options that constitute the spread, the combination is called a **calendar spread**. The absence of a uniform expiration date adds greater complication and requires that we consider calendar spreads in Chapter 5 after we introduce the pricing principles for options before expiration.

In this section, we have studied options combined with other options. However, it is also possible to combine options with other instruments to form additional profit and loss profiles. Most interestingly, options can be combined with the underlying stock and with the risk-free asset. We now turn to a consideration of combinations of options with bonds and stocks.

COMBINING OPTIONS WITH BONDS AND STOCKS

Thus far we have considered some of the most important combinations of options. We now show how to combine options with stocks and bonds to adjust payoff patterns to fit virtually any taste for risk and return combinations. These combinations show us the relationships among the different classes of securities. By combining two types of securities, we

Table 2.1 Options Combinations and Their Profits

Position	Cost	Value at Expiration	Trader Expects
Long call	C_t	$\text{MAX}\{0, S_T - X\}$	Rising stock price
Short call	$- C_t$	$- \text{MAX}\{0, S_T - X\}$	Stock price stable or falling
Long put	P_t	$\text{MAX}\{0, X - S_T\}$	Falling stock price
Short put	$- P_t$	$- \text{MAX}\{0, X - S_T\}$	Stock price stable or rising
Long straddle	$C_t + P_t$	$C_T + P_T$	Stock price volatile, rising or falling
Short straddle	$- C_t - P_t$	$- C_T - P_T$	Stock price stable
Long strangle	$C_t (S_t, X_1, T)$ $+ P_t (S_t, X_2, T)$	$C_T (S_T, X_1, T)$ $+ P_T (S_T, X_2, T)$	Stock price very volatile, rising or falling
Short strangle	$- C_t (S_t, X_1, T)$ $- P_t, (S_t, X_2, T)$	$- C_T (S_T, X_1, T)$ $- P_T (S_T, X_2, T)$	Stock price generally stable
Bull spread with calls	$C_t (S_t, X_1, T)$ $- C_t, (S_t, X_2, T)$	$C_T (S_T, X_1, T)$ $- C_T (S_T, X_2, T)$	Stock price rising
Bear spread with calls	$- C_t, (S_t, X_1, T)$ $+ C_t, (S_t, X_2, T)$	$- C_T (S_T, X_1, T)$ $+ C_T (S_T, X_2, T)$	Stock price falling
Bull spread with puts	$P_t, (S_t, X_1, T)$ $- P_t (S_t, X_2, T)$	$P_T (S_T, X_1, T)$ $- P_T (S_T, X_2, T)$	Stock price rising
Bear spread with puts	$- P_t, (S_t, X_1, T)$ $+ P_t, (S_t, X_2, T)$	$- P_T (S_T, X_1, T)$ $+ P_T (S_T, X_2, T)$	Stock price falling
Box spread	$C_t, (S_t, X_1, T)$ $- C_t, (S_t, X_2, T)$ $- P_t (S_t, X_1, T)$ $+ P_t, (S_t, X_2, T)$	$X_2 - X_1$	Riskless strategy
Long butterfly spread with calls	$C_t, (S_t, X_1, T)$ $- 2 C_t, (S_t, X_2, T)$ $+ C_t, (S_t, X_3, T)$	$C_T (S_T, X_1, T)$ $- 2 C_T (S_T, X_2, T)$ $+ C_T (S_T, X_3, T)$	Stock price stable
Short butterfly spread with calls	$- C_t, (S_t, X_1, T)$ $+ 2 C_t, (S_t, X_2, T)$ $- C_t, (S_t, X_3, T)$	$- C_T (S_T, X_1, T)$ $+ 2 C_T (S_T, X_2, T)$ $- C_T (S_T, X_3, T)$	Stock price volatile, rising or falling
Long butterfly spread with puts	$P_t, (S_t, X_1, T)$ $- 2 P_t, (S_t, X_2, T)$ $+ P_t, (S_t, X_3, T)$	$P_T (S_T, X_1, T)$ $- 2 P_T (S_T, X_2, T)$ $+ P_T (S_T, X_3, T)$	Stock price stable
Short butterfly spread with puts	$- P_t (S_t, X_1, T)$ $+ 2 P_t, (S_t, X_2, T)$ $- P_t (S_t, X_3, T)$	$- P_T (S_T, X_1, T)$ $+ 2 P_T (S_T, X_2, T)$ $- P_T (S_T, X_3, T)$	Stock price volatile, rising or falling

Table 2.1 *(continued)*

Position	Cost	Value at Expiration	Trader Expects
Long condor with calls	$C_t(S_t, X_1, T)$ $- C_t(S_t, X_2, T)$ $- C_t(S_t, X_3, T)$ $+ C_t(S_t, X_4, T)$	$C_T(S_T, X_1, T)$ $- C_T(S_T, X_2, T)$ $- C_T(S_T, X_3, T)$ $+ C_T(S_T, X_4, T)$	Stock price stable
Short condor with calls	$- C_t(S_t, X_1, T)$ $+ C_t(S_t, X_2, T)$ $+ C_t(S_t, X_3, T)$ $- C_t(S_t, X_4, T)$	$- C_T(S_T, X_1, T)$ $+ C_T(S_T, X_2, T)$ $+ C_T(S_T, X_3, T)$ $- C_T(S_T, X_4, T)$	Stock price volatile
Long condor with puts	$P_t(S_t, X_1, T)$ $- P_t(S_t, X_2, T)$ $- P_t(S_t, X_3, T)$ $+ P_t(S_t, X_4, T)$	$P_T(S_T, X_1, T)$ $- P_T(S_T, X_2, T)$ $- P_T(S_T, X_3, T)$ $+ P_T(S_T, X_4, T)$	Stock price stable
Short condor with puts	$- P_t(S_t, X_1, T)$ $+ P_t(S_t, X_2, T)$ $+ P_t(S_t, X_3, T)$ $- P_t(S_t, X_4, T)$	$- P_T(S_T, X_1, T)$ $+ P_T(S_T, X_2, T)$ $+ P_T(S_T, X_3, T)$ $- P_T(S_T, X_4, T)$	Stock price volatile
Ratio spreads	Too various to catalog		

Note: $X_1 < X_2 < X_3 < X_4$

can generally imitate the payoff patterns of a third. In addition, this section extends the concepts we have developed earlier in this chapter. Specifically, we learn more about shaping the risk and return characteristics of portfolios by using options.

In this section we consider five combinations of options with bonds or stocks. First, we consider the popular strategy of the **covered call**—a long position in the underlying stock and a short position in a call option. Second, we explore portfolio insurance. During the 1980s, portfolio insurance became one of the most discussed techniques for managing the risk of a stock portfolio. We illustrate some of the basic ideas of portfolio insurance by showing how to insure a stock portfolio. Third, we show how to use options to mimic the profit and loss patterns of the stock itself. For investors who do not want to invest the full purchase price of the stock, it is possible to create an option position that gives a profit and loss pattern much like the stock itself. Fourth, by combining options with the risk-free bond, we can synthesize the underlying stock. In this situation, the option and bond position gives the same profit and loss pattern as the stock and it has the same value as the stock as well. Finally, we show how to combine a call, a bond, and a share of stock to create a synthetic put option.

The Covered Call: Stock plus a Short Call

In a covered call transaction, a trader is generally assumed to already own a stock and writes a call option on the underlying stock. (The strategy is "covered" because the trader owns the underlying stock, and this stock covers the obligation inherent in writing the call.) This strategy is generally undertaken as an income enhancement technique. For example, assume a trader owns a share currently priced at $100. She might write a call option on this share with an exercise price of $110 and an assumed price of $4. The option premium will be hers to keep. In exchange for accepting the $4 premium, our trader realizes that the underlying stock might be called away from her if the stock price exceeds $110. If the stock price fails to increase by $10, the option she has written will expire worthless, and she will be able to keep the income from selling the option without any further obligation. As this example indicates, the strategy turns on selling an option with a striking price far removed from the current value of the stock, because the intention is to keep the premium without surrendering the stock through exercise.

While writing covered calls can often serve the purpose of enhancing income, it must be remembered that there is no free lunch in the options market. The writer of the covered call is actually exchanging the chance of large gains on the stock position in favor of income from selling the option. For example, if the stock price were to rise to $120, the trader would not receive this benefit, because the stock would be called away from her.

Figure 2.21 graphs the profits and losses at expiration for the example we have been considering. The solid line shows the profits and losses for the stock itself, while the dotted line shows the profits and losses for the covered call (the stock plus short call). For any stock price less than or equal to $110, the written call cannot be exercised against our trader and she receives whatever profits or losses the stock earns plus the $4 option premium. Thus, she is $4 better off with the covered call than she would be with the stock alone for any stock price of $110 or less. If the stock price exceeds $110, the option will be exercised against her, and she must surrender the stock. This potential exercise places an upper limit on her profit at $14. If the stock price had risen to $120 and the trader had not written the call, her profit would have been $20 on the stock investment alone. In the covered call position, she would have made only $14, because the stock would have been called away from her. The desirability of writing a covered call to enhance income depends upon the chance that the stock price will exceed the exercise price at which the trader writes the call.

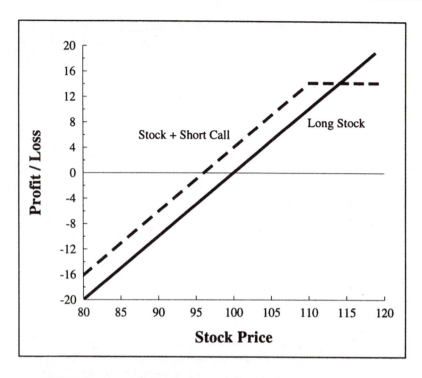

FIGURE 2.21   Profits and Losses at Expiration for a Covered Call

Portfolio Insurance: Stock plus a Long Put

Along with program trading, portfolio insurance was a dominant investing technique developed in the 1980s. **Portfolio insurance** is an investment management technique designed to protect a stock portfolio from severe drops in value. Investment managers can implement portfolio insurance strategies in various ways. Some use options, while others use futures, and still others use combinations of other instruments. We analyze a simple strategy for implementing portfolio insurance with options. Portfolio insurance applies only to portfolios, not individual stocks. Therefore, for our discussion we assume that the underlying good is a well-diversified portfolio of common stocks. We may think of the portfolio as consisting of the Standard & Poors 100. This is convenient because a popular stock index option is based on the S&P 100. Therefore, the portfolio insurance problem we consider is protecting the value of this stock portfolio from large drops in value.[7]

In essence, portfolio insurance with options involves holding a stock portfolio and buying a put option on the portfolio.[8] If we have a long position in the stock portfolio, the profits and losses from holding the portfolio consist of the profits and losses from the individual stocks. Therefore, the profits and losses for the portfolio resemble the typical stock's profits and losses.

Let S_t be the cost of the stock portfolio at time t, and let P_t be a put option on the portfolio. The cost of an insured portfolio is, therefore:

$$S_t + P_t$$

Because the price of a put is always positive, it is clear that an insured portfolio costs more than the uninsured stock portfolio alone. At expiration, the value of the insured portfolio is:

$$S_T + P_T = S_T + \text{MAX}\{0, X - S_T\} \qquad\qquad 2.13$$

As the profit on an uninsured portfolio is $S_T - S_t$, the insured portfolio has a superior performance when $\text{MAX}\{0, X - S_T\} - P_t - S_t > 0$.

As an example of an insured portfolio, consider an investment in the stock index at a value of 100.00. Figure 2.22 shows the profit and loss profiles for an investment in the index at 100 and for a put option on the index. The figure assumes that the put has a striking price of 100.00 and costs 4.00 (we are expressing all values in terms of the index). Figure 2.23 shows the effects of combining an investment in the index stocks and buying a put on the index. For comparison, Figure 2.23 also shows the profits and losses from a long position in the index itself.

The insured portfolio, the index plus a long put, offers protection against large drops in value. If the stock index suddenly falls to 90.00, the insured portfolio loses only 4.00. No matter how low the index goes, the insured portfolio can lose only 4.00 points. However, this insurance has a cost. Investment in the index itself shows a profit for any index value over 100.00. By contrast, the insured portfolio has a profit only if the index climbs above 104.00. In the insured portfolio, the index must climb high enough to offset the price of buying the insuring put option. Because the put option will expire, keeping the portfolio insured requires that the investor buy a series of put options to keep the insurance in force. In Figure 2.23, notice that the combined position of a long index and a long put gives a payoff shape that matches a long position in a call. Like a call, the insured portfolio protects against extremely unfavorable outcomes as the stock price falls. This similarity between the insured portfolio and a call position suggests that a trader might buy a call and invest the extra proceeds in a bond in order to replicate a position in an insured portfolio.

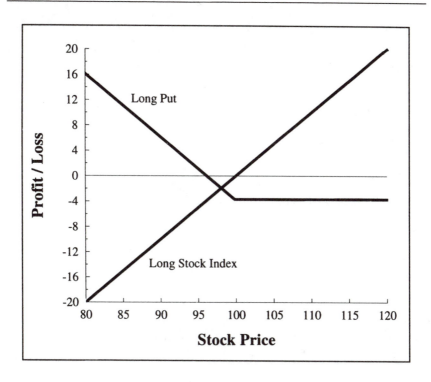

FIGURE 2.22 Profits and Losses at Expiration for a Stock Index and a Put

As a further comparison, we consider the likely profits from holding the stock portfolio and the insured portfolio. Let us assume that the option expires in one year. The stock portfolio is expected to appreciate about 10 percent and have a standard deviation of 15 percent. We also assume that the returns on the stock portfolio are normally distributed. Thus, a $100 investment in the stock portfolio would have an expected terminal value of $110 in one year. Under these assumptions, Figure 2.24 shows the probability distribution of the stock portfolio's terminal value. With a standard deviation of 15 percent there is approximately a two-thirds chance that the terminal value of the portfolio will lie between $95 and $125. This conclusion results from a feature of the normal distribution. About 67 percent of all observations from a normal distribution lie within one standard deviation of the mean.

With the insured portfolio, we have already seen that the maximum loss is $4. Therefore, the terminal value of the insured portfolio must be at least $96. However, Figures 2.23 and 2.24 imply that there is a good chance that the insured portfolio's terminal value will be $96. For the

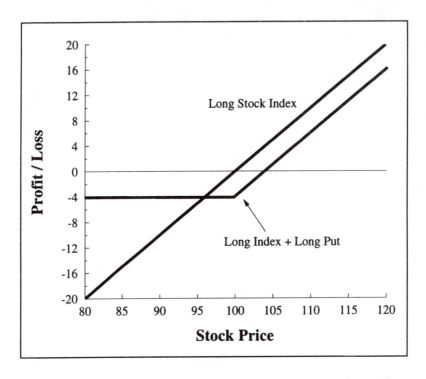

FIGURE 2.23 Profits and Losses at Expiration for an Insured Portfolio

stock portfolio, any terminal value of $100 or less gives a $96 terminal value for the insured portfolio. While the insured portfolio protects against large losses, it has a lower chance of a really large payoff. For the insured portfolio to have a terminal value of $136, for example, the stock portfolio must be worth $140. This is two standard deviations above the expected return on the stock portfolio, however, and there is little chance of such a favorable outcome.

Figure 2.25 compares the distribution of returns for the stock and for the insured portfolios. The figure presents the cumulative probability distribution for each portfolio. For the stock portfolio, the line in Figure 2.25 merely presents the cumulative probability consistent with Figure 2.24. The kinked line in Figure 2.25 corresponds to the insured portfolio. The probability of a terminal value below $96 for the insured portfolio is zero, because that is exactly what the insurance guarantees. However, there is a very good chance that the terminal value for the insured portfolio will be $96. The probability of a $96 terminal value for the insured portfolio equals the probability that the stock portfolio will be worth $100

FIGURE 2.24   Probability Distribution for a Stock Index's Terminal Value

or less. As the graph shows, this probability is 25 percent. Notice also that the probability of a $96 or lower terminal value for the stock portfolio is 18 percent. This means that there is an 82 percent chance that the stock portfolio will outperform the insured portfolio, because there is an 82 percent chance that the stock portfolio will be worth more than $96.

As we consider terminal stock portfolio values above $96, we see that the line for the insured portfolio lies above the line for the stock portfolio in Figure 2.25. Consider a $110 terminal value for the stock portfolio. Because the distribution is normal and the expected return is 10 percent, there is a 50 percent chance that the terminal value of the stock portfolio will be $110 or less. Because the line for the insured portfolio lies above the line for the stock portfolio, there is a higher probability that the insured portfolio's value will be $110 or less. The probability of a terminal value for the insured portfolio of $110 or less is 61 percent. Correlatively, there is a 50 percent chance of a terminal stock portfolio value above $110 and only a 39 percent chance of a terminal value above $110 for the insured portfolio. Thus, because the insured portfolio's cumulative

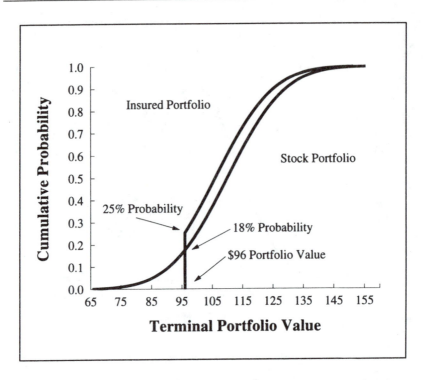

FIGURE 2.25   Comparison of Returns Distribution for an Insured and an Uninsured Stock Portfolio

probability line lies above that for the stock portfolio at higher terminal prices, the stock portfolio has a better chance of higher returns. Figure 2.25 shows that the insured portfolio sacrifices chances of a large gain to avoid the chance of a large loss. Which investment is better depends on the risk preferences of the investor. The important point to recognize is the role of options in adjusting the returns distribution for the underlying investment. With options, we can adjust the distribution to fit our tastes—subject to the risk and return trade-off governing the entire market.[9]

Finally, we also observe that the insured portfolio has the same profits and losses as a call option. In fact, the profit and loss graph for the insured portfolio matches that of a call option with a striking price of 100.00 and a price of 4.00. This does not mean, however, that the insured portfolio and such a call option would have the same value. At expiration, the call will have no residual value beyond its profit and loss at that moment. By contrast, the insured portfolio will still include the underlying value of the investment in the stock index. Therefore, for a particular time horizon, two different investments can have the same profit and loss patterns without having the same value.

Mimicking and Synthetic Portfolios

We now begin to study how European options can be combined with other instruments, notably the underlying stock and the risk-free bond, to create specialized payoff patterns at expiration. As we will see, it is possible to create portfolios of European options, the underlying stock, and the risk-free bond that simulate another instrument in key respects. We define two basic types of relationships, mimicking portfolios and synthetic instruments.[10]

A **mimicking portfolio** has the same profits and losses as the instrument or portfolio that it mimics, but it does not necessarily have the same value. A **synthetic instrument** has the same profits and losses, as well as the same value, as the instrument it synthetically replicates. For example, we will see that it is possible to create a portfolio of instruments that has the same value and the same profits and losses as a put. In this case, the portfolio would be known as a synthetic put.

Mimicking Stock: Long Call plus a Short Put. By combining a long position in a European call and a short position in a European put, we can create an option position that has the same profit and loss pattern at expiration as does the underlying stock. This long call/short put position costs:

$$c_t - p_t$$

At expiration, the payoff on this option combination is:

$$c_T - p_T = \text{MAX}\{0, S_T - X\} - \text{MAX}\{0, X - S_T\} \qquad 2.14$$

Assume for the moment that the call and put are chosen so that the exercise price equals the stock price at the time the put is purchased. That is, assume $X = S_t$. Under this special condition, the payoff on the long call/short put position is:

$$\text{MAX}\{0, S_T - S_t\} - \text{MAX}\{0, S_t - S_T\}$$

If the stock price rises, $S_T > S_t$, the call is worth $S_T - S_t$ and the put is worth nothing. Notice that $S_T - S_t$ is just the profit on the stock portfolio alone. If the stock price falls, $S_t > S_T$. In this case, the call is worth zero, and the put is worth $S_t - S_T$. As the option combination includes a short position in the put, the payoff to the portfolio is $S_T - S_t$, which is the same as the stock portfolio. Thus, the long call/short put portfolio has a value that equals the profit or loss from investing in the underlying stock. Notice again that this special condition arises when the exercise price on the options equals the stock price at the time the options combination is purchased.

To illustrate this idea, consider a stock priced at $100 and call and put options with exercise prices of $100. Assume that the call costs $7 and the put costs $3. We want to compare two investments. The first investment is buying one share of stock for $100. The second investment is buying one call for $7 and selling one put for $3.

When the options expire, the two investments have parallel profits and losses. However, the profit on the stock will always be $4 greater than the profit on the options position. For example, assume the stock price is $110 at expiration. The stock has a profit of $10 and the options investment has a profit of $6. For the options position, the put expires worthless and the call has an exercise value of $10. From this exercise value we subtract the $4 net investment required to purchase the options position. Figure 2.26 graphs the profits and losses for both options, the stock, and the combined options position.

Investing in the stock costs $100, while the options position costs only $4. Yet the options position profits mimic those of the stock fairly closely. In a sense, the options give very high leverage by simulating the stock's profits and losses with a low investment. Many options traders view this high leverage of options as one of their prime advantages. Thus, a very small investment in the options position gives a position that mimics the profits and losses of a much more costly investment in the stock. In other words, the options position is much more elastic than the similar stock position.

The profit on the stock is always $4 greater than the profit on the options position. However, the stock investment costs $100, while the options position costs only $4. Therefore, the stock costs $96 more than the options position to guarantee a certain $4 extra profit over the options position. While the long call plus short put options position mimics the profits and losses on the stock, it does not synthetically replicate the stock. As we will see, we can create a synthetic stock by adding investment in the risk-free bond to the option.

Synthetic Stock: Long Call, plus a Short Put, plus Bonds. As we have just seen, a long call combined with a short put can mimic the profit and loss pattern at the expiration date for the underlying stock. By adding an

FIGURE 2.26 Profits and Losses at Expiration for the Elements of a Mimicking Portfolio

investment in the risk-free bond, we can create a portfolio that synthesizes the stock. In this case the synthetic stock will have the same value as well as an identical profit and loss pattern as the stock being synthesized. Therefore, this section shows that a long call, plus a short put, plus the right investment in the risk-free bond, can synthesize a stock investment. (Again, we are focusing on European options throughout this discussion, which we denote as c_t and p_t for the values of European calls and puts at time t.) As we will demonstrate, the investment in the risk-free bond should be the present value of the exercise price on the call and the put. Therefore, this formula for a synthetic stock is:

$$S_t = c_t - p_t + Xe^{-r(T-t)} \qquad 2.15$$

where:

$$r = \text{risk-free rate of interest}$$

At expiration, the value of this portfolio (for both American and European options) will be:

$$c_T - p_T + X = \text{MAX}\{0, S_T - X\} - \text{MAX}\{0, X - S_T\} + X$$

We know that the stock price can be above, equal to, or below the exercise price. If the stock price at expiration exceeds the exercise price, the call is worth $S_T - X$, and the put is worthless. The value of the portfolio consists of the value of the call, plus the maturing bond, or $S_T - X + X = S_T$. This is exactly the same value as the stock at the expiration date. If the stock price is below the exercise price on the expiration date of the options, then the call is worthless and the put has a value equal to $X - S_T$. Because the portfolio consists of a short position in the put, the value of the portfolio, including the maturing bond, is $S_T - X + X = S_T$. Again, the value of the long call/short put/long bond is the same as that of the underlying stock. If the terminal value of the stock equals the exercise price, X, then both the call and put are worthless and the value of the synthetic stock portfolio is just X, the value of the maturing risk-free investment. But in this situation, it remains true that the value of the synthetic stock is equal to that of the stock itself, because $S_T = X$.

We can illustrate this synthetic stock by considering the same stock selling for $100 and the same options we considered in the previous section. Comparing just the value of the stock position versus the value of the options position at expiration, the stock position will always be worth $100 more than the options position. For example, assume the stock price is $120 at expiration. Then, the stock investment is worth $120. The options position will be worth $20, because the call can be exercised for $20 and the put will be worthless. To synthesize the stock, we need to buy a risk-free bond that pays $100 at expiration. We can think of this investment as buying a one-year Treasury bill with a face value of $100. Notice that the payoff on the Treasury bill equals the exercise price for the options. We now have two portfolios that will have identical values at the expiration date:

Investment	Cash Flow
Portfolio A	
Long position in the stock	$100
Portfolio B	
Long position in the call	−$7
Short position in the put	+3
A bond paying the exercise price of $100 at expiration	?

Thus far in the example, we have not said how much the bond should cost. However, we can employ our no-arbitrage principle for guidance. We know that both portfolios will have the same value in one year when the option expires. To avoid arbitrage, the two portfolios must have the same value now as well. This condition implies that the bond must cost $96 and that the interest rate must be 4.17 percent.

To see why the bond must cost $96, we consider the arbitrage opportunity that results with any other bond price. For example, assume that the bond costs $93. With this low bond price, Portfolio A is too expensive relative to Portfolio B. To exploit the arbitrage opportunity, we sell the overpriced Portfolio A and buy the underpriced Portfolio B, transacting as follows:

Transaction	Cash Flow
Sell the stock	$100
Buy the call	−7
Sell the put	+3
Buy the bond	−93
Net Cash Flow	+$3

When the options expire in one year, we can close out all the positions without any additional investment. To close the position, we buy back the stock and honor any obligation we have from selling the put. Fortunately, we will have $100 in cash from the maturing bond we bought. For example, if the stock price at expiration is $90, our call is worthless and the put is exercised against us. Therefore, we use the proceeds from the maturing T-bill to pay the $100 exercise price for the put that is exercised against us. We now have the stock and in return use it to close our short position in the stock. The total result at expiration is that we can honor all obligations with zero cash flow. This is true no matter what the stock price is. Therefore, the cheap price on the bond gave us an arbitrage profit of $3 when we made the initial transaction. The transactions are an arbitrage because they require no investment and offer a riskless profit. With an initial cash inflow of $3, there is clearly no investment. Also, we make a riskless profit immediately when we transact. Any bond price below $96 will permit the arbitrage transactions we have just described.

If the bond is priced higher than $96, Portfolio B is overpriced relative to Portfolio A. We then sell Portfolio B and buy Portfolio A. Again, we have an arbitrage profit. To see how to make an arbitrage profit from a bond price that is too high, assume the bond price is $98. We then transact as follows:

Transaction	Cash Flow
Buy the stock	−$100
Sell the call	7
Buy the put	−3
Sell the bond	+98
Net Cash Flow	+$2

In one year, the options will expire and the bond will mature. Selling the bond means that we borrow $98 and promise to repay $100, so we will owe $100 on the bond at expiration. However, no matter what the stock price is at expiration, we can dispose of the stock and close the options positions for a cash inflow of $100. This gives exactly what we need to pay our debt on the bond. For example, assume the stock price is $93. The call we sold expires worthless but we can exercise the put. When we exercise the put, we deliver the stock and receive the $100 exercise price. This amount repays the bond debt. Any bond price greater than $96 will permit this same kind of arbitrage transaction.

The Synthetic Put: The Put–Call Parity Relationship.   We have just seen that we can buy a call, short a put, and invest in a risk-free bond to create a synthetic stock. In fact, with any three of these four instruments, we can synthesize the fourth. This section illustrates **put–call parity**—the relationship between put, call, stock, and bond prices. Specifically, put–call parity shows how to synthesize a put option by selling the stock, buying a call, and investing in a risk-free bond. Put–call parity asserts that a put is worth the same as a long call, short stock, and a risk-free investment that pays the exercise price on the common expiration date of the put and call. The put–call parity relationship is:

$$p_t = c_t - S_t + Xe^{-r(T-t)} \qquad\qquad 2.16$$

To create a put from the other instruments, we use our previous example of a stock selling at $100, a call option worth $7 with a strike price of $100, and a bond costing $96 that will pay $100 in one year. From these securities, we can synthesize the put option costing $3 with an exercise price of $100. To create a synthetic put, we transact as follows:

Investment	Cash Flow
Portfolio C	
Buy the call	−$7
Sell the stock	+100
Buy a bond that pays the exercise price at maturity	−$96
	−$3

In buying Portfolio C, we have the same cash outflow of $3 that buying the put requires. To show that Portfolio C is equivalent to a put with a $3 price and a $100 exercise price, we consider the value of Portfolio C when the stock price equals, exceeds, or is less than $100.

If the stock price is $100 at expiration, the call in Portfolio C is worthless, but we receive $100 from the maturing bond, with which we buy the stock. This disposes of the entire portfolio. The entire portfolio is worth zero, just as the put is worth zero. For any stock price above $100, Portfolio C, like the put itself, is worthless. We can then exercise the call and use the proceeds from the bond to pay the exercise price on the call. This gives us the stock, which we owe to cover our earlier sale of the stock. Thus, we have met all obligations arising from owning Portfolio C. To illustrate this outcome, consider a terminal stock price of $105. In this case, the put would be worthless. Therefore, Portfolio C should be worthless as well. With a stock price of $105, we would exercise the call, paying for the exercise with the proceeds of our maturing bond. We receive a stock worth $105. However, we must repay our short sale of the stock by returning this share. Therefore, there is no net cash flow at the exercise date. Finally, for a stock price less than $100, Portfolio C is worth the difference between the exercise price and the stock price. If the stock price is $95, the call option expires worthless. We receive $100 on the bond investment and use $95 of this to repurchase the stock that we owe. Thus Portfolio C is worth $5, just as the put itself would be.

Considering our profits on Portfolio C, we lose $3 for any stock price of $100 or more, because Portfolio C is then worthless at expiration and it costs $3. For any stock price at expiration less than $100, Portfolio C is worth the exercise price of $100 minus the stock price. Notice that this is an exact description of the profit and losses on the put. Therefore, Portfolio C synthetically replicates the put option with an exercise price of $100 that costs $3.

Put–call parity has another important implication. Assume that $S_t = X$. In this situation, the call will be worth more than the put. To prove this principle, consider the following rearrangement of the put–call parity formula:

$$c_t - p_t = S_t - Xe^{-r(T-t)}$$

If $S_t = X$, the right-hand side of this equation must be positive, because the exercise price X is being discounted. Therefore, the quantity $c_t - p_t$ must also be positive, and this implies that the call price must exceed the put price in this special circumstance.

SUMMARY

This chapter has explored the value and profits from options positions at expiration. The concept of arbitrage provided a general framework for understanding options values and profits. We began by studying the characteristic payoffs for positions in single options, noting that there are four basic possibilities of being long or short a call or a put.

We then considered how to combine options to create special positions with unique risk and return characteristics. These options combinations included straddles, strangles, bull and bear spreads, butterfly spreads, condors, and a box spread. As we observed, a trader can either buy or sell each of these options combinations and most can be created using either puts or calls. Each gives its own risk and return profile, which differs from the position in a single option.

We also considered combinations among options, stocks, and bonds. We considered the advantages and disadvantages of covered call writing, and explored how to insure a portfolio by using a put option. We also showed that a combination of options could mimic the profit and loss profile of a stock. To create a synthetic stock we used a call, a put, and investment in a risk-free bond. The mimicking portfolio has the same profit and loss patterns, while a synthetic instrument has the identical profit and loss characteristics and the same value as the instrument being synthesized. We also showed how to create a synthetic put by trading a call, a stock, and the risk-free bond to illustrate the put–call parity relationship. In general, we conclude that put, call, bond, and stock prices are all related and that any one can be synthesized by a combination of the other three.

REVIEW QUESTIONS

1. Consider a call option with an exercise price of $80 and a cost of $5. Graph the profits and losses at expiration for various stock prices.

2. Consider a put option with an exercise price of $80 and a cost of $4. Graph the profits and losses at expiration for various stock prices.

3. For the call and put in Questions 1 and 2, graph the profits and losses at expiration for a straddle comprising these two options. If the stock price is $80 at expiration, what will be the profit or loss? At what stock price (or prices) will the straddle have a zero profit?

4. A call option has an exercise price of $70 and is at expiration. The option cost $4 and the underlying stock trades for $75. Assuming a perfect market, how would you respond if the call is an American option? State exactly how you might transact. How does your answer differ if the option is European?

5. A stock trades for $120. A put on this stock has an exercise price of $140 and is about to expire. The put trades for $22. How would you respond to this set of prices? Explain.

6. If the stock trades for $120 and the expiring put with an exercise price of $140 trades for $18, how would you trade?

7. Consider a call and a put on the same underlying stock. The call has an exercise price of $100 and costs $20. The put has an exercise price of $90 and costs $12. Graph a short position in a strangle based on these two options. What is the worst outcome from selling the strangle? At what stock price or prices does the strangle have a zero profit?

8. Assume that you buy a call with an exercise price of $100 and a cost of $9. At the same time, you sell a call with an exercise price of $110 and a cost of $5. The two calls have the same underlying stock and the same expiration. What is this position called? Graph the profits and losses at expiration from this position. At what stock price or prices will the position show a zero profit? What is the worst loss that the position can incur? For what range of stock prices does this worst outcome occur? What is the best outcome and for what range of stock prices does it occur?

9. Consider three call options with the same underlying stock and the same expiration. Assume that you take a long position in a call with an exercise price of $40 and a long position in a call with an exercise price of $30. At the same time, you sell two calls with an exercise price of $35. What position have you created? Graph the value of this position at expiration. What is the value of this position at expiration if the stock price is $90? What is the position's value for a stock price of $15? What is the lowest

value the position can have at expiration? For what range of stock prices does this worst value occur?

10. Assume that you buy a portfolio of stocks with a portfolio price of $100. A put option on this portfolio has a striking price of $95 and costs $3. Graph the combined portfolio of the stock plus a long position in the put. What is the worst outcome that can occur at expiration? For what range of portfolio prices will this worst outcome occur? What is this position called?

11. Consider a stock that sells for $95. A call on this stock has an exercise price of $95 and costs $5. A put on this stock also has an exercise price of $95 and costs $4. The call and the put have the same expiration. Graph the profit and losses at expiration from holding the long call and short put. How do these profits and losses compare with the value of the stock at expiration? If the stock price is $80 at expiration, what is the portfolio of options worth? If the stock price is $105, what is the portfolio of options worth? Explain why the stock and options portfolios differ as they do.

12. Assume a stock trades for $120. A call on this stock has a striking price of $120 and costs $11. A put also has a striking price of $120 and costs $8. A risk-free bond promises to pay $120 at the expiration of the options in one year. What should the price of this bond be? Explain.

13. In the preceding question, if we combine the two options and the bond, what will the value of this portfolio be relative to the stock price at expiration? Explain. What principle does this illustrate?

14. Consider a stock that is worth $50. A put and call on this stock have an exercise price of $50 and expire in one year. The call costs $5 and the put costs $4. A risk-free bond will pay $50 in one year and costs $45. How will you respond to these prices? State your transactions exactly. What principle do these prices violate?

15. A stock sells for $80 and the risk-free rate of interest is 11 percent. A call and a put on this stock expire in one year and both options have an exercise price of $75. How would you trade to create a synthetic call option? If the put sells for $2, how much is the call option worth? (Assume annual compounding.)

16. A stock costs $100 and a risk-free bond paying $110 in one year costs $100 as well. What can you say about the cost of a put and a call on this stock that both expire in one year and that both have an exercise price of $110? Explain.

17. Assume that you buy a strangle with exercise prices on the constituent options of $75 and $80. You also sell a strangle with exercise prices of $70 and $85. Describe the payoffs on the position you have created. Does this portfolio of options have a payoff pattern similar to that of any of the combinations explored in this chapter?

18. If a stock sells for $75 and a call and put together cost $9 and the two options expire in one year and have an exercise price of $70, what is the current rate of interest?

19. Assume you buy a bull spread with puts that have exercise prices of $40 and $45. You also buy a bear spread with puts that have exercise prices of $45 and $50. What will this total position be worth if the stock price at expiration is $53? Does this position have any special name? Explain.

20. Explain the difference between a box spread and a synthetic risk-free bond.

21. Within the context of the put–call parity relationship, consider the value of a call and a put option. What will the value of the put option be if the exercise price is zero? What will the value of the call option be in the same circumstance? What can you say about potential bounds on the value of the call and put option?

22. Using the put–call parity relationship, write the value of a call option as a function of the stock price, the risk-free bond, and the put option. Now consider a stock price that is dramatically in excess of the exercise price. What happens to the value of the put as the stock price becomes extremely large relative to the exercise price? What happens to the value of the call option?

NOTES

1. Recall that we are ignoring transaction costs. In the options market, both buyers and sellers incur transaction costs. Therefore, the options market is a negative-sum game if we include transaction costs in our analysis.

2. The arbitrage arguments used in this chapter stem from a famous paper by Robert C. Merton, "Theory of Rational Option Pricing," *Bell Journal of Economics and Management Science*, 4, Spring 1973, 141–183.

3. The buyer of a straddle need not be matched with a trader who specifically sells a straddle. Opposite the buyer of a straddle could be two individuals, one of whom sells a call and the other of whom sells a put.

4. The theoretically maximum loss for the short straddle trader occurs when the stock price goes to zero. In this case, the call cannot be exercised

against the short trader, but the put will be exercised. Thus, the trader will lose $X - S = X - 0 = X$ on the exercise. This loss will be partially offset by the funds received from selling the straddle $(C_t + P_t)$, so the total loss will be: $X - C_t - P_t$.

5. It is also possible to execute similar strategies with combinations of options and the underlying instrument.

6. The reader should note that the use of terms such as *bear spread* and *bull spread* is not standardized. While this book uses these terms in familiar ways, other traders may use them differently.

7. Three introductory studies of portfolio insurance are: Peter A. Abken, "An Introduction to Portfolio Insurance," Federal Reserve Bank of Atlanta, *Economic Review*, 72:6, November/December 1987, 2–25; and Thomas J. O'Brien, "The Mechanics of Portfolio Insurance," *Journal of Portfolio Management*, 14:3, Spring 1988, 40–47. In his paper, "Simplifying Portfolio Insurance," *Journal of Portfolio Management*, 14:1, Fall 1987, 48–51, Fischer Black shows how to insure a portfolio without using options pricing theory, and he shows how to establish an insured portfolio without a definite horizon date.

8. It is possible to create an insured portfolio without using options. These alternative strategies employ stock index futures with continuous rebalancing of the futures position. Because of this continuous rebalancing, these strategies are called "dynamic hedging" strategies. Hayne E. Leland, "Option Pricing and Replication with Transaction Costs," *Journal of Finance*, 40, December 1985, 1283–1301, discusses these dynamic strategies. With a dynamic strategy, the insurer must rebalance the portfolio very frequently, leading to a trade-off between having an exactly insured portfolio and high transaction costs. J. Clay Singleton and Robin Grieves discuss this trade-off in their paper, "Synthetic Puts and Portfolio Insurance Strategies," *Journal of Portfolio Management*, 10:3, Spring 1984, 63–69. Richard Bookstaber, "Portfolio Insurance Trading Rules," *Journal of Futures Markets*, 8:1, February 1988, 15–31, discusses some recent technological innovations in portfolio insurance strategies and foresees increasing complexity and sophistication in the implementation of insurance techniques.

9. Several studies have explored the cost of portfolio insurance. Richard J. Rendleman, Jr., and Richard W. McEnally, "Assessing the Cost of Portfolio Insurance," *Financial Analysts Journal*, 43, May/June 1987, 27–37, compare the desirability of an insured portfolio relative to a utility-maximizing strategy. They conclude that only extremely risk-averse investors will be willing to incur the costs of insuring a portfolio. Richard Bookstaber found similar results in his paper, "The Use of Options in Performance Structuring: Modeling Returns to Meet Investment Objectives," in *Controlling Interest Rate Risk: New Techniques and Applications for Money Management*, Robert B. Platt (ed.), New York, Wiley, 1986. According to Bookstaber, completely insuring a portfolio costs about 25

percent of the portfolio's total return. C. B. Garcia and F. J. Gould, "An Empirical Study of Portfolio Insurance," *Financial Analysts Journal*, July/August 1987, 44–54, find that fully insuring a portfolio causes a loss of returns of about 100 basis points. They conclude that an insured portfolio is not likely to outperform a static portfolio of stocks and T-bills. Roger G. Clarke and Robert D. Arnott study the costs of portfolio insurance directly in their paper, "The Cost of Portfolio Insurance: Trade-offs and Choices," *Financial Analysts Journal*, 43:6, November/ December 1987, 35–47. Clarke and Arnott explore the desirability of only insuring part of the portfolio, increasing the risk of the portfolio, and attempting to insure a portfolio for a longer horizon. As they conclude, transaction costs are an important factor in choosing the optimal strategy.

10. These synthetic relationships hold exactly only for European options. In Chapter 6, we explore the reasons for this restriction within the context of our discussion of American options.

3

Bounds on
Options Prices

INTRODUCTION

This chapter continues to use no-arbitrage conditions to explore options pricing principles. In the last chapter, we considered the prices options could have at expiration, consistent with no-arbitrage conditions. In this chapter, we consider options prices before expiration. Extending our analysis to options with time remaining until expiration brings new factors into consideration.

The value of an option before expiration depends on five factors: the price of the underlying stock, the exercise price of the option, the time remaining until expiration, the risk-free rate of interest, and the possible price movements on the underlying stock.[1] For stocks with dividends, the potential dividend payments during an option's life can also influence the value of the option. In this chapter, we focus on the intuition underlying the relationship between put and call prices and these factors. The next chapter builds on these intuitions to specify these relationships more formally.

We first consider how options prices respond to changes in the stock price, the time remaining until expiration, and the exercise price of the option. These factors set general boundaries for possible options prices. Later in the chapter, we discuss the influence of interest rates on options prices and we consider how the riskiness of the stock affects the price of the option.

THE BOUNDARY SPACE FOR CALL AND PUT OPTIONS

In Chapter 2, we saw that the value of a call (either European or American) at expiration must be:

$$C_T = \text{MAX}\{0, S_T - X\} \qquad\qquad 3.1$$

Similarly, the value of a put (either European or American) at expiration is:

$$P_T = \text{MAX}\{0, X - S_T\} \qquad\qquad 3.2$$

where:

C_t = the call price at time t
P_t = the put price at time t
S_t = the stock price at time t
X = the exercise price at time t
T = the expiration date of the option

Corresponding to Equations 3.1 and 3.2, we saw that call and put options had distinctive graphs that specified their values at expiration. Figure 2.4 for a call and Figure 2.6 for a put gave the value of the options at expiration. These two figures simply graph Equations 3.1 and 3.2, respectively. Now we want to consider the range of possible values for call and put options more generally. Specifically, we want to analyze the values that options can have before expiration.[2]

Said another way, we want to explore the values of options as a function of the stock price, S, the exercise price, X, and the time remaining until expiration, $T - t$. In Chapter 2, we only considered options that were at expiration, with $t = T$. Thus, we were considering option values for various ranges of stock price and exercise prices, but with zero time to expiration. Now, we want to consider option prices when the stock price, the exercise price, and the time to expiration all vary.

Before expiration, call and put values need not conform to Equations 3.1 and 3.2. Therefore, our first task is to determine the entire possible range of prices that calls and puts may have before expiration. We call this range of possibilities the **boundary space** for an option. Once we specify the largest range of possible prices, we consider no-arbitrage principles that will help us specify the price of an option more precisely.

The Boundary Space for a Call Option

To define the boundary space for a call option, we consider extreme values for the variables that affect call prices. Because we first focus on the stock price, exercise price, and the time remaining until expiration, we consider extremely high and low values for each of these variables. First, the value of a call option will depend on the stock price. We have already seen that a call option at expiration is worth more the greater the price of the stock. Second, the value of a call option depends on the exercise price of the option. Third, the value of a call can depend on the time remaining until the option expires.

The owner of a call option receives the stock upon exercise. The stock price represents the potential benefit that will come to the holder of a call, so the higher the stock price, the greater the value of a call option. We have already observed this to be true at expiration, as Equation 3.1 shows. Also, the exercise price is a cash outflow if the call owner exercises. As such, the exercise price represents a potential liability to the call owner. The lower the liability associated with a call, the better for the call owner. Therefore, the lower the exercise price, the greater the value of a call. Finally, consider the time remaining until expiration. For clarity we focus on two American options that differ only because one has a longer time remaining until expiration. Comparing these two options, we see that the one with the longer time until expiration gives every benefit that the one with the shorter time until expiration does. At a given moment, if the shorter-term option permits expiration, so does the option with a longer term until expiration. In addition, the longer-term option allows the privilege of waiting longer to decide whether to exercise. Generally, this privilege of waiting is quite valuable, so the option with the longer life tends to have a higher value. However, no matter what happens, the option with the longer life must have a price at least as great as the option with the shorter life. We will see that the same holds true for European options. The longer the time until expiration, the greater the value of the option, holding other factors constant.

We have seen that lower exercise prices and longer lives generally increase the value of an option. Therefore, the value of an option will be highest for an option with a zero exercise price and an infinite time until expiration. Similarly, the value will be lowest for an option with a higher exercise price and the shortest time until expiration. A call that is about to expire, with $t = T$, will be the call with the lowest price for a given stock price and a given exercise price. We already know the possible values that such an expiring option can have. This value is simply the call option's price at expiration, which is given by Equation 3.1. At the other extreme, the call with the highest possible value for a given stock price will be the call with a zero exercise price and an infinite time until expiration.

This call option with a zero exercise price and an infinite time until it expires allows us to exercise the option with zero cost and acquire the stock. In short, we can transform this option into the stock any time we wish without paying anything. Therefore, the value of this call must equal the price of the underlying stock. If we can get the stock for zero any time we wish, the price of the call cannot be more than the stock price. Also, the price of the call cannot exceed the stock price, because the call can only be used to acquire the stock. Therefore, we know that a call on a given stock, with a zero exercise price, and an infinite time to expiration, must have a value equal to the stock price. In this special limiting case $C_t = S_t$.

From this analysis, we have now determined the upper and lower bounds for the price of a call option before expiration. Figure 3.1 depicts the boundaries for the price of a call option as the interior area between the upper and lower bounds. The upper bound for any call option is the stock price. The figure shows this boundary as the 45-degree line from the origin. Along this line, the call option is worth the same as the stock.

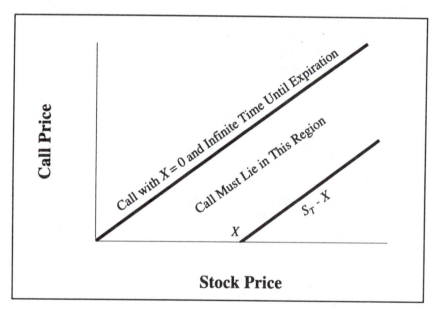

FIGURE 3.1 The Boundary Space for a Call Option

The lower bound is the value of the call option at expiration. At expiration, if the stock price is at or below the exercise price, the call is worth zero. For any stock price above the exercise price, the expiring call is worth the stock price minus the exercise price. Therefore, the value of a call option must always fall somewhere on or within the bounds given by these lines. Later in this chapter, we develop principles that help us to specify much more precisely where within these bounds the actual option price must lie.

The Boundary Space for a Put Option

We now consider the range of possible put prices. We have already considered prices for puts at expiration, and we found the value of a put at expiration to conform to Equation 3.2. Equation 3.2 gives the lower bound for the value of a put option. To find the upper bounds for a put option, we need to consider the best possible circumstances for the owner of a put option.

Upon exercise, the owner of a put surrenders the stock and receives the exercise price. The most the put holder can receive is the exercise price, and he can obtain this only by surrendering the stock. Therefore, the lower the stock price, the more valuable the put must be. This is true before expiration and at expiration, as we have already seen. The owner of an American put can exercise the option at any time. Therefore, the maximum value for an American put is the exercise price. The price of an American put equals the exercise price if the stock is worthless and is sure to remain worthless until the option expires. If the put is a European put, it cannot be exercised immediately, but only at expiration. For a European put before expiration, the maximum possible price equals the present value of the exercise price. The European put price cannot exceed the present value of the exercise price, because the owner of a European put must wait until expiration to exercise.

Figure 3.2 shows the bounds for American and European puts. The price of a put can never fall below the maximum of zero or $X - S_T$. This is the put's value at expiration, which Equation 3.2 specifies. For an American put, the price can never exceed X. For a European put, the price can never exceed the present value of the exercise price, $Xe^{-r(T-t)}$. Therefore, the interior of Figure 3.2 defines the range of possible put prices. By developing more exact no-arbitrage conditions, we can say where in this interior area the price of a put can be found.[3]

RELATIONSHIPS BETWEEN CALL PRICES

In this section we focus on price relationships between call options. These price differences arise from differences in exercise price and time until

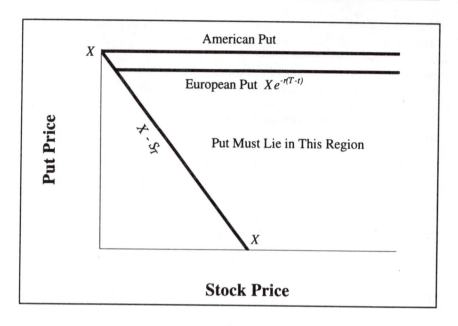

FIGURE 3.2 The Boundary Space for a Put Option

expiration. We have already seen in an informal way that the exercise price is a potential liability associated with call ownership. The greater the value of this potential liability, the lower the value of the call option. In this section, we illustrate this principle more formally by appealing to our familiar no-arbitrage arguments. We use similar no-arbitrage arguments to explicate other pricing relationships. Unless explicitly stated otherwise, all of these relationships hold for both American and European calls.

The Lower the Exercise Price, the More Valuable the Call. Let us consider a single underlying stock on which there are two call options. The two call options have the same expiration date, but one option has a lower exercise price than the other. In this section, we want to show why the option with the lower exercise price must be worth as much as or more than the option with the higher exercise price. For example, assume that two calls exist that violate this principle:

	Time until Expiration	Exercise Price	Call Price
Call A	6 months	$100	$20
Call B	6 months	95	15

These two calls violate our principle because Call A has a higher exercise price and a higher call price. These prices give rise to an arbitrage opportunity, as we now show. Faced with these prices, the trader can transact as follows:

Transaction	Cash Flow
Sell Call A	+$20
Buy Call B	−$15
Net Cash Flow	+$5

Once we sell Call A and buy Call B, we have a sure profit of at least $5. To see this, we consider profits and losses for various stock prices, such as $95 and below and $100 and above. If the stock price is $95, neither option can be exercised. If the stock price stays at $95 or below, both options expire worthless, and we keep our $5 from the initial transactions. If the stock price is greater than $100, say $105, Call A will be exercised against us. When that happens, we surrender the stock worth $105 and receive $100, losing $5 on the exercise against us. However, we ourselves exercise Call B, receiving the stock worth $105 and paying the exercise price of $95. So, we can summarize our profits and losses from the exercises that occur when the stock trades at $105.

Surrender stock	−$105
Receive $100 exercise price	+100
Pay $95 exercise price	−95
Receive stock	+105
Net Cash Flow	+$5

As the calculation shows, if Call A is exercised against us, we exercise Call B and make $5 on the double exercise. Therefore, we make a total of $10, $5 from the initial transaction and $5 on the exercises.

Next, we consider what happens if the stock price lies between $95 and $100, say at $97. This outcome is also beneficial for us, because the option we sold with a $100 strike price cannot be exercised against us. However, we can exercise our option. When we exercise, we pay the $95 exercise price and receive a stock worth $97. We add the $2 profit on this exercise to the $5 we made initially, for a total profit of $7. Figure 3.3 graphs the total profit on the position for all stock prices. With a stock price at or below $95, we make $5 because neither option can be

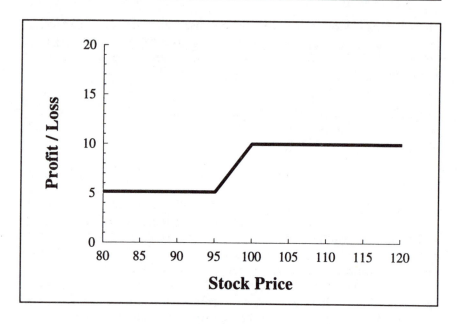

FIGURE 3.3   Arbitrage with Calls A and B

exercised. With a stock price of $100 or above, we make $10–$5 from our initial transaction and $5 from the difference between the two exercise prices. If the stock price is between $95 and $100, we make $5 from our initial transaction plus the difference between the stock price and the $95 exercise price we face.

These transactions guarantee an arbitrage profit of at least $5, and perhaps as much as $10. Figure 3.3 reflects the arbitrage profit because it shows there is at least a $5 profit for any stock price. If the profit and loss graph shows profits for all possible stock prices with no investment, then there is an arbitrage opportunity. In the real world, an investment strategy that requires no initial investment may show profits for some stock price outcomes, but it must also show losses for other stock prices. Otherwise, there is an arbitrage opportunity.

In stating our principle, we said that the call with the lower exercise price must cost at least as much as the call with the higher exercise price. Why doesn't the call with the lower exercise price have to cost more than the call with the higher exercise price? In most real market situations, the call with the lower exercise price will, in fact, cost more. However, we cannot be sure that will happen as a general rule. To see why, assume the stock underlying Calls A and B trades for $5 and there is virtually no chance that the stock price could reach $90 before the two options expire. When the underlying stock is extremely far out-of-the-money, the calls might have the same, or nearly the same, price. In such a situation, both calls would have a very low price. If it is certain that the stock price can never rise to the lower exercise price, both calls would be worthless.

The Difference in Call Prices Cannot Exceed the Difference in Exercise Prices. Consider two call options that are similar in all respects except that they have exercise prices that differ by $5. We have already seen that the price of the call with the lower exercise price must equal or exceed the price of the call with the higher exercise price. Now we show that the difference in call prices cannot exceed the difference in exercise prices. We illustrate this principle by considering two call options with the same underlying stock:

	Time until Expiration	Exercise Price	Call Price
Call C	6 months	$95	$10
Call D	6 months	100	4

The prices of Calls C and D do not meet our condition, and we want to show that these prices give rise to an arbitrage opportunity. To profit from this mispricing, we trade as follows:

Transaction	Cash Flow
Sell Call C	+$10
Buy Call D	−4
Net Cash Flow	+$6

Selling Call C and buying Call D gives a net cash inflow of $6. Because we sold a call, however, we also have the risk that the call will be exercised against us. We now show that no matter what stock price occurs, we still make a profit.

If the stock price is $95 or below, both options expire worthless, and we keep our initial cash inflow of $6. If the stock price exceeds $100, Call C is exercised against us and we exercise Call D. For example, assume the stock price is $102. We exercise, pay the $100 exercise price, and receive the stock. Call C is exercised against us, so we surrender the stock and receive the $95 exercise price. Therefore, we lose $5 on the exercise. This loss partially offsets our initial cash inflow of $6. Thus, for any stock price of $100 or more, we make $1. We now consider stock prices between

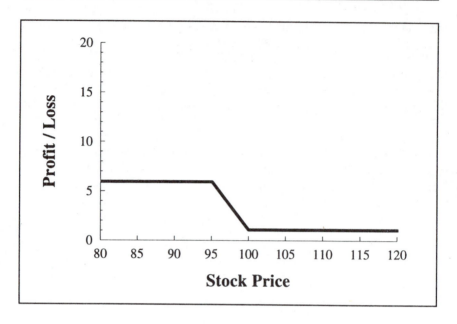

FIGURE 3.4 Arbitrage with Calls C and D

$95 and $100. If the stock price is $98, Call C will be exercised against us. We surrender the stock worth $98 and receive $95, for a $3 loss. The option we own cannot be exercised, because the exercise price of $100 exceeds the current stock price of $98. Therefore, we lose $3 on the exercise, which partially offsets our initial cash inflow of $6. This gives a $3 net profit.

Figure 3.4 shows the profits and losses on this trade for a range of stock prices. As the figure shows, we make at least $1, and we may make as much as $6. Because all outcomes show a profit with no investment, these transactions constitute an arbitrage. The chance to make this arbitrage profit stems from the fact that the call option prices differed by more than the difference between the exercise prices. In real markets, the difference between two call prices will usually be less than the difference in exercise prices. However, the difference in call prices cannot exceed the difference in exercise prices without creating an arbitrage opportunity.[4]

A Call Must Be Worth at Least the Stock Price Less the Present Value of the Exercise Price. We have already noted that a call at expiration is worth the maximum of zero or the stock price less the exercise price.

Before expiration, the call must be worth at least the stock price less the present value of the exercise price. That is:

$$C_t \geq S_t - Xe^{-r(T-t)} \qquad\qquad 3.3$$

To see why prices must observe this principle, we consider the following situation. Assume the stock trades for $103 and the current risk-free interest rate is 6 percent. A call with an exercise price of $100 expires in six months and trades for $2. These prices violate our rule, because the call option price is too low: $2 is less than the stock price less the present value of $100. These prices give rise to an arbitrage opportunity. To take advantage, we trade as follows:

Sell the stock	+$103
Buy the call option	−2
Buy a bond with remaining funds	−101
	Net Cash Flow 0

With these transactions, we owe one share of stock. However, with our call option and the money we have left from selling the stock, we can honor our obligations at any time and still have a profit. For example, at the beginning of the transactions, we can exercise our option, pay the $100 exercise price, return the stock, and keep $1.

Alternatively, we can wait until our option reaches expiration in six months. Then the bond we purchased with be worth 101e^{(.06)(.5)}$ = $104.08. Whatever the stock is worth at expiration, we can repay with profit. For example, if the stock price is higher than the exercise price, we exercise the option and pay $100 to get the stock. This gives a profit at expiration of $4.08. If the stock price is below the exercise price, we allow our option to expire. We then buy the stock in the open market and repay our debt of one share. For example, if the stock price is $95 at expiration, our option expires, and we pay $95 for the share to repay our obligation. Our profit then is $104.08 − $95 = $9.08. Figure 3.5 graphs the profits from this transaction.

From this analysis, we can see that our option must cost at least $103 −$100$e^{-(.06)(.5)}$ = $103 − $97.04 = $5.96. Any lower price allows an arbitrage profit. If the call is priced at $5.96, we have $97.04 to invest in bonds after selling the stock at $103 and buying the option at $5.96. At expiration, our bond investment pays $100, which is the exercise price. If the option sold at $5.96, the profit line in Figure 3.5 would shift down

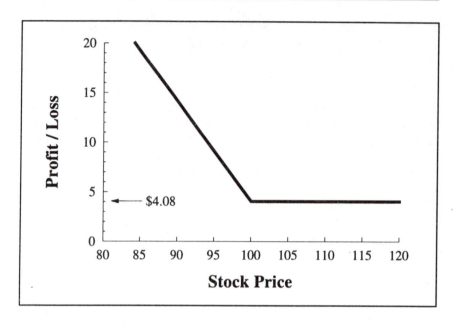

FIGURE 3.5   Arbitrage of a Call against a Stock and Bond

to show a zero profit for any stock price of $100 or more. This would
eliminate the arbitrage because there would be some stock prices that
would give zero profits. However, in real markets the price of this call
would generally be higher than $5.96. A price of $5.96 ensures against
any loss and gives profits for any stock price below $100. If there is any
chance that the stock price might be below $100 at expiration, then the
call of our example should be worth more than $5.96.

   The More Time until Expiration, the Greater the Call Price. If we
consider two call options with the same exercise price on the same underlying good, then the price of the call with more time remaining until
expiration must equal or exceed the price of the call that expires sooner.
Violating this principle leads to arbitrage, as the following example shows.

   Consider two options on the same underlying good.

	Time until Expiration	Exercise Price	Call Price
Call E	3 months	$100	$6
Call F	6 months	100	5

These prices violate our principle, which implies that Call F must cost at least as much as Call E. To capture the arbitrage profits, we trade as follows:

Transaction	Cash Flow
Sell Call E	+$6
Buy Call F	−5
Net Cash Flow	+$1

With a net cash inflow at the time of contracting, the transactions clearly require no investment. Therefore, they meet the first condition for an arbitrage. Next, we need to show that the strategy produces a profit for all stock price outcomes.

First, we show how to protect the arbitrage profit if the options are American options. Any time that Call E is exercised against us, we can exercise Call F to secure the stock to give to the holder of Call E. For example, assume that Call E is about to expire and is exercised against us with the stock price at $105. In that case, we simply exercise Call F and surrender the stock to the holder of Call E, as the following transactions show.

Assuming Call E and Call F Are American Options

Transaction	Cash Flow
Call E is exercised against us	
Receive $100 exercise price	+$100
Surrender stock worth $105	−105
Exercise Call F	
Receive stock worth $105	+105
Pay $100 exercise price	−100
Net Cash Flow	0

As these transactions show, if the call we sold is exercised against us, we can fulfill all our obligations by exercising our call. There will be no net cash flow on the exercise, and we keep the $1 profit from our original transaction.

Notice that our concluding transactions assumed that both Call E and Call F were American options. This allowed us to exercise our Call F before expiration. Had the options been European options, we could not exercise Call F when Call E was exercised against us. However, the principle still holds for European options—the European option with more time until expiration must be worth at least as much as the option with a shorter life. We can illustrate this principle for European options with the following transactions.

Assuming Call E and Call F Are European Options

Transaction	Cash Flow
Call E is exercised against us	
Receive $100 exercise price	+$100
Surrender stock worth $105	−105
Sell Call F	
Receive $S - Xe^{-r(T-t)} \geq \$5$	at least +5
Net Cash Flow	at least 0

As these transactions show, we will receive at least $5 for selling Call F. Earlier we used no arbitrage arguments to show that an in-the-money call must be worth at least the stock price minus the present value of the exercise price. The worst situation for these transactions occurs at very low interest rates. However, the arbitrage still works for a zero interest rate. Then, Call F must still be worth at least $S - X = \$105 - \$100 = \$5$. If we get $5 from selling Call F, we still have a net zero cash flow when Call E is exercised against us. If we get more, any additional net cash flow at the time of exercise is just added to the $1 cash inflow we had at the time we initially transacted.

Do Not Exercise Call Options on No-Dividend Stocks before Expiration. In this section, we show that a call option on a non-dividend-paying stock is always worth more than its mere exercise value. Therefore, such an option should never be exercised. If the trader wants to dispose of the option, it will always be better to sell the option than to exercise it.

For a call option, the **intrinsic value** or the **exercise value** of the option equals $S_t - X$. This is the value of the option when it is exercised, because the holder of the call pays X and receives S_t. We have seen that, prior to expiration, a call option must be worth at least $S_t - Xe^{-r(T-t)}$. Therefore, exercising a call before expiration discards at least the difference between X and $Xe^{-r(T-t)}$. The difference between the call price and the exercise value is the **time value** of the option. For example, consider the following values:

$$S_t = \$105$$
$$X = \$100$$
$$r = .10$$
$$T - t = 6 \text{ months}$$

The intrinsic value of this call option is \$5, or $S_t - X$. However, we know that the market price of the call option must meet the following condition:

$$C_t \geq S_t - Xe^{-r(T-t)}$$
$$\geq \$105 - \$100e^{-(.1)(.5)}$$
$$\geq \$9.88$$

Therefore, exercising the call throws away at least $X - Xe^{-r(T-t)} = \$100 - \$95.12 = \$4.88$. Alternatively it discards the difference between the lower bound on the call price and the exercise value of the call, $\$9.88 - \$5.00 = \$4.88$. For a non-dividend-paying stock, early exercise can never be optimal. This means that the call will not be exercised until expiration. However, this makes an American option on a non-dividend-paying stock equivalent to a European option. For a stock that pays no dividends, the American option will not be exercised until expiration and a European option cannot be exercised until expiration. Therefore, the two have the same price. Notice that this rule holds only for a call option on a stock that does not pay dividends. In some circumstances, it can make sense to exercise a call option on a dividend-paying stock before the option expires. The motivation for the early exercise is to capture the dividend immediately and to earn interest on those funds. We explore these possibilities in Chapter 6.

RELATIONSHIPS BETWEEN PUT PRICES

In Chapter 2, we saw that the value of either an American put or a European put at expiration is given by:

$$P_T = \text{MAX}\{0, X - S_T\}$$

Essentially, the put holder anticipates receiving the value of the exercise price and paying the stock price at expiration. Now we want to consider put values before expiration and the relationship between pairs of puts. As we did for calls, we illustrate these pricing relationships by invoking no-arbitrage conditions. Further, the relationships hold for both American and European puts unless explicitly stated otherwise.

Before Expiration, an American Put Must Be Worth at Least the Exercise Price Less the Stock Price. The holder of an American put option can exercise any time. Upon exercising, the put holder surrenders the put and the stock and receives the exercise price. Therefore, the American put must be worth at least the difference between the exercise price and the stock price.

$$P_t \geq \text{MAX}\{0, X - S_t\}$$

where P_t is the price of an American put at time t.

We illustrate this principle by showing how to reap an arbitrage profit if the principle does not hold. Consider the following data:

$$S_t = \$95$$
$$X = \$100$$
$$P_t = \$3$$

With these prices, the put is too cheap. The put's price does not equal or exceed the $5 difference between the exercise price and the stock price. To take advantage of the mispricing, we transact as shown below. With these transactions, we capture an immediate cash inflow of $2. Also, we have no further obligations, so our arbitrage is complete. Notice that these transactions involve the immediate exercise of the put option. Therefore, this kind of arbitrage is possible only for an American put option. To prevent this kind of arbitrage, the price of the American put option must be at least $5. In actual markets, the price of a put will generally exceed the difference between the exercise price and the stock price.

Transaction	Cash Flow
Buy put	−$3
Buy stock	−95
Exercise option	+100
Net Cash Flow	+$2

Before Expiration, a European Put Must Be Worth at Least the Present Value of the Exercise Price Minus the Stock Price. We have just seen that an American put must be worth at least the difference between the exercise price and the stock price, $X - S_t$. The same rule does not hold for a European put, because we cannot exercise the European put before expiration to take advantage of the mispricing. However, a similar rule holds for a European put. Specifically, the value of a European put must equal or exceed the present value of the exercise price minus the stock price:

$$p_t \geq Xe^{-r(T-t)} - S_t$$

We can illustrate this price restriction for a European put by using our same stock and option, except we treat the put as a European put. Also, the risk-free interest rate is 6 percent and we assume that the option expires in three months.

$$S_t = \$95$$
$$X = \$100$$
$$p_t = \$3$$
$$T - t = 3 \text{ months}$$
$$r = .06$$

where p_t is the price of a European put at time t. With these values, our principle states:

$$p_t \geq Xe^{-r(T-t)} - S_t = \$100e^{-(.06)(.25)} - \$95 = \$98.51 - \$95 = \$3.51$$

Because the put must be worth at least $3.51 but the actual price is only $3, we can reap an arbitrage profit by trading as follows:

Transaction	Cash Flow
Borrow $98 at 6 percent for 3 months	+$98
Buy put	−3
Buy stock	−95
Net Cash Flow	0

After making these initial transactions, we wait until the option is about to expire and we transact as follows:

Transaction	Cash Flow
Exercise option, deliver stock, and collect exercise price	+$100.00
Repay debt = $98e^{(.06)(.25)}$	−99.48
Net Cash Flow	+$0.52

These transactions give an arbitrage profit of $0.52 at expiration. Notice that there was a zero net cash flow when we first transacted, so there was no investment. These initial transactions guaranteed the $0.52 profit at expiration. Therefore, we have an arbitrage—a riskless profit with no investment.

From these two examples, we can see that an American put must be worth at least as much as a European put. The lower bound for the price of an American put is $X - S_t$, but the lower bound for the European put is $Xe^{-r(T-t)} - S_t$. Also, we know that the American put gives all the rights of the European put, plus the chance to exercise early. Therefore, the American put must be worth at least as much as the European put.

The Longer until Expiration, the More Valuable an American Put. Consider two American put options that are just alike except that one has a longer time until expiration. The put with the longer time until expiration must be worth at least as much as the other. Informally, the put with the longer time until expiration offers every advantage of the shorter-term put. In addition, the longer-term put offers the chance for greater price increases on the put after the shorter-term put expires. Without this condition, arbitrage opportunities exist.

To illustrate the arbitrage opportunity, assume the underlying stock trades for $95 and we have two American puts with exercise prices of $100 as follows:

	Time until Expiration	Put Price
Put A	3 months	$7
Put B	6 months	6

These prices permit arbitrage, because the put with the longer life is cheaper. Therefore, we sell Put A and buy Put B for an arbitrage profit, as shown below.

Transaction	Cash Flow
Sell Put A	+$7
Buy Put B	−6
Net Cash Flow	+$1

After making these transactions, we must consider what happens if Put A is exercised against us. Assume that Put A is exercised against us when the stock price is $90. In this situation, the following events occur.

Transaction	Cash Flow
On the exercise of Put A	
Receive stock worth $90	+$90
Pay exercise price of $100	−100
We exercise Put B	
Deliver stock worth $90	−90
Receive exercise price of $100	+100
Net Cash Flow	0

When the holder of Put A exercises against us, we immediately exercise Put B. No matter what the stock price may be, these transactions give a zero net cash flow. Therefore, the original transaction gave us $1, which represents an arbitrage profit of at least $1. The profit could be greater if Put A expires worthless. Then we have our $1 profit to keep, plus we still hold Put B, which may have additional value. Therefore, the longer-term American put must be worth at least as much as the shorter-term American put. Notice that this rule holds only for American puts. Our arbitrage transactions require that we exercise Put B when the holder of Put A exercises against us. This we could only do with an American option.

For European put options, it is not always true that the longer-term put has greater value. A European put pays off the exercise price only at expiration. If expiration is very distant, the payoff will be diminished in value because of the time value of money. However, the longer the life of a put option, the greater its advantage in allowing something beneficial to happen to the stock price. Thus, the longer the life of the put, the better for this reason. Whether having a longer life is beneficial to the price of a European put depends on which of these two factors dominates. We will be able to evaluate these more completely in the next chapter.

The fact that a European put with a shorter life can be more valuable than a European put with a longer life shows two important principles. First, early exercise of a put can be desirable even when the underlying stock pays no dividends. This follows from the fact that a short-term European put can be worth more than a long-term European put. Second, American and European put prices may not be identical, even when the underlying stock pays no dividends. If early exercise is desirable, the American put allows it and the European put does not. Therefore, the

American put can be more valuable than a European put, even when the underlying stock pays no dividend.

The Higher the Exercise Price, the More Valuable the Put. For both American and European put options, a higher exercise price is associated with a higher price. A put option with a higher exercise price must be worth at least as much as a put with a lower exercise price. Violations of this principle lead to arbitrage.

To illustrate the arbitrage, consider a stock trading at $90 with the following two put options having the same time until expiration:

	Exercise Price	Put Price
Put C	$100	$11
Put D	95	12

These prices violate the rule, because the price of Put D is higher, even though Put C has the higher exercise price. To reap the arbitrage profit, we transact as follows:

Transaction		Cash Flow
Sell Put D		+$12
Buy Put C		−11
	Net Cash Flow	+$1

If the holder of Put D exercises against us, we immediately exercise Put C. Assuming the stock price is $90 at the time of exercise, we consider the appropriate transactions when we face the exercise of Put D:

Transaction		Cash Flow
Exercise of Put D against us:		
Receive stock worth $90		+$90
Pay exercise price		−95
Our exercise of Put C:		
Deliver stock worth $90		−90
Receive exercise price		+100
	Net Cash Flow	+$5

No matter what the stock price is at the time of exercise, we have a cash inflow of $5 if we both exercise. Further, Put D can be exercised only

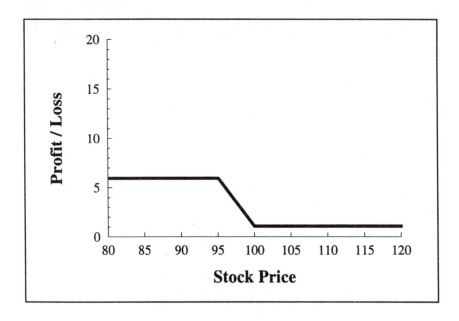

FIGURE 3.6   Arbitrage with Puts C and D

when it is profitable for us to exercise Put C. Notice that this principle holds for both American and European puts. Put C and Put D can be exercised either before expiration (for an American option) or at expiration only (for a European option). Figure 3.6 shows the profits for alternative stock prices. For any stock price of $100 or above, both puts expire worthless and we keep our initial $1 inflow. For a stock price between $95 and $100, we can exercise our option, but Put D cannot be exercised. For example, if the stock is at $97, we exercise and receive $100 for a $97 stock. This $3 exercise profit gives us a total profit of $4. If the stock price is below $95, both puts will be exercised. For example, with the stock price at $90, the exercise profit on Put D is $5, as we have seen. However, our exercise profit on Put C is $10. Thus, we lose $5 on the exercise of Put D against us, but we make $10 by exercising Put C, and we still have our $1 initial inflow, for a net arbitrage profit of $6.

   The Price Difference between Two American Puts Cannot Exceed the Difference in Exercise Prices. The prices of two American puts cannot differ by more than the difference in exercise prices, assuming other features are the same. If prices violate this condition, there will be an arbitrage opportunity. To illustrate this arbitrage opportunity, consider the following puts on the same underlying stock:

	Exercise Price	Put Price
Put E	$100	$4
Put F	105	10

These prices violate our condition, because the price difference between the puts is $6, while the difference in exercise prices is only $5. To exploit this mispricing, we transact as follows:

Transaction	Cash Flow
Sell Put F	+$10
Buy Put E	−$4
Net Cash Flow	+$6

With this initial cash inflow of $6, we have enough to pay any loss we might sustain when the holder of Put F exercises against us. For example, assume the stock trades at $95 and the holder of Put F exercises:

Transaction	Cash Flow
The exercise of Put F against us:	
Receive stock worth $95	+$95
Pay exercise price	−$105
Our exercise of Put E:	
Receive exercise price	+$100
Deliver stock worth $95	−$95
Net Cash Flow	−$5

On the exercise, we lose $5. However, we already received $6 with the initial transactions. This leaves an arbitrage profit of at least $1. As Figure 3.7 shows, we could have larger profits, depending on the stock price. If the stock price equals or exceeds $105, no exercise is possible and we keep the entire $6 of our initial transaction. For stock prices between $100 and $105, the holder of Put F can exercise against us, but we cannot exercise. For example, if the stock price is $103, we must pay $105 and receive a stock worth only $103, for a $2 exercise loss. However, with our initial cash inflow of $6, we still have a net profit of $4. For stock prices below $100, we can both exercise, as in the transactions we showed for a stock price of $95. In this case, we lose $5 on the exercise, but we still make a net profit of $1.

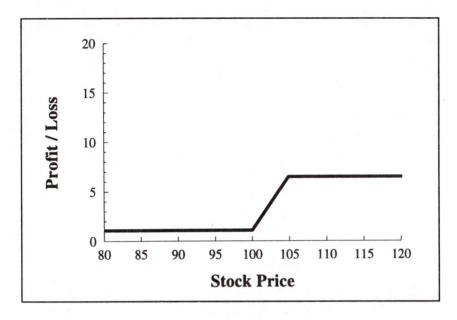

FIGURE 3.7   Arbitrage with Puts E and F

For Two European Puts, the Price Difference Cannot Exceed the Difference in the Present Value of the Exercise Prices. A similar principle holds for European puts, except the difference in put prices cannot exceed the difference in the present values of the exercise prices. If Puts E and F are European puts, the interest rate is 10 percent, and the options expire in six months, then the present values of the exercise prices are:

	Exercise Price	Present Value of Exercise Price
Put E	$100	$95.12
Put F	105	99.88

According to this principle, the price of Put F cannot exceed the price of Put E by more than $4.76 ($99.88 − $95.12). With prices of $4 and $10 for Puts E and F, there should be an arbitrage profit.

To capture the profit, we sell Put F and buy Put E, as we did with the American puts. This gives a cash inflow of $6, which we invest for six months at 10 percent. The European puts cannot be exercised until expiration, at which time our investment is worth (6e^{(.1)(.5)}$) = $6.31. The most we can lose on the exercise is $5, the difference in the exercise prices. As we saw for the American puts, this happens when the stock price is $100 or less. However, we have $6.31 at expiration, so we can easily sustain this loss. If the stock price exceeds $105, neither option can be exercised, and we keep our entire $6.31. For the European puts, the graph of the arbitrage profit is exactly like Figure 3.7, except we add $0.31 to every point. If the options had been priced $4.76 apart, our investment would have yielded $5 at expiration ($4.76$e^{(.1)(.5)}$). This $5 would protect us against any loss at expiration, but it would guarantee no arbitrage profit.

Summary

To this point, we have considered how call and put prices respond to stock and exercise prices and the time remaining until expiration. We have expressed all of these relationships as an outgrowth of our basic no-arbitrage condition: Prevailing options prices must exclude arbitrage profits. For call options, the story is very clear. The higher the stock price, the higher the call price. The higher the exercise price, the lower the call price. The longer the time until expiration, the higher the call price. For put options, the higher the stock price, the lower the put price. The higher the exercise price, the higher the put price. For time until expiration, the effects are slightly more complicated. For an American put, the longer the time until expiration, the more valuable the put. For a European put, a longer time until expiration can give rise to either a lower or higher put price.

We have also seen that no-arbitrage conditions restrict how call and put prices for different exercise prices can vary. For two call options or two American put options that are alike except for their exercise prices, the two option prices cannot differ by more than the difference in the exercise prices. For two European put options with different exercise prices, the option prices cannot differ by more than the present value of the difference in the exercise prices.

Throughout this discussion, we have been trying to tighten the bounds we can place on options prices. For example, Figure 3.1 gave the most generous bounds for call options. There we noted that the call price could never exceed the stock price as an upper bound. As a lower bound, the call price must always be at least zero or the stock price minus the exercise price, whichever is higher. The price relationships we considered in this section tighten these bounds by placing further restrictions on put and call prices. Figure 3.8 illustrates how we have tightened these bounds for call options. First, we showed that the call price must be at least zero or the stock price minus the present value of the exercise price. Figure 3.8

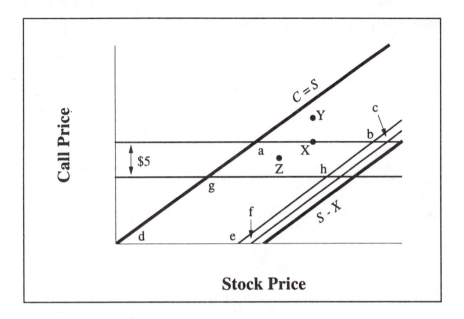

FIGURE 3.8   Call Price Relationships

reflects this restriction by pulling in the right boundary. Now we know that the call price must lie in this slightly smaller area. Also, if we consider a call with a lower exercise price, we know that the call price must be at least as high for the call with the lower exercise price.

Further, we have considered price relationships between pairs of options that differ in some respects. For example, assume that Option X in Figure 3.8 is priced correctly. We want to consider Option Y, which is another call like X, except it has a longer time until expiration. With its longer time until expiration, the price of Y must equal or exceed the price of X. For example, Y in Figure 3.8 would have to lie on or above the horizontal line abc that runs through X. Based on our information, Y in Figure 3.8 has a permissible location.

Consider another option, Z, which is just like X except Z has an exercise price that is $5 higher than X's. The price of Z can never fall below the stock price minus the present value of Z's exercise price. Therefore, the right boundary for the stock price minus the present value of Z's exercise price gives a floor for the price of Z. The price of Z must lie above the line eb. With a higher exercise price, the price of Option Z cannot exceed the price of X. Therefore, the price of Z must lie on or below the line abc. Combining these two restrictions, we know that the price of Z must lie in the area given by abcd.

However, we can locate the price of Z more exactly. We know from our discussion that two calls that differ only in their exercise prices must have prices that differ no more than their exercise prices. In our example, the exercise price of Z is $5 more than the exercise price of X. In Figure 3.8, line gh is $5 below line abc. Therefore, continuing to assume that the price of X is correct, Z must have a price that lies on or above gh. If it did not, the price of Z would be too low relative to X. Putting these principles together, we know that the price of Z must lie within the area defined by abhg. Z in Figure 3.8 conforms to these rules.

We cannot specify exactly where Z must lie within area abhg. Options prices also depend on two additional factors that we must now consider: interest rates and the way in which the stock price moves. After considering these additional factors in this chapter and in Chapter 4, we will be able to pinpoint the price that an option must have.

OPTIONS PRICES AND THE INTEREST RATE

We now apply our no-arbitrage approach to examine the effect of interest rates on options prices. For a call option, the exercise price represents a potential liability the owner of a call option faces at expiration. Before expiration, the lower the present value of the liability associated with owning a call, the better for the call owner. Therefore, as we show in the following section, call options prices increase with higher interest rates. The result may seem counterintuitive because we generally associate higher asset prices with lower interest rates. This is not so for call options, as our no-arbitrage argument shows. The owner of a put option may exercise and receive the exercise price in exchange for surrendering the stock, so the exercise price represents a potential asset for a put owner. The lower the interest rate, the higher the present value of that potential asset. Therefore, the lower the interest rate, the higher the price of a put. This section presents a no-arbitrage argument to show why the price of a put must fall as interest rates rise.

Call Prices and Interest Rates

We have already observed that the price of either an American or a European call must equal or exceed the larger of zero or the stock price minus the present value of the exercise price:

$$C_t \geq \text{MAX}\{0, S_t - Xe^{-r(T-t)}\} \qquad\qquad 3.4$$

In Equation 3.3, $Xe^{-r(T-t)}$ is the present value of the exercise price. The larger the interest rate, r, the smaller that present value, and thus a higher interest rate gives a larger value for $S_t - Xe^{-r(T-t)}$. This makes sense because the exercise price is a liability the call owner incurs upon exercise.

We can also show that the call price must rise if interest rates rise by the following no-arbitrage example. Consider a call option on a stock trading at $100. The exercise price of the call is $100. The option expires in six months and the current interest rate is 10 percent. From Equation 3.3, the price of this call must equal or exceed $4.88:

$$C_t \geq \text{MAX}\{0, \$100 - \$100e^{-(.1)(.5)}\} \geq \$4.88$$

For convenience, we assume that the option is correctly priced at $4.88.[5]

Suddenly, interest rates jump from 10 to 12 percent, but the option price remains at $4.88. Now the option price does not meet the condition in Equation 3.3. The option price is too low, so we want to transact to guarantee an arbitrage profit. Accordingly, we trade as follows:

Transaction	Cash Flow
Sell stock	+$100.00
Buy call	−4.88
Buy bond maturing in 6 months and yielding 12 percent	−95.12
Net Cash Flow	0

In six months, the option is at expiration and our bond matures. The bond will pay $101.

How we deal with the call and stock depends on the stock price relative to the option price. If the stock trades for $100, the call option is worthless. In this case, we buy the stock for $100 and return it, leaving a profit of $1. If the stock price is less than $100, our profit increases. For example, with a $95 stock price, the option is worthless and we buy the stock for $95. These transactions leave a total profit of $6. If the stock price exceeds $100, we exercise our call and pay the exercise price of $100. After exercising and returning the stock, we still have $1. Therefore, we have a profit at expiration with no investment. This arbitrage opportunity arose because the option price did not increase as the interest rate rose. With our example, the price of the call should have risen to at least $5.82 to exclude arbitrage:

$$C_t \geq \text{MAX}\{0, S_t - Xe^{-r(T-t)}\} \geq \text{MAX}\{0, \$100 - \$100e^{-(.12)(.5)}\} \geq \$5.82$$

Because the price did not respond, we were able to reap an arbitrage profit. To exclude arbitrage, the price of a call must be higher the higher the interest rate. Otherwise, a riskless profit without investment will be possible.

Put Prices and Interest Rates

Interest rates also affect put prices. When exercising, the holder of a put receives the exercise price. Therefore, for a put owner, the exercise price is a potential cash inflow. The greater the present value of that potential inflow, the higher will be the value of the put. As a consequence, the put price should be higher the lower the interest rate. If a put price fails to adjust to changing interest rates, there will be an arbitrage opportunity. This rule holds for both American and European puts.

To show how put prices depend on interest rates, consider a stock trading at $90. A European put option on this stock expires in six months and has an exercise price of $100. Interest rates are at 10 percent. We know that the European put price must meet the following condition:

$$p_t \geq \text{MAX}\{0,\ Xe^{-r(T-t)} - S_t\} \geq \text{MAX}\{0,\ \$100 e^{-(.1)(.5)} - \$90\} \geq \$5.12$$

For convenience, we assume that the put is priced at $5.12.

Let us now assume that interest rates suddenly fall to 8 percent, but that the put price does not change. Our principle asserts that the put should be worth at least $6.08 now. With the put price staying at $5.12, when it should be $6.08, we trade as follows:

Transaction	Cash Flow
Borrow $95.12 at 8 percent	+$95.12
Buy stock	−90.00
Buy put	−5.12
Net Cash Flow	0

With these transactions in place, we wait until expiration in six months to reap our arbitrage profit. At expiration, we owe $99 on our borrowings. From the stock and the put, we must realize enough to cover that payment. Any remaining money will be profit. If the stock price at expiration is $100, we allow our put to expire and we sell the stock. We receive $100, from which we pay $99. This leaves a $1 profit. If the stock price at expiration is below $100, we exercise our put. For example, with a stock price of $95, we exercise our put, deliver the stock, and collect $100. This gives a $1 profit. We make exactly $1 at expiration for any stock price of $100 or less. For any stock price above $100, our put is worthless and our profit equals the difference between the stock price and our $99 debt. From these transactions, we see that we will make at least $1 at expiration. This we achieve with zero investment. Therefore, the failure of the put option price to adjust to changing interest rates generates an arbitrage opportunity. The put price must rise as interest rates fall.

OPTIONS PRICES AND STOCK PRICE MOVEMENTS

Up to this point, we have studied the way in which four factors constrain call and put prices. These factors are the stock price, the exercise price, the time remaining until expiration, and the interest rate. Even with these four factors, we cannot say exactly what the option price must be before expiration. There is a fifth factor to consider—stock price movements before expiration. If we consider a stock with options on it that expire in six months, we know that the stock price can change thousands of times before the option expires. Further, for two stocks, the pattern of changes and the volatility of the stock price changes can differ dramatically. However, if we can develop a model for understanding stock price movements, we can use that model to specify what the price of an option must be.

We now make a drastic, but temporary, simplifying assumption. Between the current moment and the expiration of an option, we assume that the stock price will rise by 10 percent or fall by 10 percent. With this assumption about the stock's price movement, we can use our no-arbitrage approach to determine the exact value of a European call or put. Therefore, knowing the potential pattern of stock price movements gives us the final key to understanding options prices. This chapter illustrates how to determine options prices based on this simplified model of stock price movements. The next chapter shows how to apply more realistic models of stock price movements to compute accurate options prices.

Let us assume that a stock trades for $100. In the next year, the price can rise or fall exactly 10 percent. Therefore, the stock price next year will be either $90 or $110. Both a put and a call option have exercise prices of $100 and expire in one year. The current interest rate is 6 percent. We want to know how much the put and call will be worth. With these data, the call price is $7.55, and the put is worth $1.89. Other prices create arbitrage opportunities. This section shows that the options must have these prices. Chapter 4 explains why these no-arbitrage relationships must hold. (As we consider a single period in this section, we employ discrete compounding.)

The Call Price

We have asserted that the call price must be $7.55, given our other data, if the call price is to exclude an arbitrage opportunity. If the option price is lower, we will enter arbitrage transactions that include buying the option. Similarly, if the option price is higher, our arbitrage transactions will include selling the call. We illustrate each case in turn. Let us begin by assuming that the call price is $7, which is below our no-arbitrage price of $7.55. If the call price is too low, we transact as follows:

Transaction	Cash Flow
Sell 1 share of stock	+$100.00
Buy 2 calls	−14.00
Buy bond	−86.00
Net Cash Flow	0

At expiration, the stock price will be either $110 or $90. If the stock price is $110, the calls will be worth $10 each—the stock price minus the exercise price. If the stock price is $90, the calls are worthless. In either case, the bond will pay $91.16. If the stock price is $90, we repurchase a share with our bond proceeds for $90. This leaves a profit of $1.16. If the stock price is $110, we sell our two options for $20. Adding this $20 to our bond proceeds, we have $111.16. From this amount, we buy a share for $110 to repay the borrowing of a share. This leaves a profit of $1.16. Therefore, we make $1.16 whether the stock price rises or falls. We made this certain profit with zero investment, so we have an arbitrage profit.

Now assume the call price is $8, exceeding $7.55. In this case, the call price is too high, so we sell the call as part of the following transactions.

Transaction	Cash Flow
Buy 1 share of stock	−$100.00
Sell 2 calls	+16.00
Sell a bond (borrow funds)	+84.00
Net Cash Flow	0

At expiration, we know we must repay $89.04. If the stock price at expiration is $90, the calls cannot be exercised against us. So we sell our stock for $90 and repay our debt of $89.04. This leaves a profit of $.96.

If the stock price goes to $110, the calls we sold will be exercised against us. To fulfill one obligation, we deliver our share of stock and receive the exercise price of $100. We then buy back the other call that is still outstanding. It costs $10, the difference between the stock price and the exercise price. This leaves $90, from which we repay our debt of $89.04. Now we have completed all of our obligations and we still have $0.96. Therefore, with a call priced at $8, we will have a profit of $0.96 from these transactions no matter whether the stock price goes up or down. We captured this sure profit with zero investment, so we have an arbitrage profit.

To eliminate arbitrage, the call must trade for $7.55. If that call price prevails, both transaction strategies fail. For example, we might try to transact as follows if the call price is $7.55.

Transaction	Cash Flow
Buy 1 share of stock	−$100.00
Sell 2 calls	+15.10
Sell a bond (borrow funds)	+84.90
Net Cash Flow	0

At expiration, we owe $90. If the stock price is $90, our calls are worthless. However, we can sell our share for $90 and repay our debt. Our net cash flow at expiration is zero. If the stock price is $110, the calls will be exercised against us. We deliver our one share and receive $100. From this $100 we repay our debt of $90. This leaves $10, the exact difference between the stock and exercise price. Therefore, we can use our last $10 to close our option position. Our net cash flow is zero. With a call price of $7.55, our transactions cost us zero and they yield zero. This is exactly the result we expect in a market that is free from arbitrage opportunities.[6]

The Put Price

Based on the same data we have just considered for the call option, the put price must be $1.89 to avoid arbitrage. We can see that this must be the case in two ways. First, we show that put–call parity requires a price of $1.89. Second, we show how any other price leads to arbitrage opportunities similar to those that occurred when the call was priced incorrectly.

From Chapter 2 we know that put–call parity expresses the value of a European put as a function of a similar call, the stock, and investment in the risk-free bond.

$$p_t = c_t - S_t + Xe^{-r(T-t)}$$

where $Xe^{-r(T-t)}$ is the present value of the exercise price. For our example, we know that the correct call price is $7.55 and that the stock trades for $100. With one year remaining until expiration, the present value of the exercise price is $94.34. According to put–call parity for our example:

$$p_t = \$7.55 - \$100.00 + \$94.34 = \$1.89$$

If the put is not worth $1.89, arbitrage opportunities arise. This makes sense because the put–call parity relationship is itself a no-arbitrage condition.[7]

We now show how to reap arbitrage profits if the put does not trade for $1.89. We consider the transactions if the put price is above or below its correct price of $1.89. First, let us assume that the put price is $1.50. In this case, the put is too cheap relative to other assets. The other assets that replicate the put are too expensive, taken together. These are the call, stock, bond combination on the right-hand side of the put–call parity formula. The put–call parity relationship suggests that we should buy the relatively overpriced put and sell the relatively overpriced portfolio that replicates the put. To initiate this strategy, we transact as follows:

Transaction	Cash Flow
Buy put	−$1.50
Sell call	+7.55
Buy stock	−100.00
Borrow $93.95 and invest at 6 percent for one year	+94.34
Net Cash Flow	0

In one year, our debt is $99.59 and the put and call are at expiration. The stock price will be either $90 or $110. We consider the value of our position for both possible stock prices. If the stock price is $90, we exercise our put and deliver our share of stock. This gives a cash flow of $100, from which we repay our debt of $99.59. We have no further obligations, yet $0.41 remains. Thus, we make a profit with no initial investment.

If the stock price is $110, our put is worthless and the stock will be called away from us. When the call is exercised against us, we receive $100. From this $100, we repay our debt of $99.59. Again, this leaves us with $0.41. No matter whether the stock goes to $90 or to $110, we make $0.41. We achieved this profit with no initial investment. Consequently, we have a certain profit with zero investment, a sure sign of an arbitrage profit.

We now consider how to transact if the put price is higher than $1.89. Let us assume that the put trades for $2. With the put being too expensive, we sell the relatively overpriced put and purchase the relatively under-priced portfolio that replicates the put. In this case, our transactions are just the reverse of those we made when the put price was too low. We transact as follows:

Transaction	Cash Flow
Sell put	+$2.00
Buy call	−7.55
Sell stock	+100.00
Lend $94.45 at 6 percent for one year	−94.45
Net Cash Flow	0

In one year, our loan matures, so we collect $100.12. If the stock price is $90, our call is worthless and the put will be exercised against us. We must accept the $90 stock and pay the $100 exercise price. This leaves one share of stock and $0.12. We use the share to cover our original sale of stock, and we have $0.12 after meeting all obligations.

If the stock price goes to $110, the put we sold will expire worthless. We exercise our call, paying the $100 exercise price to acquire the stock. We now have $0.12 and one share, so we cover our original share sale by returning the stock. Again, we have completed all transactions and $0.12 remains. Therefore, no matter whether the stock goes to $90 or $110 over the one-year investment horizon, we make $0.12. We did this with zero investment, so we have an arbitrage profit.

These transactions illustrate why the put must trade for $1.89 in our example. Any other price allows arbitrage. If the put price is $1.89, both of the transactions we have just considered will cost zero to execute, but they will be sure to return zero when the options expire. In a market free of arbitrage opportunities, this is just what we expect.

OPTIONS PRICES AND THE RISKINESS OF STOCKS

As we have seen, options prices depend on several factors, including stock prices. In this section, we explore how stock price changes affect options prices. Specifically, we consider how the riskiness of the stock affects the price of the put or call. We use a simple model of the way a stock price changes to illustrate a very important result: The riskier the underlying stock, the greater the value of an option. This principle holds for both put and call options. While it may seem odd for an option price to be higher if the underlying good is riskier, we can use no-arbitrage arguments to show why this must be true.

Essentially, a call option gives its owner most of the benefits of rising stock prices and protects the owner from suffering the full cost of a drop in stock prices. Thus, a call option offers insurance against falling stock prices and holds out the promise of high profits from surging stock prices. The riskier the underlying stock, the greater the chance of an extreme stock price movement. If the stock price falls dramatically, the insurance feature of the call option comes into play. This limits the call holder's loss. However, if the stock price increases dramatically, the call owner participates fully in the price increase. The protection against large losses, coupled with participation in large gains, makes call options more valuable when the underlying stock is risky.

For put options, risk has a parallel effect. Put owners benefit from large stock price drops and suffer from price increases. However, a put protects the owner from the full force of a stock price rise. In effect, a put embodies insurance against large price rises. At the same time, the put allows its owner to benefit fully from a stock price drop. Because the put incorporates protection against rising prices and allows its owner to capture virtually all profits from falling prices, a put is more valuable the riskier the underlying stock.

In the preceding section, we used a very simple model of stock price movement to show how to price put and call options. In this section, we extend the same model and example to evaluate the effect of riskiness on stock prices. Earlier, we assumed a stock traded for $100 and that its price would go to either $90 or $110 in one year. We assumed that the risk-free rate of interest was 6 percent and that a call and put option both had exercise prices of $100 and expired in one year. Under these circumstances, the call was worth $7.55 and the put was worth $1.89. Any other price for the put or call led to arbitrage opportunities. To explore the effect of risk, we consider two other possible outcomes for the stock price. First, we assume that the stock is not risky. In this case, the stock price increases by the risk-free rate of 6 percent with certainty. Second, we consider stock price movements in which the stock price goes to either $80 or $120.

Options Prices for Riskless Stock

If the stock is risk free, its value grows at the risk-free rate. Otherwise, there would be an arbitrage opportunity between the stock and the risk-free bond.[8] Consequently, we consider prices of our example options assuming that the stock price in one year will be $106 with certainty. Under these circumstances, the call option will be worth $5.66 and the put will be worth zero.

The put will be worth zero one year before expiration because it is sure to be worth zero at expiration. If the stock price is sure to be $106 at expiration, the put only gives the right to force someone to accept a stock worth $106 for $100. Thus, the put is worthless, because there is no chance the stock price will be below the exercise price of the put.

The call has a certain payoff at expiration, because the stock price is certain. At expiration, the call is worth $MAX\{0, S_T - X\} = \$6$. With a riskless stock, the call is also riskless. Investment in the call pays a certain return of $6 in one year, so the call must be worth the present value of $6, or $5.66. Any other price for the call creates an arbitrage opportunity. For example, if the option trades at $5.80, we sell the call and invest the $5.80 at 6 percent. In one year, our investment is worth $6.15 and the exercise of the call against us costs us $6. This yields a $0.15 arbitrage profit. For any other price of either the put or the call, our familiar transactions guarantee an arbitrage profit.

Earlier, we placed the following bound on the European call price before expiration:

$$c_t \geq MAX\{0, S_t - Xe^{-r(T-t)}\}$$

Now we see that this relationship holds exactly if the stock is risk free. In other words, the European call price is on the lower boundary if the stock has no risk. Therefore, holding the other factors constant, any excess value of the call above the boundary is due solely to the riskiness of the stock.

Comparing our two examples of stock price movements, we saw that the risk-free stock implied a call price of $5.66. If the stock price was risky, moving up or down 10 percent in the next year, the call price was $7.55. This call price difference is due to the difference in the riskiness of the stock. As we now show, higher risk implies higher options prices.

Riskier Stocks Result in Higher Options Prices

In our model of stock price movements, we assumed that stock prices change over a year in a very specific way. When we assumed that stock prices could increase or decrease 10 percent, we found certain options prices. We now consider the same circumstances but allow for more radical stock price movements of 20 percent up or down. All other factors remain the same. In summary, a stock trades today at $100. In one year, its price will be either $80 or $120. The risk-free interest rate is 6 percent. A call and put each have an exercise price of $100 and expire in one year. Under these circumstances, the call price must be $12.26, and the put price must be $6.60. Any other prices create arbitrage opportunities. Therefore, we have observed the price effects of the following three stock price movements on options prices.

Stock Price Movement	Call Price	Put Price
Stock price increases by a certain 6 percent	$5.66	$0.00
Stock price rises or falls by 10 percent	7.55	1.89
Stock price rises or falls by 20 percent	12.26	6.60

In these examples, we held other factors constant. Each example used options with the same exercise price and time to expiration. Also, each example employed the same risk-free rate. As these examples illustrate, greater risk in the stock increases both put and call prices.

SUMMARY

In this chapter, we discussed the relationships that govern options prices. We began by considering general boundary spaces for calls and puts. By linking relationships between options features, such as time to expiration and exercise prices, we specified price relationships between options. For example, we saw that the price of a call with a lower exercise price must equal or exceed the price of a similar call with a higher exercise price. We discussed the five factors on which options prices depend: the exercise price, the stock price, the risk-free interest rate, the time to expiration, and the riskiness of the stock. We found that options prices have a definitive relationship to these factors, as Table 3.1 summarizes. We explore these price reactions in detail in Chapter 5.

Understanding these factors helps us place bounds on call and put prices. However, to determine an exact price, we must specify how the stock price can move. To illustrate the important influence of stock price movements on options prices, we considered a very simple model of stock price movements. For example, we assumed that the stock prices can change 10 percent in the next year. With this assumption, we were able to find exact options prices. However, this assumption about the

Table 3.1 Options Price Response to Changes in Underlying Variables

For an Increase in the:	The Call Price	The Put Price
Stock Price	Rises	Falls
Exercise Price	Falls	Rises
Time until Expiration	Rises	May rise or fall
Interest Rate	Rises	Falls
Stock Risk	Rises	Rises

movement of stock prices is very unrealistic. A year from now, a stock may have a virtually infinite number of prices, not just two. With unrealistic assumptions about stock price movements, the options prices we compute are likely to be unrealistic as well. In the next chapter, we work toward more realistic assumptions about stock price movements and we develop a more exact options pricing model.

REVIEW QUESTIONS

1. What is the maximum theoretical value for a call? Under what conditions does a call reach this maximum value? Explain.
2. What is the maximum theoretical value for an American put? When does it reach this maximum? Explain.
3. Answer Question 2 for a European put.
4. Explain the difference in the theoretical maximum values for an American and a European put.
5. How does the exercise price affect the price of a call? Explain.
6. Consider two calls with the same time to expiration that are written on the same underlying stock. Call 1 trades for $7 and has an exercise price of $100. Call 2 has an exercise price of $95. What is the maximum price that Call 2 can have? Explain.
7. Six months remain until a call option expires. The stock price is $70 and the exercise price is $65. The option price is $5. What does this imply about the interest rate?
8. Assume the interest rate is 12 percent and four months remain until an option expires. The exercise price of the option is $70 and the stock that underlies the option is worth $80. What is the minimum value the option can have based on the no-arbitrage conditions studied in this chapter? Explain.
9. Two call options are written on the same stock that trades for $70 and both calls have an exercise price of $85. Call 1 expires in six months and Call 2 expires in three months. Assume that

Call 1 trades for $6 and that Call 2 trades for $7. Do these prices allow arbitrage? Explain. If they do permit arbitrage, explain the arbitrage transactions.

10. Explain the circumstances that make early exercise of a call rational. Under what circumstances is early exercise of a call irrational?

11. Consider a European and an American call with the same expiration and the same exercise price that are written on the same stock. What relationship must hold between their prices? Explain.

12. Before exercise, what is the minimum value of an American put?

13. Before exercise, what is the minimum value of a European put?

14. Explain the differences in the minimum values of American and European puts before expiration.

15. How does the price of an American put vary with time until expiration? Explain.

16. What relationship holds between time until expiration and the price of a European put?

17. Consider two puts with the same term to expiration (six months). One put has an exercise price of $110, the other has an exercise price of $100. Assume the interest rate is 12 percent. What is the maximum price difference between the two puts if they are European? If they are American? Explain the difference, if any.

18. How does the price of a call vary with interest rates? Explain.

19. Explain how a put price varies with interest rates. Does the relationship vary for European and American puts? Explain.

20. What is the relationship between the risk of the underlying stock and the call price? Explain in intuitive terms.

21. A stock is priced at $50 and the risk-free rate of interest is 10 percent. A European call and a European put on this stock both have exercise prices of $40 and expire in six months. What is the difference between the call and put prices? (Assume continuous compounding.) From the information supplied in this question, can you say what the call and put prices must be? If not, explain what information is lacking.

22. A stock is priced at $50 and the risk-free rate of interest is 10 percent. A European call and a European put on this stock both have exercise prices of $40 and expire in six months. Assume that the call price exceeds the put price by $7. Does this represent an arbitrage opportunity? If so, explain why and state the transactions you would make to take advantage of the pricing discrepancy.

NOTES

1. The price of an option depends on these five factors when the underlying stock pays no dividends. As we will discuss in Chapter 5, if the underlying stock pays a dividend, the dividend is a sixth factor that we must consider.
2. Like Chapter 2, the discussion of these rational bounds for options prices relies on a paper by Robert C. Merton, "Theory of Rational Option Pricing," *Bell Journal of Economics and Management Science*, 4, 1973, 141–183.
3. Scholars have tested market data to determine how well puts and calls meet these boundary conditions. Dan Galai was the first to test these relationships in his paper, "Empirical Tests of Boundary Conditions for CBOE Options," *Journal of Financial Economics*, 6, June/September 1978, 182–211. Galai found some violations of the no-arbitrage conditions in the reported prices. However, these apparent arbitrage opportunities disappeared if a trader faced a 1 percent transaction cost. Mihir Bhattacharya conducted similar, but more extensive, tests in his paper, "Transaction Data Tests on the Efficiency of the Chicago Board Options Exchange," *Journal of Financial Economics*, 1983, 161–185. Like Galai, Bhattacharya found that a trader facing transaction costs could not exploit apparent arbitrage opportunities. However, both studies found that a very-low-cost trader, such as a market maker, could have a chance for some arbitrage returns.
4. As we discuss in Chapter 5, differences between European and American call options require some slight revisions of these rules. In this section, we have said that the difference in the price of two calls cannot exceed the difference in exercise prices. Our arbitrage arguments for this principle assumed immediate exercise before expiration, thus implicitly assuming that the option is American. For a similar pair of European options, the price differential cannot exceed the present value of the difference between the two exercise prices. The arbitrage profit equals the excess difference between the exercise prices. With European options, this excess differential is not available until expiration, when traders can exercise. Therefore, for European options, the arbitrage profit will be the excess difference in the exercise prices discounted to the present.
5. Assuming that the option is correctly priced at the lower bound implicitly assumes that the stock price has no risk. In other words, we implicitly assume that the stock price will not change before expiration. Making this assumption does not affect the validity of our example, because we are focusing on the single effect of a change in interest rates.
6. The next chapter explains why we need to buy one share of stock and sell two calls in this example. In brief, by combining a bond, a stock, and the right number of calls, we can form a riskless portfolio.
7. The put–call parity relationship was first addressed by Hans Stoll, "The Relationship Between Put and Call Option Prices," *Journal of Finance*, 24, May 1969, 801–824. Robert C. Merton extended the concept in his

paper, "The Relationship Between Put and Call Option Prices: Comment," *Journal of Finance*, 28, 183–184. Robert C. Klemkosky and Bruce G. Resnick tested the put–call parity relationship empirically with market data. Their two papers are: "An Ex-Ante Analysis of Put–Call Parity," *Journal of Financial Economics*, 8, 1980, 363–372 and "Put–Call Parity and Market Efficiency," *Journal of Finance*, 34, 1979, 1141–1155. While they find that market prices do not agree perfectly with the put–call parity relationship, the differences are not sufficiently large to generate trading profits after considering all transaction costs.

8. If the stock earned a riskless rate above the risk-free rate, we would borrow at the risk-free rate and invest in the stock. Later, we could sell the stock, repay our debt, and have a certain return from the difference in the two riskless rates. If the stock earned a riskless rate below the risk-free rate, we would sell the stock and invest the proceeds in the higher rate of the risk-free bond. Therefore, for a given horizon, there is only one risk-free rate.

4

European Options Pricing

INTRODUCTION

In Chapter 3 we showed how to compute call and put prices assuming that stock prices behave in a highly simplified manner. Specifically, we assumed that stock prices could rise by a certain percentage or fall by a certain percentage for a single period. After that single period, we assumed that the option expired. Under these unrealistic and highly restrictive assumptions, we found that calls and puts must each have a unique price; any other price leads to arbitrage. In this chapter, we develop similar options pricing models, but we use more realistic models of stock price movement.

To develop a more realistic options pricing model, this chapter first analyzes options pricing under the simple percentage change model of stock price movements. Now, however, we show how to find the unique prices that the no-arbitrage conditions imply. This framework is the **Single-Period Binomial Model**. Analyzing the single-period model leads to more realistic models of stock price movements. One of these more realistic models is the **Multi-Period Binomial Model**. By considering several successive models of stock price changes, we eventually come to one of the most elegant models in all of finance—the **Black–Scholes Options Pricing Model**.

Throughout this chapter, we focus on European options. Later, in Chapter 6, we consider American options pricing and the complications arising from the potential for early exercise. At the beginning of this chapter, we focus on stocks with no dividends. Later in this chapter, we consider the complications that dividends bring in evaluating the prices of European options.

THE SINGLE-PERIOD BINOMIAL MODEL

In Chapter 3, we considered a stock priced at $100 and assumed that its price would be $90 or $110 in one year. In this example, the risk-free interest rate was 6 percent. We then considered a call and put on this stock, with both options having an exercise price of $100 and expiring in one year. The call was worth $7.55, and the put was worth $1.89. As we showed in Chapter 3, any other option price creates arbitrage opportunities.

Now we want to create a synthetic European call option—a portfolio that has the same value and profits and losses as the call being synthesized. Consider a portfolio comprised of one-half share of stock plus a short position in a risk-free bond that matures in one year and has an initial purchase price of $42.45. In one year, the portfolio's value depends on whether the stock price is $110 or $90. Depending on the stock price, the half-share will be worth $55 or $45. In either event, we will owe $45 to repay our bond. If the stock price rises, the portfolio will be worth $10. If the stock price falls, the portfolio will be worth zero. These are exactly the payoffs for the call option. Therefore, the value of the portfolio must be the same as the value of the call option. Figure 4.1

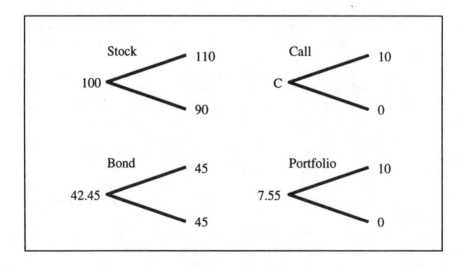

FIGURE 4.1 One-Period Payoffs

shows values for the stock, the call, the risk-free bond, and the portfolio value at the outset and one year later. The stock price moves to $110 or $90, and the call moves accordingly to $10 or zero. The risk-free bond increases at a 6 percent rate no matter what the stock does, so borrowing $42.45 generates a debt of $45 due in one year. Likewise, our portfolio of one-half share and a $42.45 borrowing will be worth $10 or zero in one year, depending on the stock price. The diagrams appearing in Figure 4.1 are known as binomial "trees" or "lattices."

Because our portfolio and the call option have exactly the same payoffs in all circumstances, they must have the same initial value. Otherwise, there would be an arbitrage opportunity. This means that an investment of one-half share of stock, S_t, and a bond, B_t, of $42.45 must equal the value of the call.

$$c_t = 0.5S_t - \$42.45 = \$50 - 42.45 = \$7.55$$

Therefore, the call must be worth $7.55. This is the same conclusion we reached in Chapter 3. This result shows that a combined position in the stock and the risk-free bond can replicate a call option for a one-period horizon.

We now show how to find the replicating portfolio made of the stock and the risk-free investment. At the outset, $T - t = 1$, the value of the portfolio, $PORT_t$, depends on the stock price, the number of shares, N, and the price of the bond, B_t.

$$PORT = NS_t - B_t$$

At the end of the horizon, $T - t = 0$, the debt equals the amount borrowed, B_t, plus interest, $B_T = RB_t$. The portfolio's value also depends on the stock price. If the stock price rises, the value of the portfolio will be:

$$PORT_{U,T} = NUS_T - RB_t$$

where:

$$PORT_{U,T} = \text{value of the replicating portfolio at time } T$$
$$\text{if the stock price goes up}$$
$$U = 1 + \text{percentage of stock price increase}$$
$$R = 1 + r$$

Likewise, if the stock price falls, the value of the portfolio will be:

$$PORT_{D,T} = NDS_T - RB_t$$

where:

$$PORT_{D,T} = \text{value of the replicating portfolio at time } T$$
$$\text{if the stock price goes down}$$
$$D = 1 - \text{percentage of stock price decrease}$$

At expiration, $T - t = 0$, the value of the call also depends on whether the stock price rises or falls. For each circumstance, we represent the call's price as c_U and c_D.

As our example showed, we can choose the number of shares to trade, N, and the amount of funds to borrow, B_t, to replicate the call. Replicating the call means that the portfolio will have the same payoff. Therefore, if the stock price rises:

$$PORT_{U,T} = NUS_T - RB_t = c_U$$

If the stock price falls:

$$PORT_{D,T} = NDS_T - RB_t = c_D$$

After these algebraic manipulations, we have two equations with two unknowns, N and B_t. Solving for the values of the unknowns that satisfy the equations, N^* and B_t^*, we find:

$$N^* = \frac{c_U - c_D}{(U - D) S_t}$$
$$B_t^* = \frac{c_U D - c_D U}{(U - D) R}$$

Therefore,

$$c_t = N^*S_t - B_t^* \qquad\qquad 4.1$$

This is the **Single-Period Binomial Call Pricing Model**. It holds for a call option expiring in one period when the stock price will rise by a known percentage or fall by a known percentage. The model shows that the value of a call option equals a long position in the stock, plus some borrowing at the risk-free rate. Applying our new notation to our example, we have:

$$c_U = \$10$$
$$c_D = \$0$$
$$U = 1.1$$
$$D = .9$$
$$R = 1.06$$
$$B_t^* = \frac{c_U D - c_D U}{(U - D) R}$$
$$= \frac{10(0.9) - 0(1.1)}{(1.1 - 0.9)(1.06)} = \$42.45$$
$$N^* = \frac{c_U - c_D}{(U - D) S_t} = \frac{10 - 0}{(1.1 - 0.9) 100} = 0.5$$

The Role of Probabilities

In discussing the single-period binomial model, we have not used the concept of probability. For example, we have not considered the likelihood that the stock price will rise or fall. While we have not explicitly used probabilistic concepts, the array of prices does imply a certain probability that the stock price will rise, if we are willing to assume that investors are risk neutral.[1] We assume a risk-neutral economy in this section to show the role of probabilities. The option prices that we compute under the assumption of risk neutrality are the same as those we found from strict no-arbitrage conditions without any reference to probabilities.

Assuming risk neutrality and given the risk-free interest rate and the up and down percentage movements, we can compute the probability of a stock price increase. Using our definitions of N^* and B_t^*, the call is worth:

$$c_t = \left(\frac{c_U - c_D}{(U - D) S_t}\right) S_t - \frac{c_U D - c_D U}{(U - D) R}$$

Simplifying, we have:

$$c_t = \frac{c_U - c_D}{U - D} - \frac{c_U D - c_D U}{(U - D) R}$$

Isolating the c_U and c_D terms gives:

$$c_t = \frac{\left(\dfrac{R-D}{U-D}\right)c_U + \left(\dfrac{U-R}{U-D}\right)c_D}{R}$$

In this equation, the call value equals the present value of the future payoffs from owning the call. If the stock price goes up, the call pays C_U at expiration. If the stock goes down, the call pays C_D. The numerator of this equation gives the expected value of the call's payoffs at expiration. Therefore, the probability of a stock price increase is also the probability that the call is worth c_U. The probability of a stock price increase is $(R-D)/(U-D)$, and the probability of a stock price decrease is $(U-R)/(U-D)$.

For our continuing example, we have the following values: $c_U = \$10$, $c_D = \$0$, $U = 1.1$, $D = 0.9$, $R = 1.06$. Therefore, the probability of an increase in the stock price (π_U) is 0.8 and the probability of a decrease (π_D) is 0.2. The value of the call in our single-period model is:

$$c_t = \frac{\pi_U c_U + \pi_D c_D}{R} = \frac{0.8 \times 10 + 0.2 \times 0}{1.06} = \$7.55$$

This result shows that the value of a call equals the expected payoff from the call at expiration, discounted to the present at the risk-free rate, assuming a risk-neutral economy.

Summary

Our single-period model is a useful tool. We have seen how to replicate an option by combining a long position in stock with a short position in the risk-free asset. Also, we used the single-period model to show that the value of a call equals the present value of the call's expected payoffs at expiration. Nonetheless, our single-period model suffers from two defects. First, it holds only for a single period. We need to be able to value options that expire after many periods. Second, our assumption about stock price changes is still unrealistic. Obviously we do not really know how stock prices can change in one period. In fact, if we define one year as a period, we know that stock prices can take almost an infinite number of values by the end of the period. We now proceed to refine our model to consider these objections.

THE MULTI-PERIOD BINOMIAL MODEL

The principles that we developed for the single-period binomial model also apply to a multi-period framework.[2] Here we illustrate the underlying principles by considering a two-period horizon. Over two periods, the stock price must follow one of four patterns. For the two periods, the stock can go: up–up, up–down, down–up, or down–down. Assuming fixed down and up percentages, the up–down and down–up sequences result in the same terminal stock price. For each terminal stock price, a call option has a specific value. Figure 4.2 shows the binomial trees for the stock and call. To clarify the notation, S_{UU} indicates the terminal stock price if the stock price goes up in both periods. C_{UU} is the resulting call price at expiration when the stock price rises in both periods. For the two-period case, the notation π_{UU} indicates the probability of an up–up sequence of price movements, and π_{DD} indicates the probability of a down–down sequence of price movements. We define other patterns accordingly.

We can express the value of a call option two periods before expiration as:

$$c_t = \frac{\pi_{UU}c_{UU} + \pi_{UD}c_{UD} + \pi_{DU}c_{DU} + \pi_{DD}c_{DD}}{R^2}$$

In this equation, the call value equals the expected value of the payoffs at expiration discounted at the risk-free rate.

We continue to use our example of a $100 stock that can rise or fall by 10 percent. The probability that the stock price will increase is 0.8, so this gives a 0.2 probability of a price drop. Also, the probability of an

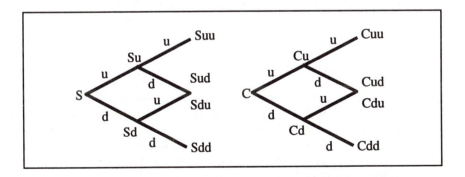

FIGURE 4.2 Two-Period Payoffs

increase in one period is independent of the probability of an increase in any other period. We now assume that the call is two periods from expiration and that the stock trades for $100. In the first period, the stock can go up or down, giving $US_t = \$110$, $DS_t = \$90$. After the second period, there are four possible patterns with three actually different stock prices: $UUS_t = \$121$, $DDS_t = \$81$, and $UDS_t = DUS_t = \$99$. The probabilities of these different terminal stock prices are: $\pi_{UU} = (0.8)(0.8) = 0.64$, $\pi_{UD} = (0.8)(0.2) = 0.16$, $\pi_{DU} = (0.2)(0.8) = 0.16$, and $\pi_{DD} = (0.2)(0.2) = 0.04$. The call price at expiration equals the terminal stock price minus the exercise price of $100, or zero, whichever is larger. Therefore, we have $C_{UU} = \$21$, $C_{DD} = 0$, $C_{DU} = C_{UD} = 0$.

To determine the call price two periods before expiration, we apply our formula for a call option two periods before expiration. In doing so, we compute the expected value of the call at expiration and discount for two periods:

$$c = \frac{0.64\,(\$21) + 0.16\,(0) + 0.16\,(0) + 0.04\,(0)}{1.06^2} = \frac{\$13.44}{1.06^2} = \$11.96$$

If the call expires in two periods and the stock trades for $100, the call will be worth $11.96. Notice that our sample call pays off at expiration only if the stock price rises twice. Any other pattern of stock price movement in our example gives a call that is worthless at expiration. With one period until expiration and the stock trading at $100, we saw that the call was worth $7.55. With the same initial stock price and two periods until expiration, the call is worth $11.96. This price difference reflects the difference in the present value of the expected payoffs from the call.

In the single-period binomial model, there are two possible stock price outcomes. With two periods until expiration, there are four possible stock price patterns. In general, there are 2^n possible stock price patterns, where n is the number of periods until expiration. Thus, the number of stock and call outcomes increases very rapidly. For example, if the option is just 20 periods from expiration, there are more than 1 million stock price outcomes and the same number of call outcomes to consider.[3] It quickly becomes apparent that we need a more general formula for the multi-period binomial pricing model. Also, for options with many periods until expiration, we need a computer.

We have explored the single-period and two-period binomial model in detail, and we have analyzed examples for each. The principles we have developed remain true no matter how many periods we consider. However, the computations become more numerous and cumbersome, as we just saw. Therefore, we now make a mathematical jump to present the formula, which we discuss in intuitive terms.

The Multi-Period Binomial Call Pricing Model

In this section, we begin by introducing the Multi-Period Binomial Call Pricing Model. As Equation 4.2 shows, it is undeniably complex. However, a little study will show that the equation is not really so intimidating.

$$c_t = \frac{\sum_{j=0}^{n} \left(\frac{n!}{j! \, (n-j)!} \right) [\pi_U^j \, \pi_D^{n-j}] \, \text{MAX} \, [0, \, U^j D^{n-j} S_t - X]}{R^n} \qquad 4.2$$

To understand this formula, we need to break it into simpler elements. From our previous discussion, we know that the formula gives the present value of the expected payoffs from the call at expiration. The denominator R^n is the discount factor raised to n, the number of periods until expiration. The numerator gives the expected payoff on the call option. Thus, we need to focus on the numerator.

With the multi-period model, we are analyzing an option that expires in n periods. As a feature of the binomial model, we know that the stock price either goes up or down each period. Let us say that it goes up j of the n periods. Then the stock price must fall $n - j$ periods. Our summation runs from $j = 0$ to $j = n$, which includes every possibility. When $j = 0$, we evaluate the possibility that the stock price never rises. When $j = n$, we evaluate the possibility that the stock price rises every period. The summation considers these extreme possibilities and every intermediate possibility.

For any random number of stock price increases, j, the numerator expresses three things about the call for the j stock price increases among the n periods. First, starting from the right, the numerator gives the payoff on the option if the stock price rises j times. This is our familiar expression beginning with MAX. The value of the call at expiration is either zero, or the stock price minus the exercise price, whichever is greater. The expression $U^j D^{n-j} S_t$ gives the stock price at expiration if the stock price rises j periods and falls the other $n - j$ periods. Second, the numerator expresses the probability of exactly j stock price increases and $n - j$ stock price decreases. Earlier, we saw how to find the probability of up and down movements. Therefore, $\pi_U^j \pi_D^{n-j}$ gives the probability of observing j up movements and $n - j$ down movements. Third, more than one sequence of stock price movements can result in the same terminal stock price. For instance, in the two-period model we saw that UDS_t gave the same terminal stock price as DUS_t. The numerator also computes the number of different combinations of stock price movements that result in the same terminal stock price. The expression:

$$\frac{n!}{j!\,(n-j)!}$$

computes the number of possible combinations of j rises from n periods. In essence, the combination weights the possibility of exactly n rises and $n-j$ falls by the number of different patterns that result in exactly j rises and $n-j$ falls. For example, only one pattern results in n rises—the stock must rise in every period. By contrast, if $j = n - j$, there will usually be many patterns that can give j rises and $n-j$ falls.

In the expression for the combination, $n!$ is called n-factorial. Its value equals n multiplied by $n-1$ times $n-2$ and so on down to 1:

$$n! = n(n-1)(n-2)(n-3)\dots \quad (1)$$

To illustrate, if $n = 5$, then $5! = 5(4)(3)(2)(1) = 120$. For example, with the two-period model we could have the pattern up–down or down–up resulting in the same stock price. Thus, there are two combinations of one increase over two periods. The increase could be first or second. For any j value, the numerator in Equation 4.2 computes the number of combinations of j increases from n periods, times the probability of having exactly j increases times the payoff on the call if there are j increases. The summation ensures that the numerator reflects all possible j values.

In our two-period example, the option pays off at expiration only if the stock price rises both times. In general, many stock price patterns leave the option out-of-the-money at expiration. For valuing the option, stock price patterns that leave the option out-of-the-money are a dead end, because they result in a zero option price. As a consequence, we do not need to fully evaluate stock price patterns that leave the option out-of-the-money at expiration. Instead, we only need to evaluate those values of j for which the option expires in-the-money. In our two-period example, we do not need to compute the entire formula for $j = 0$ and $j = 1$. If the stock price never goes up or goes up only once, the option expires out-of-the-money. For our two-period example, we need only consider what happens to the option when the stock price rises twice, that is, when $j = 2$. Only then does the option finish in-the-money. Let us define m as the number of times the stock price must rise for the option to finish in-the-money. Thus, when the stock price rises exactly m times, it must fall $n - m$ times. However, this pattern still leaves the option in-the-money, because the stock price rose the needed m times. Then we need only consider values of $j = m$ to $j = n$. In our two-period example, $m = 2$ because the stock price must rise in both periods for the option to finish in-the-money. Therefore, the following formula gives an alternative expression for the value of an option:

$$c_t = \frac{\sum_{j=m}^{n} \left(\frac{n!}{j!\,(n-j)!}\right) (\pi_U^j\, \pi_D^{n-j})\, [U^j D^{n-j}\, S_t - X]}{R^n} \qquad 4.3$$

Notice that the summation begins with m, the minimum number of stock price increases needed to bring the option into-the-money. Because we consider only the events that put the option in-the-money, we no longer need to worry about the call being worth the maximum of zero or the stock price less the exercise price at expiration. With at least m stock price rises, the option will be worth more than zero because it necessarily finishes in-the-money. Now we divide the formula into two parts—one associated with the stock price and the other associated with the exercise price.

$$c_t = S_t \left[\sum_{j=m}^{n} \left(\frac{n!}{j!\,(n-j)!}\right) (\pi_U^j\, \pi_D^{n-j}) \frac{U^j D^{n-j}}{R^n} \right]$$
$$- XR^{-n} \left[\sum_{j=m}^{n} \left(\frac{n!}{j!\,(n-j)!}\right) \pi_U^j\, \pi_D^{n-j} \right] \qquad 4.4$$

This version of the binomial formula starts to resemble our familiar expression for the value of the call as the stock price minus the present value of the exercise price. If the option is in-the-money and the stock price is certain to remain unchanged until expiration, the call price equals the stock price minus the present value of the exercise price. Our formula has exactly that structure except for the two complicated expressions in brackets. These two expressions reflect the riskiness of the stock. This uncertainty or riskiness about the stock gives the added value to the call above the stock price minus the present value of the exercise price.

The multi-period binomial model can reflect numerous stock price outcomes, if there are numerous periods. Just 20 periods gives more than 1 million stock price movement patterns. In our examples, we kept the period length the same and added more periods. This lengthened the total time until expiration. As an alternative, we could keep the same time to expiration and consider more periods of shorter duration. For example, we originally treated a year as a single period. For that year, we could regard each trading day as a period, giving about 250 periods per year. We could evaluate an option with the multi-period model by assuming that the stock price could change once a day.

The binomial model requires that the price move up a given percentage or down a given percentage. Therefore, if we shorten the period, we need to adjust the stock price movements to correspond to the shorter period. While up or down 10 percent might be reasonable for a period of one year, it certainly would not be reasonable for a period of one day. Similarly, a risk-free rate of 6 percent makes sense for a period of one year, but not for a period of one day.

By adjusting the period length, the stock price movement, and the interest rate, we can refine the binomial model as much as we wish. For example, we could assume that the stock price could move one-hundredth of a percent every minute of the year if we wished. Under this assumption, the model would have finer partitions than exist in the market for most stock. However, with the price changing every minute and a time to expiration of one year, we would have trillions of possible stock price outcomes to consider. While having so many periods would be computationally expensive, we could apply the model if we wished. Conceptually, we could make each period so short that the stock price would change continuously. However, if the stock price truly changed continuously, there would be an infinite number of periods to consider. While we cannot compute binomial model values for an infinite number of periods, mathematical techniques do exist to compute options prices when stock prices change continuously.

BINOMIAL PUT OPTIONS PRICING

In discussing binomial options pricing, we have used call options as an example. However, the model also applies to put options. To value put options, we follow the same reasoning process that we have considered in detail for call options. Rather than detail all of the reasoning leading to the formula, we begin with the formula for the price of a European put option.

$$p_t = \frac{\sum_{j=0}^{n} \left(\frac{n!}{j!\,(n-j)!}\right) (\pi_U^j\, \pi_D^{n-j})\ \mathrm{MAX}\ [0,\, X - U^j D^{n-j}\, S_t]}{R^n} \qquad 4.5$$

This formula matches our binomial call formula, except we substitute the expression for the value of a put at expiration, $X - U^j D^{n-j} S_t$, in place of the value of a call at expiration.

In pricing the call option, we only considered stock price patterns that left the call in-the-money at expiration. The same is true for the put. The put finishes in-the-money if the stock price does not increase often enough to make the stock price exceed the exercise price. We defined m as the number of price increases needed to bring the call into-the-money. If the price increases $m - 1$ or fewer times, the put finishes in-the-money. Therefore, we can also write the formula for the put as follows:

$$p_t = \frac{\sum_{j=0}^{m-1} \left(\frac{n!}{j!\,(n-j)!}\right) (\pi_U^j \, \pi_D^{n-j})[X - U^j D^{n-j} S_t]}{R^n} \qquad 4.6$$

Rearranging terms gives:

$$P_t = XR^{-n} \left(\sum_{j=0}^{m-1} \left(\frac{n!}{j!\,(n-j)!}\right) (\pi_U^j \, \pi_D^{n-j}) \right)$$

$$- S_t \left(\sum_{j=0}^{m-1} \left(\frac{n!}{j!\,(n-j)!}\right) (\pi_U^j \, \pi_D^{n-j})\frac{U^j D^{n-j}}{R^n} \right) \qquad 4.7$$

This formula for the put parallels our familiar expression for the put as equaling the present value of the exercise price minus the stock price. As with the call, the two bracketed expressions account for the risky movement of the stock price.

We can also value the put through put–call parity. We have the value of the call under the binomial model as given above. Put–call parity tells us that:

$$p_t = c_t - S_t + Xe^{-r(T-t)}$$

Both approaches must necessarily give the same answer.

STOCK PRICE MOVEMENTS

In actual markets, stock prices change to reflect new information. During a single day, a stock price may change many times. From the ticker, we can observe stock prices when transactions occur. When trading ceases overnight, however, we cannot observe the stock price for hours at a time. Where the price wanders during the night, no one can know. Our observations are also limited, because stock prices are quoted in eighths of a dollar. The true stock price need not jump from one eighth to the next, but the observed stock price does. Sometimes the observed price remains the same from one transaction to another. But just because we observe the same price twice in succession does not mean it remained at that price between the two observations. From these reflections, we see that we can never know exactly how stock prices change because we cannot observe the true stock price at every instant. Therefore, any model of stock price behavior deviates from an exact description of how stock prices move. Nonetheless, it is possible to develop a realistic model of stock price movements. In this section, we review a particular model that has been very successful in a wide range of finance applications.

Let us consider the random information that affects the price of a stock. We assume that the information arrives continuously and that each bit of information is small in importance. Under this scenario, we consider a stock price that rises or falls a small proportion in response to each bit of information. We know that finance depends conceptually on the twin ideas of expected return and risk. Thus, we might also think of a stock as having a positive expected rate of return. In the absence of special events, we expect the stock price to grow along the path of its expected rate of return. However, the world is risky. Information about the stock is sometimes favorable and sometimes unfavorable. As this random information becomes known, it pushes the stock away from its expected growth path. When the information is better than expected, the stock price jumps above its growth path. Negative information has the opposite effect; it pushes the stock price below its expected growth path. Thus, we might imagine the stock price growing along its expected growth path just as a drunk walks across a field. We expect the drunk to reach the other side of the field, but we also think he will wander and stumble in unpredictable short-term deviations from the straight path. Similarly, we expect a stock price to rise, because it has a positive expected return, but we also expect it to wander above and below its growth path, due to new information.

Finance uses a standard mathematical model that is consistent with the story of the preceding paragraph. It assumes that the stock grows at an expected rate μ with a standard deviation σ over some period of time Δt:

$$\Delta S = S_{t+1} - S_t = S_t \mu \Delta t + S_t N(0,1)\sigma \sqrt{\Delta t} \qquad 4.8$$

where:

S_t = the stock price at the beginning of the interval
ΔS = the stock price change during time Δt
$S_t \mu \Delta t$ = expected value of the stock price change during time Δt
$N(0,1)$ = normally distributed random variable with $\mu = 0$, $\sigma = 1$
σ = standard deviation of the stock price

Equation 4.8 says that the stock price change during Δt depends on two factors: the expected growth rate in the price and the variability of the growth. First, the expected growth in the stock price over a given interval depends on the mean growth rate, μ, and the amount of time, Δt. Therefore, if the stock price starts at S_t, the expected stock price increase after an interval of Δt equals $S_t \mu \Delta t$. However, this is only the expected stock price increase after the interval. Due to risk, the actual price change can be greater or lower. Deviations from the expected stock price depend on chance and on the volatility of the stock. The equation captures risk by using the normal distribution. For convenience, the model uses the standard normal distribution, which has a zero mean and a standard deviation of 1. The standard deviation represents the variability of a particular stock. We multiply the standard deviation of the stock by a random drawing from the normal distribution to capture the riskiness of the stock. Also, the equation says that the variability increases with the square root of the interval Δt. In other words, the further into the future we project the stock price with our model, the less certain we can be about what the stock price will be.

Dividing both sides of Equation 4.8 by the original stock price, S_t, gives the percentage change in the stock price during Δt:

$$\frac{\Delta S}{S_t} = \mu \, \Delta t + N(0,1) \, \sigma \, \sqrt{\Delta t}$$

From this equation, it is possible to show that the percentage change in the stock price is normally distributed:

$$\frac{\Delta S}{S_t} \sim N[\mu \Delta t, \sigma \sqrt{\Delta t}] \qquad\qquad 4.9$$

Figure 4.3 shows two stock price paths over the course of a year, with both stock prices starting at \$100. The straight line graphs a stock that grows at 10 percent per year with no risk. The jagged line shows a stock price path with an expected growth rate of 10 percent and a standard deviation of 0.2 per year. We generated the second price path by taking

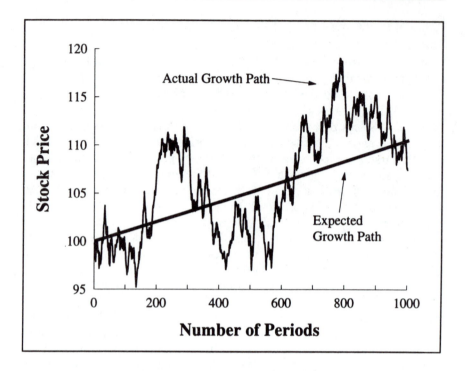

FIGURE 4.3 Two Stock Price Paths

repeated random samples from a normal distribution to create price changes according to Equation 4.8. As the jagged line in Figure 4.3 shows, a stock might easily wander away from its growth path due to the riskiness represented by its standard deviation.

To construct Figure 4.3, we used 1000 periods per year and a growth rate of 10 percent. To construct the straight line, we assumed that the stock price increased by 0.1/1000 each period. However, this gives an ending stock price of $110.51, not the $110 we expect if the stock price grows at 10 percent per year. This difference results from using 1000 compounding intervals during the year.

However, we hypothesize that information arrives continuously, so that the stock price could always change. To avoid worrying about the compounding interval, we now employ continuous compounding. Therefore, we focus on logarithmic stock returns. For example, consider a beginning stock price of $100 and an ending price of $110 a year later. The logarithmic stock return over the year is $\ln(S_t/S_0) = \ln(\$110/\$100) = \ln(1.1) = .0953$. The logarithmic stock return is just the continuous growth rate that takes the stock price from its original value to its ending value. Thus, $\$100e^{\mu t} = \$100e^{.0953(1)} = \$110$. We now need a continuous growth model of stock prices that is consistent with our model for the percentage change stock price model of Equation 4.9. With some difficult math, it is possible to prove the following result:

$$\ln\left(\frac{S_t + \Delta t}{S_t}\right) \sim N[(\mu - 0.5 \, \sigma^2)(\Delta t), \, \sigma\sqrt{\Delta t}] \qquad 4.10$$

This expression asserts that logarithmic stock returns are distributed normally with the given mean and standard deviation. For a later time, $t + \Delta t$, the expected stock price and the variance of the stock price are:

$$E\,(S_{t + \Delta t}) = S_t e^{\mu \Delta t}$$
$$VAR\,(S_{t + \Delta t}) = S_t^2 e^{2\mu \Delta t}\,(e^{\sigma^2 \Delta t} - 1)$$

Thus, the expected stock price at $t + \Delta t$ depends on the original stock price, S_t, the expected growth rate, μ, and the amount of time that elapses, Δt. Similarly, the variance of the stock price depends on the original stock price, the expected growth rate, and the elapsed time as well. The longer the time horizon, the larger will be the variance. The increasing variance reflects our greater uncertainty about stock prices far in the future.

As an example, consider a stock with an initial price of $100 and an expected growth rate of 10 percent. If the stock has a standard deviation of 0.2 per year, we can compute the expected stock price and variance for six months into the future. For this example, we have the following values:

$$S_t = \$100$$
$$\mu = .1$$
$$\sigma = .2$$
$$\Delta t = .5$$
$$E\,(S_{t + \Delta t}) = \$100 \; e^{0.1(0.5)} = \$105.13$$
$$VAR(S_{t + \Delta t}) = (\$100)(\$100)(e^{2(0.1)(0.5)})(e^{(0.2)(0.2)(0.5)} - 1) = \$223.26$$

The standard deviation of the price over period Δt is $14.94. Figure 4.4 shows stock price realizations that are consistent with this example. We found these prices by drawing random values from a normal distribution and using our example growth rate and standard deviation. Each dot in the figure represents a possible stock price realization. Notice that the price tends to drift higher over time, consistent with a rising expected

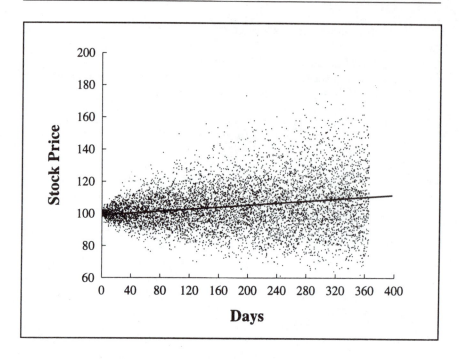

FIGURE 4.4   Possible Stock Prices

value. This is shown by the regression line that is fitted through the points. However, there is considerable uncertainty about what the price will be at any future date. The further we go into the future, the greater that uncertainty becomes.

Research on actual stock price behavior shows that logarithmic stock returns are approximately normally distributed. So we say that, as an approximation, stock returns follow a **log-normal distribution**. Stock returns themselves are not normally distributed. As an example, Figure 4.5 shows a distribution of stock returns with a mean of 1.2 and a standard deviation of 0.6. It is easy to see that this distribution is not normal because it is skewed to the right. There is a greater chance of larger returns than one would expect with a normal distribution. Figure 4.6 shows the log-normal distribution that corresponds to the values in Figure 4.5. The values graphed in Figure 4.6 are the logarithms of the values used to construct Figure 4.5. The graph in Figure 4.6 shows a normal distribution. We will assume that stock returns are distributed as Figure 4.6 shows, except the mean and standard deviation differ from stock to stock.

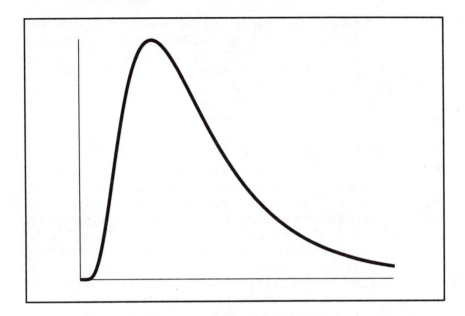

FIGURE 4.5 A Log-Normal Distribution

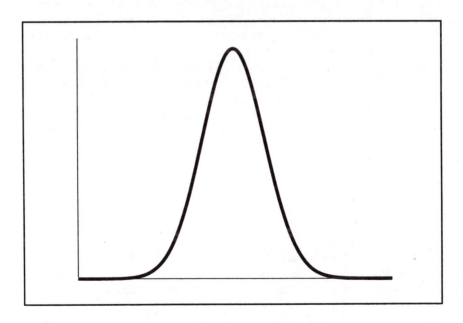

FIGURE 4.6 The Normal Distribution

While the log-normal distribution only approximates stock returns, it has two great virtues. First, it is mathematically tractable, so we can obtain solutions for the value of call options if stock returns are log-normally distributed. Second, the resulting call option prices that we compute are very good approximations of actual market prices. In the remainder of this chapter, we treat stock returns as log-normally distributed with a specified mean and variance.

THE BINOMIAL APPROACH TO THE BLACK–SCHOLES MODEL

We have seen how to generalize the binomial model to any number of periods. Increasing the number of periods allows for many possible stock price outcomes at expiration, thereby increasing the realism of the results. However, three problems remain. First, as the number of periods increases, computational difficulties begin to arise. Second, increasing the number of periods while holding the time until expiration constant means that the period length becomes shorter. We must adjust the up and down movement factors, U and D, and the risk-free rate to fit the time horizon. Obviously, we cannot use factors with a scale appropriate to a year when the period length is, say, one day. Third, we have worked with more or less arbitrarily selected up and down factors. The price that the model gives can only be as good as its inputs. The example inputs we have been considering serve well as illustrations, but they are not appropriate for analyzing real options. Therefore, we need a better way to determine the up and down factors.

Modeling stock returns by a log-normal process solves these three problems simultaneously. If stock returns are log-normally distributed with the mean return given by μ and a standard deviation of σ for some unit of calendar time Δt, then we define the following binomial inputs as:

$$
\begin{aligned}
U &= e^{\sigma \sqrt{\Delta t}} \\
D &= \frac{1}{U} \\
\pi_u &= \frac{e^{\mu \Delta t} - D}{U - D}
\end{aligned}
\qquad 4.11
$$

As the entire analysis takes place within a risk-neutral framework μ, the expected return on the stock must equal the risk-free rate. Therefore, the probability of an upward stock price movement becomes:

$$
\pi_u = \frac{e^{r \Delta t} - D}{U - D}
\qquad 4.12
$$

Notice that the values of R, U, and D adjust automatically as the tree is adjusted to include more and more periods during the fixed calendar interval $T - t$. The absolute value of each becomes smaller, exactly as we would expect for a shorter time period. The values for U and D depend on the riskiness of the stock returns. The probability of a stock price increase depends upon the mean return on the stock. Thus, if we can estimate the standard deviation of stock returns, we have reasonable inputs to the binomial model. These can replace the arbitrary example values that we have been using.[4]

To illustrate how the binomial model gives increasingly refined estimates as the number of periods increases, consider a European call option that has one year until expiration and an exercise price of $100. Assume that the underlying stock trades for $100, with a standard deviation of 0.10. The risk-free rate of interest is 6 percent. Figure 4.7 shows how the binomial prices converge to the true option price of $7.46 as the number

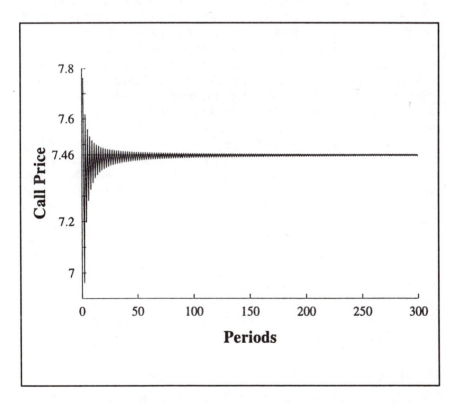

FIGURE 4.7 Convergence of Binomial Prices as the Number of Periods Increases

of periods increases. The binomial prices oscillate around the true price: For a single-period binomial model, the price is $7.76. With two periods, the binomial model gives a price of $6.96. With 20 periods, the binomial price is $7.40, and with 100 periods, the binomial price is $7.45. In general, the greater the number of periods in the lattice, the more accurate is the computed binomial price.

As we show in the next section, using the model of stock returns discussed in this section allows us to compute the value of an option with an infinite number of periods until expiration. With the strict binomial model, we could never employ an infinite number of periods because it would take forever to add all the individual results.

THE BLACK–SCHOLES OPTIONS PRICING MODEL

To this point, we have developed the binomial options pricing model. We have discussed the log-normal distribution of stock returns and have presented up and down factors for the binomial model that are consistent with the log-normal distribution of stock returns. Also, we have seen how to adjust the precision of the binomial model by dividing a given unit of calendar time into more and more periods. As we deal with more periods, however, the calculations in the binomial model become cumbersome. As the number of periods in the binomial model becomes very large, the binomial model converges to the famous Black–Scholes Options Pricing Model.

Fischer Black and Myron Scholes developed their options pricing model under the assumptions that asset prices adjust to prevent arbitrage, that stock prices change continuously, and that stock returns follow a log-normal distribution.[5] Also, their model holds for European call options on stocks with no dividends. Further, they assume that the interest rate and the volatility of the stock remain constant over the life of the option. The mathematics they used to derive their result include stochastic calculus, which is beyond the scope of this text. In this section, we present their model and illustrate the basic intuition that underlies it. We show that the form of the Black–Scholes model parallels the bounds on options pricing that we have already observed. In fact, the form of the Black–Scholes model is very close to the binomial model we have just been considering.

The Black–Scholes Call Option Pricing Model

The following expression gives the Black–Scholes options pricing model for a call option:

$$c_t = S_t N(d_1) - Xe^{-r(T - t)} N(d_2) \qquad 4.13$$

where:

$N(\cdot)$ = cumulative normal distribution function

$$d_1 = \frac{\ln\left(\frac{S_t}{X}\right) + (r + .5\,\sigma^2)(T - t)}{\sigma\sqrt{T - t}} \qquad 4.14$$

$$d_2 = d_1 - \sigma\sqrt{T - t}$$

This model has the general form we have long considered—the value of a call must equal or exceed the stock price minus the present value of the exercise price:

$$c_t \geq S_t - Xe^{-r(T - t)}$$

To adapt this formula to account for risk, as in the Black–Scholes model, we multiply the stock price and the exercise price by some factors to account for risk, giving the general form:

$$c_t = S_t \times \text{Risk Factor 1} - Xe^{-r\,(T - t)} \times \text{Risk Factor 2}$$

The binomial model shares this general form with the Black–Scholes model. With the binomial model, the risk adjustment factors were the large bracketed expressions of Equation 4.2. With the Black–Scholes model, the risk factors are $N(d_1)$ and $N(d_2)$. In the Black–Scholes model, these risk adjustment factors are the continuous time equivalent of the bracketed expressions in the binomial model.

Computing Black–Scholes Options Prices

In this section, we show how to compute Black–Scholes options prices. Assume that a stock trades at $100 and the risk-free interest rate is 6 percent. A call option on the stock has an exercise price of $100 and expires in one year. The standard deviation of the stock's returns is 0.10 per year. We compute the values of d_1 and d_2 as follows:

$$d_1 = \frac{\ln\left(\frac{100}{100}\right) + (.06 + .5\,(.01))1}{.1\,\sqrt{1}} = .65$$

$$d_2 = .65 - .1 \times 1 = .55$$

Next, we find the cumulative normal values associated with d_1 and d_2. These values are the probability that a normally distributed variable with a zero mean and a standard deviation of 1.0 will have a value equal to or less than the d_1 or d_2 term we are considering. Figure 4.8 shows a graph of a normally distributed variable with a zero mean and a standard deviation of 1.0. It shows the values of d_1 and d_2 for our example. For illustration, we focus on d_1, which equals 0.65. In finding $N(d_1)$, we want to know which portion of the area under the curve lies to the left of 0.65. This is the value of $N(d_1)$. Clearly, the value we seek is larger than 0.5, because d_1 is above the mean of zero. We can find the exact value by consulting a table of the cumulative normal distribution for this variable. We present this table as Appendix A. For a value of 0.65 drawn from the border of the table, we find our probability in the interior: $N(0.65) = 0.7422$. Similarly, $N(d_2) = N(0.55) = 0.7088$. We now have:

$$c_t = \$100 \times 0.7422 - \$100 \times 0.9418 \times 0.7088 = \$7.46$$

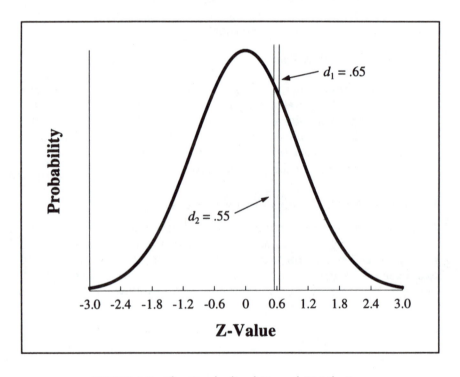

FIGURE 4.8 The Standardized Normal Distribution

We chose these values for our example because they parallel the values from our original binomial example. There we also assumed that the stock traded for $100 and that the risk-free rate was 6 percent. We assumed an up factor of 10 percent and a down factor of −10 percent. With a single-period binomial model and these values, we found that a call must be priced at $7.55. The two results are close. However, if we use more periods in the Binomial Model and use up and down factors that are consistent with a log-normal distribution of stock returns, the Binomial Model will converge to the Black–Scholes model price.

The Black–Scholes Put Option Pricing Model

Black and Scholes developed their options pricing model for calls only. However, we can find the Black–Scholes model for European puts by applying put–call parity:

$$p_t = c_t - S_t + Xe^{-r(T-t)}$$

Substituting the Black–Scholes call formula in the put–call parity equation gives:

$$p_t = S_t N(d_1) - Xe^{-r(T-t)}N(d_2) - S_t + Xe^{-r(T-t)}$$

Collecting like terms simplifies the equation to:

$$p_t = S_t[N(d_1) - 1] + Xe^{-r(T-t)}[1 - N(d_2)]$$

If we consider the cumulative distribution of all values from $-\infty$ to $+\infty$, the maximum value is 1.0. For any value of d_1 we consider, part of the whole must lie at or below the value and the remainder must lie above it. For example, if $N(d_1)$ is 0.7422, for $d_1 = 0.65$, then 0.2578 of the total area under the curve must lie at values greater than 0.65. Now we apply a principle of normal distributions. The normal distribution is symmetrical, so the same percentage of the area under the curve that lies above d_1 must lie below $-d_1$. Therefore, for any symmetrical distribution and any arbitrary value, w:

$$N(w) + (-w) = 1$$

Following this pattern and substituting for $N(d_1)$ and $N(d_2)$ gives the equivalent Black–Scholes value for a put option.

$$p_t = Xe^{-r(T-t)} N(-d_2) - S_t N(-d_1) \qquad 4.15$$

This equation has the familiar form that we have been exploring since Chapter 2. We emphasize that the Black–Scholes model for puts holds only for European puts.

INPUTS FOR THE BLACK–SCHOLES MODEL

We have seen that the Black–Scholes model for the price of an option depends on five variables: the stock price, the exercise price, the time until expiration, the risk-free rate, and the standard deviation of the stock. Of these, the stock price is observable in the financial press or on a trading terminal. The exercise price and the time until expiration can be known with certainty. We want to consider how to obtain estimates of the other two parameters: the risk-free interest rate and the standard deviation of the stock.

Estimating the Risk-Free Rate of Interest

Estimates of the risk-free interest rate are widely available and are usually quite reliable.[6] There are still a few points to consider, however. First, we need to select the correct rate. Because the Black–Scholes model uses a risk-free rate, we can use the Treasury bill rate as a good estimate. Quoted interest rates for T-bills are expressed as discount rates. We need to convert these to regular interest rates and express them as continuously compounded rates. As a second consideration, we should select the maturity of the T-bill carefully. If the yield curve has a steep slope, yields for different maturities can differ significantly. With T-bills maturing each week, we choose the bill that matures closest to the option expiration.

We illustrate the computation with the following example. Consider a T-bill with 84 days until maturity. Its bid yield is 8.83 and its asking yield is 8.77. Letting BID and ASK be the bid and asked yields, the following formula gives the price of a T-bill as a percentage of its face value:

$$P_{TB} = 1 - 0.01 \left(\frac{\text{BID} + \text{ASK}}{2} \right) \left(\frac{\text{Days until Maturity}}{360} \right)$$

$$= 1 - 0.01 \left(\frac{8.83 + 8.77}{2} \right) \left(\frac{84}{360} \right)$$

$$= 0.97947$$

In this formula, we average the bid and asked yields to estimate the unobservable true yield, which lies between the observable bid and asked yields. For our example, the price of the T-bill is 97.947 percent of its face value. To find the corresponding continuously compounded rate, we solve the following equation for r:

$$e^{r(T - t)} = \frac{1}{P_{TB}}$$
$$e^{r(0.23)} = 1/0.97947$$
$$0.23r = \ln (1.02096) = 0.0207$$
$$r = 0.0902$$

In the equation, $T - t = 0.23$ because 84 days is 23 percent of a year. Thus, the appropriate interest rate in this example is 9.02 percent. Securing good estimates of the risk-free interest rate is fairly easy. However, having an exact estimate is not critical, as options prices are not very sensitive to the interest rate.

Estimating the Stock's Standard Deviation

Estimating the standard deviation of the stock's returns is more difficult and more important than estimating the risk-free rate. The Black–Scholes model takes as its input the current, instantaneous standard deviation of the stock. In other words, the immediate volatility of the stock is the riskiness of the stock that affects the options price. The Black–Scholes model also assumes that the volatility is constant over the life of the option.[7] There are two basic ways to estimate the volatility. The first method uses historical data, while the second technique employs fresh data from the options market itself. This second method uses options prices to find the options market's estimate of the stock's standard deviation. An estimate of the stock's standard deviation that is drawn from the options market is called an **implied volatility**. We consider each method in turn.[8]

Historical Data.   To estimate volatility using historical data, we compute the price relatives, logarithmic price relatives, and the mean and standard deviation of the logarithmic price relatives. Letting PR_t indicate the price relative for day t so that $PR_t = P_t/P_{t-1}$, we give the formulas for the mean and variance of the logarithmic price relatives as follows:

$$\overline{PR} = \frac{1}{T} \sum_{t=1}^{T} \ln PR_t$$
$$VAR\ (PR) = \frac{1}{T - 1} \sum_{t=1}^{T} (\ln PR_t - \overline{PR})^2$$

As an example, we apply these formulas to data in the following table, which gives 11 days of price information for a stock. With 11 price observations, we compute ten daily returns. The first column tracks the day, while the second column records the stock's closing price for the day. The third column computes the price relative from the prices in column 2. The fourth column gives the log of the price relative in column 3. The last column contains the result of subtracting the mean of the logarithmic price relatives from each observation and squaring the result.

Day	P_t	PR_t	$\ln(PR_t)$	$[\ln PR_t - PR_\mu]^2$
0	100.00			
1	101.50	1.0150	0.0149	0.000154
2	98.00	0.9655	−0.0351	0.001410
3	96.75	0.9872	−0.0128	0.000234
4	100.50	1.0388	0.0380	0.001264
5	101.00	1.0050	0.0050	0.000006
6	103.25	1.0223	0.0220	0.000382
7	105.00	1.0169	0.0168	0.000205
8	102.75	0.9786	−0.0217	0.000582
9	103.00	1.0024	0.0024	0.000000
10	102.50	0.9951	−0.0049	0.000053
		Sums	0.0247	0.004294

Sample μ = 0.0247/10 = 0.00247
Sample σ^2 = 0.004294/9 = 0.000477
Sample σ = 0.021843

The mean, variance, and standard deviation that we have calculated are all based on our sample of daily data. We use the sample standard deviation as an input to the Black–Scholes model.

Three inputs to the Black–Scholes model depend on the unit of time. These inputs are the interest rate, the time until expiration, and the standard deviation. We can use any single measure we wish, but we need to express all three variables in the same time units. For example, we can use days as our time unit and express the time until expiration as the number of days remaining. Then we must also use a daily estimation of the standard deviation and the interest rate for a single day. Generally, one year is the most convenient common unit of time. Therefore, we need to convert our daily standard deviation into a comparable yearly estimate. We have estimated our daily standard deviation of ten days. However, these are ten trading days, not calendar days. Accordingly, we recognize that we are working in trading time, not calendar time. Deleting weekend days and holidays, each year has about 250–252 trading days. We use 250 trading days per year.

We have already seen that stock prices are distributed with a standard deviation that increases as the square root of time. Accordingly, we can adjust the time dimension of our volatility estimate by multiplying it by the square root of time. For example, we convert from our daily standard deviation estimate to an equivalent yearly value by multiplying the daily estimate times the square root of 250.[9]

$$\text{Annualized } \sigma = \text{Daily } \sigma \times \sqrt{250} \qquad\qquad 4.16$$

For our daily estimate of 0.021843, the estimated standard deviation in annual terms is 0.3454.

In our example, we have used ten days of data. In actual practice, we face a trade-off between using the most recent possible data and using more data. In statistics, we almost always get more reliable estimates by using more data. However, the Black–Scholes model takes the instantaneous standard deviation as an input. This gives great importance to using current data. If we use the last year of historical data, then we have a rich data set for estimating the old volatility. Using just ten days, as we did in our example, emphasizes current data, but it is really not very much data for getting a reliable estimate.

To emphasize the importance of using current data, consider the Crash of 1987. On Bloody Monday, October 19, 1987, the market lost about 22 percent of its value. If we used a full year of daily data to estimate a stock's historical volatility the next day, our estimate would be too low. In the light of the Crash, the instantaneous volatility had surely increased.

Implied Volatility. To overcome the limitations inherent in using historical data to estimate standard deviations, some scholars have turned to techniques of implied volatility. In this section, we show how to use market data and the Black–Scholes model to estimate a stock's volatility. There are five inputs to the Black–Scholes model, which the model relates to a sixth variable, the call price. With a total of six variables, any five imply a unique value for the sixth. The technique of implied volatility uses known values of five variables to estimate the standard deviation. The estimated standard deviation is an implied volatility because it is the value implied by the other five variables in the model.[10]

To find implied volatilities, we begin with established values for the stock price, exercise price, interest rate, time until expiration, and the call price. We use these to find the implied standard deviation. However, the standard deviation enters the Black–Scholes Model through the values for d_1 and d_2, which are used to determine the values of the cumulative normal distribution. As a result, we cannot solve for the standard deviation directly. Instead, we must search for the volatility that makes the Black–Scholes equation hold. To do this, we need a computer. Otherwise, we would have to try an estimate of the standard deviation, make all of the Black–Scholes computations by hand, and adjust the standard deviation for the next try. This would be cumbersome and time-consuming. Therefore, implied volatilities are almost always found using a computer.

For most stocks with options, several options with different expirations trade at once. Some researchers have argued that all of these options should be used to find the volatility implied by each. The resulting estimates are then given weights and averaged to find a single volatility estimate. The single estimate is known as a **weighted implied standard deviation**. In principle, this is a good idea because it uses more information. Other things being equal, estimates based on more information should dominate estimates based on less information. However, some options trade infrequently, which makes their prices less reliable for computing implied volatilities. In addition, options way out-of-the-money give somewhat spurious volatility estimates. Virtually all weighting schemes give the highest weight to options closest to-the-money. At-the-money options tend to give the least biased volatility estimates, and many options traders derive implied volatilities by focusing on at-the-money options.[11]

Standard Deviation	Corresponding Call Price	
0.1	$ 3.41	too low
0.5	11.03	too high
0.3	7.16	too high
0.2	5.24	too high
0.15	4.31	too low
0.175	4.78	too low
0.18	4.87	too low
0.185	4.97	too low
0.19	5.06	too high
0.188	5.02	too high
0.187	5.00	success

EUROPEAN OPTIONS AND DIVIDENDS

Most of the stocks that underlie stock options pay dividends. Yet the Black–Scholes model assumes that the underlying stock pays no dividends. While the Black–Scholes model might be elegant and provide a great deal of insight into options pricing, successful real-world application of the model depends upon resolving the dividend problem. In this section, we consider the impact of dividends on options values and we show how slight adjustments in the Black–Scholes model allow it to apply to options on dividend-paying stocks. We continue to focus on European options.

The Effect of Dividends on Options Prices

As we have seen, the value of a call option at expiration equals the maximum of zero or the stock price minus the exercise price, and a put option at expiration is worth the maximum of zero or the exercise price minus the stock price. In our familiar notation:

$$c_T = \text{MAX}\{0, S_T - X\}$$
$$p_T = \text{MAX}\{0, X - S_T\}$$

For both the call and the put, anything that affects the stock price at expiration will affect the price of the option. Dividends that might be paid during the life of the option can obviously affect the stock price. We may regard a dividend as a repayment of a portion of the share's value to the shareholder. As such, we would expect the stock price to fall by the amount of the dividend payment.[12] As a metaphor, we might think of the dividend on a stock as a leakage of value from the stock. As the value of the stock drops due to the leakage of dividends, the changing stock price will affect the value of options on the stock.

A drop in the stock price due to a dividend will have an adverse effect on the price of a call and a beneficial effect on the price of a put. For a call, the stock price at expiration will be lower than it would have been had there been no dividend. Thus, the dividend will reduce the quantity $S_T - X$, thus reducing the value of the call at expiration. For the put, the dividend will reduce the stock price at expiration, and it will therefore increase the quantity $X - S_T$.

We can illustrate the effect of dividends with an example of a call and put that have a common exercise price of $100. Assume the options are moments from expiration, and that the stock price is $102. Without bringing dividends into consideration, the value of the options would be:

$$c_T = \text{MAX}\{0, S_T - X\} = \text{MAX}\{0, \$102 - \$100\} = \$2$$
$$p_T = \text{MAX}\{0, X - S_T\} = \text{MAX}\{0, \$100 - \$102\} = \$0$$

Just before expiration, the stock pays a dividend of $3, causing the stock price to drop from $102 to $99. With a stock price of $99 at expiration, the call option will be worth zero, and the put will be worth $1. Failing to take into account the looming dividend payment could cause large pricing errors from a blind application of the Black–Scholes model. We now turn to adjustments in the Black–Scholes model that reflect dividends.

Adjustments for Known Dividends

For most stocks, the dividend payments likely to occur during the life of an option can be forecast with considerable precision. If we are looking ahead to a dividend forecasted to occur in three months, we expect the stock price to drop by the amount of the dividend when the stock goes ex-dividend. At the present moment, three months before the ex-dividend date, we can build that looming dividend into our analysis. To do so, we subtract the present value of the dividend from the current stock price. We then apply the Black–Scholes model as usual, except we use the adjusted stock price as an input to the model instead of the current stock price.

As an example, consider call and put options with a common exercise price of $100 and 150 days until expiration. Assume that the underlying stock trades for $102, and that you expect the stock to pay a $3 dividend in 90 days. The risk-free rate is 9 percent, and the standard deviation for the stock is 0.30. The present value of the $3 dividend is:

$$\$3e^{-r\,(90/365)} = \$2.93$$

According to this technique, we reduce the stock price now by the present value of the dividend, giving an adjusted stock price of $99.07. We then apply the Black–Scholes model in the usual way, except we use the adjusted stock price of $99.07 instead of the current price of $102. The following table shows the results of applying the adjusted and unadjusted models to the call and the put.

Black–Scholes Model Price	Call	Put
Adjusted for Known Dividends	8.91	6.21
Unadjusted	10.74	5.11

Applying the Black–Scholes model, with the adjustment for known dividends that we have just discussed, gives a call value of $8.91 and a put value of $6.21. With no adjustment for dividends, the Black–Scholes prices are $10.74 for the call option and $5.11 for the put option. The difference in prices is substantial, amounting to almost 20 percent. Also, as we hypothesized, subtracting the present value of the dividends from the stock price reduces the value of the call and increases the value of the put.

The same technique applies in situations when there are several dividends. The stock price should be adjusted by subtracting the present value of all dividends that are expected to occur before the expiration date of the option. Dividends expected after the option expires can be ignored, because the option will already have been exercised or allowed to expire before those dividends affect the value of the stock.

Adjustments for Continuous Dividends—Merton's Model

Robert Merton has shown how to adjust the Black–Scholes model to account for dividends when the dividend is paid at a continuous rate. Instead of focusing on the quarterly dividends that characterize individual stocks, Merton's model applies when the dividend is paid continuously. Essentially, the adjustment for continuous dividends treats the dividend rate as a negative interest rate. We have already seen that dividends reduce the value of a call option, because they reduce the value of the stock that underlies the option. In effect, we have a continuous leakage of value from the stock that equals the dividend rate. We let the Greek letter delta, δ, represent this rate of leakage.[13]

Merton's model applies particularly well to options on goods such as foreign currency. In such an option, the foreign currency is treated as paying a continuous dividend equal to the foreign interest rate. (We explore options on foreign currency in Chapter 7.) Merton's model also applies fairly well to options on individual stocks, if we treat the quarterly dividends as being earned at a continuous rate. Merton's adjustment to the Black–Scholes model for continuous dividends is:

$$c_t^M = e^{-\delta\,(T\,-\,t)}\,S_t N(d_1^M) - Xe^{-r\,(T\,-\,t)}\,N(d_2^M)$$

$$d_1^M = \frac{\ln\left(\dfrac{S_t}{X}\right) + (r - \delta + 0.5\,\sigma^2)(T - t)}{\sigma\sqrt{T - t}}$$

$$d_2^M = d_1^M - \sigma\sqrt{T - t}$$

4.17

where δ = the continuous dividend rate on the stock

To adjust the regular Black–Scholes model, we replace the current stock price with the stock price adjusted for the continuous dividend. That is, we replace S_t with:

$$e^{-\delta(T-t)}S_t$$

Substituting this expression into the formulas for d_1 and d_2 gives d_1^M and d_2^M as shown above. Merton's adjusted put value is:

$$p_t^M = Xe^{-r(T-t)}N(-d_2^M) - Se^{-\delta(T-t)}N(-d_1^M) \qquad 4.18$$

When $\delta = 0$, Merton's model reduces immediately to the Black–Scholes model. Thus, the Merton model is a more general model than the original Black–Scholes and it will appear repeatedly in the remainder of the text. As an example of how to apply the continuous dividend adjustment, consider the following data:

$$S_t = \$60$$
$$X = \$60$$
$$r = 0.09$$
$$\sigma = 0.2$$
$$T - t = 180 \text{ days}$$

The stock will pay a quarterly dividend of $2 in 90 days, implying a continuous dividend rate, δ, of 13.75 percent. We compute the call price, c_t^M, as follows:

$$d_1^M = \frac{\ln\left(\dfrac{60}{60}\right) + [0.09 - 0.1375 + 0.5\,(0.2)(0.2)]\left(\dfrac{180}{365}\right)}{.2\sqrt{\dfrac{180}{365}}}$$

$$= \frac{0 - 0.01356}{0.14045} = -0.09656$$

$$d_2^M = -0.09656 - 0.2\sqrt{\frac{180}{365}} = -0.23701$$

$N(d_1^M) = N(-0.09656) = 0.4615$, and $N(d_2^M) = N(-0.23701) = 0.4063$. Therefore, $N(-d_1^M) = 0.5385$, and $N(-d_2^M) = 0.5937$. The call and put values adjusted for continuous dividends are:

$$c_t^M = 60\, e^{-0.1375(180/365)}\,(0.4615) - 60\, e^{-0.09(180/365)}\,(0.4063) = \$2.55$$
$$p_t^M = 60\, e^{-0.09(180/365)}\,(0.5937) - 60\, e^{-0.1375(180/365)}\,(0.5385) = \$3.88$$

The Binomial Model and Dividends

The binomial model can evaluate European options prices for options on dividend paying stocks. There are three alternative dividend treatments within the context of the binomial model, and all involve adjusting the lattice to reflect the impact of dividends on the stock price. The first considers options on stocks paying a continuous dividend. This binomial approach is the analog to the Merton model that we considered earlier. The second binomial approach applies to options on a stock that will pay a known dividend yield at a certain time. For example, a stock might pay a dividend equal to some fraction of its value on a certain date, such as a dividend of 3 percent of the stock's value 120 days from now. The third approach applies to a known dollar dividend that will occur at a certain time. For example, 90 days from now a stock might pay a $1 dividend. The binomial model can accommodate any number of dividend payments between the present and the expiration of the option.

Continuous Dividends. To apply the Binomial Model to options on a stock paying a continuous dividend, we need to adjust the binomial parameters to reflect the continuous leakage of value from the stock that the dividend represents. For Merton's model for European options on a stock paying a continuous dividend, we saw that the adjustment largely involved subtracting the continuous dividend rate, δ, from the risk-free rate, r. This is exactly the adjustment required for the binomial model. For options on a stock paying a continuous dividend δ, the U, D, and π_U factors are:

$$U = e^{\sigma \sqrt{\Delta t}}$$
$$D = \frac{1}{U} \qquad\qquad 4.19$$
$$\pi_U = \frac{e^{(r - \delta)\Delta t} - D}{U - D}$$

We illustrated Merton's model by considering a call option on a stock with a price of $60, a standard deviation of 0.2, and a continuous dividend rate of 13.75 percent. The call had an exercise price of $60 and expired in 180 days. The risk-free rate was 9 percent. We saw that the price of this option according to Merton's model was $2.5557. According to the binomial model, with 200 periods, the price would be $2.5516, which is almost identical. For the same data, the European put according to Merton's model was worth $3.8845. The binomial model with 200 periods gives a put price of $3.8805.

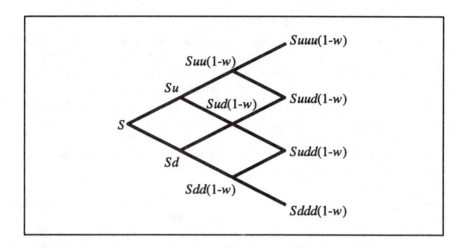

FIGURE 4.9   The Binomial Tree for a Stock with a Known Dividend Yield

Known Dividend Yield.   Consider a stock that will pay w percent of its value as a dividend in 55 days. An option on the stock expires in 120 days, and we model the price of the option using a three-period binomial model. In this situation, the dividend will occur in the second period. The binomial tree for the stock will appear as shown in Figure 4.9. At the second period in the binomial tree, the stock price will be reduced to $(1 - w)$ percent of its value. If the stock price rose in each of the first two periods, the stock price at period 2 would be $S_t UU(1 - w)$. Because of the known dividend yield occurring at day 55, the value of the stock is reduced by the w percent dividend. Given that the stock price went up the first two periods, the value of the stock in the third period could be either $S_t UUU(1 - w)$ if the stock price goes up again, or it could be $S_t UUD(1 - w)$ if the stock price falls in the final period. To value either a call or a put in the context of the binomial model with a known dividend yield, we apply the usual technique to work from the terminal stock prices back to the current stock price and current options price.

Extending this example, let us assume that the initial stock price is $80, that the exercise price for a call and a put is $75, that the standard deviation of the stock is 0.3, and the risk-free rate of interest is 7 percent. The percentage dividend that will be paid is 3 percent, so $w = 0.03$. With 120 days until expiration and a three-period binomial model, $\Delta t = 40/365 = 0.1096$. Therefore:

$$U = e^{0.3\sqrt{0.1096}} = 1.1044$$

$$D \quad \frac{1}{1.1044} = 0.9055$$

$$\pi_U = \frac{1.0077 - 0.9055}{1.1044 - 0.9055} = 0.5138$$

The discounting factor for a single period is $e^{-r\Delta t} = e^{-0.07(40/365)} = 0.9924$. Figure 4.10 shows the binomial tree for the stock of our example. In the

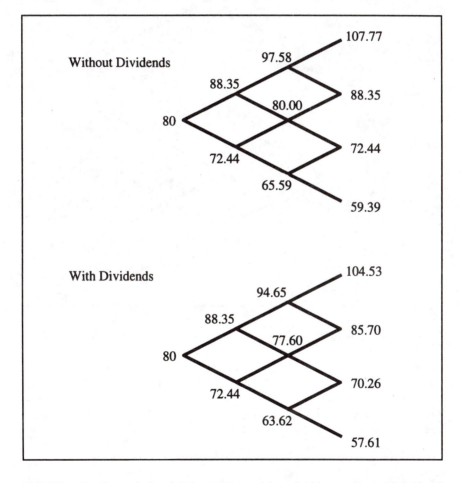

FIGURE 4.10 Example Stock Price Lattices with and without a Known Dividend Yield

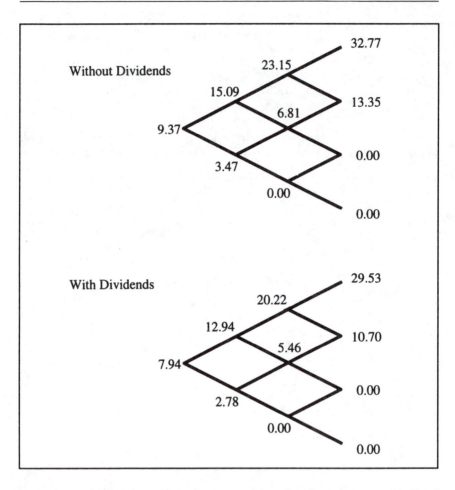

FIGURE 4.11 Example Call Price Lattices with and without a Known Dividend Yield

top panel, the stock price without dividends appears, while the bottom tree shows the effect of the 3 percent dividend on the stock price. For example, in the bottom tree reflecting dividends, the stock price pattern generated by a rise, a rise, and a fall is:

$$S_t UUD(1 - w) = \$80(1.1044)(1.1044)(0.9055)(1.0 - .03)$$
$$= \$85.70$$

Figure 4.11 shows two binomial trees for the call option. The top tree in Figure 4.11 does not reflect the dividends and shows that the option's

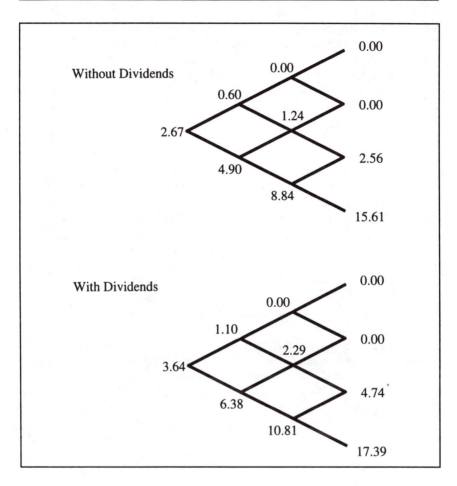

FIGURE 4.12 Example Put Price Lattices with and without a Known Dividend Yield

value would be $9.37. The bottom tree, which does reflect the 3 percent dividend yield, shows that the call is worth $7.94. The difference in the two prices is due entirely to taking account of the dividend.

Figure 4.12 parallels Figure 4.11, except it shows trees for the put option. The top tree ignores the dividend and shows that the put's value would be $2.67 if there were no dividend. Taking account of the dividend in the bottom tree gives a put price of $3.64. The effect of the dividend increases the put's value by 36 percent, from $2.67 to $3.64, and decreases the call's value by 15 percent, from $9.37 to $7.94. Clearly dividends can have a profound effect on options prices.

Known Dollar Dividend.   Most stocks that underlie stock options pay a fixed dollar dividend, rather than pay a dividend that equals some percentage of their value. This presents a complication, because the tree may develop a tremendous number of branches. For example, assume that the stock price is initially $80 and that $U = 1.1$. Therefore, $D = 0.9091$. After one period, the stock price is either $88 or $72.73, as Figure 4.13 shows. Assume that a $2 dividend is paid just before the first period. Taking the dividend payment into account, the stock price will be either $86 or $70.73 at the first period. In the next period the stock price will either rise or fall. If it was $86, it will then be $94.60 if the price rises again or $78.18 if the price falls. If the stock price fell in the first period, so that it was $70.73 after the dividend payment, in the second period it will either rise to $77.80 or fall to $64.30. Figure 4.13 shows that there are four possible prices after two periods: $94.60, $78.18, $77.80, or $64.30. In the normal tree, there would be only three prices to consider, because $S_t UD = S_t DU$. That is not the case with known dollar dividends. Letting DIV$ indicate a given dollar dividend, $(S_t U - \text{DIV\$})D$ does not equal $(S_t D - \text{DIV\$})U$. For many periods and multiple dividend payments, the number of nodes to evaluate can explode, making this model very difficult to apply.

We can avoid these difficulties by making a simplifying assumption. We assume that the stock price reflects the dividend, which is known with certainty, and all other factors that might affect the stock price, which are uncertain. We then adjust the uncertain component of the stock price for the impending dividends and model the uncertain component of the

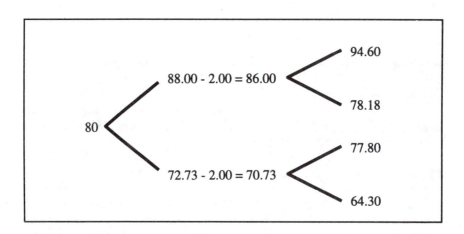

FIGURE 4.13   A Stock Price Lattice Unadjusted for a Known Dollar Dividend

stock price with the binomial tree adding back the present value of all future dividends at each node. Specifically, we follow these steps:

1. Compute the present value of all dividends to be paid during the life of the option as of the present time $= t$.
2. Subtract this present value from the current stock price to form $S_t' = S_t - PV$ of all dividends.
3. Create the binomial tree by applying the up and down factors in the usual way to the initial stock price S_t'.
4. After generating the tree, add to the stock price at each node the present value of all future dividends to be paid during the life of the option.
5. Compute the options values in the usual way by working through the binomial tree.

To make this discussion more concrete, consider again the tree that failed to recombine in Figure 4.13. The initial stock price was $80, $U = 1.1$, $D = 0.9091$, and a dividend was to be paid just before the time of the first period. We now additionally assume that one period is 0.25 years and the interest rate is 10 percent. Therefore, the one-period discount factor is:

$$e^{-r\,(\Delta t)} = e^{-0.1(0.25)} = 0.9753$$

At the outset, the present value of the dividend is $1.95 = 0.9753($2)$. To form S_t' we subtract this present value from S_t:

$$S_t' = S_t - \text{PV of all dividends} = \$80 - \$1.95 = \$78.05$$

Figure 4.14 shows the binomial tree generated from a starting price of $78.05. Notice that the present value of the dividends ($1.95) has been added to the first node only, because only the first node represents a time before the payment of the dividend. Notice also that the tree recombines at the second period, in contrast to Figure 4.13.

Summary

In this section, we have considered the effect of dividends on European options. In general, a dividend on a stock reduces the value of the stock

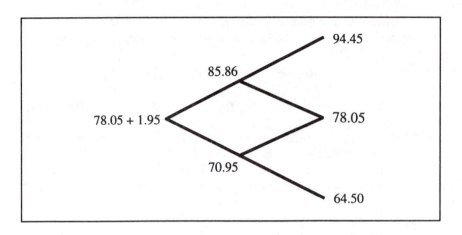

FIGURE 4.14 Stock Price Lattice Adjusted for a Known Dollar Dividend

by the amount of the dividend. Dividends reduce the value of call options because they reduce the stock price. Dividends increase the value of put options because the dividend reduces the price of the stock. The Black–Scholes model as originally developed pertained only to options on non-dividend-paying stocks. However, the stocks that underlie most stock options do pay dividends, so the limitation of the Black–Scholes model is potentially serious.

There are several adjustments to the Black–Scholes model to account for dividends. The first one adjusts for known dividends by subtracting the present value of the dividends from the stock price and then applying the Black–Scholes model in the usual way. When the underlying stock pays a continuous dividend, Merton showed how to adjust the Black–Scholes model to account for the dividend.

We also considered adjustments to the binomial model to account for dividends. When the stock pays a known dividend yield at a given date, the binomial model can reflect the impact of this dividend on the stock price and the option quite easily. When the dividend is a given dollar amount, the binomial model requires a more elaborate adjustment, but it too can adjust the stock price and compute options values that reflect the impact of the dividend.

TESTS OF THE OPTIONS PRICING MODEL

If the Black–Scholes options pricing model correctly captures the factors that affect options prices, the price computed according to the model should correspond closely to the price observed in the market. Otherwise, either the model is inadequate or prices in the market are irrational. Therefore, each of the tests that we will consider in this section test a joint hypothesis—adequacy of the options pricing model and market rationality. If we find a discrepancy between the two, we can account for this divergence by claiming that the model is inadequate or by allowing that market participants are foolish. Note, however, that the Black–Scholes model was derived under the assumption that prices should not permit arbitrage. Accordingly, any major discrepancy between the model price and the market price would be serious indeed.

The Black–Scholes Study

The first empirical study of options pricing was conducted by Black and Scholes.[14] In this 1972 test, they examined over-the-counter options prices, because listed options did not yet trade. Black and Scholes computed a theoretical option price based on their model. If the market price exceeded their theoretical price, they assumed that they sold the option. Similarly, if the market price was below the price they computed, they assumed that they bought the option. In both cases, they assumed that they held a stock position in conjunction with the option that gave a riskless position. (In other words, if they were long the call option, they would hold $-N(d_1)$ shares of stock as well.) This risk-free position should earn the risk-free rate if options prices in the market and their model are identical. They maintained this position until expiration, adjusting the portfolio as needed to maintain its riskless character. Their results showed significant profit opportunities. In other words, actual market prices differed significantly from the theoretical price given by the model. However, this difference was statistically significant, but not economically important. When Black and Scholes considered transaction costs, they found that the costs of trading would erode any potential profit. Therefore, options traders could not follow their strategy and make a profit. This result helped to show the strong correspondence between market prices and options prices computed from theoretical models, such as the Black–Scholes model.

The Galai Studies

As in the Black–Scholes study, Galai created hedged portfolios of options and stock and used these portfolios to study the correspondence between the Black–Scholes model price and actual market prices for options.[15] In contrast to the Black–Scholes study, Galai used listed options data from the Chicago Board Options Exchange. With options trading on an exchange, Galai had access to daily price quotations. Therefore, he was able to compute the rate of return on the hedged option–stock portfolio for each option for each day. He also adjusted the hedge ratio each day to maintain the neutral hedge—neutral in the sense that a change in the stock price would not change the overall value of the combined option–stock position. Comparing market prices to Black–Scholes model prices, Galai assumed that he sold overpriced options and bought underpriced options each day.

Galai's results showed that this strategy could earn excess returns. In other words, his initial results seemed to be inconsistent with an efficient market. However, this apparent result disappeared when Galai considered transaction costs. If transaction costs were only 1 percent, the apparent excess returns disappeared. Most traders outside the market face transaction costs of 1 percent or higher. However, market makers can transact for less than 1 percent transaction costs. This suggests that market makers could have followed Galai's strategy to earn excess returns. Yet even market makers face some additional transaction costs implied by their career choice. For instance, the market maker must buy or lease a seat on the exchange and the market maker must forego alternative employment. When Galai brought these additional implicit transaction costs into the analysis, the market maker's apparent excess returns diminished or disappeared. At any rate, Galai's results showed that Black–Scholes model prices closely match actual market prices for options.

The Bhattacharya Study

Mihir Bhattacharya used an approach like the Black–Scholes and Galai studies to analyze the correspondence between actual market prices and theoretical prices.[16] Bhattacharya discussed the adherence of market prices to theoretical boundaries implied by no-arbitrage conditions. We focus on one of his three boundaries. As we discussed in Chapter 3, a call option should be worth more than its exercise value if time remains until expiration. Bhattacharya compiled a sample of 86,000 transactions and examined them to determine if immediate exercise was profitable. He found 1100 such exercise opportunities, meaning that the stock price exceeded the exercise price plus the call price. As we argued in Chapter 3, such a price relationship should not exist. However, these exercise opportunities assumed that the exercise could be conducted without transaction costs. When Bhattacharya considered transaction costs, these apparently profitable exercise opportunities disappeared. The apparent violation of the boundary condition was observed only because transaction costs were not considered. This means that traders could not exploit the deviation from the boundary condition to make a profit.

The MacBeth–Merville Study

James MacBeth and Larry Merville used the Black–Scholes model to compute implied standard deviations for the underlying stocks.[17] They assumed that the Black–Scholes model correctly prices at-the-money options with at least 90 days until expiration. Based on these assumptions and the estimated standard deviation, they evaluated how well the Black–Scholes model prices options that are in-the-money or out-of-the-money and how well the model prices options that have fewer than 90 days until expiration. They found some systematic discrepancies between market prices and Black–Scholes model prices. First, the Black–Scholes prices tended to be less than market prices for in-the-money options and the Black–Scholes prices tended to be higher than market prices for out-of-the-money options. Second, this first effect is larger the further the options are from the money. However, it is smaller the shorter the time until expiration. Therefore, we expect to find the greatest discrepancy between market prices and the Black–Scholes model price for options with a long time until expiration and options that are way-in- or way-out-of-the-money.

The Rubinstein Study

Mark Rubinstein compared market prices with theoretical options prices from the Black–Scholes model and other models of options prices.[18] Some other models outperformed the Black–Scholes model in some respects, yet none did so consistently. Further, Rubinstein confirmed some of the biases noted by MacBeth and Merville for the Black–Scholes model. However, none of the other models was consistently free of bias either. In general, Rubinstein was unable to conclude that there was a single model superior to the others.

Summary

Testing of the options pricing model is far from complete. Recently, attention has turned to the information inherent in options prices that might not be reflected in stock prices or that might be reflected first in options prices and later in stock prices. For example, Joseph Anthony finds that trading volume in call options leads trading volume in the underlying stock by one day.[19] While this lead–lag relationship does not necessarily imply any inefficiency in either market, it does seem to suggest that information that reaches the market affects options first.[20] In recent years the proliferation of many new kinds of options has attracted attention away from options on individual stocks. The kinds of studies on options on individual stocks that were conducted by Black and Scholes, Galai, Bhattacharya, and Rubinstein have recently been conducted for these new kinds of options. In large part, these new results corroborate the earlier results that were found for options on individual stocks. In this section, it has been possible to discuss only some of the most famous studies. There are many other worthwhile studies that have been conducted and many more still that remain to be conducted.

SUMMARY

We began this chapter by developing the binomial model. We showed that the single-period binomial model emerges directly from no-arbitrage conditions that govern all asset prices. We extended the single-period model to the multi-period binomial model. With this model, we found that we could apply our no-arbitrage principles to value options with numerous periods remaining until expiration. Throughout this development, we considered price movements that were somewhat arbitrary.

Researchers have studied the actual price movements of stocks in great detail. We found that logarithmic stock returns are distributed approximately normally and that this model of stock price movements has proven to be very useful as a working approximation of stock price behavior. Using this model of stock price behavior, a binomial model with many periods until expiration approaches the Black–Scholes model. The Black–Scholes model gives an elegant equation for pricing a call option as a function of five variables: the stock price, the exercise price, the risk-free rate, the time until expiration, and the standard deviation of the stock. Only two of these variables, the interest rate and the standard deviation, are not immediately observable. We showed how to estimate these two parameters.

REVIEW QUESTIONS

1. What is binomial about the binomial model? In other words, how does the model get its name?
2. If a stock price moves in a manner consistent with the binomial model, what is the chance that the stock price will be the same for two periods in a row? Explain.

3. Assume a stock price is $120 and in the next year it will either rise by 10 percent or fall by 20 percent. The risk-free interest rate is 6 percent. A call option on this stock has an exercise price of $130. What is the price of a call option that expires in one year? What is the chance that the stock price will rise?

4. Based on the data in Question 3, what would you hold to form a risk-free portfolio?

5. Based on the data in Question 3, what will the price of the call option be if the option expires in two years and the stock price can move up 10 percent or down 20 percent in each year?

6. Based on the data in Question 3, what would the price of a call with one year to expiration be if the call has an exercise price of $135? Can you answer this question without making the full calculations? Explain.

7. A stock is worth $60 today. In a year, the stock price can rise or fall by 15 percent. If the interest rate is 6 percent, what is the price of a call option that expires in three years and has an exercise price of $70? What is the price of a put option that expires in three years and has an exercise price of $65?

8. Consider our model of stock price movements given in Equation 4.8. A stock has an initial price of $55 and an expected growth rate of 0.15 per year. The annualized standard deviation of the stock's return is 0.4. What is the expected stock price after 175 days?

9. A stock sells for $110. A call option on the stock has an exercise price of $105 and expires in 43 days. If the interest rate is 0.11 and the standard deviation of the stock's returns is 0.25, what is the price of the call according to the Black–Scholes model? What would be the price of a put with an exercise price of $140 and the same time until expiration?

10. Consider a stock that trades for $75. A put and a call on this stock both have an exercise price of $70 and they expire in 150 days. If the risk-free rate is 9 percent and the standard deviation for the stock is 0.35, compute the price of the options according to the Black–Scholes model.

11. For the options in Question 10, now assume that the stock pays a continuous dividend of 4 percent. What are the options worth according to Merton's model?

12. Consider a Treasury bill with 173 days until maturity. The bid and asked yields on the bill are 9.43 and 9.37. What is the price of the T-bill? What is the continuously compounded rate on the bill?

13. Consider the following sequence of daily stock prices: $47, $49, $46, $45, $51. Compute the mean daily logarithmic return for this share. What is the daily standard deviation of returns? What is the annualized standard deviation?

14. A stock sells for $85. A call option with an exercise price of $80 expires in 53 days and sells for $8. The risk-free interest rate is 11 percent. What is the implied standard deviation for the stock?

15. For a particular application of the binomial model, assume that $U = 1.09$, $D = 0.91$, and that the two are equally probable. Do these assumptions lead to any particular difficulty? Explain. (Note: These are specified up and down movements and are not intended to be consistent with the Black–Scholes model.)

16. For a stock that trades at $120 and has a standard deviation of returns of 0.4, use the Black–Scholes model to price a call and a put that expire in 180 days and that have an exercise price of $100. The risk-free rate is 8 percent. Now assume that the stock will pay a dividend of $3 on day 75. Apply the known dividend adjustment to the Black–Scholes model and compute new call and put prices.

17. A call and a put expire in 150 days and have an exercise price of $100. The underlying stock is worth $95 and has a standard deviation of 0.25. The risk-free rate is 11 percent. Use a three-period binomial model and stock price movements consistent with the Black–Scholes model to compute the value of these options. Specify U, D, and π_u, as well as the values for the call and put.

18. For the situation in Problem 17, assume that the stock will pay 2 percent of its value as a dividend on day 80. Compute the value of the call and the put under this circumstance.

19. For the situation in Problem 17, assume that the stock will pay a dividend of $2 on day 80. Compute the value of the call and the put under this circumstance.

20. Consider the first tree in Figures 4.10 and 4.12. If the stock price falls in both of the first two periods, the price is $65.59. For the first tree in Figure 4.12, the put value is $8.84 in this case. Given that the exercise price on the put is $75, does this present a contradiction? Explain.

21. Consider the second tree in Figures 4.10 and 4.11. If the stock price increases in the first period, the price is $88.35. For the second tree in Figure 4.11, the call price is $12.94 in this case. Given that the exercise price on the put is $75, does this present a contradiction? Explain.

NOTES

1. A risk-neutral investor considers only the expected payoffs from an investment. For such an investor, the risk associated with the investment is not important. Thus, a risk-neutral investor would be indifferent between an investment with a certain payoff of $50 or an investment with a 50 percent probability of paying $100 and a 50 percent probability of paying zero.

2. The development of the binomial model stems from two seminal articles: R. Rendleman and B. Bartter, "Two-State Option Pricing," *Journal of Finance*, 34, December 1979, 1093–1110, and J. Cox, S. Ross, and M. Rubinstein, "Option Pricing: A Simplified Approach," *Journal of Financial Economics*, 7, September 1979, 229–263. J. Cox and M. Rubinstein develop and discuss the binomial model in their book *Option Pricing*, Prentice Hall, 1973, and their paper "A Survey of Alternative Option Pricing Models," which appears in *Option Pricing*, edited by M. Brenner, Lexington, D. C. Heath, 1983, 3–33.

3. Not every one of these stock price outcomes will be unique. Even in the two-period model we saw that $UDS = DUS$. Strictly speaking, with 20 periods, there are more than 1 million stock price paths.

4. To this point, we have considered the binomial model in some detail and we have considered the log-normal model of stock prices. In essence, each different assumption about stock price movements leads to a different class of options pricing models. For instance, we have already observed that assuming stock prices can either rise or fall by a given amount in a period leads to the binomial model. The log-normal assumption that we have just been considering assumes that the stock price path is continuous. In other words, for the stock price to go from $100 to $110, the price must pass through every value between the two. Another entire class of assumptions about stock price movements assumes that the stock price follows a jump process—the stock price jumps from one price to another without taking on each of the intervening values. A quick test to distinguish these two models is to determine whether the stock price path can be drawn without lifting pen from paper. If so, then the stock price path is continuous. The following papers analyze options pricing under alternative assumptions about stock price movements: J. Cox and S. Ross, "The Valuation of Options for Alternative Stochastic Processes," *Journal of Financial Economics*, 3, January–March 1976, 145–166; R. Merton, "Option Pricing When Underlying Stock Returns Are Discontinuous," *Journal of Financial Economics*, 3, January–March 1976, 125–144; F. Page and A. Saunders, "A General Derivation of the Jump Process Option Pricing Formula," *Journal of Financial and Quantitative Analysis*, 21:4, December 1986, 437–446; C. Ball and W. Torous, "On Jumps in Common Stock Prices and Their Impact on Call Option Pricing," *Journal of Finance*, 40:1, March 1985, 155–173; and E. Omberg,

"Efficient Discrete Time Jump Process Models in Option Pricing," *Journal of Financial and Quantitative Analysis*, 23:2, June 1988, 161–174.

5. F. Black and M. Scholes, "The Pricing of Options and Corporate Liabilities," *Journal of Political Economy*, May 1973, 637–659, provides the classic statement of the model. In his paper, "Fact and Fantasy in the Use of Options," *Financial Analysts Journal*, 1975, May/June, 31:4, 36–41 and 61–72, Fischer Black develops many of the same ideas in a more intuitive manner. More recently, Fischer Black has told the story of how Myron Scholes and he discovered the options pricing formula. See F. Black, "How We Came Up with the Option Formula," *Journal of Portfolio Management*, Winter 1989, 4–8.

6. In imperfect markets, there may not be a single interest rate, but traders may face a borrowing rate and a lending rate. J. Gilster and W. Lee consider this possibility in their paper, "The Effects of Transaction Costs and Different Borrowing and Lending Rates on the Option Pricing Model: A Note," *Journal of Finance*, 39:4, September 1984, 1215–1221. They also consider transaction costs and show that considering both imperfections in the debt market and transaction costs results in two offsetting influences. As such, they conclude, neither has a strong effect on the estimation of the option price, and Black–Scholes options prices conform well to actual prices observed in the market. Thus, neither market imperfection is too important because the two imperfections tend to cancel each other.

7. Of course, it is possible that the stock volatility could change over the life of the option. But shifting volatilities present difficulties in finding an options pricing model. J. Hull and A. White, "The Pricing of Options on Assets with Stochastic Volatilities," *Journal of Finance*, 42:2, June 1987, 281–300, address this issue. While Hull and White acknowledge that no formula for an option price assuming changing volatility has been found, they develop techniques for approximating the value of an option with changing volatility. In doing so, they assume that changes in volatility are correlated with changes in the stock price. This problem has also been studied by L. Scott, "Option Pricing When the Variance Changes Randomly: Theory, Estimation, and an Application," *Journal of Financial and Quantitative Analysis*, 22:4, December 1987, 419–438. Scott uses simulation techniques to approximate options prices, but concedes that no formula for an option price under shifting volatilities has been found. Finally, James Wiggins explores this problem as well in his paper, "Option Values under Stochastic Volatility: Theory and Empirical Estimates," *Journal of Financial Economics*, 19:2, December 1987, 351–372. He also acknowledges that an actual formula for the price of an option under shifting volatilities is lacking. Wiggins applies a numerical estimation technique to develop estimates of options prices assuming that volatility follows a continuous process. Under this assumption, Wiggins is able to compute estimated options prices.

8. There is a third potentially useful method that we do not consider in this book. M. Parkinson, "The Random Walk Problem: Extreme Value Method for Estimating the Variance of the Displacement," *Journal of Business*, 53, January 1980, 61–65, showed that focusing on high and low prices for a few days could give as good an estimate as using historical data for five times as many days. His model assumes that stock prices are distributed log-normally. Compared with the use of historical data on the closing price for a given day, Parkinson's method uses both the high and low prices for the day. This method would allow a good estimate from more recent historical data than simply focusing on the history of closing prices. M. Garman and M. Klass, "On the Estimation of Security Price Volatilities from Historical Data," *Journal of Business*, 53:1, 1980, 67–78 pointed out some difficulties with Parkinson's approach. First, his method is very sensitive to any errors in the reported high and low prices. Further, if trading during the day is sporadic, Parkinson's method will generate biased estimates of volatility. In particular, with discontinuities in the trading, the reported high will almost certainly be lower than the high that would have been observed with continuous trading. Similarly, the reported low will be higher than the value that would have been achieved under continuous trading. Garman and Klass also show how to improve Parkinson's type of estimate.

9. Similarly, assume that we estimate the standard deviation with weekly data. We would convert this raw data to annualized data by multiplying the weekly standard deviation times the square root of 52. Similarly, if we begin with monthly data, we annualize our monthly standard deviation by multiplying it times the square root of 12.

10. In principle, we can take any five of the values as given and solve for the sixth. For example, Menachem Brenner and Dan Galai, "Implied Interest Rates," *Journal of Business*, 59, July 1986, 493–507, find that interest rates implied in the options market correspond to other short-term rates of interest. These implied rates are nearer to the borrowing rate than to the lending rate. Further, in situations where early exercise is imminent, the interest rates implied in the options markets can differ widely from short-term rates on other instruments. Steve Swidler takes this approach a step further in his paper, "Simultaneous Option Prices and an Implied Risk-Free Rate of Interest: A Test of the Black-Scholes Model," *Journal of Economics and Business*, 38:2, May 1986, 155–164. Swidler uses two options, which allow him to estimate two parameters simultaneously—two equations in two unknowns. Swidler estimates the implied interest and the implied standard deviation. While the standard deviation can differ from stock to stock, there should be a common interest rate for all options on a given date. For most of the stocks he examines, Swidler finds that a single interest rate can be found. Accordingly, he regards his evidence as supporting the reasonableness of the Black–Scholes model.

11. For a discussion of these weighting techniques, see Henry A. Latane and Richard J. Rendleman, Jr., "Standard Deviations of Stock Price Ratios Implied in Option Prices," *Journal of Finance,* 31, 1976, 369–382; Donald P. Chiras and Steven Manaster, "The Information Content of Option Prices and a Test of Market Efficiency," *Journal of Financial Economics,* 6, 1978, 213–234; and Robert E. Whaley, "Valuation of American Call Options on Dividend Paying Stocks: Empirical Tests," *Journal of Financial Economics,* 10, 1982, 29–58. Stan Beckers, in his paper, "Standard Deviations Implied in Option Prices as Predictors of Future Stock Price Variability," *Journal of Banking and Finance,* 5, 1981, 363–382, concludes that using the option with the highest sensitivity to the standard deviation provides the best estimate of future volatility.

12. In fact, considerable research shows that the stock price falls when a stock goes ex-dividend, but the drop in the stock price does not equal the full amount of the dividend. In this text, we make the simplifying assumption that the stock price falls by the amount of the dividend. Alternatively, the reader may regard the dividend as being equal to the amount of the fall in the stock price occasioned by the dividend payment.

13. This is not the same as capital delta, Δ, which stands for the sensitivity of the call option price to a change in the stock price.

14. F. Black and M. Scholes, "The Valuation of Option Contracts and a Test of Market Efficiency," *Journal of Finance,* 27:2, 1972, 399–417.

15. D. Galai, "Tests of Market Efficiency of the Chicago Board Options Exchange," *Journal of Business,* 50:2, April 1977, 167–197, and "Empirical Tests of Boundary Conditions for CBOE Options," *Journal of Financial Economics,* 6:2/3, June–September 1978, 182–211.

16. M. Bhattacharya, "Transaction Data Tests on the Efficiency of the Chicago Board Options Exchange," *Journal of Financial Economics,* 12:2, 1983, 161–185.

17. J. D. MacBeth and L. J. Merville, "An Empirical Examination of the Black–Scholes Call Option Pricing Model," *Journal of Finance,* 34:5, 1979, 1173–1186.

18. M. Rubinstein, "Nonparametric Tests of Alternative Option Pricing Models Using All Reported Trades and Quotes on the 30 Most Active CBOE Option Classes from August 23, 1976 through August 31, 1978," *Journal of Finance,* 40:2, 1985, 455–480. The other models tested were extensions of the Black–Scholes model based on changing assumptions about how stock prices move. For instance, they included options models based on the assumption that stock prices jump from one price to another, rather than moving continuously through all intervening prices as the stock price moves from one price to another. Rubinstein tested the following models: the Black–Scholes model, the jump model, the mixed diffusion jump model, the constant elasticity of variance model, and the displaced diffusion model.

19. J. H. Anthony, "The Interrelation of Stock and Options Market Trading-Volume Data," *Journal of Finance,* 43:4, September 1988, 949–964.

20. Options prices may react before stock prices due to the trading preferences of informed traders. We have already seen that options markets often offer lower transaction costs than the market for the underlying good. For traders with good information, the options market may be the preferred market to exploit their information. On this scenario, we would expect to see options prices and volume change before stock prices and volume. The trading of the informed traders would move options prices, and the arbitrage linkages between options and stocks would lead to an adjustment of the corresponding stock prices.

5

Options Sensitivities and Options Hedging

INTRODUCTION

Chapter 4 developed the principles of pricing for European options. There we analyzed options pricing within the framework of the binomial model and extended the discussion to encompass the Black–Scholes model, which gives a closed-form solution for the price of a European option on a nondividend stock. We also considered the Merton model, which provides a solution for the price of a European option on a stock paying a continuous dividend.

In this chapter, we continue our exploration of these models by focusing on the response of options prices to the factors that determine the price. Specifically, we noted in Chapter 4 that the price of a European option depends on the price of the underlying stock, the exercise price, the interest rate, the volatility of the underlying stock, and the time until expiration. This chapter analyzes the sensitivity of options prices to these factors and shows how a knowledge of these relationships can direct trading strategies and can improve options hedging techniques.

OPTIONS SENSITIVITIES IN THE MERTON AND BLACK–SCHOLES MODELS

Throughout this chapter, we focus on the Merton model (given in Equations 4.17 and 4.18) and the sensitivity of options prices in this model to the underlying factors. This approach embraces the Black–Scholes model (presented in Equations 4.13–4.15), as we may regard the Merton model simply as the Black–Scholes model extended to account for stocks that pay continuous dividends. As we saw in Chapter 4, the Merton model simplifies to the Black–Scholes model if we assume that the underlying stock pays no dividends. Similarly, the sensitivities of options prices in the Merton model reduce to those for the Black–Scholes model if we assume that the underlying stock pays no dividends.

The options price sensitivities that we consider in this chapter all derive from calculus. For example, the sensitivity of the option price with respect to the stock price is simply the first derivative of the options pricing formula with respect to the stock price. For readers unfamiliar with calculus, we illustrate this basic idea in two ways. The first derivative of the call price with respect to the stock price is just the change in the call price for a change in the stock price:

$$\frac{\Delta c}{\Delta S}$$

This change in the call price is measured for an extremely small change in the stock price. In fact, in terms of calculus, the change in the call price is measured for an infinitesimal change in the stock price. As a second illustration, consider a European call option on a stock priced at $100 with a standard deviation of 0.3. The option expires in 180 days, has a striking price of $100, and the current risk-free rate of interest is

Table 5.1 Call Prices for Various Stock Prices

Call Price	Stock Price	$N(d_1)$
$9.1111	$98.00	0.5780
$9.4024	$98.50	0.5874
$9.6984	$99.00	0.5967
$9.9991	$99.50	0.6060
$10.1512	$99.75	0.6105
$10.3044	$100.00	0.6151
$10.3660	$100.10	0.6169
$10.4587	$100.25	0.6196
$10.6142	$100.50	0.6241
$10.9284	$101.00	0.6330
$11.2472	$101.50	0.6418
$11.5702	$102.00	0.6505

8 percent. Table 5.1 shows the value of this call for stock prices in the neighborhood of $100. It also shows the value of $N(d_1)$ computed at each price as well. Consider a change in the stock price from $100 to $102. For this change of $2 in the stock price, the call price changes from $10.3044 to $11.5702. Therefore:

$$\frac{\Delta c}{\Delta S} = \frac{1.2658}{2.00} = 0.6329$$

Next consider a change in the stock price from $100 to $100.10. In this case the call price would change from $10.3044 to $10.3660, giving:

$$\frac{\Delta c}{\Delta S} = \frac{0.0616}{0.10} = 0.6160$$

For these two cases, we now compare the relative change in call prices to $N(d_1)$. For a stock price of $100, $N(d_1) = 0.6151$, and our $\Delta c/\Delta S$ term has a value in that neighborhood. We also note that for a $2 stock price change, $\Delta c/\Delta S$ is 0.6329, but for a $0.10 change, $\Delta c/\Delta S = 0.6160$. As the change becomes smaller, the value for $\Delta c/\Delta S$ approaches the value of $N(d_1)$ for a stock price of $100, which is 0.6151. For an infinitesimally small change in the stock price, the change in the value of the call option will exactly equal $N(d_1)$. In fact, $N(d_1)$ is the first derivative of the call price with respect to the stock price for a nondividend stock. The line for the call in Figure 5.1 shows how the value of our example option changes as a function of the stock price. The straight line tangent to the option price curve in the the top graph of Figure 5.1 shows the instantaneous rate of change in the call price for a change in the stock price. The slope of this straight line is the first derivative of the call price with respect to the stock price. As the figure shows, the straight line indicates the slope of the call price curve at a stock price of $100, which is 0.6151.

All of the sensitivity measures we consider in this chapter are similarly conceived and derived. They all derive from calculus, and they all express the sensitivity of an option price to a change in one of the underlying parameters. In the common calculus notation for our example, the first derivative of the call price with respect to the stock price is denoted as $\partial c/\partial S$. Table 5.2 presents the standard sensitivities used in options analysis for the Merton model as it applies to calls, while Table 5.3 gives the same equations for puts. (See Chapter 4 for the equations for the two models and other terms.)

FIGURE 5.1   Call and Put Prices as a Function of the Stock Price
$X = \$100$; $\sigma = .3$; $r = .08$; $T - t = 180$ days

Table 5.2 Call Sensitivities for the Merton Model

Name	Sensitivity
DELTA$_c$	$\dfrac{\partial c}{\partial S} = e^{-\delta\,(T\,-\,t)}\,N(d_1^M)$
THETA$_c$	$-\dfrac{\partial c}{\partial(T-t)} = -\dfrac{SN'(d_1^M)\,\sigma\,e^{-\delta\,(T\,-\,t)}}{2\sqrt{T-t}}$
	$+\ \delta\,S\,N(d_1^M)\,e^{-\delta\,(T\,-\,t)} - r\,Xe^{-r\,(T\,-\,t)}\,N(d_2^M)$
VEGA$_c$	$\dfrac{\partial c}{\partial\sigma} = S\sqrt{T-t}\,N'(d_1^M)\,e^{-\delta\,(T\,-\,t)}$
RHO$_c$	$\dfrac{\partial c}{\partial r} = X(T-t)\,e^{-r(T\,-\,t)}\,N(d_2^M)$
GAMMA$_c$	$\dfrac{\partial\ \text{DELTA}_c}{\partial S} = \dfrac{\partial^2 c}{\partial S^2} = \dfrac{N'(d_1^M)\,e^{-\delta\,(T\,-\,t)}}{S\sigma\sqrt{T-t}}$
Note:	$N'(d_1^M) = \dfrac{1}{\sqrt{2\,\pi}}e^{-0.5\,(d_1^M)^2}$

Table 5.3 Put Sensitivities for the Merton Model

Name	Sensitivity
DELTA$_p$	$\dfrac{\partial p}{\partial S} = e^{-\delta\,(T\,-\,t)}\,[N(d_1^M) - 1]$
THETA$_p$	$-\dfrac{\partial p}{\partial(T-t)} = -\dfrac{SN'(d_1^M)\,\sigma\,e^{-\delta\,(T\,-\,t)}}{2\sqrt{T-t}}$
	$-\ \delta\,S\,N(-d_1^M)\,e^{-\delta\,(T\,-\,t)} + r\,Xe^{-r\,(T\,-\,t)}\,N(-d_2^M)$
VEGA$_p$	$\dfrac{\partial p}{\partial\sigma} = S\sqrt{T-t}\,N'(d_1^M)\,e^{-\delta\,(T\,-\,t)}$
RHO$_p$	$\dfrac{\partial p}{\partial r} = -X(T-t)\,e^{-r(T\,-\,t)}\,N(-d_2^M)$
GAMMA$_p$	$\dfrac{\partial\ \text{DELTA}_p}{\partial S} = \dfrac{\partial^2 p}{\partial S^2} = \dfrac{N'(d_1^M)\,e^{-\delta\,(T\,-\,t)}}{S\sigma\sqrt{T-t}}$
Note:	$N'(d_1^M) = \dfrac{1}{\sqrt{2\,\pi}}e^{-0.5\,(d_1^M)^2}$

As we saw in Chapter 4, the Black–Scholes model is the same as the Merton model in the special case of there being no dividends on the stock. Similarly, we can derive the sensitivities for the Black–Scholes model from those of the Merton model if we assume that the stock pays no dividends. Tables 5.4 and 5.5 parallel Tables 5.2 and 5.3 and give the sensitivities for the Black–Scholes model.

Earlier we considered a call option on a stock priced at $100 with a standard deviation of 0.3 and no dividend. The call had 180 days until expiration, and we assumed a risk-free rate of 8 percent. Table 5.6 shows all of the sensitivities for calls and puts for both the Black–Scholes model (assuming no dividend) and the Merton model (assuming a continuous dividend of 3 percent).

DELTA

DELTA is the first derivative of an option's price with respect to a change in the price of the stock. As such, DELTA measures the sensitivity of the option's price to changing stock prices. $DELTA_c$ is always positive, while $DELTA_p$ is always negative. Thus, the value of a call increases with a stock price increase, while the value of a put decreases if the stock price

Table 5.4   Call Sensitivities for the Black–Scholes Model

Name	Sensitivity
$DELTA_c$	$$\frac{\partial c}{\partial S} = N(d_1)$$
$THETA_c$	$$-\frac{\partial c}{\partial (T-t)} = -\frac{SN'(d_1)\,\sigma}{2\sqrt{T-t}}$$ $$- r\,Xe^{-r(T-t)}\,N(d_2)$$
$VEGA_c$	$$\frac{\partial c}{\partial \sigma} = S\sqrt{T-t}\,N'(d_1)$$
RHO_c	$$\frac{\partial c}{\partial r} = X(T-t)\,e^{-r(T-t)}\,N(d_2)$$
$GAMMA_c$	$$\frac{\partial\,DELTA_c}{\partial S} = \frac{\partial^2 c}{\partial S^2} = \frac{N'(d_1)}{S\sigma\sqrt{T-t}}$$
Note:	$$N'(d_1) = \frac{1}{\sqrt{2\pi}}e^{-0.5(d_1)^2}$$

Table 5.5 Call Sensitivities for the Black–Scholes Model

Name	Sensitivity
DELTA$_p$	$\dfrac{\partial p}{\partial S} = N(d_1) - 1$
THETA$_p$	$-\dfrac{\partial p}{\partial (T - t)} = -\dfrac{S N'(d_1) \sigma}{2\sqrt{T - t}}$ $+ r X e^{-r(T - t)} N(-d_2)$
VEGA$_p$	$\dfrac{\partial p}{\partial \sigma} = S\sqrt{T - t}\, N'(d_1)$
RHO$_p$	$\dfrac{\partial p}{\partial r} = -X(T - t)\, e^{-r(T - t)} N(-d_2)$
GAMMA$_p$	$\dfrac{\partial\, \text{DELTA}_p}{\partial S} = \dfrac{\partial^2 p}{\partial S^2} = \dfrac{N'(d_1)}{S \sigma \sqrt{T - t}}$
Note:	$N'(d_1) = \dfrac{1}{\sqrt{2\pi}} e^{-0.5(d_1)^2}$

Table 5.6 Options Sensitivities
$S = \$100; \; X = \$100; \; r = 0.08; \; \sigma = 0.3; \; T - t = 180 \text{ days}$

	Black–Scholes Model $\delta = 0.0$		Merton Model $\delta = 0.03$	
	Call	Put	Call	Put
Option prices	$10.3044	$6.4360	$9.4209	$7.0210
DELTA	0.6151	−0.3849	0.5794	−0.4060
THETA	−12.2607	−4.5701	−10.3343	−5.5997
VEGA	26.8416	26.8416	26.9300	26.9300
RHO	25.2515	−22.1559	23.9250	−23.4823
GAMMA	0.0181	0.0181	0.0182	0.0182

increases. In Table 5.6 for the options on a nondividend stock, DELTA$_c$ = .6151 and DELTA$_p$ = −0.3849. These sensitivities can be interpreted as follows. If the stock price rises by $1, the price of the call will rise by approximately $0.6151, while the price of the put will fall by about $0.3849.

These estimations of the change in the option price are only approximate. If the change in the stock price were infinitesimal, the DELTAs would give us an exact price change for the options. Because a $1 change in the stock price is discrete, our computed prices remain estimates. If the stock price is $101, we have $c = \$10.9284$, and $p = \$6.0601$. Thus, the call price increases by $0.6240 (compared to the predicted $0.6151), and the put price falls by $0.3759 (compared to the predicted fall of $0.3849).

The lower graph of Figure 5.1 shows how the put price of our example varies with the stock price. Notice that the price of a European put can be less than its intrinsic value, as we discussed in Chapter 4. As the two panels of Figure 5.1 indicate, options prices are extremely dependent upon stock prices, and the price of the underlying stock is the key determinant of an option price. Therefore, DELTA is the most important of all of the sensitivity measures that we consider in this chapter.

DELTA-Neutral Positions

Consider a portfolio, P, of a short position of one European call on a nondividend stock combined with a long position of DELTA units of the stock. The portfolio would have the value:

$$P = -c + N(d_1)S \qquad\qquad 5.1$$

Continuing to use our sample options of Table 5.6, the cost of the portfolio, assuming a current stock price of $100, would be:

$$P = -c + N(d_1)S = -\$10.3044 + 0.6151(\$100.00) = \$51.2056$$

If the stock price were to suddenly change to $100.10, the portfolio's value would be:

$$P = -c + N(d_1)S = -\$10.3660 + 0.6151(\$100.10) = \$51.2055$$

Thus, the value of the portfolio would change by only $0.0001 for a $0.10 change in the stock price. If the change in the stock price were infinitesimal, the price of the portfolio would not change at all. If the change in the stock price were larger, the change in the value of the portfolio would be larger, but it would still be quite small relative to the change in the stock price. For example, if the stock price rose from $100 to $110, the portfolio's value would be:

$$P = -c + N(d_1)S = -\$17.2821 + 0.6151(\$110.00) = \$50.3789$$

In this case, a change of $10 in the stock price caused a change of $0.8267 in the value of the portfolio. Figure 5.2 shows how the value of this portfolio changes for changes in the stock price.

A portfolio like the one we are considering, and described by Equation 5.1, is known as a **DELTA-neutral portfolio**. It is DELTA-neutral because an infinitesimal change in the price of the stock does not affect the price of the portfolio. Put another way, we could say that the DELTA of this portfolio is zero; the value of the portfolio is insensitive to the value of the stock.

As we saw in Chapter 4, the Black–Scholes model assumes that the stock price changes continuously. Imagine now that we can trade shares and options continuously as the stock price changes. We see from the equation for DELTA in Table 5.2 that DELTA changes when the stock price changes. (DELTA also changes when other factors change as well, such as the standard deviation and the time remaining until the option expires.) Assume now that we trade continuously to rebalance our portfolio as the stock price changes. In rebalancing, we seek to maintain the condition of Equation 5.1. In particular, we trade continuously to main-

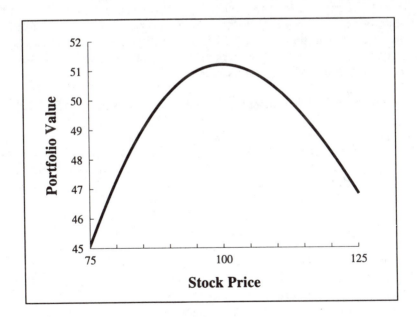

FIGURE 5.2   Value of a DELTA-Neutral Portfolio as a Function of the Stock Price (Portfolio includes −1 call and 0.6151 shares) $X = \$100$; $\sigma = 0.3$; $r = 0.08$; $T - t = 180$ days

tain our portfolio as a DELTA-neutral portfolio. By trading continuously, the portfolio is DELTA-neutral at every instant and never loses or gains value in response to changes in the stock price. By following this strategy of continuously rebalancing our portfolio, we know that it has zero price risk as a function of changing stock prices. In effect, by continuously rebalancing we have created a risk-free portfolio. Further, if the portfolio is risk-free, it must earn the risk-free rate of return.

This is the key intuition of the Black–Scholes model. Black and Scholes realized that continuous trading could maintain a DELTA-neutral portfolio as a risk-free portfolio earning the risk-free rate. This was an important step that enabled them to find a solution for their options pricing model.

As a practical matter, creating a DELTA-neutral portfolio in the manner described appears to be a difficult way of buying a risk-free security. Why not just buy a Treasury bill? Later in this chapter, we explore the extremely valuable practical consequences of using DELTA-oriented hedging technologies. However, at the present we can easily see how the idea of a DELTA-neutral portfolio can be very useful in adjusting the riskiness of a stock trading strategy.

For the call option and the stock that we have been considering, assume that an outright investment in the stock is too risky. An investor in this position could use the idea of DELTA-neutrality to shape the risk characteristics of the investment to her particular needs. For example, assume that a trader holds a portfolio as follows:

$$-0.5c + N(d_1)S = -0.5(\$10.3044) + 0.6151(\$100.00) = \$56.3578$$

This portfolio is similar to the DELTA-neutral portfolio that we considered earlier, except instead of selling a call, the investor sells only one-half of a call. In considering the DELTA-neutral portfolio, we saw that selling the call in conjunction with investing in the stock gave a risk-free portfolio. Now, by selling one-half of a call, the investor diminishes the risk, but does not totally eliminate it. Figure 5.3 shows how the value of the DELTA-neutral portfolio and this new portfolio will vary as the stock price changes. This new portfolio has some risk exposure to changing stock prices, but it is much less risky than the stock itself. Later in this chapter, we consider a variety of strategies for using options to accept, avoid, or transform various investment risks.

As we noted earlier, DELTA changes as the stock price and other parameters of the options pricing model change. For our continuing example, Figure 5.4 shows how the DELTAs of the call and put vary with changing stock prices. $DELTA_c$ tends to approach 1.0 when the call option

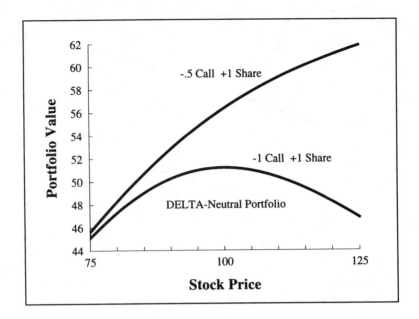

FIGURE 5.3   Value of a DELTA-Neutral Portfolio as a Function of the Stock Price (One portfolio includes −1 call and 0.6151 shares, and one portfolio includes −0.5 calls and 0.6151 shares) $X = \$100$; $\sigma = 0.3$; $r = 0.08$; $T - t = 180$ days

is deep-in-the-money. Similarly, when the call is deep-out-of-the-money, $DELTA_c$ approaches zero. When the stock price is near the exercise price, $DELTA_c$ is most sensitive to a change in the stock price. For $DELTA_p$, similar principles apply. $DELTA_c$ is always greater than zero, while $DELTA_p$ is always less than zero. The DELTA of a deep-in-the-money put approaches −1, while the DELTA of a deep-out-of-the-money put approaches zero.

THETA

If the stock price and all other parameters of the options pricing model remain constant, the price of options will still change with the passage of time. THETA is the negative of the first derivative of the option price with respect to the time remaining until expiration. $THETA_c$ and $THETA_p$ can be greater or less than zero depending upon circumstances. However, $THETA_c$ and $THETA_p$ are generally less than zero.[1]

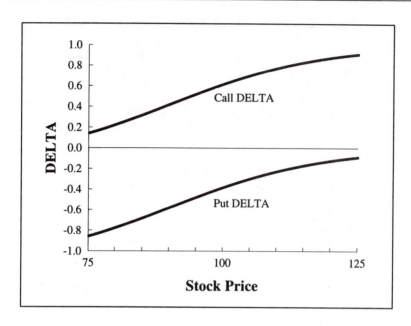

FIGURE 5.4 Call and Put DELTAs as a Function of the Stock Price
$X = \$100$; $\sigma = 0.3$; $r = 0.08$; $T - t = 180$ days

The tendency for options prices to change due merely to the passage of time is known as **time decay**. To see how the passage of time affects options prices, consider our continuing example of call and put options with $S = \$100$, $X = \$100$, $\sigma = 0.3$, $r = 0.08$, and $T - t = 180$ days. For these values, we noted earlier that $c = \$10.30$, and $p = \$6.44$. For these values, $\text{THETA}_c = -12.2607$, and $\text{THETA}_p = -4.5701$. These values of THETA are expressed in terms of years. Suppose that the time to expiration changes by 0.1 years (37 days) from 180 days until expiration to 143 days. Recalling that THETA is the negative of the first derivative of the options price with respect to time until expiration, we would expect the call and put prices to be $c = \$10.30 + 0.1(-12.2607) = \$9.07$, and $p = \$6.44 + 0.1(-4.5701) = \$5.98$. Recalling that all of these computed prices are approximations, the actual prices would be $c = \$9.01$, and $p = \$5.92$.

If all parameters remain constant, except the expiration date draws nearer, both options will have to fall in value. Both the call and the put will be worthless at expiration, because $S = X = \$100$. Therefore, the call and put options will lose their entire value through time decay. Figure 5.5 illustrates time decay for our sample options.

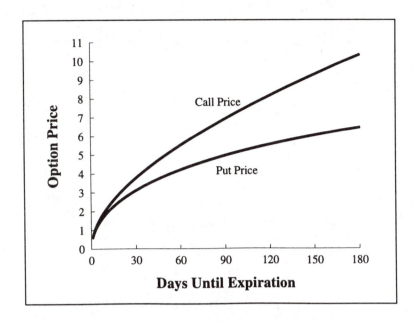

FIGURE 5.5 Call and Put Prices as a Function of the Time until Expiration $S = \$100$; $X = \$100$; $\sigma = 0.3$; $r = 0.08$

THETA$_c$ and THETA$_p$ both vary with changing stock prices and with the passage of time. For the options of our continuing example, Figure 5.6 shows how the call and put THETAs vary with the stock price. (Notice that the graph shows how a put that is deep-in-the-money can have a positive THETA.) THETA$_c$ and THETA$_p$ also both change with the passage of time. If the stock price is near the exercise price, THETA$_c$ and THETA$_p$ will become quite negative as expiration nears, as Figure 5.7 shows. However, this is not true for options that are deep-in-the-money or deep-out-of-the-money. Figure 5.7 shows how THETA$_c$ and THETA$_p$ change in very different manners depending upon whether the options are in-the-money or out-of-the-money. For example, a European put that is in-the-money will have a positive THETA as expiration nears.

VEGA

VEGA is the first derivative of an option's price with respect to the volatility of the underlying stock. VEGA$_c$ and VEGA$_p$ are identical and always positive. (VEGA is sometimes known as kappa, lambda, or sigma as well. We use the term VEGA throughout.)

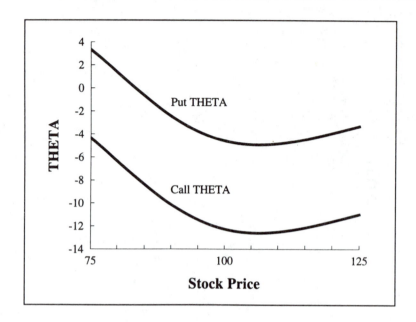

FIGURE 5.6 Call and Put THETAs as a Function of the Stock Price
$X = \$100; \sigma = 0.3; r = 0.08; T - t = 180$ days

The VEGA is an important determinant of options prices. A sudden substantive change in the standard deviation of the underlying stock can cause a dramatic change in options values. As we noted for our example options, $c = \$10.30$ and $p = \$6.44$ when $\sigma = 0.3$. If volatility were to suddenly increase by 0.2 so that $\sigma = 0.5$, we would expect new prices of $c = \$10.30 + 0.2(26.8416) = \$15.67$ and $p = \$6.44 + 0.2(26.8416) = \$11.81$.

The actual call and put prices with $\sigma = 0.5$ would be $c = \$15.69$ and $p = \$11.82$, causing a price increase of 52 percent for the call and 84 percent for the put. During and immediately following the Crash of 1987 (when the stock market lost 20–25 percent of its value in one day), the perceived volatility for stocks increased tremendously causing an increase in options values. (Of course, calls generally lost value due to falling prices, and puts increased in value for the same reason.) Figure 5.8 shows how call and put prices vary with the standard deviation for our example options.

VEGA tends to be greatest for an option near-the-money. When an option is deep-in-the-money or deep-out-of-the-money, the VEGA is low and can approach zero. Figure 5.9 shows how VEGA varies with respect

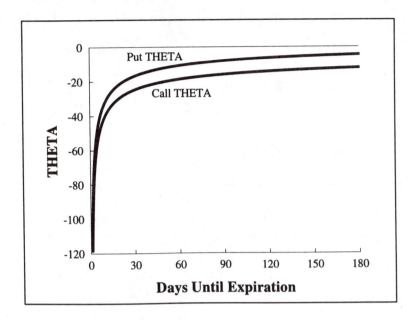

FIGURE 5.7 Call and Put THETAs as a Function of the Time until Expiration $X = \$100$; $\sigma = 0.3$; $r = 0.08$

to the stock price for the call and put of our continuing example. Because the two example options are at-the-money, VEGA is at its maximum. For calls or puts in-the-money or out-of-the-money, the VEGA will be lower.

RHO

RHO is the first derivative of an option's price with respect to the interest rate. RHO_c is always positive, while RHO_p is always negative. In general, options prices are not very sensitive to RHO. In Table 5.6, $RHO_c = 25.2515$, and $RHO_p = -22.1559$. If the interest rate were to increase by 1 percent, then the call price should increase by $0.01(25.2515) = \$0.2525$, while the price of the put should fall by $0.01(-22.1559) = \$0.2216$. Figure 5.10 shows how the prices of our example options would change given varying interest rates. Large changes in the interest rate have relatively little effect on options prices.

RHO changes as a function of both the stock price and the time until expiration. RHO_c tends to be low for an option that is deep-out-of-the-money and high for a deep-in-the-money call. RHO_c tends to be sensitive

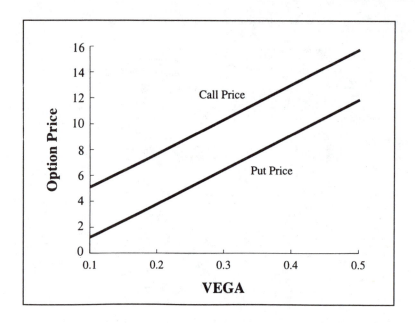

FIGURE 5.8 Call and Put Prices as a Function of the Standard Deviation
$S = \$100; X = \$100; r = 0.08; T - t = 180$ days

to the stock price when a call is near-the-money. For a deep-in-the-money put, RHO_p is generally low, and RHO_p is generally large for a deep-out-of-the-money put. When the put is near-the-money, RHO_p tends to be more sensitive to the stock price. Figure 5.11 illustrates the sensitivity of RHO_c and RHO_p to the stock price for the options in our continuing example.

RHO_c and RHO_p change as time passes, with both tending toward zero as expiration approaches. The interest rate affects the price of an option in conjunction with the time remaining until expiration mainly through the time value of money. If little time remains until expiration, the interest rate is relatively unimportant, and the price of an option becomes less sensitive to the interest rate. For our example options, Figure 5.12 shows how RHO_c and RHO_p tend to zero as expiration approaches.

GAMMA

Unlike the other sensitivity measures we have considered thus far, GAMMA does not measure the sensitivity of the price of an option to one of the parameters. Instead, GAMMA measures how DELTA changes

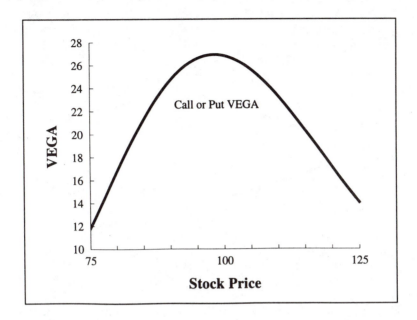

FIGURE 5.9 Call and Put VEGA as a Function of the Stock Price
$X = \$100$; $r = 0.08$; $T - t = 180$ days

with changes in the stock price. The GAMMA of a put and a call are always identical, and GAMMA can be either positive or negative. (In terms of calculus, GAMMA is the second derivative of the option price with respect to the stock price.) GAMMA is the only second-order effect that we consider, but it is an important one.

From our example computations in Table 5.6, we see that $GAMMA_c = GAMMA_p = 0.0181$. The table also shows $DELTA_c = 0.6151$, and $DELTA_p = -0.3849$. If the stock price were to increase by \$1 from \$100 to \$101, we would expect the two DELTAs to change. The new expected $DELTA_c = 0.6151 + 1(0.0181) = 0.6332$, and the new expected $DELTA_p = -0.3849 + 1(0.0181) = -0.3668$. With a stock price of \$101, the actual values are: $DELTA_c = 0.6330$, and $DELTA_p = -0.3670$.

GAMMA tends to be large when an option is near-the-money. A large GAMMA for a given stock price simply means that the DELTA is highly sensitive to changes in the stock price around its current level. For our sample options, Figure 5.4 shows that $DELTA_c$ and $DELTA_p$ are sensitive to the stock price when the price is near the exercise price of \$100. When an option is deep-in-the-money, the DELTA is near 1.0 and is not very sensitive to changing stock prices. Because of DELTA's low sensitivity

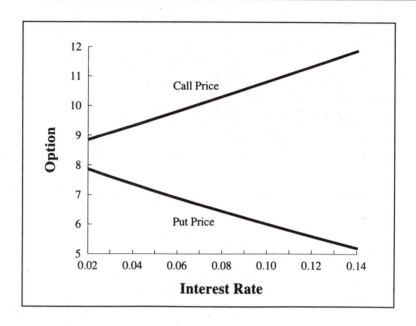

FIGURE 5.10 Call and Put Prices as a Function of the Interest Rate
$S = \$100; X = \$100; \sigma = 0.3; T - t = 180$ days

to stock prices, the GAMMA for a call or a put that is deep-in-the-money must be low. A similar principle applies for a call or a put that is deep-out-of-the-money. In such a situation, the DELTA of either a call or a put will be quite low, and it will be insensitive to changing stock prices. Due to this low sensitivity, the GAMMA will be small for either a call or a put that is deep-out-of-the-money.

Figure 5.4 shows how $DELTA_c$ and $DELTA_p$ vary with the stock price for our sample options. GAMMA essentially measures the slope of the graphs in Figure 5.4. Because the slopes of the graphs in Figure 5.4 are near zero for calls or puts that are deep-in-the-money or deep-out-of-the-money, GAMMA must be low as well. When the call or put are near-the-money, the rate of change in the DELTA as a function of the stock price is high—that is, the slope of the graph in Figure 5.4 is high. Therefore, for near-the-money options, GAMMA must be large.

Figure 5.13 shows how GAMMA varies with the stock price for our sample options. The figure applies to both the put and the call, because the GAMMAs are the same for a put and call with the same underlying instrument, time to expiration, and strike price. As the figure shows, GAMMA is large when the option is near-the-money and small when

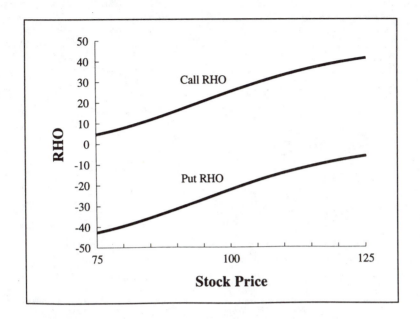

FIGURE 5.11 Call and Put RHOs as a Function of the Stock Price
$X = \$100; \sigma = 0.3; r = 0.08; T - t = 180$ days

the option is deep-in-the-money or when it is deep-out-of-the-money.

GAMMA also varies with the time remaining until expiration. For an option that is near-the-money, GAMMA increases as expiration approaches. This large GAMMA reflects the heightened sensitivity of the DELTA to the stock price when the option is near-the-money and expiration is near. For an option that is deep-out-of-the-money or deep-in-the-money, GAMMA will fall dramatically as expiration becomes very close. For in-the-money or out-of-the-money options, with expiration distant, the GAMMA will tend to rise as time passes. However, it is difficult to make solid generalizations about how GAMMA will change without actually calculating the effects of the passage of time. Both our example options are at-the-money, so the GAMMAs of the call and put will rise as expiration nears. Figure 5.14 shows how GAMMA varies with time remaining until expiration for options at-the-money, in-the-money, and out-of-the-money.

Positive and Negative GAMMA Portfolios

Earlier in this chapter, we created an example of a DELTA-neutral portfolio. For our sample call option, we saw that we could create a DELTA-

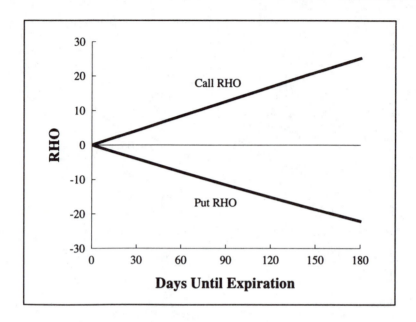

FIGURE 5.12 Call and Put RHOs as a Function of the Time until Expiration $S = \$100$; $X = \$100$; $\sigma = 0.3$; $r = 0.08$

neutral portfolio consisting of a long position of 0.6151 shares of the underlying stock and a short position of one call. Figure 5.2 shows how the value of this portfolio changes as the stock price changes. As the price of the stock moves away from $100, the value of the portfolio decreases.

The underlying stock has a DELTA of 1.0, which never changes. The change in the value of the stock is always 1:1 for changes in the value of the stock. Because the DELTA of the stock never changes, its GAMMA must be zero; the DELTA of the stock is completely insensitive to changes in the stock price. For our example call, the GAMMA is 0.0181. Because we have sold one call with a GAMMA of 0.0181 and 0.6151 shares with a GAMMA of zero, the GAMMA of this portfolio must be -0.0181. Because the portfolio has a negative GAMMA, the DELTA of the portfolio must decrease if the stock price changes.

For small changes in the stock price, we know that the price of the portfolio of -1 call and 0.6151 shares will not change, because the portfolio was constructed to be DELTA-neutral. For large changes in the stock price, however, the value of this portfolio will fall. The following data show the value of the elements of the portfolio and the total portfolio for stock prices of $90, $100, and $110.

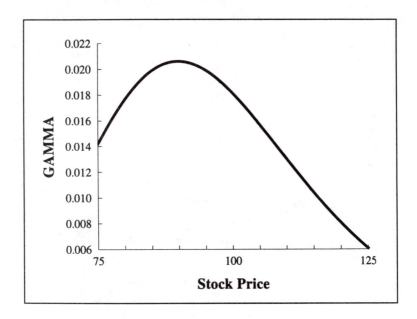

FIGURE 5.13 GAMMA as a Function of the Stock Price $X = \$100$; $\sigma = 0.3$; $r = 0.08$; $T - t = 180$ days

Stock Price	Call Price	0.6151 Shares	Portfolio Value (−1 Call + 0.6151 Shares)
$ 90	$ 5.12	$55.36	$50.24
$100	$10.30	$61.51	$51.21
$110	$17.28	$67.66	$50.38

The negative GAMMA of this portfolio ensures that large changes in the stock price will make the portfolio lose value. This is true whether the stock price rises or falls.

By contrast, consider a DELTA-neutral portfolio with a positive GAMMA. We can construct such a portfolio by combining our example put with the underlying stock to form a new portfolio. From Table 5.6, $p = \$6.4360$, $\text{DELTA}_p = -0.3849$, and $\text{GAMMA}_p = 0.0181$. A portfolio of one put and 0.3849 shares of stock will be DELTA-neutral, will be worth $44.926, and will have a GAMMA of 0.0181. The following table shows how the value of this positive GAMMA portfolio will vary with large changes in the stock price.

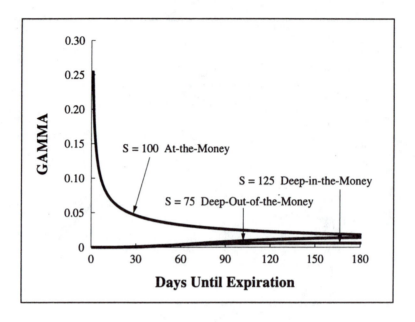

FIGURE 5.14 GAMMA as a Function of the Time until Expiration
$X = \$100;\ \sigma = 0.3;\ r = 0.08;\ T - t = 180$ days

Stock Price	Put Price	0.3849 Shares	Portfolio Value (1 Put + 0.3849 Shares)
$ 90	$11.25	$34.64	$45.89
$100	$ 6.44	$38.49	$44.93
$110	$ 3.41	$42.34	$45.75

These examples of a negative GAMMA portfolio and a positive GAMMA portfolio show the desirability of positive GAMMAs. If a trader holds a position with a positive GAMMA, large changes in the stock price will cause the portfolio value to increase. We have explored this within the context of a DELTA-neutral portfolio, but the principle holds for all portfolios.

CREATING NEUTRAL PORTFOLIOS

We have seen that a trader can create a DELTA-neutral portfolio from a stock and a call or from a stock and a put. In some situations, a trader might like to create a position that is neutral with respect to some other parameter, such as the THETA or VEGA of a portfolio. We now focus on stock-plus-option portfolios, and show how to ensure various types of neutrality for these portfolios.

We saw that a stock-plus-call or a stock-plus-put portfolio could be created as a DELTA-neutral portfolio. In general, a stock plus a single option portfolio can be made neutral with respect to just one parameter. For example, when we created the DELTA-neutral portfolios analyzed earlier, we found that the resulting portfolios were not GAMMA-neutral. A portfolio comprising a stock and a single option can never be DELTA-neutral and GAMMA-neutral unless the GAMMA of the option happens to be zero. However, we can control both the DELTA and the GAMMA of a stock-plus-option portfolio by creating a portfolio of a stock and two different options.

To illustrate this idea, we introduce another call option on the same underlying stock that we have been considering throughout this chapter. This call option has the same time to expiration, but its exercise price is $X = \$110$. For this call, we have $c = \$6.06$, $\text{DELTA}_c = 0.4365$, and $\text{GAMMA}_c = 0.0187$. To create a portfolio that is DELTA-neutral and GAMMA-neutral using our stock and these two calls, we create a portfolio that meets the two following conditions:

$$N_s \, \text{DELTA}_s + N_1 \text{DELTA}_1 + N_2 \text{DELTA}_2 = 0$$
$$N_s \, \text{GAMMA}_s + N_1 \text{GAMMA}_1 + N_2 \text{GAMMA}_2 = 0$$

where N_s, N_1, and N_2 are the number of shares, the number of the first call (with $X = \$100$), and the number of the second call (with $X = \$110$) to be held in the portfolio. We choose to create the portfolio with one share of stock, so $N_s = 1$. This leaves two equations with two unknowns, N_1 and N_2. We must choose these values to meet the two neutrality conditions.

For our example stock and options, we have:

$$1(1) + N_1(0.6151) + N_2(0.4365) = 0$$
$$1(0) + N_1(0.0181) + N_2(0.0187) = 0$$

If $N_1 = -5.1917$ and $N_2 = 5.0251$, the conditions will be met. Therefore, we create a DELTA-neutral and GAMMA-neutral portfolio by buying one share, selling 5.1917 calls with $X = \$100$, and buying 5.0251 calls with $X = \$110$. The resulting portfolio will be both DELTA-neutral and GAMMA-neutral.

This portfolio may be DELTA-neutral and GAMMA-neutral, but its value will still be sensitive to other parameters, such as the standard deviation of the underlying stock or the time until expiration. If we wanted to make the portfolio neutral with respect to DELTA, GAMMA, and VEGA, for example, we would need to add a third option to the portfolio. In general, we need to use one option for each sensitivity parameter that we want to control.

OPTIONS SENSITIVITIES AND OPTIONS TRADING STRATEGIES

Thus far in this chapter, we have seen that a trader can use a knowledge of options sensitivities to control risk. By the same token, this knowledge can be used to guide speculative trading strategies as well. By knowing the sensitivities of the various positions, a trader can create strategies to exploit certain expectations efficiently. Further, a trader should be aware of the various sensitivities of a position so she does not suffer unpleasant surprises.

In Chapter 2, we considered a wide variety of strategies, such as straddles, strangles, butterfly spreads, and condors, and we evaluated the profitability of these trades at expiration. Now, armed with the Black–Scholes model and the Merton model, we can understand how the value of these positions will behave prior to expiration. Further, given a knowledge of the sensitivities, we can analyze how a given trading strategy is likely to behave when the stock price changes, when volatility changes, or when the option approaches expiration. To explore the characteristics of options strategies, we consider the sample options shown in Table 5.7, which we use to illustrate some of the typical strategies.

The Straddle

Consider a long straddle consisting of call $C2$ and put $P2$ from Table 5.7. The cost of this position is $16.74. If the stock price at expiration is $100, which is the common exercise price for the two options, the position will expire worthless. At expiration, the value of the straddle will equal the intrinsic value of the call if the stock price exceeds $100, or it will equal the intrinsic value of the put if the stock price is below $100.

At the present, 180 days before expiration, the straddle has a DELTA of 0.2302, so the value of the straddle will vary directly with the stock price, but at a much reduced rate. The GAMMA of the straddle is 0.0362, so large shifts in the stock price will be beneficial. The VEGA of the straddle is 53.6832, indicating that any increase in volatility will increase the value of the position. The THETA of the straddle is -16.8308, emphasizing that the passage of time will reduce the value of the position.

Table 5.7 Sample Options
$S = \$100; r = 0.08; \sigma = 0.3; \delta = 0$

	Calls			
	C1 $X = \$90;$ $T - t = 180$ days	C2 $X = \$100;$ $T - t = 180$ days	C3 $X = \$110;$ $T - t = 180$ days	C4 $X = \$100;$ $T - t = 90$ days
Price	16.33	10.30	6.06	6.91
DELTA	0.7860	0.6151	0.4365	0.5820
GAMMA	0.0138	0.0181	0.0187	0.0262
THETA	−11.2054	−12.2607	−11.4208	−15.8989
VEGA	20.4619	26.8416	27.6602	19.3905
RHO	30.7085	25.2515	18.5394	12.6464

	Puts			
	P1 $X = \$90;$ $T - t = 180$ days	P2 $X = \$100;$ $T - t = 180$ days	P3 $X = \$110;$ $T - t = 180$ days	P4 $X = \$100;$ $T - t = 90$ days
Price	2.85	6.44	11.80	4.95
DELTA	−0.2140	−0.3849	−0.5635	−0.4180
GAMMA	0.0138	0.0181	0.0187	0.0262
THETA	−4.2839	−4.5701	−2.9612	−8.0552
VEGA	20.4619	26.8416	27.6602	19.3905
RHO	−11.9582	−22.1559	−33.6087	−11.5295

In fact, if the stock price remains at $100 for the 180 days that remain until expiration, the value of the straddle will decay from $16.74 to zero over this period. A single day is 0.00273973 years. Therefore, with a THETA of −16.8303, we would expect a loss in the value of the straddle from day 180 to day 179 of −$0.046, assuming the stock price remains steady at $100. While the straddle might lose only about $0.05 of its value per day due to time decay, it will decay to just $11.86 in 90 days. Figure 5.15 shows how the profit and loss from this straddle varies for 180, 90, and zero days to expiration as a function of the stock price.

Time decay works to the benefit of the seller of this strangle, reducing the potential liability each day. By the same token, the seller is exposed to volatility risk. If the volatility of the underlying stock increases, both option values will rise and the short straddle position will lose. Finally,

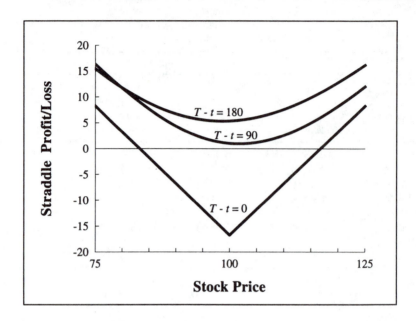

FIGURE 5.15 The Profit/Loss of a Straddle as a Function of the Stock Price with Various Times Remaining until Expiration $X = \$100$; $\sigma = 0.3$; $r = 0.08$

the positive GAMMA on the straddle is unfortunate from the point of view of the seller.

The Strangle

As we saw in Chapter 2, a strangle is similar to a straddle because it involves the purchase of a put and a call. Unlike a straddle, however, the striking prices of the put and call are not identical. To purchase a strangle, the trader buys a call with a lower exercise price and purchases a put with a higher exercise price. Here we consider two different strangle purchases using the example options detailed in Table 5.7.

The first strangle covers the exercise price range from $90 to $110. To purchase the strangle, the trader buys $C1$ with an exercise price of $90 and buys $P3$ with an exercise price of $110. For $C1$ we have $c = \$16.33$, DELTA $= 0.7860$, GAMMA $= 0.0138$, THETA $= -11.2054$, VEGA $= 20.4619$, and RHO $= 30.7085$. For $P3$, $p = 11.80$, DELTA $= -0.5635$, GAMMA $= 0.0187$, THETA $= -02.9612$, VEGA $= 27.6602$, and RHO $= -33.6087$. Because both options are $10 into-the-money, they are fairly expensive, and the total cost of this strangle is $28.13. $C1$ has a large DELTA, due to its being well into-the-money. For $C1$ RHO is positive, but RHO is negative for $P3$. As a result the strangle is not very sensitive to interest rates.

As a second strangle, we focus on an exercise price range from $100 to $110. This strangle requires the purchase of $C2$ and $P3$. For $C2$, $c =$ 10.30, DELTA $= 0.6151$, GAMMA $= 0.0181$, THETA $= -12.2607$, VEGA $= 26.8416$, and RHO $= 25.2515$. $P3$ is the same put we considered in the preceding paragraph, as it is used in both strangles that we consider. This second strangle costs $22.10. The DELTA of the call (0.6151) and put (-0.5635) almost offset each other, so this strangle is almost DELTA-neutral. However, the strangle has a positive GAMMA, and a high positive sensitivity to volatility. The RHOs of $C2$ (25.2515) and $P3$ (-33.6087) have different signs and largely offset each other. Therefore, the strangle has a low sensitivity to interest rates.

Figure 5.16 shows the profit and loss profiles for both strangles as a function of the current stock price. At the current stock price of $100, the profit or loss on the two positions is equal. For any stock price below

FIGURE 5.16 The Profit/Loss of Two Strangles as a Function of the Stock Price with Various Times Remaining until Expiration $\sigma = 0.3$; $r = 0.08$

$100, the first strangle has a greater profit (or a smaller loss). If the stock price moves above $100, the second strangle has a greater profit.

Notice that the two strangles have quite different risk profiles. As we noted earlier, the first strangle (with $X_1 = \$90$ and $X_2 = \$110$) is almost DELTA-neutral. The second strangle (with $X_1 = \$100$ and $X_2 = \$110$) is much more sensitive to changes in the stock price around $S = \$100$. The VEGA for the first strangle is 48.1221, while the VEGA for the second strangle is 54.5018. As both strangles employ the same put ($P3$), this difference in VEGA is due to the difference in VEGA between $C1$ and $C2$, and demonstrates the greater sensitivity to risk of the first strangle.

The Butterfly Spread with Calls

In a butterfly spread, a purchaser employs calls with three different exercise prices with the same underlying good and the same expiration. To illustrate the investment characteristics of this position, we use calls $C1$–$C3$ from Table 5.7. To purchase a butterfly spread, the trader would buy $C1$ (with $X = \$90$), buy $C3$ (with $X = \$110$), and sell two $C2$ (with $X = \$100$). Thus the position is long $C1$, long $C3$, and short two $C2$. This position costs $1.79:

$$16.33 - 2(10.30) + 6.06 = \$1.79$$

At a price of $1.79, we might expect future payoffs to be unlikely and small, and we should be aware of potential risks. From Chapter 2, we know that a butterfly spread with calls has the greatest payoff at expiration if the stock price equals the exercise price of the calls that were sold. For our example, that price would be $100. If the stock price at expiration were $100, $C1$ (with $X = \$90$) would be worth $10, and all other options in the spread would expire worthless.

The DELTA of this butterfly spread is:

$$0.7860 - 2(0.6151) + 0.4365 = -0.0077$$

Thus, the DELTA of the spread is almost zero, but just slightly negative. Any change in the stock price will cause a slight fall in the value of the position. Further, the GAMMA is near zero, but also slightly negative:

$$0.0138 - 2(0.0181) + 0.0187 = -0.0037$$

There is also little to hope for from a change in volatility, because the VEGA for the spread is negative:

$$20.4619 - 2(26.8416) + 27.6602 = -5.5611$$

Therefore, the position is not very sensitive to volatility, but an increase in volatility would cause some loss in value.

The butterfly spread has a RHO of -1.2551:

$$30.7085 - 2(25.2515) + 18.5394 = -1.2551$$

The value of the butterfly spread will vary inversely with interest rates, but the position is not very sensitive to interest rates.

The THETA for the butterfly spread is:

$$-11.2054 - 2(-12.2607) - 11.4208 = 1.8952$$

The positive THETA indicates that time decay will increase the value of the position.

These relationships are clear from Figure 5.17. As we noted, DELTA for the spread is slightly negative. In Figure 5.17, this leads to a shallow

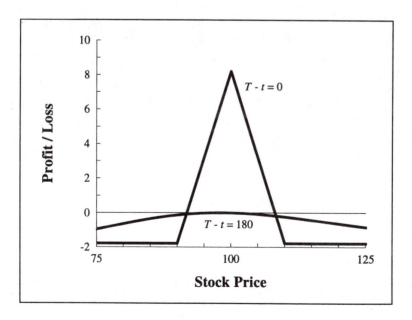

FIGURE 5.17 The Profit/Loss of a Butterfly Spread as a Function of the Stock Price $\sigma = 0.3$; $r = 0.08$; $T - t = 180$ days; $X_1 = \$90$; $X_2 = \$100$; $X_3 = \$110$

curve for the figure, but with a downward slope for stock prices greater or less than $100. The negative GAMMA is shown in the figure as the increasing downward curvature of the line. Figure 5.17 also shows the profit and loss on the butterfly spread as a function of the stock price at expiration. If the stock price remains at $100, time decay will cause the value of the butterfly spread to rise to $10 at expiration. Thus, time decay increases the value of this position, consistent with the positive THETA noted earlier.

The Bull Spread with Calls

To create a bull spread with calls, a trader purchases a call with a lower exercise price and sells a call with a higher exercise price. The two calls have the same underlying good and same term to expiration. We illustrate the bull spread with calls by considering options $C1$ and $C2$ from Table 5.7. These calls have exercise prices of $90 and $100, respectively. Option $C1$ costs $16.33, and Option $C2$ costs $10.30. Therefore, the spread will cost $6.03.

The sensitivities for the spread are: DELTA = $0.7860 - 0.6151 = 0.1709$; GAMMA = $0.0138 - 0.0181 = -0.0043$; THETA = $-11.2054 + 12.2607 = 1.0553$; VEGA = $20.4619 - 26.8416 = -6.3797$; and RHO = $30.7085 - 25.2515 = 5.4570$. Therefore, we see that a stock price increase will cause an increase in the value of the spread, which will be partially offset for large stock price changes by the negative GAMMA. Time decay will cause an increase in the value of the spread, as shown by the positive THETA. The spread has a negative VEGA, indicating that an increase in the stock's volatility will cause a decrease in the value of the spread. Finally, the RHO is positive, so an increase in interest rates will cause the spread to increase in value.

Figure 5.18 shows the profit and loss profile for the spread as a function of the price of the underlying stock. The graph shows that the value of the spread is positively related to the stock price. Further, Figure 5.18 illustrates that time decay will cause an increase in profits on the position. If no other parameters change, the profit and loss profile for the spread will collapse to its value at expiration as shown in the graph.

The VEGA of the option with the higher exercise price ($C2$ with $X = \$100$) is larger than that of $C1$ (with $X = \$90$). Because the position is long $C1$ and short $C2$, the spread's VEGA is negative. Therefore, an increase in volatility will cause the price of the spread to fall. Figure 5.19 shows the profitability of the spread as a function of the standard deviation.

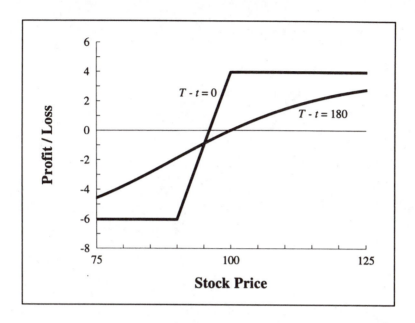

FIGURE 5.18 The Profit/Loss of a Bull Spread with Calls as a Function of the Stock Price $\sigma = 0.3$; $r = 0.08$; $T - t = 180$ days; $X_1 = \$90$; $X_2 = \$100$

A Ratio Spread with Calls

As discussed in Chapter 2, there are infinitely many possible ratio spreads, because a new position can be created merely by changing the ratio between the options that comprise the spread. Therefore, we illustrate the general technique of ratio spreads with a fairly simple ratio spread using just two options.

Earlier we considered the straddle composed of call $C2$ and put $P2$ from Table 5.7. We noted that the straddle costs \$16.74 and has a DELTA $= 0.6151 - 0.3849 = 0.2302$. The straddle had a VEGA $= 26.8416 + 26.8416 = 53.6832$. Thus, the straddle is essentially a volatility strategy with a relatively low DELTA and a high VEGA.

Consider now a trader's desire to create a position with most of the characteristics of a straddle, but to make it more purely a volatility strategy. In other words, the trader anticipates a volatility increase for the underlying stock, but does not wish to take a position on whether stock prices might rise or fall. Therefore, this trader would like to create a DELTA-neutral position with a high VEGA. The trader can create such a position by using a ratio spread that is similar to the straddle. However,

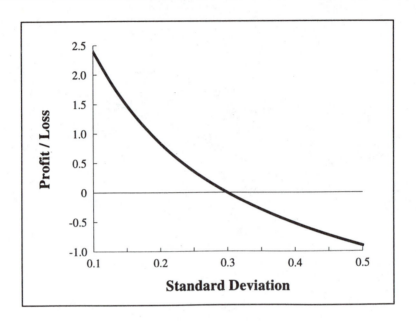

FIGURE 5.19 The Profit/Loss of a Bull Spread with Calls as a Function of the Standard Deviation $S = \$100; r = 0.08; T - t = 180$ days; $X_1 = \$90; X_2 = \$100$

instead of buying one $C2$ and one $P2$, the trader decides to buy one $C2$ and to buy enough puts ($P2$) to create a DELTA-neutral position. Therefore, the trader buys one $C2$ and 1.5981 $P2$, which costs: $\$10.30 + 1.5981(6.44) = \$20.59$. This position is DELTA-neutral because the DELTA of the spread is:

$$DELTA = 0.6151 + 1.5981(-0.3849) = 0.0$$

The other sensitivities for the ratio spread are: GAMMA $= 0.0181 + 1.5981(0.0181) = 0.0470$; THETA $= -12.2607 + 1.5981(-4.5701) = -19.5642$; VEGA $= 26.8416 + 1.5981(26.8416) = 69.7372$; and RHO $= 25.2515 + (1.5981)(-22.1559) = -10.1558$. Therefore, this ratio spread has zero DELTA, and a high VEGA. The value of the spread will suffer from time decay and will fall if interest rates rise.

Figure 5.20 shows the profitability of the straddle and the ratio spread as a function of the stock price. The ratio spread is much less sensitive to changing stock prices. This is consistent with its creation as a DELTA-neutral position. Both the straddle and the spread are essentially a bet

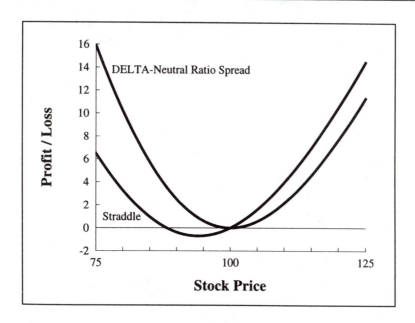

FIGURE 5.20 The Profit/Loss of a Straddle and a Ratio Spread as a Function of the Stock Price $\sigma = 0.3$; $r = 0.08$; $T - t = 180$ days; $X = \$100$

on increasing volatility. However, the ratio spread is a purer bet on volatility because it is insensitive to stock price changes. Figure 5.21 shows how the profitability of the straddle and the ratio spread change with changing volatility. Clearly, the ratio spread is more sensitive to changing volatility, as is shown by its greater slope in Figure 5.21.

One of the advantages of ratio spreads is the ability to avoid risk exposure to one parameter and to accept risk exposure to another. For example, one could use a ratio spread of the form we have considered to create a position that is VEGA-neutral but with a large DELTA, indicating a high sensitivity to changes in the stock price. This VEGA-neutral position could be created by buying $C2$ and selling $P2$ in a ratio of 1:1. The resulting spread would have a DELTA = 1.0. Thus, with a ratio spread of two options, one can maintain neutrality with respect to one parameter and accept sensitivity with respect to a second parameter.

The Calendar Spread

All of the options strategies we have considered thus far have employed options with the same expiration date. A **calendar spread** or a **time spread**

FIGURE 5.21 The Profit/Loss of a Straddle and a Ratio Spread as a Function of the Standard Deviation $S = \$100$; $r = 0.08$; $T - t = 180$ days; $X = \$100$

is an option combination that employs options with different expiration dates but a common underlying stock. These spreads all have a horizon that terminates by the time the near-expiration option expires.

By using calendar spreads, a trader can adopt speculative strategies designed to exploit beliefs about future stock prices. Bullish and bearish calendar spreads are both possible. The trader can also exploit differential sensitivities to create positions that are neutral with respect to some options parameter, while selecting exposure to others. For example, a trader might create a DELTA-neutral calendar spread that will profit with time decay.

A Calendar Spread with Calls. As a first example of a calendar spread, consider calls $C2$ and $C4$ in Table 5.7. These calls are identical, except call $C2$ expires in 180 days, while $C4$ expires in 90 days. Assume that a trader creates a calendar spread by buying $C2$ and selling $C4$. The cost of this position is: $\$10.30 - \$6.91 = \$3.39$. The sensitivities for the spread are: DELTA $= 0.6151 - 0.5820 = 0.0331$; GAMMA $= 0.0181 - 0.0262 = -0.0081$; THETA $= -12.2607 - (-15.8989) = 3.6382$;

VEGA $= 26.8416 - 19.3905 = 7.4511$; and RHO $= 25.2515 - 12.6464 = 12.6051$. In purchasing this position, the trader has obtained a position that will gain value for an increase in the stock price, volatility, and interest rate. Further, the position will increase in value with time decay.

Figure 5.22 shows the profitability of the calendar spread at the time it is initiated (with 180 days until $C2$ expires and 90 days until $C4$ expires). It also shows the value of the spread in 90 days (when $C4$ expires and $C2$ has 90 days remaining until expiration). We first consider the value profile of the spread at the time it is initiated. At $S = \$100$, the spread is worth 3.39, the price the trader paid. As we have seen, it is essentially DELTA-neutral and GAMMA-neutral, with a relatively low sensitivity to the standard deviation and the interest rate. The spread does have a positive THETA, however, indicating that time decay will increase the value of the position.

This positive time decay is also shown in Figure 5.22, because the figure shows the profitability of the position in 90 days, when $C4$ expires. If the stock price is at 100, $C4$ will expire worthless, but $C2$ will be worth 6.91. Therefore, the price of the spread will rise from 3.39 to

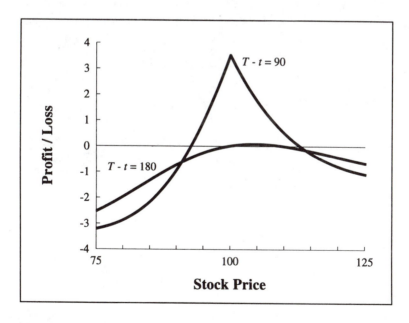

FIGURE 5.22 The Value of a Calendar Spread with Calls as a Function of the Stock Price $r = 0.08$; $T_1 - t = 180$ days; $T_2 - t = 90$ days; $X_1 = X_2 = \$100$

$6.91 over 90 days if the stock price does not change. This increase in profits is due strictly to time decay. Therefore, this type of calendar spread with calls is essentially an attempt to take advantage of time decay.

A Calendar Spread with Puts. Consider the spread in which a trader buys a put with a distant expiration and sells a put with a nearby expiration. We illustrate this spread by considering puts P2 and P4 from Table 5.7. The trader buys P2 for $6.44 and sells put P4 for $4.95, for a total cost of $1.49.

The sensitivities for the spread are: DELTA $= -0.3849 - (-0.4180) = 0.0331$; GAMMA $= 0.0181 - 0.0262 = -0.0081$; THETA $= -4.5701 - (-8.0552) = 3.4851$; VEGA $= 26.8416 - 19.3905 = 7.4511$; and RHO $= -22.1559 - (-11.5295) = -10.6264$. The most important features of this spread are its low DELTA and its significantly positive THETA. The position is not very sensitive to changes in stock prices, but it should appreciate with time decay. Figure 5.23 shows the profitability of this spread as a function of the stock price at the time it is initiated (when P2 has 180 days until expiration and P4

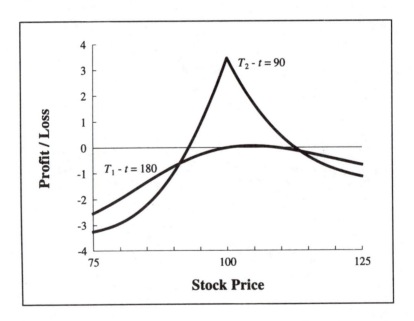

FIGURE 5.23 The Value of a Calendar Spread with Puts as a Function of the Stock Price $r = 0.08$; $T_1 - t = 180$ days; $T_2 - t = 90$ days; $X_1 = X_2 = \$100$

has 90 days until expiration). The figure also shows the profitability of the spread at the expiration date of the nearby put. Notice that this graph is almost (but not quite) identical to Figure 5.22. Implementing a calendar spread with puts or calls gives virtually the same profit and loss profile. If the stock price remains constant at $S = \$100$, the value of the spread will rise from $1.49 to $4.95 over the 90 days until $P4$ expires. Thus, this calendar spread with puts is essentially an attempt to exploit time decay.

SUMMARY

This chapter has explored the sensitivity of options prices to the key parameters that determine the price of an option—the stock price, the standard deviation of the stock's returns, the interest rate, and the time remaining until expiration. We explored these measures within the context of the Merton model, and showed that the Merton model embraces the Black–Scholes model. Given a knowledge of these sensitivities, a trader can use options more effectively, both for hedging and for speculating.

We have seen that DELTA measures the sensitivity of the price of an option to the price of the underlying stock. GAMMA measures the tendency for DELTA to change as the stock price changes, providing a measure of a second order for the key sensitivity DELTA. VEGA gauges the sensitivity of an option's price to the volatility of the underlying stock, while RHO measures the sensitivity of the option price to the interest rate. Finally, THETA measures the sensitivity of the option price to the time to expiration of the option.

By combining options with the underlying stock, or by combining options into portfolios, the trader can create positions with exactly the desired risk exposures. For example, we saw that a trader could use a stock and a call to create a portfolio that is DELTA-neutral. A DELTA-neutral portfolio does not change in value as the stock price changes infinitesimally. We also saw how to use two options in conjunction with a stock to make a portfolio both DELTA-neutral and GAMMA-neutral.

In many instances, a trader will seek exposure to one or more of the options parameters as a speculative technique. For example, we saw how traders can use straddles to accept exposure to volatility while minimizing exposure to changes in the stock price. Such a strategy is essentially a bet on increasing volatility, if the trader buys a straddle. We also observed that strangles created with different pairs of exercise prices could have substantially different DELTAs, even when all other factors are equal. A speculator interested in making money is well advised to master these relationships. A hedger needs to know how a given position responds to changing parameters to understand a hedge completely and to create more effective hedges. Given a knowledge of these sensitivities, a speculator or a hedger can understand the full spectrum of risk entailed by a position.

REVIEW QUESTIONS

1. Consider Call A, with: $X = \$70$; $r = 0.06$; $T - t = 90$ days; $\sigma = 0.4$; and $S = \$60$. Compute the price, DELTA, GAMMA, THETA, VEGA, and RHO for this call.
2. Consider Put A, with: $X = \$70$; $r = 0.06$; $T - t = 90$ days; $\sigma = 0.4$; and $S = \$60$. Compute the price, DELTA, GAMMA, THETA, VEGA, and RHO for this call.
3. Consider a straddle comprised of Call A and Put A. Compute the price, DELTA, GAMMA, THETA, VEGA, and RHO for this straddle.
4. Consider Call A. Assuming the current stock price is $60, create a DELTA-neutral portfolio consisting of a short position of one call and the necessary number of shares. What is the value of this portfolio for a sudden change in the stock price to $55 or $65?
5. Consider Call A and Put A from above. Assume that you create a portfolio that is short one call and long one put. What is the DELTA of this portfolio? Can you find the DELTA without computing? Explain. Assume that a share of stock is added to the short call/long put portfolio. What is the DELTA of the entire position?
6. What is the GAMMA of a share of stock if the stock price is $55 and a call on the stock with $X = \$50$ has a price $c = \$7$ while a put with $X = \$50$ has a price $p = \$4$? Explain.
7. Consider Call B written on the same stock as Call A with: $X = \$50$; $r = 0.06$; $T - t = 90$ days; $\sigma = 0.4$; and $S = \$60$. Form a bull spread with calls from these two instruments. What is the price of the spread? What is its DELTA? What will the price of the spread be at expiration if the terminal stock price is $60? From this information, can you tell whether THETA is positive or negative for the spread? Explain.
8. Consider again the sample options, $C2$ and $P2$, of the chapter discussion as given in Table 5.7. Assume now that the stock pays a continuous dividend of 3 percent per annum. See if you can tell how the sensitivities will differ for the call and a put without computing. Now compute the DELTA, GAMMA, VEGA, THETA, and RHO of the two options if the stock has a dividend.
9. Consider three calls Call C, Call D, and Call E, all written on the same underlying stock. $S = \$80$; $r = 0.07$; $\sigma = 0.2$. For Call C,

$X = \$70$, and $T - t = 90$ days. For Call D, $X = \$75$, and $T - t = 90$ days. For Call E, $X = \$80$, and $T - t = 120$ days. Compute the price, DELTA, and GAMMA for each of these calls. Using Calls C and D, create a DELTA-neutral portfolio assuming that the position is long one Call C. Now use calls C, D, and E to form a portfolio that is DELTA-neutral and GAMMA-neutral, again assuming that the portfolio is long one Call C.

NOTE

1. THETA$_p$ could be positive for a put that is deep-in-the-money. For example, if $S = \$50$, $X = \$100$, $r = 0.08$, $\sigma = 0.3$, and $T - t = 180$ days, $p = \$46.1354$, and THETA$_p = 7.6377$. Notice that the put is worth less than $X - S$, because the put is European and the owner cannot exercise. However, if none of the parameters change over the life of the option, the put price must rise to $50 at the expiration date.

6

American Options Pricing

INTRODUCTION

Chapter 4 considered the principles of pricing for European options—those that can be exercised only at the expiration of the option. There we considered the binomial model and saw how it could be extended logically to the Black–Scholes model. Strictly speaking, the Black–Scholes model holds only for European options on non-dividend-paying stocks. However, we saw that it is possible to extend the Black–Scholes model to account for dividends by several adjustment procedures, such as the known dividend adjustment, and Merton's model, which accounts for continuous dividends. In addition, we saw that the binomial model can price options on stocks that pay dividends, either in the form of a proportional dividend or an actual dollar dividend. Therefore, the tools for pricing European options are quite robust. However, all of the models considered in Chapter 4 pertain strictly to European options.

This chapter focuses on American options—those that can be exercised at any time during the option's life. Most options that are publicly traded are American options, so it is important to develop techniques for pricing these instruments. However, the early-exercise feature of American options brings with it substantial complexity. As we will see, there are no general closed-form pricing models for American options that would parallel the Black–Scholes model for European options.

This chapter begins by analyzing the differences between American and European options. It then turns to consider some attempts to estimate the value of American options. Also, we consider a special case in which there is an exact options pricing formula. Later in the chapter, we return to the binomial model and show how it can be used to price American options with a high degree of accuracy.

AMERICAN VERSUS EUROPEAN OPTIONS

Consider two calls or two puts that are just alike in terms of having the same underlying good, the same exercise price, and the same time to expiration, but one option is American and the other is European. In this context, American options are just like European options, except the American option allows the privilege of early exercise. Because of this parallel between the two kinds of options, we analyze American options by contrasting them with the simpler European options that we have already considered, under the assumption that the options are parallel—have the same underlying good, the same exercise price, and the same time until expiration. The difference in price between parallel American and European options must stem from the early exercise feature of the American option. Thus, if we know the price of a European option, we can price the parallel American option by determining the impact of the early exercise privilege. The value of the right to exercise before expiration is the **early exercise premium**. Much of our analysis of American options will concentrate on valuing the early exercise premium.

Because an American option affords every benefit of a parallel European option, plus the potentially valuable benefit of early exercise, we know that, for parallel options:

$$C_t \geq c_t \text{ and } P_t \geq p_t$$

where American options are denoted by uppercase C or P, and European options are indicated by lowercase c or p. While the American option must be worth at least as much as the parallel European option, it may not actually be worth more—the early exercise premium may have no value in some circumstances. In some situations, however, the early exercise premium may be extremely valuable, and the American option can be worth much more than the parallel European option.

American versus European Puts

In Chapter 3, we considered various boundary conditions that limited the arbitrage-free range of options prices. Due to its early exercise feature, an American put can always be converted into its exercise value $X - S_t$. Therefore:

$$P_t \geq X - S_t$$

For a European put we saw in Chapter 3 that:

$$p_t \geq Xe^{-r(T - t)} - S_t$$

The difference in prices of parallel American and European options depends largely on the extent to which the option is in-the-money, the interest rate, and the amount of time remaining until expiration. The early exercise of an American put discards the value of waiting to see how stock prices evolve. On the other hand, by exercising immediately, the owner of an American put captures the exercise value, $X - S_t$, and can invest those proceeds from the time of exercise until the expiration date of the option. The greater this amount of time, and the higher the interest rate, the greater the incentive for early exercise.

To illustrate this idea consider a European put option with an exercise price of $100 and 180 days until expiration. The underlying stock has a standard deviation of 0.1 and the risk-free rate is 10 percent. If the stock price is $100, the European put is worth $0.9749, well above its immediate exercise value of zero. However, if the stock price is $85, the European put is worth $10.33, well below $X - S_t = \$15$. With a stock price of $85, we know that the parallel American put would be worth at least $15. Figure 6.1 graphs the value of this European put and the quantity $X - S_t$ for various stock prices. As the graph shows, for stock prices near $85, the value of the European put approaches its lower bound of $Xe^{-r(T-t)} - S_t$ and changes almost 1:1 for changes in the stock price. Figure 6.1 suggests why American puts can be worth considerably more than their parallel European puts—the American put gives its owner the right to capture the exercise value immediately. With lower interest rates or a shorter time to expiration, the difference between $X - S_t$ would be lower relative to the value of the European put. For example, for this option with a stock price of $85 and only 20 days until expiration, the European put would be worth $14.45, much closer to the exercise value of $15.

Notice that this substantial difference in the value of American and European puts arises without any consideration of dividends, because the stock considered in our previous example had no dividends. As Figure 6.1 shows, the difference between $X - S_t$ and the value of a European put is larger when the put is deep-in-the-money. For a put, large dividends reduce the value of the underlying stock substantially and tend to push

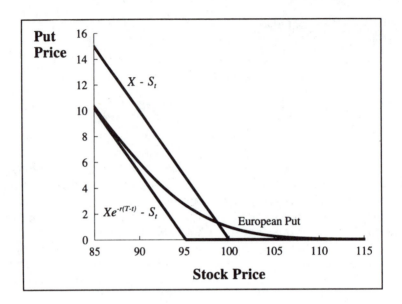

FIGURE 6.1 The Boundary Space for European and American Puts

a put deeper into-the-money. Thus, dividends can also increase the difference in value between European and American puts.

For an American put on a dividend-paying stock, the optimal time to exercise is generally immediately after a dividend payment. Certainly, exercising just before a dividend payment would not make sense; it would be much better to wait for the dividend payment to reduce the stock price and push the put further into-the-money.

In this discussion of early exercise of American puts, the critical point to realize is that a substantial difference between European and American puts can arise even when there are no dividends. Further, it can be quite rational to exercise an American put before expiration on a non-dividend-paying stock. Later in this chapter, we will see exactly when it is rational to exercise an American put before expiration.

American versus European Calls

In understanding the differences between American and European calls, we begin with the simpler situation in which the underlying stock pays no dividends. For calls on a non-dividend-paying stock, early exercise is never rational, and the price of an American and European call will be the same.

In Chapter 3, we explored boundary conditions for European call options and showed that before expiration the call must be worth at least as much as the stock price minus the present value of the exercise price. That is:

$$c_t \geq S_t - Xe^{-r(T - t)}$$

The immediate exercise value of a call is only $S_t - X$. As long as there is some time remaining until expiration and the interest rate is not zero, the European call will be worth more than the immediate exercise value.

Relative to its parallel European call, an American call gives benefits from the right to exercise early. However, the boundary condition on the call shows that early exercise is never desirable if the underlying stock pays no dividend. Therefore, the right to exercise early that is inherent in the American call can have no value, and for calls on a non-dividend-paying stock, the price of an American call is the same as the price of a parallel European call.

We now consider the importance of dividends on call values. If the underlying stock pays a dividend, it can be rational to exercise early, and an American call can be worth more than its parallel European call. We emphasize this point by considering a radical situation. Assume that a stock trades for $80 and the firm has announced that it will pay a liquidating dividend of $80 one minute before the options on this stock expire. Assume that American and European calls on this share have an exercise price of $60 and the present time is two minutes before expiration. (The time is just before expiration in this example so that we can ignore the time value of money.) What would be the value of the American and European calls?

For the owner of the American call, the strategy is clear. The owner should exercise the option immediately, paying the exercise price of $60 and receiving the liquidating dividend of $80. This gives a cash flow of +$20, so the value of the American call must be $20. The European call cannot be exercised until expiration. But, under the terms of this example, the stock will be worth zero at the expiration of the option due to the payment of the liquidating dividend one minute before expiration. Therefore, the European call must be worth zero. Another way to see that the European call is worth zero is from the adjustment for known dividends, discussed in Chapter 4. There we saw that one could adjust the stock price by subtracting from the stock price the present value of all dividends to be paid during the life of the option. The Black–Scholes model could then be applied as usual if we substituted this dividend-adjusted stock price for the current stock price as an input to the model. In our present example, we would subtract the $80 dividend from the $80 stock price, giving an adjusted stock price of zero. Because the call is at expiration, it will be worth the maximum of zero or the adjusted stock price minus the exercise price. Therefore, the European call will be worth zero in the extreme circumstance we are considering.

In less extreme circumstances—when the dividend is smaller relative to the value of the stock and when there is more time remaining until expiration—it can still be rational to exercise before expiration. The decision to exercise early depends mainly on the amount of the dividend, the interest rate, and the time remaining until expiration. Our extreme example shows a general principle about early exercise. If there is to be early exercise of a call, it should occur immediately before a dividend payment. Later in this chapter, we will explore more fully the conditions that lead to the early exercise of calls. We now turn to models for pricing American options.

PSEUDO-AMERICAN CALL OPTION PRICING

The **Pseudo-American Call Option Pricing Model** was created by Fischer Black.[1] It does not provide an exact pricing technique for American calls, but provides an estimated call price that draws on the intuitions of the Black–Scholes model. Later we explore more exact methods for pricing American calls, but the pseudo-American model is important because it clearly shows the factors that lead to early exercise, and it highlights the differences between European and American calls. Essentially, the valuation technique requires four steps.

1. From the current stock price, subtract the present value of all dividends that will be paid before the option expires. So far, this is the same procedure we followed for the known dividend adjustment for European calls.
2. For each dividend date, reduce the exercise price by the present value of all dividends yet to be paid, including the dividend that is about to go ex-dividend.
3. Taking each dividend date and the actual expiration date of the option as potential expiration dates, compute the value of a European call using the adjusted stock and exercise prices.
4. Select the highest of these European call values as the estimate of the value of the American call.

Each step has a clear rationale. In the first step, we adjust the stock price to reflect its approximate value after it pays the dividends. In the second step, we effectively add back the value of dividends to be received from the stock if we exercise. This is accomplished by reducing the liability of the exercise price by the present value of the dividends we will capture if we exercise. In the third step, we evaluate different exercise decisions. If we exercise, we will do so just before a dividend payment to capture the dividend from the stock. Thus, in the third step we consider the payoffs from each potential exercise date. Finally, in the fourth step, we compare the different payoffs associated with each exercise strategy that we computed in the third step. Assuming that we plan to follow the best exercise strategy, we approximate the current American call price as the highest of these computed European call prices.

As an example, consider the following data.

$$S_t = \$60$$
$$X = \$60$$
$$T - t = 180 \text{ days}$$
$$r = 0.09$$
$$\sigma = 0.2$$
$$D_1 = \$2, \text{ to be paid in 60 days}$$
$$D_2 = \$2, \text{ to be paid in 150 days}$$

What is the pseudo-American call worth? The present value of the dividends is:

$$D_1 e^{-rt} + D_2 e^{-rt} = \$2e^{-(0.09)(60/365)} + \$2e^{-(0.09)(150/365)} = \$3.90$$

We subtract this present value from the stock price, so we use $56.10 as our stock price in all subsequent calculations. We will use this adjusted stock price to compute call values, assuming the option expires at three different times: the actual expiration date, the date of the last dividend, and the date of the first dividend. Three inputs remain constant for each computation: $S = \$56.10$, $r = 0.09$, and $\sigma = 0.2$. The time until expiration will vary, and we must adjust the exercise price for different dividend amounts.

We begin with the actual expiration date. Applying the Black–Scholes model with $T - t = 180$ days and $X = \$60$ gives a call value of $2.57. (This is the same as the known dividend adjustment for European calls discussed in Chapter 4.) Next, we deal with each dividend date, starting with the final dividend. The dividend is just about to be paid, so we adjust the exercise price by subtracting $2. Thus, for $X = \$58$ and $T - t = 150$ days, the call value is $2.97. Next, we consider the date of the first dividend. The present value of the dividends at that time consists of the dividend that is just about to be paid, $2, plus the present value of the second dividend that will be paid in 90 days, $2e^{-(0.09)(90/365)} = $1.96. Together, these dividends have a present value of $3.96, so we adjust the exercise price to $56.04. Therefore, for $X = \$56.04$ and $T - t = 60$ days, the call price is $2.28.

Now we have three estimated call prices corresponding to two dividend dates and the actual expiration date of the option. The estimates are $2.28 for the first dividend date, $2.97 for the second date, and $2.57 for the actual expiration date. Therefore, we take the largest value, $2.97, as the estimate of the pseudo-American call value. According to Whaley, the average error for this pseudo-American model is about 1.5 percent.[2]

The strategy behind the pseudo-American options technique is to realize that an American call on a dividend-paying stock can be analyzed as consisting of a series of options. Given that early exercise is only optimal just prior to a dividend payment, we may think of the American call as consisting of a portfolio of European options that expire just before each dividend and at the actual exercise date. In the pseudo-American technique, we evaluate each of those European options, and treat the American option as being worth the maximum of all of the European options.

EXACT AMERICAN CALL OPTION PRICING

In general, there is no closed-form solution to the value of an American call option on a dividend-paying stock. However, an exact pricing formula is possible in one special case. It is possible to compute the exact price for an option on a stock that pays a single dividend during the life of the option.[3] The model is also known as the **Compound Option Model**.

As discussed in the previous section on the pseudo-American model, an American call option really consists of a series of options that expire just before the various dividend dates and at the actual expiration of the option. We now focus on the situation when there is just one dividend between the present and the expiration date of the option, time T. We assume that the dividend occurs at time t_1. The time line in Figure 6.2 shows the decision points that we must consider. As t_1 approaches, the owner of the call must decide whether to exercise. If she exercises, she does so the instant before t_1 and receives the stock with dividends and pays the exercise price. If she does not exercise, the stock pays the dividend and she continues to hold a call on the stock, now without the dividend. The instant after the dividend payment occurs, the call is effectively a European call, because there are no more dividend payments

FIGURE 6.2 Decision Points for Options on a Dividend-Paying Stock

and early exercise on a European call is never rational. Letting S_1 be the stock price just after the dividend, D_1, is paid, and letting C_1 be the call price just after the dividend is paid, her choice is:

Exercise: Receive stock with dividend; pay the exercise price.
$$S_1 + D_1 - X$$

Don't Exercise: Own call on the stock with the stock's value reduced by the dividend amount.
$$C_1$$

Considering the American call before the dividend date, we can see that it is really a compound option, or an option on an option. It is an option on an option because she has the option to refrain from exercising and to own a European option.

The exercise decision as t_1 approaches depends principally on the stock price. If the stock reaches some critical level, the owner should exercise. If it is below that level, the call owner will be better off not exercising and owning the resulting (effectively European) call. The critical stock price, S^*, is the stock price at which the owner is indifferent about the exercise decision, and the owner will be indifferent if the exercise decision leaves her wealth unchanged. The critical stock price is the stock price that makes the two outcomes equal:

$$S^* + D_1 - X = C_1 \qquad\qquad 6.1$$

For example, assume that the dividend date t_1 is at hand and that 90 days remain until the option expires. The exercise price is \$100, the standard deviation of the stock is 0.2, the risk-free rate is 10 percent, and the dividend that is to be paid is \$5. If the stock price immediately after the dividend is paid is $100.67, the call option is worth $5.67. For these data, $S^* = \$100.67$, because:

$$\$100.67 + \$5.00 - \$100.00 = \$5.67$$

If the stock price is higher than $100.67 the instant before t_1, the call owner should exercise. If the stock price is less than $100.67, she should not exercise.

We now turn to the valuation of the American call before the dividend date. In this case, the value of the call is:

$$
\begin{aligned}
C_t = {} & (S - D_1 e^{-r(t_1-t)})\, N(b_1) - (X - D_1)e^{-r(t_1-t)}\, N(b_2) \\
& + (S - D_1 e^{-r(t_1-t)})\, N_2\left(a_1;\, -b_1;\, -\sqrt{\frac{t_1 - t}{T - t}}\right) \\
& - Xe^{-r(T - t)}\, N_2\left(a_1;\, -b_1;\, -\sqrt{\frac{t_1 - t}{T - t}}\right)
\end{aligned}
\qquad 6.2
$$

where:

$$a_1 = \frac{\ln\left(\dfrac{S - D_1\, e^{-r(t_1-t)}}{X}\right) + (r + 0.5\,\sigma^2)(T - t)}{\sigma\,\sqrt{T - t}}$$

$$a_2 = a_1 - \sigma\sqrt{T - t}$$

$$b_1 = \frac{\ln\left(\dfrac{S - D_1\, e^{-r(t_1-t)}}{S^*}\right) + (r + 0.5\,\sigma^2)(t_1 - t)}{\sigma\,\sqrt{T_1 - t}}$$

$$b_2 = b_1 - \sigma\sqrt{t_1 - t}$$

The function $N_2(a;\, b;\, \rho)$ is the standardized cumulative bivariate normal distribution. For two variables, x and y, that are distributed according to the standardized bivariate normal function, and have a correlation of ρ, $N_2(a;\, b;\, \rho)$ is the probability that $x \leq a$ and that $y \leq b$. N_2 is like the standard normal function used in the Black–Scholes model, except it takes into account two variables that are correlated. Considered singly, variables x and y are distributed normally with a mean of zero and a standard deviation of 1.0. Assume for the moment that $a = 0$, $b = 0$, and the correlation between x and y is zero, so $\rho = 0$. In that case, N_2 would give the probability of both x and y being less than or equal to zero. Considered alone, the chance that $x \leq 0$ is 50 percent, and the same is true of y considered by itself. Because we assume that the correlation between the two is zero, the joint probability of both x and y being less than 0 is just the product of the two individual probabilities, or 25 percent.

We now turn to a close examination of the formula, which bears close similarities to the Black–Scholes model. At time t, the value of the call must equal the present value of the expected payoffs on the option. We have already seen that these are somewhat complex. First, at the dividend date, if the stock price exceeds the critical stock price, the call owner will exercise. In that case the payoff is the stock with dividend minus the exercise price, and this payoff occurs at t_1. If the stock price is less than the critical price at t_1, she will not exercise. The payoffs from the option then become either zero, if the exercise price equals or exceeds the stock price at expiration, or the stock price less the exercise price, if the stock price exceeds the exercise price at expiration. In the exact American call pricing formula the cumulative normal (N) and bivariate cumulative normal (N_2) express various probabilities of certain stock price outcomes. These probabilities give different weights to possible outcomes from the option investment. For example, the term:

$$N_2 \left(a_2; -b_2; -\sqrt{\frac{t_1 - t}{T - t}} \right) \qquad 6.3$$

measures the probability that $S^* + D_1 \leq S_t$ and that $S_T \geq X$. This probability would be associated with the payoff that arises when the owner does not exercise the option at the dividend date, but the option is in-the-money at expiration. Thus, without exploring all of the mathematics, we see that the call price is a function of the payoffs that arise in the various possible circumstances, such as not exercising and having the call finish in the money, coupled with the probability of those circumstances arising.

We now show how to compute the exact value of an American call on a stock with one dividend according to this model. Continuing with our example, we have an American call with an exercise price of \$100 on a stock with a standard deviation of 0.2. The risk-free rate is 10 percent. The stock will pay a \$5 dividend when the option has 90 days remaining until expiration. We will find the price of the call when it has 180 days remaining until expiration and the stock price is $110.

The first step is to compute the value of the stock less the present value of the dividend:

$$S - D_1 e^{-r(t_1 - t)} = \$110 - \$5e^{-0.1(90/365)} = \$105.12$$

Other terms are:

$$a_1 = \frac{\ln\left(\dfrac{110.00 - 4.88}{100.00}\right) + [0.1 + 0.5\,(0.2)\,(0.2)](180/365)}{0.2\,\sqrt{180/365}}$$

$$= \frac{0.0499 + 0.0592}{0.1404} = 0.7771$$

$$a_2 = 0.7771 - 0.2\,\sqrt{180/365} = 0.6367$$

$$b_1 = \frac{\ln\left(\dfrac{110.00 - 4.88}{100.67}\right) + [0.1 + 0.5\,(0.2)\,(0.2)](180/365)}{0.2\,\sqrt{90/365}}$$

$$= \frac{0.0433 + 0.0296}{0.0993} = 0.7341$$

$$b_2 = 0.7341 - 0.2\,\sqrt{90/365} = 0.6348$$

$$\sqrt{\frac{t_1 - t}{T - t}} = \sqrt{\frac{90}{180}} = 0.7071$$

Given these values, we now compute the cumulative normal and cumulative bivariate normal terms.

$$N\,(b_1) = N\,(0.7341) = 0.768556$$
$$N\,(b_2) = N\,(0.6348) = 0.737221$$

$$N_2\left(a_1;\, -b_1;\, -\sqrt{\frac{t_1 - t}{T - t}}\right) = N_2\,(0.7771;\, -0.7341;\, -0.7071) = 0.099098$$

$$N_2\left(a_2;\, -b_2;\, -\sqrt{\frac{t_1 - t}{T - t}}\right) = N_2\,(0.6367;\, -0.6348;\, -0.7071) = 0.101320$$

We now compute the value of the American call as:

$$
\begin{aligned}
C_t &= (105.12)(0.768556) + (105.12)(0.099098) \\
&\quad - 100\, e^{-0.1(180/365)}(0.101320) - (100.00 - \\
&\quad 5.00)e^{-0.1(90/365)}(0.737221) \\
&= 80.79 + 10.42 - 9.64 - 68.33 \\
&= \$13.24
\end{aligned}
$$

Thus, with 180 days until expiration, this American call should be worth $13.24. This compares with a pseudo-American value in the same circumstances of $12.91.

Strictly speaking, this model holds only for an American call on a stock paying a single dividend before the option's expiration date. However, when there is more than one dividend, exercise is normally rational only for the final dividend. Therefore, we can use the exact pricing model if we subtract the present value of all dividends other than the final one from the stock price and then use the adjusted stock price in all computations. (Notice that this parallels the logic of the known dividend adjustment to the Black–Scholes model.)

As we have just noted, it is only for this special case of a call with one dividend that we can compute an exact American option price. For all other circumstances, we must use a variety of approximation techniques. Fortunately, these techniques work very well, and we turn now to a consideration of them.

ANALYTICAL APPROXIMATIONS OF AMERICAN OPTIONS PRICES

In Chapter 4, we considered the Merton model, which extended the Black–Scholes model to European options on stocks that pay a continuous dividend at a constant rate. The analytical approximations that we now consider apply to American options on an underlying instrument that pays a continuous dividend at a constant rate. The Merton model provides a closed-form solution to the problem of European options on stocks with continuous dividends. For American options, no closed-form solutions are available. The analytical approximations for American options considered in this section are extremely accurate and computationally inexpensive.

To understand the incentive for early exercise of an option on a stock with a continuous dividend, consider again the Merton model developed in Chapter 4.

$$
c_t^M = Se^{-\delta(T - t)}N(d_1^M) - Xe^{-r(T - t)}N(d_2^M)
$$

The difference in value between this European option and a parallel American option arises from the potential benefits of early exercise. Thus, we focus on an option that is deep-in-the-money. In such a situation, d_1^M will be large, and d_2^M will be large as well. Consequently, $N(d_1^M)$ and $N(d_2^M)$ will approach 1.0. In the limit then, for an option that is extremely deep in-the-money, Merton's model approaches:

$$c_t = S_t\, e^{-\delta(T - t)} - Xe^{-r\,(T - t)}$$

By contrast, an American option would have to be worth at least its immediately available exercisable proceeds:

$$C_t \geq S_t - X$$

If a trader owns the American option, she has a choice between these two quantities. Which is preferable depends upon how deep-in-the-money the option is, the dividend rate on the stock, δ, the interest rate, r, and the time remaining until the option expires, $T - t$. If the stock price reaches a critical level, S^*, such that:

$$S_t^* - X = c(S^*,\, X,\, T - t) + \text{early exercise premium} \qquad 6.4$$

the owner of an American option is indifferent about exercising. If the stock price exceeds S^* she will exercise immediately to capture the exercise proceeds $S_t - X$. If the stock price is below S^* she will not exercise. Figure 6.3 presents a graph of these relationships. Notice that the European call in Figure 6.3 can be worth less than $S_t - X$, because of the dividend. (As we noted above, a deep-in-the-money European call will tend to its lower bound of $S_t e^{-\delta(T - t)} - Xe^{-r(T - t)}$.) At the critical stock price, S^*, the European call is worth exactly $S^* - X$. For any stock price greater than S^*, the European call will be worth less than the exercisable proceeds for the American call. This explains why the owner of the American call is indifferent about exercise at a stock price of S^*; at that stock price the American and European calls are worth the same—$S^* - X$. For higher stock prices, the value of the European call falls below that of the American, and the value of the American call becomes equal to its exercisable proceeds. Thus, the owner of the American call should exercise to capture the quantity $S_t - X$. Those funds can then be invested from the exercise date to the expiration date to earn a return that will be lost if the option is not exercised.

FIGURE 6.3 American Calls and the Incentive for Early Exercise

A similar argument applies to American put options. As the stock price falls well below the exercise price, there comes a point at which:

$$X - S^{**} = p(S^{**}, X, T - t) + \text{early exercise premium} \qquad 6.5$$

S^{**} is the critical stock price for an American put. If the stock price falls below S^{**}, the American put should be exercised to capture the exercised proceeds of $X - S_t$. Figure 6.4 presents a graph of this relationship for the European and American put. As the graph shows, for any stock price less than S^{**}, the American put should be exercised immediately.

While a complete discussion of the mathematics is beyond the scope of this text, we present the formulas for an analytic approximation of the American call and put options, and we discuss the computation of call and put values under the terms of the model.

The analytic approximation for an American call is:

$$\begin{aligned} C_t &= c_t + A_2\left(\frac{S_t}{S^*}\right)^{q_2} && \text{if } S_t < S^* \\ &= S_t - X && \text{if } S_t \geq S^* \end{aligned} \qquad 6.6$$

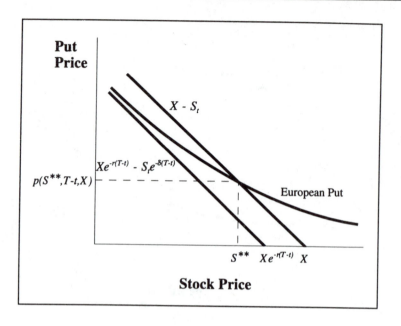

FIGURE 6.4 American Puts and the Incentive for Early Exercise

where:

$$A_2 = \frac{S^* \left[1 - e^{-\delta(T - t)} N(d_1)\right]}{q_2}$$

and S^* is the solution to:

$$S^* - X = c_t(S^*, X, T - t) + \{1 - e^{-\delta(T - t)} N(d_1)\}(S^*/q_2) \quad 6.7$$

$N(d_1)$ and $p(S^*, X, T - t)$ are evaluated at S^*. To find S^* requires an iterative search for the value that makes the equation balance. Other terms are:

$$q_2 = \frac{1 - n + \sqrt{(n - 1)^2 + 4k}}{2}$$

$$n = \frac{2(r - \delta)}{\sigma^2}, \quad k = \frac{2r}{\sigma^2(1 - e^{-r(T - t)})}$$

For an American put, the analytic approximation is:

$$P_t = p_t + A_1 \left(\frac{S_t}{S^{**}}\right)^{q_1} \quad \text{if } S_t > S^{**}$$
$$= X - S_t \qquad\qquad \text{if } S_t \leq S^{**}$$

6.8

where:

$$A_1 = \frac{S^{**}\,[1 - e^{-\delta(T - t)}N(-d_1)]}{q_1}$$

$$q_1 = \frac{1 - n - \sqrt{(n - 1)^2 + 4k}}{2}$$

S^{**} is found by an iterative search to make the following equation hold:

$$X - S^{**} = p_t(S^{**}, X, T - t) - [1 - e^{-\delta(T - t)}N(-d_1)](S^{**}/q_1) \quad 6.9$$

$N(-d_1)$ and $p_t(S^{**}, X, T - t)$ are evaluated at the critical stock price S^{**}.

To illustrate the application of this model, consider an American call option on an underlying stock that is currently priced at $60, has a standard deviation of 0.2, and pays a continuous dividend of 13.75 percent. The call has a striking price of $60 and 180 days until expiration. The risk-free rate is 9 percent. In Chapter 4, we illustrated the Merton model with a European call having the same terms and found that the price of the European call was $2.5557.

The first step in computing the value of this American call is to find the value of the intermediate terms n, k, and q_2. They are:

$$n = \frac{2(0.09 - 0.1375)}{(0.2)(0.2)} = -2.375$$

$$k = \frac{2(.09)}{(0.2)(0.2)\left[1 - e^{-0.09\left(\frac{180}{365}\right)}\right]} = 103.6555$$

$$q_2 = \frac{1 - (-2.375) + \sqrt{(-2.375 - 1)^2 + 4(103.6555)}}{2} = 12.007537$$

We next search for the critical stock price, S^*, and find that $S^* = 70.2336$. (This search must be done by trial-and-error until the correct one is discovered.) If the actual stock price equaled the critical price, the European call would be worth \$9.0152. Then, d_1 and $N(d_1)$, computed at that critical stock price of \$70.2336, would be 1.024716 and 0.847251, respectively. Based on these values, we calculate A_2 as:

$$A_2 = \frac{70.2336\left[1 - e^{-0.1375\left(\frac{180}{365}\right)} 0.847251\right]}{12.007537} = 1.218344$$

We can now compute the American call price. Because the current stock price of \$60 lies below the critical price of \$70.2336, the value of the American call is:

$$C_t = 2.5557 + 1.218344\left(\frac{60}{70.2336}\right)^{12.007537}$$
$$= 2.5557 + 0.183878 = 2.7395$$

Thus, the early exercise premium is \$0.18. Because this computation involves an iterative search for S^*, it is quite tedious to perform without a computer.

THE BINOMIAL MODEL AND AMERICAN OPTIONS PRICES

Thus far in this chapter, we have considered various options pricing models for finding the value of American options on dividend-paying stocks. As we have seen, there is no general exact solution for this problem. In fact, only for the case of an American call on a stock paying a single dividend during the option's life is it possible to compute an exact price. In all other circumstances, we must rely on estimation techniques. The analytic approximation method we have studied in this chapter applies only to continuous dividends. With stocks typically paying discrete dividends, the need for other estimation techniques is particularly important.

The binomial model is particularly important for American options because it applies to both American calls and puts on stocks with all kinds of dividend payments. These include the case of no dividends, continuous dividends, known dividend yields, and known dollar dividends. There is a common strategy for applying the binomial model that applies to all types of dividend patterns, and we begin our discussion by analyzing the underlying strategy for the binomial model for American options. We then consider each of the different dividend strategies in turn.

No Dividends

In Chapter 3, we explored the boundary conditions on the pricing of European options on stocks paying no dividends. For nondividend stocks we saw that it can never be optimal to exercise a call before expiration. This means that the American call and the European call on a nondividend stock must have the same value. Therefore, for the case of a call on a nondividend stock we can price the American call as if it were a European call. It can often be advantageous to exercise puts on nondividend stocks, so the value of European and American puts can differ substantially. We illustrate this point for an American put and explicate the basic strategy for applying the binomial model to American options.

The Basic Strategy

In Chapter 4, we explored the binomial model for European options on stocks with and without dividends. For European options on nondividend stocks, we derived the possible stock prices at expiration and determined the value of the option (call or put) at expiration from our no-arbitrage condition. We then computed the value of an option one period before expiration as the expected value of the option at expiration discounted for one period. We continued this strategy, working through the binomial lattice, until we found the value of the option at the current time.

For options on stocks with dividends, we applied the binomial model by creating a lattice for the stock that reflected the timing and amount of dividend payments that the stock would make. These adjustments affected the distribution of possible stock values at the expiration date. We then computed the option values in the usual way by working from the exercise date back to the present.

To apply the binomial model for American options, we follow the same basic valuation strategy as for European options. There is, however, one important difference. For the option lattice for an American option, the option value is set equal to the maximum of:

1. The expected option value in one period discounted for one period at the risk-free rate.

2. The immediate exercise value of the option, $S_t - X$ for a call, or $X - S_t$ for a put.

Except for this treatment of each node in the lattice for an American option, the binomial model for an American option is applied in exactly the same way as it is for a European option.

We illustrate this technique by considering an American put on a stock that pays no dividend. We assume the following data:

$$S_t = \$80$$
$$X = \$75$$
$$r = 0.07$$
$$\sigma = 0.3$$
$$T = 120 \text{ days}$$

Assuming a three-period binomial model, a single period is 40 days or 0.1096 years. This gives a discount factor of 0.9924 per period, and the following parameter values:

$$U = 1.1044$$
$$D = 0.9055$$
$$\pi_u = 0.5138$$

Figure 6.5 shows the stock price tree consistent with these data. (The careful reader may recall the same example from Figure 4.10.) The upper tree of Figure 6.6 repeats the upper tree from Figure 4.12, which is the

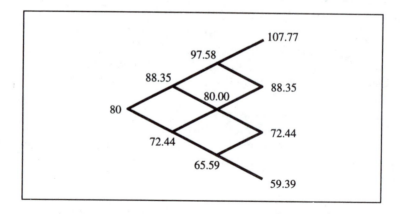

FIGURE 6.5 Three-Period Stock Price Lattice

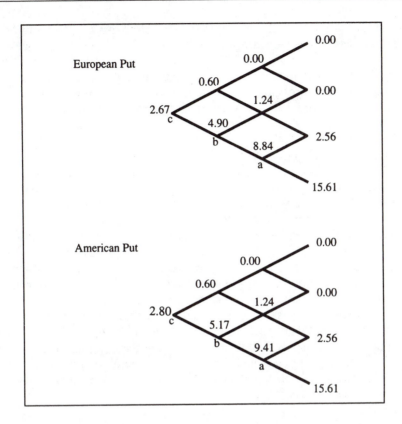

FIGURE 6.6 Three-Period Price Lattices for a European and an American Put

binomial tree for a European put option on this stock. As the tree shows, the value of the European put is $2.67 at node c. The lower tree in Figure 6.6 is the binomial tree for an American put. Aside from the upper tree being for a European put and the lower tree pertaining to an American put, all other circumstances are the same. An examination of the two trees shows that they are identical except for the prices at nodes a, b, and c.

Before turning to the differences at nodes a, b, and c, we first consider why the other nodes are identical. First, consider the nodes at expiration. At expiration, European and American options are identical. Both can be exercised and both have the same payoffs from the exercise decision. Therefore, European and American options at expiration must have the same value. Second, consider a node one period before expiration, such as the middle node of the tree at which the stock price is $80 and both the European and American put prices are $1.24. If the stock price one period prior to expiration is $80, the American put cannot be exercised because the put is out-of-the-money. Therefore, it offers no advantage over the parallel European put. Consequently, the value must be the same.

These reflections lead us to see a condition for an American and a European option to have identical prices at a given node: If the option cannot be exercised at the given node, and if all nodes that can be reached subsequent to the node under consideration have identical prices for American and European options, then the price of the American and European options must be identical at the node in question. We can illustrate this point from the same tree by considering the node two periods before expiration in which the stock price is $88.35 and the value of the put (either European or American) is $0.60. The American put cannot be exercised at that node, because it is out-of-the-money with a stock price of $88.35. Further, all subsequent nodes have identical prices for the American and European puts. Therefore, the price of the European and American puts must be the same at that node.

We now turn to consider those nodes at which prices differ for the European and American put. At node a, the stock price is $65.59, the European put price is $8.84, and the American put price is $9.41. The European put price is just the expected value of the put's expiration values contingent upon the stock's rising or falling. The value at node a for the American put is:

$$P = \text{MAX}(X - S, p) = \text{MAX}(\$75 - \$65.59, \$8.84) = \$9.41$$

If the stock price reaches node a, the holder of an American put should exercise and capture the exercise value of $9.41. This is higher than the present value of the expected payoff at expiration, which is the price of the European put—$8.84. As this example shows, the American put derives its higher value from its right to exercise early when conditions warrant.

At node b, the stock price is $72.44, and the European put is worth $4.90. The owner of the American put could exercise immediately for an exercise value of $75 - $72.44 = $2.56, but this would be foolish. One period later, the put will be worth $1.24 if the stock price rises or $9.41 if the stock price falls. Given that the probability of a stock price rise is 0.5138, the present value of the put's expected value in one period is:

$$[0.5138\,(\$1.24) + 0.4862\,(\$9.41)]e^{-0.07\left(\frac{40}{365}\right)}$$
$$= \$5.21\,(0.9924) = \$5.17$$

The value of the put at node b is therefore:

$$MAX\{\$2.56, \$5.17\} = \$5.17$$

Therefore, at node b, the put should not be exercised, and it is worth $5.17—the present value of the expected put value in one period.

At node c, the present time at which we want to value the option, the same rule applies. The American put cannot be exercised rationally, because it is out-of-the-money with $75 − $80 = −$5. The present value of the expected value of the put in one period is:

$$[0.5138 \, (\$0.60) + 0.4862 \, (\$5.17)]e^{-0.07\left(\frac{40}{365}\right)} = \$2.80$$

The value of the American put at node c, which represents the present time, is:

$$MAX\{-\$5.00, \$2.80\} = \$2.80$$

Because the exercise value (−$5.00) is negative, the value of the American put equals the present value of the expected value in one period ($2.80), and the American put should not be exercised.

This example illustrates the basic principle of applying the binomial model to American options. As we work back through the tree, discounting the next period's expected option values, we must ask at every node whether the immediate exercise value or the computed present value is greater. The value at the node is the maximum of those two quantities. Further, we may note that the stock tree is unaffected by whether the option we are analyzing is an American or a European option. We now consider how to apply the binomial model to American options on dividend-paying stocks.

Continuous Dividends

In Chapter 4, we explored Merton's model, which adjusts the Black–Scholes model to price European options on stocks that pay a continuous dividend. We also showed how to use the binomial model to price European options on stocks that pay continuous dividends. There we saw that the parameters for the binomial model for a stock paying a continuous dividend were:

$$U = e^{\sigma \sqrt{\Delta t}}$$

$$D = \frac{1}{U}$$

$$\pi_U = \frac{e^{(r - \delta)\Delta t} - D}{U - D}$$

6.10

As we have discussed in this chapter, the stock price tree is identical whether we are pricing European or American options. Therefore, these parameters apply to generating the binomial tree of stock prices for American options on stocks paying a continuous dividend. As an examination of these parameters shows, the stock price tree will be identical in both cases. However, the probability of a stock price increase varies inversely with the level of the continuous dividend rate, δ.

To illustrate the binomial model for pricing options on stocks with continuous dividends, consider the following data:

$$S_t = \$60$$
$$X = \$60$$
$$T = 180 \text{ days}$$
$$\sigma = 0.2$$
$$r = 0.09$$

Based on these data, consider a European and an American call option on this stock in the context of a two-period binomial model:

$$U = e^{\sigma \sqrt{\Delta t}} = e^{0.2\sqrt{\frac{90}{365}}} = 1.104412$$

$$D = \frac{1}{U} = 0.905460$$

$$\pi_U = \frac{e^{(r - \delta)\Delta t} - D}{U - D} = \frac{e^{(0.09 - 0.1375)\left(\frac{90}{365}\right)} - 0.905460}{1.104412 - 0.905460} = 0.416663$$

The single-period discount factor is $e^{-0.09(90/365)} = 0.978053$. Figure 6.7 gives the two-period stock price tree for these data, while Figure 6.8 shows the trees for a European and an American call. At expiration, the call will be in-the-money only if the stock price rises twice to a terminal price of $73.18. In this case, both the European and American calls are worth

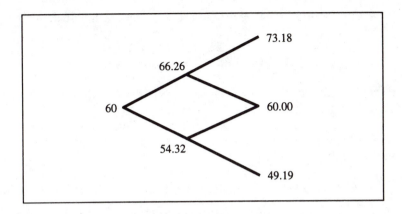

FIGURE 6.7   Two-Period Stock Price Lattice

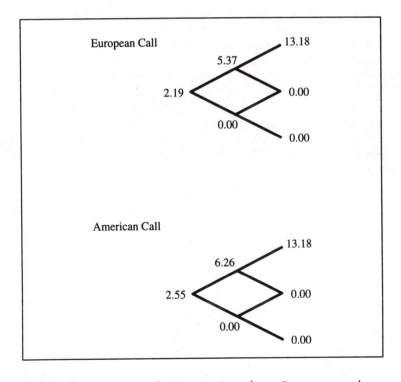

FIGURE 6.8   Two-Period Price Lattices for a European and an American Call

$13.18. One period before expiration, the present value of the expected terminal call value is:

$$\$13.18(0.416663)(0.978053) = \$5.37$$

This is the value of the European call at the node with a stock price of $66.26. For the American call, the same expected value prevails, but the owner of the American call could exercise. The exercise value of the American call is $66.26 − $60 = $6.26. Therefore, the value of the American call is:

$$C = \text{MAX}\{S - X, c\} = \text{MAX}\{\$6.26, \$5.37\} = \$6.26$$

Therefore, if the stock price reaches $66.26 in one period, the holder of the American call should exercise. In terms of the binomial tree for the American call, the value at this node becomes $6.26. At the present time, the present values of the expected call values one period hence are $2.19 for the European call and $2.55 for the American call. Thus, the current price of the European call is $2.19. At the present, the stock price and exercise price are both $60, so the American option cannot be exercised rationally. This means that the current American call price is $2.55, based on a two-period tree. With 200 periods, the European call value is $2.55 and the American call price is $2.73. Table 6.1 shows how the two call prices converge to their true value as the number of periods in the binomial tree ranges from one to 200. For comparison, the Merton model price for the European option is $2.5557 and the American analytic approximation is $2.7395. Thus, the binomial method provides estimates that are extremely close to other model prices that we have explored.

Table 6.1   The Convergence of European and American Call Prices

Number of Periods	European Call	American Call
1	3.3129	3.3129
2	2.1894	2.5530
3	2.8139	2.9399
4	2.3625	2.6380
5	2.7099	2.8517
10	2.4763	2.6909
25	2.5861	2.7554
50	2.5396	2.7216
100	2.5476	2.7256
200	2.5516	2.7275

Known Dividend Yields

In Chapter 4, we considered options on a stock that pays a known dividend yield at a certain date. For example, a stock might pay a dividend equal to 1 percent of its value in 90 days. The dividend payment obviously affects the stock price tree for the binomial model, and the loss of value from the stock will affect the value of calls and puts. This is true for both European and American options. While the existence of the dividend will affect the value of European calls and puts, they do not call for European option owners to make any special decisions, as they cannot exercise even if they wished. For the holder of an American call or put, there is an exercise decision, because the American option owner can exercise immediately before the dividend payment (in the case of a call), exercise immediately after the dividend payment (in the case of a put), or not exercise. While the dividend will affect the stock price tree, we note again that the stock price tree will be identical whether we are considering a European or an American option.

To apply the binomial model for an American call or put, we begin with the terminal stock price and the value of the option at expiration and work from expiration back to the present in the normal way. However, at each node, we must take account of the potential for early exercise. As we have seen, we take early exercise into account by finding the value of a European option at each node and compare this value with the exercise value of the American option. If the exercise value exceeds the European value, the option price at the node should be the exercise value. Otherwise, the price at the node should be the European option price.

To see how to apply the binomial model to compute American options prices on a stock with a known dividend yield, consider the following data. A stock is currently priced at $80 and it will pay a dividend equal to 3 percent of its value in 55 days. The standard deviation of the stock is 0.3, and the risk-free rate is 7 percent. A call option on this stock has 120 days until expiration and an exercise price of $75. Based on these data, and with a three-period binomial model, $\Delta t = 40/365 = 0.1096$. Therefore:

$$U = e^{0.3\sqrt{0.1096}} = 1.1044$$

$$D = \frac{1}{1.1044} = 0.9055$$

$$\pi_U = \frac{1.0077 - 0.9055}{1.1044 - 0.9055} = 0.5138$$

The discounting factor for a single period is $e^{-rΔt} = e^{-0.07(40/365)} = 0.9924$. Figure 6.9 shows the stock price tree for this example. (This same example was considered in Chapter 4 for European calls.) In terms of Figure 6.9, the dividend occurs between time 1 (day 40) and time 2 (day 80). The call owner might exercise at time 1 before the dividend is paid, but if she waits until time 2, the dividend will already be paid, and the dividend's value will be lost from the stock.

Figure 6.10 shows options price trees for European and American calls consistent with the stock price tree of Figure 6.9. At expiration and the period prior to expiration, the European and American call option trees are identical. This is because the exercise value for the American option never exceeds the value of the European call. In the first period, if the stock price rises from $80 to $88.35, the owner of an American call should exercise. We can see the desirability of exercise in this case as follows. At the node with a stock price of $88.35, the present value of the expected value of the call in the next period is $12.94, the value of the European call. With a stock price of $88.35 and an exercise price of $75, the American call can (and should) be exercised for an exercise value of $13.35. Thus, in the tree for the American call, the value at this node is the exercise value of $13.35. This difference in the two trees affects the current value of the European and American calls, which are $7.94 and $8.15, respectively. With 200 periods, the European and American calls are worth $7.61 and $8.04, respectively. The binomial model applies to options on stocks with any number of dividend yields during the life of the option.

For these options, none of the other models we have considered apply. From the valuation date, the dividend amount is uncertain, as it will be

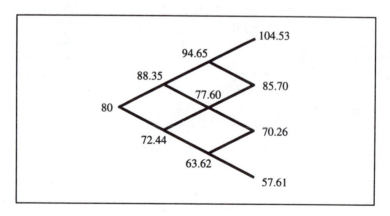

FIGURE 6.9 Three-Period Stock Price Lattice

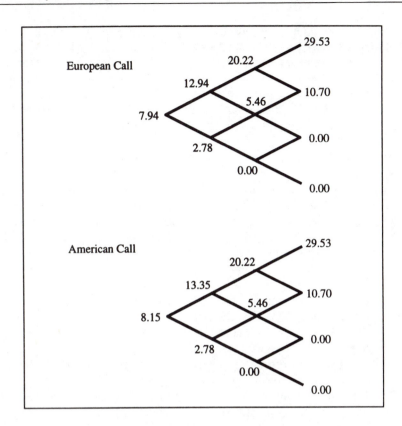

FIGURE 6.10 Three-Period Price Lattices for a European and an American Call

3 percent of whatever stock price prevails in 55 days. Therefore, the exact American options pricing model does not apply. Further, the analytic approximation method for American options does not apply because the dividend is not continuous. For European options, we cannot apply the known dividend adjustment, because the dollar amount of the dividend is unknown. Similarly, we cannot apply the Merton model because the dividend is not continuous. Of all the methods we have studied, only the binomial model can deal with the known dividend yield for an American option.

Known Dollar Dividends

For options on stocks with known dollar dividends, the binomial model can be applied in a manner almost identical to that appropriate for known dividend yields. The first step is to generate the tree describing the potential stock price movements. As we saw in Chapter 4 when we considered the pricing of European options on stocks with known dollar dividends, there can be a problem with the tree failing to recombine after the dividend has been paid. In this situation, the number of nodes can increase dramatically, particularly when there are many periods and several dividends. (For details on why the tree fails to recombine, see Chapter 4.)

We can solve this problem as we did in Chapter 4 by making a simplifying assumption. We assume that the stock price reflects the dividend, which is known with certainty, and all other factors that might affect the stock price, which are uncertain. We then adjust the uncertain component of the stock price for the impending dividends and model the uncertain component of the stock price with the binomial tree adding back the present value of all future dividends at each node. Specifically, we follow these steps:

1. Compute the present value of all dividends to be paid during the life of the option as of the present time $= t$.
2. Subtract this present value from the current stock price to form $S_t' = S_t -$ PV of all dividends.
3. Create the binomial tree by applying the up and down factors in the usual way to the initial stock price S_t'.
4. After generating the tree, add to the stock price at each node the present value of all future dividends to be paid during the life of the option.
5. Compute the option values in the usual way by working through the binomial tree.

These were exactly the steps we used in Chapter 4 to resolve this difficulty.

The application of this procedure to American options is exactly the same as with European options, with one exception. In working through the tree to generate the options price tree, we must compare the present value of next period's expected option value with the exercise value of the option. The option price at the node is the higher of the present value or the exercise value. The computation of the value at a node is exactly the same as in other cases we have already considered, such as the application of the binomial model to options on stocks with known dividend yields.

We illustrate the application of the binomial model to options on stocks with a known dollar dividend by considering a comprehensive example. A stock now trades for $50, has a standard deviation of 0.4, and will pay a dividend of $2 in 90 days. An American call and put on this stock expire in 120 days, and both have an exercise price of $50. The risk-free rate of interest is 9 percent, and we will model the price of the options with a five-period binomial model.

According to the five steps outlined earlier, we begin by subtracting the present value of the dividends to be paid during the life of the option from the current stock price. The present value of the dividend is $1.96, so the adjusted stock price, S', is $48.04. A single period is 24 days, and the discount factor for one period is 0.9941. The parameters for the binomial model with five periods are:

$$\Delta t = \frac{24}{365} = 0.065753 \text{ years}$$

$$U = e^{\sigma \sqrt{\Delta t}} = e^{0.4 \sqrt{0.065753}} = 1.108015$$

$$D = \frac{1}{U} = 0.902515$$

$$\pi_U = \frac{e^{r\Delta t} - D}{U - D} = \frac{e^{0.09(0.065753)} - 0.902515}{1.108015 - 0.902515} = 0.503262$$

The top panel of Figure 6.11 shows the stock price lattice generated with a starting price of $48.04 and the up and down factors shown above. This upper lattice does not reflect the dividend. Having generated this lattice, we account for dividends by adding the present value of all future dividends to be paid during the life of the option to each node. The bottom lattice of Figure 6.11 shows the adjusted stock prices. As the dividend will be paid in 90 days, the dividend falls between the third and fourth periods. This means that for periods 4 and 5, there are no dividends to consider, and the two lattices have identical stock prices in periods 4 and 5. For all periods before the dividend, the stock price at each node is adjusted by adding the present value of the dividend. For example, the node for the second period represents a time that is 48 days from now. At that time, the dividend will be 42 days away, and the present value of the dividend at that point is $1.98. Therefore, if we compare the stock prices in the two lattices for period 2, the prices in the bottom lattice will exceed their counterparts in the upper lattice by $1.98. All other stock prices in periods 1–3 are adjusted similarly. The bottom stock price lattice in Figure 6.11 is the lattice that we will use to compute the option prices.

In Figure 6.12, the upper lattice pertains to the American call, while the lower lattice prices the American put. Some prices are preceded by an asterisk, indicating that the price represents the exercise value of the

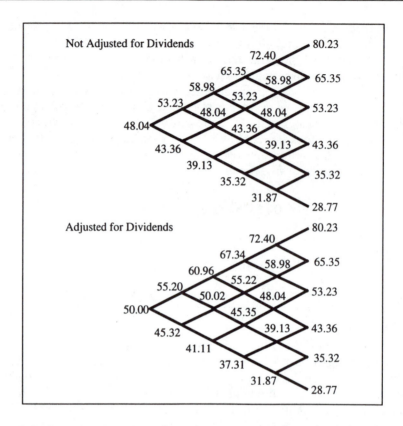

FIGURE 6.11 Five-Period Stock Price Lattices Unadjusted and Adjusted for a Known Dollar Dividend

option at that node. For example, the call lattice has a price of $17.34 in period 4. The present value of the two option values in period 4 is $15.93. However, the stock price at that node is $67.34, implying an exercise value of $17.34. Because the exercise value exceeds $15.93, the call value at that node is $17.34. Working back through the lattice to the present shows an American call value of $4.48 and an American put value of $4.90. With the five-period lattice, the European call and put are worth $4.31 and $4.81, respectively. For the same data, except using a lattice with 200 periods, the American call is worth $4.59, and the American put is $4.78. With a 200-period lattice, the European call and put are $4.17 and $4.66, respectively. We also note that this example can be solved using the exact American call option pricing model, which gives a call price of $4.59, the same as the binomial model with 200 periods.

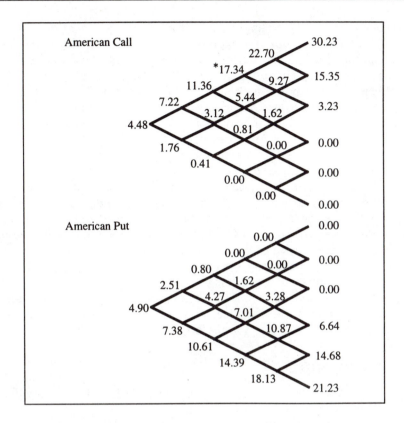

FIGURE 6.12 Five-Period Price Lattices for an American Call and Put on a Stock with a Known Dollar Dividend

SUMMARY

This chapter explored the pricing of American options. We began by reviewing the differences between American and European options. For nondividend stocks, the American and European calls have the same value, as early exercise is never desirable. For puts, however, we showed that there are incentives to early exercise even when there are no dividends. Therefore, the price of an American put can exceed that of a European put even in the absence of dividends. When the underlying stock pays dividends, circumstances can arise in which it would be desirable to exercise a call and a put before expiration, and the prices of American and European options diverge.

The discussion then turned to models for pricing American options, beginning with Black's pseudo-American options pricing model. We then considered the exact pricing model for an American call with a single dividend before the option's expiration. We noted that this is the only situation in which an exact pricing formula exists for American options. In all other pricing situations, we must use approximation techniques.

When the underlying stock pays a continuous dividend, an approximation for American options applies. This analytical approximation is analogous to the Merton model for European options, and it accurately estimates the prices of American calls and puts when the underlying instrument pays a continuous dividend.

Most stocks pay discrete dividends, so the analytical approximation does not apply. Accordingly, we turned to the binomial model and showed how it can apply to American options when the underlying good pays dividends in a variety of different ways. We considered the binomial model for American options when the underlying good pays a continuous dividend, when it pays a known dividend yield, and when it pays a known dollar dividend. In the last two cases, the binomial model can accommodate any number of dividends.

Many of the calculations of this chapter are quite tedious and time-consuming. (Imagine, for instance, the tedium of computing the binomial model price for a lattice of 100 periods.)

REVIEW QUESTIONS

1. Explain why American and European calls on a nondividend stock always have the same value.
2. Explain why American and European puts on a nondividend stock can have different values.
3. Explain the circumstances that might make the early exercise of an American put on a nondividend stock desirable.
4. What factors might make an owner exercise an American call?
5. Do dividends on the underlying stock make the early exercise of an American put more or less likely? Explain.
6. Do dividends on the underlying stock make the early exercise of an American call more or less likely? Explain.
7. Explain the strategy behind the pseudo-American call pricing strategy.
8. Consider a stock with a price of $140 and a standard deviation of 0.4. The stock will pay a dividend of $2 in 40 days and a second dividend of $2 in 130 days. The current risk-free rate of interest is 10 percent. An American call on this stock has an exercise price of $150 and expires in 100 days. What is the price of the call according to the pseudo-American approach?

9. Could the exact American call pricing model be used to price the option in Question 8? Explain.
10. Explain why the exact American call pricing model treats the call as an "option on an option."
11. Explain the idea of a bivariate cumulative standardized normal distribution. What would be the cumulative probability of observing two variables both with a value of zero, assuming that the correlation between them was zero? Explain.
12. In the exact American call pricing model, explain why the model can compute the call price with only one dividend.
13. What is the critical stock price in the exact American call pricing model?
14. Explain how the analytical approximation for American options values is analogous to the Merton model.
15. Explain the role of the critical stock price in the analytic approximation for an American call.
16. Why should an American call owner exercise if the stock price exceeds the critical price?
17. Consider the binomial model for an American call and put on a stock that pays no dividends. The current stock price is $120, and the exercise price for both the put and the call is $110. The standard deviation of the stock returns is 0.4, and the risk-free rate is 10 percent. The options expire in 120 days. Model the price of these options using a four-period tree. Draw the stock tree and the corresponding trees for the call and the put. Explain when, if ever, each option should be exercised. What is the value of a European call in this situation? Can you find the value of the European call without making a separate computation? Explain.
18. Consider the binomial model for an American call and put on a stock whose price is $120. The exercise price for both the put and the call is $110. The standard deviation of the stock returns is 0.4, and the risk-free rate is 10 percent. The options expire in 120 days. The stock will pay a dividend equal to 3 percent of its value in 50 days. Model and compute the price of these options using a four-period tree. Draw the stock tree and the corresponding trees for the call and the put. Explain when, if ever, each option should be exercised.
19. Consider the binomial model for an American call and put on a stock whose price is $120. The exercise price for both the put and the call is $110. The standard deviation of the stock returns is 0.4, and the risk-free rate is 10 percent. The options expire in

120 days. The stock will pay a \$3 dividend in 50 days. Model and compute the price of these options using a four-period tree. Draw the stock tree and the corresponding trees for the call and the put. Explain when, if ever, each option should be exercised.

20. Consider the analytic approximation for American options. A stock sells for \$130, has a standard deviation of 0.3, and pays a continuous dividend of 3 percent. An American call and put on this stock both have an exercise price of \$130, and they both expire in 180 days. The risk-free rate is 12 percent. Find the value of the call and put according to this model. Demonstrate that you have found the correct critical stock price for both options.

21. An American call and put both have an exercise price of \$100. An acquaintance asserts that the critical stock price for both options is \$90 under the analytic approximation technique. Comment on this claim and explain your reasoning.

NOTES

1. Fischer Black first proposed this idea in his paper "Fact and Fantasy in the Use of Options," *Financial Analysts Journal*, July/August 1975, 36–72.

2. R. E. Whaley, "Valuation of American Call Options on Dividend Paying Stocks: Empirical Tests," *Journal of Financial Economics*, 10, March 1982, 29–58.

3. This model was developed in a series of papers: R. Roll, "An Analytical Formula for Unprotected American Call Options on Stocks with Known Dividends," *Journal of Financial Economics*, 5, 1977, 251–258; R. Geske, "A Note on an Analytic Valuation Formula for Unprotected American Call Options on Stocks with Known Dividends," *Journal of Financial Economics*, 7, 1979, 375–380; R. Whaley, "On the Valuation of American Call Options on Stocks with Known Dividends," *Journal of Financial Economics*, 9, 1981, 207–211; R. Geske, "Comments on Whaley's Note," *Journal of Financial Economics*, 9, 1981, 213–215.

7
Options on Stock Indexes, Foreign Currency, and Futures

INTRODUCTION

This chapter considers three different kinds of options: options on stock indexes, options on foreign currency, and options on futures. We consider these different types of options together because the principles that determine the price of these options are almost identical. In essence, the three types of options considered in this chapter are united by the fact that the good underlying each option can be treated as paying a continuous dividend. The pricing of these options is further unified by the conceptual connections among the different options. For example, we will consider options on stock index futures as well as options on stock indexes themselves, and we analyze options on foreign currency futures as well as options on foreign currencies alone.

While there may be common principles for the pricing of these three types of options, the markets for each of these options are quite large and have their own features. These were explored in Chapter 1. Consequently, this chapter begins by analyzing the pricing principles for these options. As noted above, the underlying instruments may all be treated as paying a continuous dividend—particularly when we think of a dividend as a leakage of value from the instrument paying the dividend. For a stock index, the continuous dividend really is a dividend—the aggregate dividends on the stocks represented in the index. For a foreign currency, we may treat the foreign interest rate as a continuous dividend. For a futures, the cost of financing and storing the underlying good (a bond, 5000 bushels of wheat, or the proverbial pork bellies) is a leakage of value from the commodity.

Because the underlying good pays a continuous dividend, we know that the Merton model, which was discussed in Chapter 4, pertains directly to pricing these three types of European options. Also, the binomial model directly applies as well. For American options, discussed in Chapter 6, two approaches are clearly applicable. First, the analytic approximation technique works extremely well in pricing the types of options discussed in this chapter. Second, we can also apply the binomial model under the assumption of continuous dividends.

EUROPEAN OPTIONS PRICING

In Chapter 4, we considered the Merton model, which extends the Black–Scholes model, to provide an exact pricing model for European options on stocks that pay dividends at a continuous rate. We also discussed the binomial model and saw that it can apply to European options pricing on stocks that pay a continuous dividend. In this section, we extend both of these models to the pricing of European options on stock indexes, foreign currency, and futures.

Merton's Model

Merton's model extends the Black–Scholes model by treating continuous dividends as a negative interest rate. In Chapter 4, we saw how dividends reduce the value of a call option, because they reduce the value of the stock that underlies the option. In effect, a continuous dividend implies a continuous leakage of value from the stock that equals the dividend rate. We let the Greek letter delta, δ, represent this rate of leakage.[1] Merton's adjustment to the Black–Scholes model for continuous dividends is:

$$c_t^M = e^{-\delta (T - t)} S_t N(d_1^M) - X e^{-r(T - t)} N(d_2^M)$$

$$d_1^M = \frac{\ln\left(\frac{S_t}{X}\right) + (r - \delta + 0.5\,\sigma^2)\,(T - t)}{\sigma\sqrt{T - t}}$$

7.1

$$d_2^M = d_1^M - \sigma\sqrt{T - t}$$

where δ = the continuous dividend rate on the stock

To adjust the regular Black–Scholes model, we replace the current stock price with the stock price adjusted for the continuous dividend. That is, we replace S_t with:

$$e^{-\delta(T - t)}S_t \qquad 7.2$$

Substituting this expression into the formulas for d_1 and d_2 gives d_1^M and d_2^M as shown above. Merton's adjusted put value is:

$$p_t^M = Xe^{-r(T - t)}N(-d_2^M) - Se^{-\delta(T - t)}N(-d_1^M) \qquad 7.3$$

When $\delta = 0$, Merton's model reduces immediately to the Black–Scholes model.

We can determine the price of options on stock indexes, foreign currency, and futures if we can determine the correct term to substitute for expression 7.2 in the Black–Scholes model.

The Binomial Model

In Chapter 4, we saw that the price at time t of a European call, c_t, and a European put, p_t, could be expressed as follows under the terms of the binomial model.

$$c_t = \frac{\sum_{j=m}^{n}\left(\frac{n!}{j!(n - j)!}\right)\left(\pi_U^j\pi_D^{n-j}\right)\left[U^jD^{n-j}S_t - X\right]}{R^n} \qquad 7.4$$

$$p_t = \frac{\sum_{j=0}^{n}\left(\frac{n!}{j!(n - j)!}\right)\left(\pi_U^j\pi_D^{n-j}\right)\text{MAX}\left[0, X - U^jD^{n-j}S_t\right]}{R^n} \qquad 7.5$$

where:

$U = 1 +$ percentage increase in a period if the stock price rises
$D = 1 -$ percentage decrease in a period if the stock price falls
$R = 1 +$ risk-free rate per period
$\pi_U =$ probability of a price increase in any period
$\pi_D =$ probability of a price decrease in any period

These pricing models apply for any time span divided into n periods, where m is the minimum number of price increases to bring the call into-the-money at expiration.

To apply the binomial model to options on goods paying a continuous dividend, we need to adjust the binomial parameters to reflect the continuous leakage of value from the stock that the dividend represents and to accurately reflect the price movements on the stock. For Merton's model for European options on a stock paying a continuous dividend, we saw that the adjustment largely involved subtracting the continuous dividend rate, δ, from the risk-free rate, r. This is exactly the adjustment required for the binomial model. For options on a good paying a continuous dividend δ, the U, D, and π_U factors are:

$$U = e^{\sigma \sqrt{\Delta t}}$$

$$D = \frac{1}{U}$$

$$\pi_U = \frac{e^{(r - \delta)\Delta t} - D}{U - D}$$

7.6

We can apply this binomial model to options on stock indexes, foreign currency, or futures by determining the appropriate δ and the correct price of the instrument to take the place of S_t in the binomial model.

Options on Stock Indexes

The Merton model and the binomial model apply directly to pricing options on stock indexes. Because a stock index merely summarizes the performance of some set of stocks, we may think of the stock index as representing a portfolio of stocks, some of which pay dividends. Because we are pricing an option on this portfolio of stocks, we are concerned only with the dividends on the entire portfolio—we need to consider the dividend on individual stocks only insofar as they determine the overall dividend for the portfolio. Almost all individual stocks pay periodic discrete dividends (usually following a quarterly payment pattern). However, for stock indexes, including many stocks, the assumption of a continuous dividend payment is fairly realistic. In general, the greater the number of stocks represented in a stock index, the more realistic the assumption of continuous dividends.[2]

To illustrate the application of Merton's model to pricing options on stock indexes, consider a stock index that has a current value of $350. The standard deviation of returns for the index is 0.2, the risk-free rate is 8 percent, and the continuous dividend rate on the index is 4 percent. European call and put options on this stock index expire in 150 days and have a striking price of $340. Therefore, the dividend rate of 4 percent takes the role of δ in the Merton model and the index value of 350 takes the role of S_t. For these data, we find the value of the call and put in index units as follows:

$$d_1^M = \frac{\ln\left(\frac{350}{340}\right) + [0.08 - 0.04 + 0.5(0.2)(0.2)]\left(\frac{150}{365}\right)}{0.2\sqrt{\frac{150}{365}}}$$

$$= \frac{0.028988 + 0.024658}{0.128212} = 0.418413$$

$$d_2^M = 0.418413 - 0.2\sqrt{\frac{150}{365}} = 0.290201$$

$N(d_1^M) = N(0.418413) = 0.662177$; $N(d_2^M) = N(0.290201) = 0.614169$; $N(-d_1^M) = N(-0.418413) = 0.337823$, and $N(-d_2^M) = N(-0.290201) = 0.385831$. Therefore, the call and put are worth:

$$c_t^M = e^{-0.04(150/365)}\, 350.00\, (0.662177) - 340.00\, e^{-0.08(150/365)}\, (0.614169) = \$25.92$$

$$p_t^M = 340.00\, e^{-0.08(150/365)}\, (0.385831) - 350.00\, e^{-0.04(150/365)}\, (0.337823) = \$10.63$$

For a five-period binomial model price on the same options, the call is worth $26.37, while the put is worth $11.08. With 200 periods, the call price is $25.94, and the put price is $10.65. (The calculations for the binomial model are not shown here, but similar calculations for other options appear later in this chapter.)

Options on Foreign Currency

We now explore the application of the Merton model to pricing options on a foreign currency. We assume that we are looking at the issues from the point of view of a U.S. options trader. In terms of the Merton model, the dollar value of the foreign currency takes the role of the stock price, S_t, and the foreign interest rate takes the role of the continuous dividend rate, δ. The standard deviation in the Merton model is that of the underlying asset, so the correct standard deviation to use in the model is the standard deviation of the foreign currency.

As an example, consider a European call and a European put option on the British pound. The pound is currently worth $1.40, and has a standard deviation of 0.5, reflecting difficulties in the European Monetary System (EMS). The current British risk-free rate is 12 percent, while the U.S. rate is 8 percent. The call and put both have a striking price of $1.50 per pound, and they both expire in 200 days.

According to the Merton model, the call is worth $0.1452, while the put value is $0.2700. Both of these prices are the dollar price for an option on a single British pound. We illustrate the computation of the price of the currency options using a five-period binomial model. The binomial parameters are:

$$U = e^{\sigma \sqrt{\Delta t}} = e^{0.5 \sqrt{0.1096}} = 1.1800$$

$$D = \frac{1}{U} = 0.847452$$

$$\pi_U = \frac{e^{(r - \delta)\Delta t} - D}{U - D} = 0.445579$$

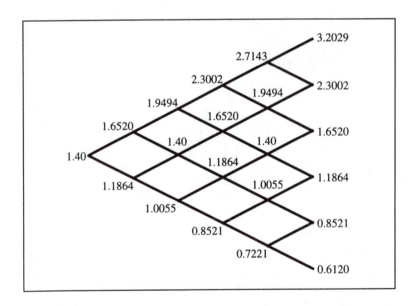

FIGURE 7.1 A Five-Period Binomial Lattice for the British Pound

The one-period discount factor is $e^{-0.08(40/365)} = 0.9913$. Figure 7.1 shows the five-period binomial lattice for the foreign currency price, while Figure 7.2 shows the lattices for the call and the put. The price of the call is $0.1519, and the put is worth $0.2766. For a 200-period lattice, the call is worth $0.1454 and the put is worth $0.2702. These 200-period binomial estimates are extremely close to the values from the Merton model.

Options on Futures

In simplest terms, a futures contract is an agreement entered at one date calling for the delivery of some good at a future date. The price is established at the time the contract is entered, and the exchange of goods for the contract price occurs at the expiration of the futures contract. For

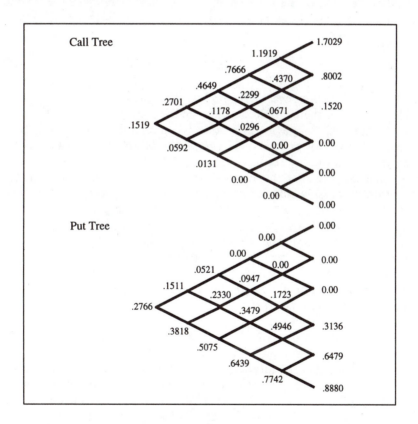

FIGURE 7.2 The Five-Period Lattices for Foreign Currency Call and Put Prices

example, a trader might buy a futures contract for 100 Troy ounces of gold for delivery in one year at a price of $400 per ounce. The current cash market price of gold might be $361.94 at the time of contracting. The trader has the obligation to pay $400 per ounce for the gold and take delivery of the metal in one year. The seller of the futures has complementary obligations. The purchaser of the futures contract profits if the price of the good at delivery exceeds the futures contract price. By contrast, the seller of the futures hopes that the futures contract price will exceed the price of the underlying good at expiration.[3]

Consider a good such as gold that has a large stock relative to consumption, that is easily storable, does not have a seasonal production pattern (like wheat), and does not have a seasonal consumption pattern (like gasoline). Further, assume that it is possible to sell gold short and to obtain the use of the proceeds from the short sale.[4] When these conditions hold, the futures price at time t, F_t, for delivery of the good at time T is given by:

$$F_t = \text{SPOT}_t e^{r(T - t)} \qquad\qquad 7.7$$

If this relationship between the spot, or cash, price and the futures price did not prevail, there would be immediate arbitrage opportunities.

For example, assume a continuously compounded risk-free rate of 10 percent. If the spot price is $361.94 and the futures calls for delivery in one year, then the futures price must be $400 to avoid arbitrage. To see this, first assume that the futures price is too high—say $410. In this situation a trader would borrow $361.94 for 10 percent for one year, would use the borrowed funds to buy the gold for $361.94 per ounce, would sell the futures contract at a price of $410, and would store the gold for one year until the expiration of the futures. (We ignore market imperfections and storage costs for simplicity.) In one year, the trader could deliver the gold against the futures and collect $410, the futures contract price. From this $410, the trader would repay the debt, which would be $400, leaving a profit of $10. Notice that the trader had a zero cash flow at the outset of these transactions and that the profit was certain once those initial transactions were made. Thus, the $10 is an arbitrage profit.

Now assume that the futures price is too low relative to the spot price. If the futures is $380, for example, the trader would transact as follows: Sell the gold short and receive $361.94, invest $361.94 for one year at 10 percent, and buy the futures contract for $380. In one year, the trader's loan will be worth $400. From this $400, the trader will pay $380 to receive one ounce of gold in completion of the futures contract. The trader will then complete the short sale by returning the ounce of gold to the party from whom it was borrowed to consummate the short sale. The trader now has $20, which represents a riskless profit with no investment. The trader had a zero net cash flow at the outset, and once the transactions were in place, the profit was assured.

The only price relationship that rules out arbitrage is one that conforms to Equation 7.7. The futures price must equal the cash price compounded at the risk-free rate of interest from the contract date to the expiration of the futures. The relationship expressed in Equation 7.7 is called the **cost-of-carry model**. In general, all precious metals (gold, silver, platinum, and palladium) and all financial instruments (equities and debt) conform almost perfectly to this relationship. To the degree that a commodity fails to conform to the cost-of-carry model, the pricing techniques discussed in this chapter do not pertain to pricing futures options on that commodity.

In terms of the Merton model, the rate at which the spot price grows, r, takes the place of δ, and the futures price takes the place of the stock price in Equation 7.1. In other words, for futures on commodities that conform to the cost-of-carry model, $\delta = r$.[5] When we make this substitution in Equation 7.1, the formula becomes considerably simpler due to the equivalence of δ and r. For European futures options, the price of the futures call, c_t^F, and put, p_t^F, are:

$$c_t^F = e^{-r(T-t)}[F_t N(d_1^F) - X N(d_2^F)]$$

$$p_t^F = e^{-r(T-t)}[X N(-d_2^F) - F_t N(-d_1^F)] \qquad 7.8$$

$$d_1^F = \frac{\ln\left(\dfrac{F_t}{X}\right) + (0.5\,\sigma^2)(T-t)}{\sigma\sqrt{T-t}}$$

$$d_2^F = d_1^F - \sigma\sqrt{T-t}$$

Equation 7.8 employs the standard deviation of the futures price.[6]

The binomial model also applies to options on futures, and the parameters of Equations 7.4 and 7.5 can be applied directly. Notice that the probability of a futures price increase becomes:

$$\pi_U = \frac{e^0 - D}{U - D} = \frac{1 - D}{U - D}$$

As an example, consider European options on a stock index futures that expire in one year. The current cash market price of the index is 480, and the risk-free rate is 7 percent. Therefore, according to the cost-of-carry model, the futures price must be:

$$F_t = 480.00 \; e^{0.07 \; (365/365)} = 514.80$$

European call and put options on this futures contract have an exercise price of 500, and the standard deviation of the futures price is 0.2. The price of the call and put according to the Merton/Black model must be:

$$d_1^F = \frac{\ln\left(\dfrac{514.80}{500.00}\right) + 0.5(0.2)(0.2)}{0.2} = 0.24582$$
$$d_2^F = 0.245852 - 0.2 = 0.045852$$

$N(d_1^F) = 0.597102$, and $N(d_2^F) = 0.518286$. Therefore, the call and put prices are:

$$c_t^F = e^{-0.07}[514.80 \, (0.597102) - 500.00 \, (0.518286)] = \$44.98$$
$$p_t^F = e^{-0.07} [500.00 \, (0.481714) - 514.80 \, (0.402898)] = \$31.18$$

For a binomial model with five periods, the call and put prices are $46.49 and $32.69, respectively. With 200 periods the binomial model gives prices of $44.95 and $31.15 for the call and put, respectively.

Options on Futures versus Options on Physicals

For some goods, such as foreign currencies, options trade on the futures contract and on the good itself. For example, in Chapter 1 we saw that the Philadelphia Stock Exchange trades options on foreign currencies, while the Chicago Mercantile Exchange trades options on foreign currency futures. The differences between options on futures and options on the underlying good itself depends critically on whether the option is a European or an American option.

At the expiration of a futures contract, the futures price must equal the spot price. This is necessary to avoid arbitrage. For example, in the gold market if the spot price is $400 per ounce and the futures contract is at expiration, the futures contract price must also be $400. If it were not, there is a simple and immediate arbitrage opportunity. If the futures price at expiration exceeds the spot price, a trader would buy the physical good and deliver it in the futures market to capture the higher futures price. By contrast, if the futures price is below the spot price, the arbitrageur would buy a futures contract, take delivery of gold, and sell the gold for the higher spot price. To avoid both of these potential arbitrage plays, the spot price and the futures price must be equal at the expiration of the futures contract.

The no-arbitrage condition has important implications for pricing European futures options. Because a European option can be exercised only at expiration, a European futures option can be exercised only when the futures price and the spot price are identical. This restriction on exercise means that the payoffs on European futures options and options on physicals are identical. Therefore, the price of a European futures option and a European option on the physical must always be identical.

For American options, the analysis is more complex, because the trader can exercise an American option at any time. The relationship between prices of American options on futures and physicals depends on the relationship between the futures price and the spot price prevailing at a given time prior to expiration. For precious metals and financials, the futures price before expiration almost always exceeds the spot price. In the markets for some commodities, the spot price often exceeds the futures price. This happens in markets for industrial metals such as copper, in markets for agricultural goods, and in the energy market. While a complete explanation for why these price relationships arise lies beyond the scope of this book, we offer a very brief explanation. In essence, the futures price will lie above the spot price if supplies of the underlying good are large relative to consumption, if the underlying good is easily storable and transportable, if the market for the underlying good is well developed, if supply of and demand for the underlying good are free of seasonal fluctuations, and if it is easy and cheap to effect short sales for the underlying good. These conditions prevail for precious metals and financials. By contrast, industrial metals, agricultural commodities, and energy products are strongly affected by supply and demand seasonalities, by poorly developed cash markets, and by costly transportation and storage. These factors allow the spot price to exceed the futures price on occasion.[7]

Without regard to the economic factors that cause the futures price or the spot price to be higher, the relationship between the futures and spot price determines the relationship between prices for American futures options and American options on the physical. When the futures price exceeds the spot price, the price of an American futures call must exceed the price of an American call on the physical, and the price of an American futures put must be less than the price of an American put on the physical. When the spot price exceeds the futures price, the price of an American futures call must be below the price of an American call on the physical and the price of an American futures put must exceed the price of an American put on the physical.

OPTIONS SENSITIVITIES

In Chapter 5, we considered the sensitivity of options prices to changes in the underlying parameters. Our exploration focused on the Merton model and we analyzed the DELTA, GAMMA, THETA, VEGA, and RHO of European calls and puts. In this section, we extend that analysis to options on stock indexes, options of foreign currencies, and options on futures. The principles are virtually identical, but we must make slight substitutions in the definitions of the sensitivities to account for differences in the underlying instruments. Tables 7.1 and 7.2 present the call and put sensitivities for the Merton model. These are the same tables discussed in Chapter 5. These same sensitivities apply to options on stock indexes, options on foreign currencies, and options on futures with the following substitutions:

Sensitivities of Options on Stock Indexes. Interpret S_t as the price of the stock index, and interpret δ as the continuous dividend yield on the

Table 7.1 Call Sensitivities for the Merton Model

Name	Sensitivity
DELTA$_c$	$\dfrac{\partial c}{\partial S} = e^{-\delta (T - t)} N(d_1^M)$
THETA$_c$	$-\dfrac{\partial c}{\partial (T - t)} = -\dfrac{SN'(d_1^M)\, \sigma\, e^{-\delta (T - t)}}{2\sqrt{T - t}}$ $+ \delta\, S\, N(d_1^M)\, e^{-\delta (T - t)} - r\, Xe^{-r (T - t)}\, N(d_2^M)$
VEGA$_c$	$\dfrac{\partial c}{\partial \sigma} = S\sqrt{T - t}\, N'(d_1^M)\, e^{-\delta (T - t)}$
RHO$_c$	$\dfrac{\partial c}{\partial r} = X(T - t)\, e^{-r(T - t)}\, N(d_2^M)$
GAMMA$_c$	$\dfrac{\partial\, \text{DELTA}_c}{\partial S} = \dfrac{\partial^2 c}{\partial S^2} = \dfrac{N'(d_1^M)\, e^{-\delta (T - t)}}{S\, \sigma\, \sqrt{T - t}}$
Note:	$N'(d_1^M) = \dfrac{1}{\sqrt{2\, \pi}} e^{-0.5 (d_1^M)^2}$

Table 7.2　Put Sensitivities for the Merton Model

Name	Sensitivity
DELTA$_p$	$\dfrac{\partial p}{\partial S} = e^{-\delta\,(T-t)}\,[N(d_1^M) - 1]$
THETA$_p$	$-\dfrac{\partial p}{\partial (T-t)} = -\dfrac{SN'(d_1^M)\,\sigma\,e^{-\delta\,(T-t)}}{2\sqrt{T-t}}$ $+\ \delta\,S\,N(-d_1^M)\,e^{-\delta\,(T-t)} + r\,Xe^{-r\,(T-t)}\,N(-d_2^M)$
VEGA$_p$	$\dfrac{\partial p}{\partial \sigma} = S\sqrt{T-t}\,N'(d_1^M)\,e^{-\delta\,(T-t)}$
RHO$_p$	$\dfrac{\partial p}{\partial r} = -X(T-t)\,e^{-r(T-t)}\,N(-d_2^M)$
GAMMA$_p$	$\dfrac{\partial\,\text{DELTA}_p}{\partial S} = \dfrac{\partial^2 p}{\partial S^2} = \dfrac{N'(d_1^M)\,e^{-\delta\,(T-t)}}{S\,\sigma\,\sqrt{T-t}}$
Note:	$N'(d_1^M) = \dfrac{1}{\sqrt{2\,\pi}}e^{-0.5\,(d_1^M)^2}$

stock index. Adjust the computation of d_1 and d_2 by making these same substitutions.

Sensitivities of Options on Foreign Currency.　Interpret S_t as the price of the foreign currency, and interpret δ as the continuous interest rate on the foreign risk-free instrument. Adjust the computation of d_1 and d_2 by making these same substitutions.

Sensitivities of Options on Futures.　Interpret S_t as the price of the futures contract, and interpret δ as being equal to the risk-free rate, so that $r - \delta = 0$. Adjust the computation of d_1 and d_2 by making these same substitutions.

　　Because these sensitivities are so similar, we illustrate all with an example of a a European option on the British pound. The current value of a British pound is $1.56. The U.S. risk-free rate of interest is 8 percent, while the risk-free rate on the British pound is 11 percent. The standard deviation of the British pound is 0.25, and the option expires in 90 days. The exercise price of the options we consider is $1.50. In terms of the Merton model, our inputs would be $S = \$1.56$, $X = \$1.50$, $\sigma = 0.25$, $T - t = 90$ days, $\delta = 0.11$, and $r = 0.08$. With these values a European call is worth $0.1002, and a European put is worth $0.0526. Table 7.3 shows the sensitivity values for this option.

PRICING AMERICAN OPTIONS

Chapter 6 explored the pricing of American stock options. There we saw that exact solutions for pricing American-style options are generally not available. Further, we noted that the key feature that made American call options pricing distinct from European call options pricing was the payment of dividends by the underlying good. In this section, we explore the pricing of American options on stock indexes, foreign currency, and futures.

As we have discussed earlier in this chapter, we may regard futures, foreign currencies, and stock indexes as goods that pay continuous dividends. This makes them particularly well suited to analysis by the Barone–Adesi and Whaley analytic approximation. Therefore, we begin our analysis of American options on stock indexes, foreign currency, and futures by applying the analytic approximation to these instruments.

The binomial model also applies to these instruments, and we consider it in detail later in this chapter. The binomial model has special applicability to options on stock indexes, because stock indexes actually have dividend payment patterns that are discrete. As we will see later in this chapter, there are certain periods of the year when stocks tend to pay dividends. This seasonality in dividend payments from stocks implies that stock indexes will also exhibit a seasonal dividend pattern. The binomial model is particularly well suited to handling this type of dividend pattern.

Table 7.3   Foreign Currency Option Sensitivities
$S = \$1.56; X = \$1.50; \sigma = 0.25; T - t = 90$ days; $r - 0.08; \delta = 0.11$

	Merton Model	
	Call	Put
Options Prices	$0.1002	$0.0526
DELTA	0.6082	−0.3650
THETA	−0.1085	−0.1578
VEGA	0.2859	0.2859
RHO	0.2093	−0.1534
GAMMA	1.9058	1.9058

Analytical Approximations

As we discussed in Chapter 6, we may analyze the value of an American option as being comprised of the value of a corresponding European option, plus an early exercise premium. The value of an American option must always be at least the amount of its immediately available exercisable proceeds. For a call:

$$C_t \geq S_t - X$$

If a trader owns the American option, she has a choice between the exercisable proceeds or the value of the European call. Which is preferable depends upon how deep-in-the-money the option is, the dividend rate on the stock, δ, the interest rate, r, and the time remaining until the option expires, $T - t$. If the stock price reaches a critical level, S^*, such that:

$$S_t^* \, X = c(S^*, X, T - t) + \text{early exercise premium} \qquad 7.9$$

the owner of an American call option is indifferent about xercising. If the stock price exceeds S^*, she will exercise immediately to capture the exercise proceeds $S_t - X$. If the stock price is below S^*, she will not exercise. At the critical stock price, S^*, the European call is worth exactly $S^* - X$. For any stock price greater than S^*, the European call will be worth less than the exercisable proceeds for the American call. This explains why the owner of the American call is indifferent about exercise at a stock price of S^*; at that stock price the American and European calls are worth the same—$S^* - X$. For higher stock prices, the value of the European call falls below that of the American, and the value of the American call becomes equal to its exercisable proceeds. Thus, the owner of the American call should exercise to capture the quantity $S - X$. Those funds can then be invested from the exercise date to the expiration date to earn a return that will be lost if the option is not exercised.

A similar argument applies to American put options. As the stock price falls well below the exercise price, there comes a point at which:

$$X - S^{**} = p(S^{**}, X, T - t) + \text{early exercise premium} \qquad 7.10$$

S^{**} is the critical stock price for an American put. If the stock price falls below S^{**}, the American put should be exercised to capture the exercised proceeds of $X - S_t$. From Chapter 6, the analytic approximation for an American call on a stock is:

$$C_t = c_t + A_2\left(\frac{S_t}{S^*}\right)^{q_2} \quad \text{if } S_t < S^*$$
$$= S_t - X \qquad\qquad \text{if } S_t \geq S^* \qquad\qquad 7.11$$

where:

$$A_2 = \frac{S^*\,[1 - e^{-\delta(T - t)}N(d_1)]}{q_2}$$

and S^* is the solution to:

$$S^* - X = c_t(S^*, X, T - t) + \{1 - e^{-\delta(T - t)}N(d_1)\}(S^*/q_2) \quad 7.12$$

$N(d_1)$ and $p(S^*, X, T - t)$ are evaluated at S^*. To find S^* requires an iterative search for the value that makes the equation balance. Other terms are:

$$q_2 = \frac{1 - n + \sqrt{(n - 1)^2 + 4k}}{2}$$

$$n = \frac{2(r - \delta)}{\sigma^2}, \quad k = \frac{2r}{\sigma^2\,(1 - e^{-r(T - t)})}$$

For an American put, the analytic approximation is:

$$P_t = p_t + A_1\left(\frac{S_t}{S^{**}}\right)^{q_1} \quad \text{if } S_t > S^{**}$$
$$= X - S_t \qquad\qquad \text{if } S_t \leq S^{**} \qquad\qquad 7.13$$

where:

$$A_1 = \frac{S^{**}\,[1 - e^{-\delta(T - t)}N(-d_1)]}{q_1}$$

$$q_1 = \frac{1 - n - \sqrt{(n - 1)^2 + 4k}}{2}$$

S^{**} is found by an iterative search to make the following equation hold:

$$X - S^{**} = p_t(S^{**}, X, T - t) - [1 - e^{-\delta(T - t)}N(-d_1)](S^{**}/q_1) \quad 7.14$$

$N(-d_1)$ and $p_t(S^{**}, X, T - t)$ are evaluated at the critical stock price S^{**}. We now consider how this model can apply to options on stock indexes, foreign currency, and futures.

The Analytic Approximation for Options on Stock Indexes. To apply the Barone–Adesi and Whaley model to options on stock indexes, we merely need to reinterpret certain parameters in the model. Specifically, we interpret S in the model to indicate the price of the stock index in question, and we interpret δ as the aggregate dividend rate on all of the stocks represented in the index. S^* and S^{**} are the critical levels of the stock index that would trigger exercise.

As an example, assume that a stock index has a current value of 400, that the risk-free rate of interest is 7 percent, that the continuous dividend rate on the stocks comprising the index is 3.5 percent, that the standard deviation of the stock index is 0.18, that the time to expiration is 140 days, and that the exercise price is 380. For these values, the Barone–Adesi and Whaley model gives a call price $C = 32.14$ and a put price $P = 7.41$, where these option values are expressed in index units. For the call, the critical price is $S^* = 822.31$, while for the put the critical price is $S^{**} = 328.50$. Because the current index value is below S^* and above S^{**}, there is no incentive to exercise.

The Analytic Approximation for Options on Foreign Currencies. As with options on stock indexes, we can apply the Barone–Adesi and Whaley model to American options on foreign currencies by reinterpreting Equations 7.11 and 7.13. To apply these equations to options on foreign currency, we interpret S as the current value of the foreign currency. The dividend rate, δ, is interpreted as the risk-free rate of interest on the foreign currency.

Earlier in this chapter, we considered an example of a British pound in the context of the Merton model. In that example, the pound was currently worth $1.40 and had a standard deviation of 0.5. The British risk-free rate is 12 percent, while the U.S. rate is 8 percent. The exercise price for both a call and a put is $1.50, and the two options expire in 200 days. Using the Merton model, we found that the European option values would be $c = \$0.1452$ and $p = \$0.2700$. For these same parameter values, American options would be worth: $C = \$0.1498$ and $P = \$0.2718$. The critical prices are $S^* = \$2.52$ and $S^{**} = \$0.69$. Thus, it would be unwise to exercise either the call or the put. These values were found by letting the spot value of the pound ($1.40) take on the role of S in the analytic approximation formula, while the British interest rate (12 percent) played the role of the dividend, δ.

The Analytic Approximation for Options on Futures.   The Barone–Adesi and Whaley model applies with equal facility to options on futures. In Equations 7.11 to 7.13, we interpret S as the futures price, and we assume that the rate of return on the underlying asset equals the risk-free rate. That is, we assume that $r = \delta$. This assumption is valid if the futures contract is a financial asset or a precious metal.

To apply this model to futures, consider an American call and put on platinum. The cost-of-carry model holds very well for this precious metal, justifying our assumption that $r = \delta$. Assume that the current spot price of platinum is $500 per ounce, that the risk-free rate of interest is 11 percent, that an American futures call and put expire in 75 days, and that the two options have an exercise price of $500. If platinum conforms to the cost-of-carry, the futures price must be:

$$F = S e^{r(T - t)} = \$500 \; e^{\,0.11(75/365)} = \$511.43$$

The volatility of the futures price is 0.25. In applying Equations 7.11 to 7.13 above, we replace S with the futures price of $511.43, and replace δ with the risk-free rate of 11 percent. For these data, the American option prices are $C = \$28.5323$ and $P = \$17.2875$, with critical futures prices $S^* = \$622.98$ and $S^{**} = \$401.2984$. For the corresponding European options, the prices are: $c = \$28.37$ and $p = \$17.1955$. The early exercise premium on the call is about $0.16 and for the put the premium is about $0.09.

Earlier we noted that the value of an American call on a futures would be higher than the value of an American call on the physical good if the futures price exceeded the spot price. We also said that the American put on the futures would be worth less than the corresponding American put on the physical if the futures price exceeded the cash price. This example confirms that point, because the prices of options on physical platinum (given the spot price of $500 and assuming the same standard deviation of 0.25 pertains to the futures price and to the spot price) are: $C = \$22.09$ and $P = \$22.09$. Thus, the call price on the physical good is lower and the put price on the physical good is higher than the corresponding option on the futures.[8]

Summary.   In this section, we have seen that the Barone–Adesi and Whaley analytical approximation applies not only to options on stocks, but to options on stock indexes, options on foreign currency, and options on futures. To apply the model to these disparate instruments, we merely need to reinterpret some of the parameters in the model in the way we have explored in this section.

It is worth emphasizing that the Barone–Adesi and Whaley model assumes that the underlying good in each case pays at a continuous rate, whether it be dividends on a stock index, the foreign interest rate for foreign currency options, or the cost-of-carry rate on the good underlying a futures contract. This assumption is virtually without flaw for options on foreign currency and options on futures, and it is quite reasonable for options on stock indexes. However, we must note that the dividend flow from stock indexes is not really continuous. To deal with discontinuous dividend flows, we now turn to a consideration of the binomial model and its applications to options on stock indexes, foreign currency, and futures.

The Binomial Model

In Chapter 6, we considered the application of the binomial model to pricing American options when the underlying good paid no dividend, a continuous dividend, a known dividend yield, or a known dollar dividend. Because this chapter considers options on stock indexes, foreign currency, and futures, we are most interested in applying the binomial model to a dividend payment stream that is continuous or that pays known dividends. As Chapter 6 has already shown how to apply the binomial model to the nondividend case and to the case of known dividend yields, we focus on the dividend patterns of greatest interest, continuous dividends and known dollar dividends.

Review of the Basic Strategy for the Binomial Model. As we have seen in Chapters 4 and 6, we follow a common strategy for computing options prices under the binomial model. For options on stocks with dividends, we applied the binomial model by creating a lattice for the stock that reflected the timing and amount of dividend payments that the stock would make. These adjustments affected the distribution of possible stock values at the expiration date. We then computed the option values in the usual way by working from the exercise date back to the present.

To apply the binomial model for American options, we follow the same basic valuation strategy, with one important difference. For the options lattice for an American option, the option value is set equal to the maximum of:

1. The expected option value in one period discounted for one period at the risk-free rate.
2. The immediate exercise value of the option, $S_t - X$ for a call, or $X - S_t$ for a put.

Except for this treatment of each node in the lattice for an American option, the binomial model for an American option is applied in exactly the same way as it is for a European option. As we work back through the tree, discounting the next period's expected option values, we must ask at every node whether the immediate exercise value or the computed present value is greater. The value at the node is the maximum of those two quantities. Further, we may note that the stock tree is unaffected by whether the option we are analyzing is an American or a European option.

Review of the Binomial Model and Continuous Dividends. In Chapter 4, we explored Merton's model, which adjusts the Black–Scholes model to price European options on stocks that pay a continuous dividend. We also showed how to use the binomial model to price European options on stocks that pay continuous dividends. There we saw that the parameters for the binomial model for a stock paying a continuous dividend were:

$$U = e^{\sigma \sqrt{\Delta t}}$$
$$D = \frac{1}{U}$$
$$\pi_U = \frac{e^{(r - \delta)\Delta t} - D}{U - D}$$

7.15

As we have discussed in this chapter, the stock price tree is identical whether we are pricing European or American options. Therefore, these parameters apply to generating the binomial tree of stock prices for American options on stocks paying a continuous dividend. As an examination of these parameters shows, the stock price tree will be identical in both cases. However, the probability of a stock price increase varies inversely with the level of the continuous dividend rate, δ.

Review of the Binomial Model and Known Dollar Dividends. To apply the binomial model to options on goods with known dollar dividends, the first step is to generate the tree describing the potential stock price movements. As we saw in Chapter 4 when we considered the pricing of European options on stock with known dollar dividends, there can be a problem with the tree failing to recombine after the dividend has been paid. In this situation, the number of nodes can increase dramatically, particularly when there are many periods and several dividends. (For details on why the tree fails to recombine, see Chapter 4.)

We can solve this problem as we did in Chapter 4 by making a simplifying assumption. We assume that the stock price reflects the dividend, which is known with certainty, and all other factors that might affect the stock price, which are uncertain. We then adjust the uncertain component of the stock price for the impending dividends and model the uncertain component of the stock price with the binomial tree adding back the present value of all future dividends at each node. Specifically, we follow these steps:

1. Compute the present value of all dividends to be paid during the life of the option as of the present time $= t$.
2. Subtract this present value from the current stock price to form $S_t' = S_t - $ PV of all dividends.
3. Create the binomial tree by applying the up and down factors in the usual way to the initial stock price S_t'.
4. After generating the tree, add to the stock price at each node the present value of all future dividends to be paid during the life of the option.
5. Compute the option values in the usual way by working through the binomial tree.

These were exactly the steps we used in Chapter 6 to resolve this difficulty.

The application of this procedure to American options is exactly the same as with European options, with a single exception. In working through the tree to generate the options price tree, we must compare the present value of next period's expected option value with the exercise value of the option. The option price at the node is the higher of the present value or the exercise value. The computation of the value at a node is exactly the same as in other cases we have already considered.

The Binomial Model for Options on Stock Indexes.   As we have just discussed, the binomial model can apply to options on stock indexes for both a continuous dividend on the stock index and for specific dividends at certain times. Stock indexes in fact tend to pay dividends in a discrete manner, with higher dividend payments coming at certain times of the year. Figure 7.3 shows the typical dividend pattern on the S&P 500 index, and is a function of the tendency of firms to pay dividends at the end of each calendar quarter.

In this section, we explore how to apply the binomial model to options on stock indexes with discrete dividend patterns of the type shown in Figure 7.3. Later in this chapter, we show how to apply the binomial model to continuous payments on futures options and foreign currency.

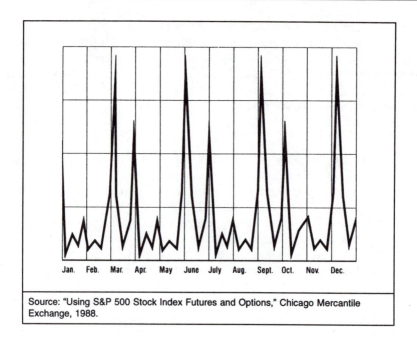

Jan. Feb. Mar. Apr. May June July Aug. Sept. Oct. Nov. Dec.

Source: "Using S&P 500 Stock Index Futures and Options," Chicago Mercantile
Exchange, 1988.

FIGURE 7.3 The Seasonal Pattern of Dividends on the S&P 500 Stock
Index

To make the discussion more concrete, let us consider a stock index
with a current value of 1200. An American call and put option on the
index expire in 125 days and have a common exercise price of 1250. The
volatility of the index is 0.2. The current risk-free interest rate is 8 percent.
During the life of these options, the index will pay two dividends. The
first dividend occurs on day 15 and will be 15 index units, while the
second falls on day 120 and will be 20 index units. The present value of
the two dividends at the present date is:

$$PV = 15.00e^{-0.08(15/365)} + 20.00e^{-0.08(120/365)} = 34.4316$$

The next step is to subtract this value from the current index to form
$S_t' = 1200.00 - 34.4316 = 1165.5684$.

We now compute the up and down factors and apply them to S_t' to
form the stock index tree. We will form a tree with five periods, so each
period consists of 25 days.

$$\Delta t = \frac{25}{365} = 0.0685 \text{ years}$$

$$U = e^{\sigma\sqrt{\Delta t}} = e^{0.2\sqrt{0.0685}} = 1.0537$$

$$D = \frac{1}{U} = 0.9490$$

$$\pi_U = \frac{e^{r\Delta t} - D}{U - D} = \frac{e^{0.08(0.0685)} - 0.9490}{1.0537 - 0.9490} = 0.5396$$

The upper panel in Figure 7.4 shows the stock index lattice for this example. However, we must still adjust this lattice by adding to each node the present value of all dividends to be received from that point to the expiration date of the option. The nodes occur at 0, 25, 50, 75, 100, and 125 days from the present. The first dividend occurs in 15 days,

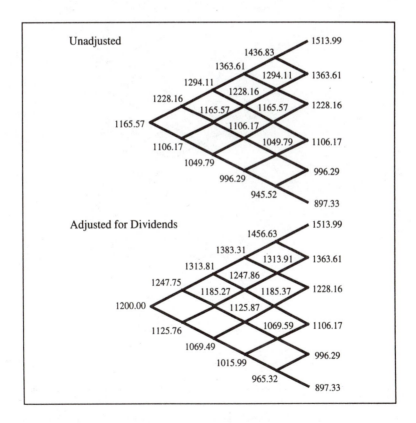

FIGURE 7.4   The Five-Period Stock Index Price Lattice

so it will affect only the node representing the present. The second dividend occurs in 120 days, so it will affect all nodes, except those at expiration. The lower panel of Figure 7.4 shows the stock index lattice adjusted for the present value of the dividends. For the present, we already know that the present value of both dividends is 34.43. All later periods occur after the first dividend, so we need to consider only the second dividend for subsequent nodes. At period 1, 25 days from now, the present value of the final dividend is:

$$20.00\,e^{-0.08(120\ -\ 25)/365} = 19.59$$

The other present values (19.70, 19.80, and 19.91) are found similarly, and are included in the stock index lattice in the bottom panel of Figure 7.4.

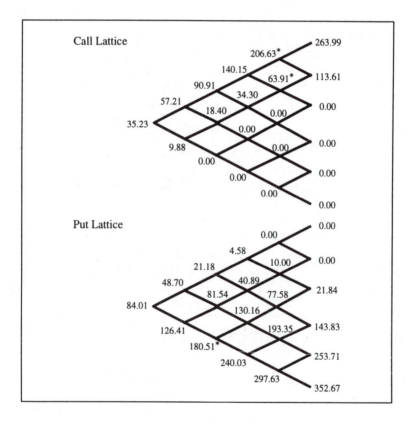

FIGURE 7.5 The Five-Period Lattice for an American Call and Put on the Stock Index

To compute the price of an option, we create a parallel lattice, starting at the expiration date. Figure 7.5 shows the call and put lattices for the American options we are considering. For the option, the value at expiration is simply the intrinsic value of the option at that point. We then consider the nodes representing one period before expiration, and compute the expected value of the payoffs one period later and discount that expected payoff for one period. For example, if the stock index value falls in four periods, it will be at 996.29 at expiration, while if it falls every period, it will be at 897.33. For a put at expiration, the payoffs will be 253.71 and 352.67, respectively, as the adjusted lattice for the stock index shows. One period earlier, the discounted expected value of these two payoffs is:

$$\{0.5396(253.71) + 0.4604(352.67)\} \times 0.9945 = 297.63$$

In terms of the adjusted lattice for the stock index, this corresponds to a stock index price at time four of 965.32.

Because we are working with American options, the holder of the put has the right to exercise at any time. At the fourth period, if the stock index price is 965.32, the immediate exercise value is $1250.00 - 965.32 = 284.68$. The holder of the put faces the following choice at the node we are considering. She may exercise the option for an immediate cash inflow of 284.68 index units, or continue to hold the put, with its expected present value of 297.63 index units. A rational trader would hold at this point. The node in the put lattice that we are considering must have the maximum of the immediate exercise value (284.68) or the discounted expected value of the payoffs in one period (297.63). Thus, the node in the put lattice in Figure 7.5 has the value 297.63. Asterisks in the option lattices indicate an entry resulting from an exercise. For example, if the stock price falls in both of the first two periods, the put holder should exercise. Figure 7.5 shows that the value of an American call on the stock index would be 35.23 index units, while the American put is worth 84.01 index units. As the figure also shows, early exercise of either option is unlikely.

The Binomial Model for Options on Foreign Currency. We now illustrate how the binomial model applies to options on foreign currency by considering the binomial model with continuous dividends. This continuous dividends approach applies to stock index options and options on futures as well. We illustrate the application of the binomial model to American options on foreign currency with the same example considered earlier in this chapter, except we now allow the option to be an

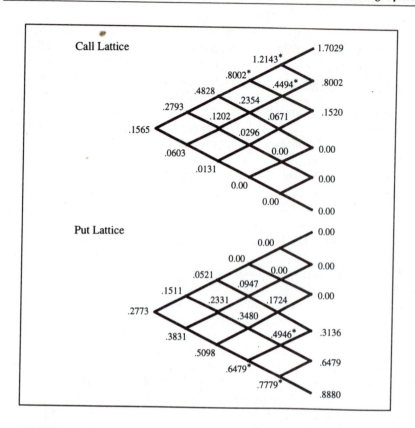

FIGURE 7.6 The Five-Period Lattice for an American Call and Put on the British Pound

American option. Earlier, we analyzed a European call and put option on the British pound. The pound is currently worth \$1.40, and has a standard deviation of 0.5. The current British risk-free rate is 12 percent, while the U.S. rate is 8 percent. The call and put both have a striking price of \$1.50 per pound, and they both expire in 200 days.

With a five-period binomial model, we found that the parameters were $U = 1.1800$; $D = 0.847452$; and $\pi_U = 0.445579$. The one-period discount factor is $e^{-0.08(40/365)} = 0.9913$. All of these values are the same whether the option under consideration is European or American. Consequently, the lattice for the foreign currency remains the same as well. As we saw for the European options, the five-period lattice gave a call price of \$0.1519 and a put price of \$0.2766. For a 200-period lattice the call was

$0.1454 and the put was $0.2702. For comparison, the Merton model gave a call price of $0.1452 and a put price of $0.2700.

To compute the price of American options on the foreign currency, we apply our familiar technology of constructing and evaluation lattices for the call and the put. For each node we compute the expected value of the payoffs one period later and discount them for one period. Because we are now analyzing American options, we must check each node to determine whether the intrinsic value or our discounted expected value is greater. The node in question takes on the maximum of these two values.

Figure 7.6 gives the call and put lattices for these American options. An asterisk indicates a node at which early exercise is optimal. Because early exercise is optimal in some instances for both the call and the put, the price of these American options must be greater than the European counterpart. The price of the American call is $0.1565, and the American put is $0.2773. This gives an early exercise premium of $0.0046 on the call and $0.0007 for the put.

The Binomial Model for Options on Futures.   We now apply the binomial model to options on futures. Generally, the goods underlying futures contracts may be thought of as paying a rate of return that equals the cost-of-carry. Earlier we saw that this rate must equal the risk-free rate of interest to avoid arbitrage—at least if markets were sufficiently perfect. Equation 7.6 gave the parameters for the binomial model as it applies to options on goods paying a continuous return. For futures, we assume that $r = \delta$. The parameters for the binomial model are the same whether we consider a European or an American option.

As an example, we consider again the option on the stock index futures contract that we analyzed above. A stock index stands at $480 and the risk-free rate of interest is 7 percent. A call and a put on the stock index futures contract expire in one year. Therefore, the futures prices must be 514.80, as we saw above. If the standard deviation of the futures contract is 0.2 and the exercise price on both the call and put is $500, we saw that the five-period binomial prices for the European call and put were 46.49 and 32.69, respectively.

For these options, the binomial parameters are:

$$U = e^{\sigma \sqrt{\Delta t}} = e^{0.2 \sqrt{0.2}} = 1.0936$$

$$D = \frac{1}{U} = 0.9144$$

$$\pi_U = \frac{e^{(r - \delta)\Delta t} - D}{U - D} = 0.4777$$

FIGURE 7.7 The Five-Period Lattice for the Platinum Futures Price

The discount factor per period is 0.9861. Figure 7.7 shows a five-period binomial lattice for the futures price. At the end of one year, the futures price will range between $329.11 and $805.25. Figure 7.8 shows the American call and put lattices for options on this futures contract. The asterisks indicate nodes at which the exercise value was substituted for the computed present value of the next period's expected payoffs. As we saw earlier in this chapter, the five-period binomial price for European options was $46.49 and $32.69 for the call and put, respectively. As Figure 7.8 shows, the American option prices from a five-period binomial analysis are $47.28 and $33.28 for the call and put, respectively.

SUMMARY

This chapter has applied familiar ideas to new instruments—options on stock indexes, options on foreign currency, and options on futures contracts. We considered both European and American options. For European options on stock indexes, foreign currency, and futures, we saw that they can be priced by the Merton model or by the binomial model. For American options we analyzed the analytic approximation of Barone–Adesi and Whaley, and we considered the binomial model.

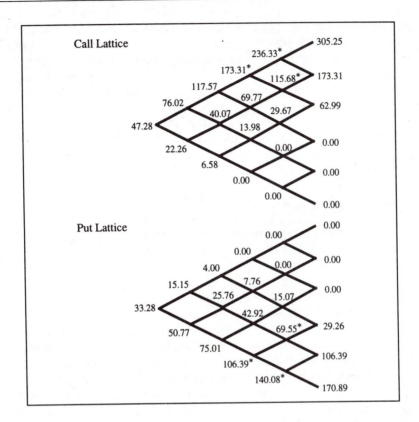

FIGURE 7.8 The Five-Period Lattice for the American Call and Put Futures Options

In essence, the Merton model applies directly, given a slight reinterpretation of the parameters of the model. The reinterpretation requires that we substitute the stock index value, the foreign currency value, or the futures price for the stock price in the Merton model. We also substitute the dividend rate on the stock index, the foreign interest rate on the foreign currency, or the cost-of-carry on the futures, which we presume to equal the risk-free rate. With these substitutions, we can apply the Merton model to price the options considered in this chapter. The binomial model applies in a straightforward way to European stock index options, options on foreign currency, and options on futures.

For American options, we saw that both the Barone–Adesi and Whaley model and the binomial model are well suited to analyzing the options considered in this chapter. It is extremely reasonable to regard foreign currencies and futures as paying a continuous yield, and it is a reasonable assumption for stock indexes as well. Thus, the analytic approximation works quite well for the types of options considered in this chapter.

The binomial model applies to all of the American options discussed in this chapter as well. It is particularly well suited to pricing options on stock indexes. While it may be reasonable to assume that stock indexes pay a continuous dividend, we saw that there are significant discontinuities in the dividend stream for many real-world stock indexes. The binomial model is ideal for pricing options on goods that pay discrete dividends.

REVIEW QUESTIONS

1. Explain why interest payments on a foreign currency can be treated as analogous to a dividend on a common stock.

2. Why do we assume that the cost-of-carry for a futures is the same as the risk-free rate?

3. Explain verbally how to adjust a price lattice for an underlying good that makes discrete payments.

4. If a European and an American call on the same underlying good have different prices when all of the terms of the two options are identical, what does this difference reveal about the two options? What does it mean if the two options have identical prices?

5. Consider an option on a futures contract within the context of the binomial model. Assume that the futures price is 100, that the risk-free interest rate is 10 percent, that the standard deviation of the futures is 0.4, and that the futures expires in one year. Assuming that a call and a put on the futures also expire in one year, compute the binomial parameters U, D, and π_U. Now compute the expected futures price in one period. What does this reveal about the expected movement in futures prices?

6. For a call and a put option on a foreign currency, compute the Merton model price, the binomial model price for a European option with three periods, the Barone–Adesi and Whaley model price, and the binomial model price with three periods for American options. Data are as follows: The foreign currency value is 2.5; the exercise price on all options is 2.0; the time until expiration is 90 days; the risk-free rate of interest is 7 percent; the foreign interest rate is 4 percent; the standard deviation of the foreign currency is 0.2.

7. Consider a call and a put on a stock index. The index price is 500, and the two options expire in 120 days. The standard deviation

of the index is 0.2, and the risk-free rate of interest is 7 percent. The two options have a common exercise price of 500. The stock index will pay a dividend of 20 index units in 40 days. Find the European and American option prices according to the binomial model, assuming two periods. Be sure to draw the lattices for the stock index and for all of the options that are being priced.

8. Consider two European calls and two European put options on a foreign currency. The exercise prices are $0.90 and $1, giving a total of four options. All options expire in one year. The current risk-free rate is 8 percent, the foreign interest rate is 5 percent, and the standard deviation of the foreign currency is 0.3. The foreign currency is priced at $0.80. Find all four option prices according to the Merton model. Compare the ratios of the option prices to the ratio of the exercise prices. What does this show?

NOTES

1. This is not the same as capital delta, Δ, which stands for the sensitivity of the call option price to a change in the stock price.
2. Even large indexes, such as the S&P 500, exhibit a distinct seasonal pattern in their index payments. Therefore, continuous dividends for a stock index represents something of an assumption.
3. Our discussion of futures abstracts form considerable institutional detail that is very important in the market. For instance, there is a fairly complex margining system that essentially requires traders to pay any paper losses in cash each day between the futures contracting date and the delivery date. Further, it is fairly easy to complete futures contract obligations without actually making delivery.
4. When these conditions are not met, the pricing relationships discussed in this section do not hold. Slight deviations from these idealized conditions lead to slight pricing discrepancies, while some commodities do not obey the pricing rule at all. For details see Robert W. Kolb, *Understanding Futures Markets*, 4e, Miami, Kolb Publishing Company, 1994, Chapters 1–3.
5. Notice that this equivalence of δ and r implies that the expected change in the futures price is zero. As the futures requires no investment and we are employing risk-neutrality arguments, the expected payoff from all investments is the risk-free rate. The risk-free rate applied to zero investment gives a zero expected profit.
6. The application of this model to options on futures was first presented in Fischer Black, "The Pricing of Commodity Contracts," *Journal of Financial Economics*, 3, March 1976, 167–179.

7. For a detailed explanation of these pricing relationships see Chapter 3 of *Understanding Futures Markets*, 4e, Miami, Kolb Publishing Company, 1994.

8. Notice that the call and put on the physical have the same price of $22.09. This will always be the case if the price of the spot good equals the exercise price.

8

The Options Approach
to Corporate Securities

INTRODUCTION

In this chapter, we apply the concepts developed in this book to the analysis of corporate securities such as stocks and bonds. We will see that virtually all securities have options features, and the options approach to corporate securities can help us understand these securities more fully.

Since the Black–Scholes model first appeared in the early 1970s, research on options has expanded rapidly. Options theory has given insight into several areas of finance, one of the most fruitful being corporate finance. In this chapter, we explore the insights that options theory brings to understanding corporate securities. By thinking of corporate securities as embracing options, we can build a deeper understanding of the value of securities such as stocks and bonds.[1]

The chapter begins by considering a firm with a simple capital structure of equity and a single pure discount bond. We show that the equity of the firm can be regarded as a call option on the entire firm with an exercise price equal to the obligation to the bondholders. Similarly, we can analyze the bond as involving an option as well. For this simple case, we show that the corporate bond can be regarded as consisting of a risk-free bond plus a short position in a put option. Of course, most firms have a more complex financial structure, but considering this simple case introduces the options dimension of most corporate securities.

In more realistic situations, the options embedded in corporate securities are more complex. In many firms, some debt is subordinated to more senior debt, meaning that the firm pays on the junior debt only after the senior debt claims have been satisfied. We show that the options approach to junior and senior debt analyzes these bonds as involving different exercise prices. When a firm has equity and coupon bonds, the analysis of the equity shows that the stock owners have a series of options. As another example, convertible debt includes a specific option—the option to convert the debt instrument into shares of the firm. The option to convert debt to equity is an option purchased by and held by the bond owner. Most corporate bonds are callable, so the issuer of the bond is entitled to retire the bond under specified circumstances. This call feature gives the issuer of the bond options with specified exercise prices. Understanding the options features of these different debt instruments gives a clearer understanding of their pricing. As we will see, these options features of corporate bonds have value, and they definitely affect the value of the bonds in which they are embedded.

A **warrant** is a security that gives the owner the option to convert the warrant into a new share of the issuing firm by paying a stated exercise price. This definition shows that a warrant is very similar to an option. However, there is an important difference. An option has an existing share as its underlying good. By contrast, the exercise of a warrant requires that the firm issue a new share of stock. As we will see, this difference leads to a slight difference in the valuation of options and warrants.

EQUITY AND A PURE DISCOUNT BOND

We begin our analysis of corporate securities by focusing on a firm with an extremely simple capital structure. This firm has common stock and a single bond for its financing. The bond is a pure discount bond that matures in one year. In this section, we want to understand these securities from the options point of view.

Common Stock as a Call Option

For this firm financed by common stock and a single pure discount bond, we assume the bond issue is a pure discount bond, with face value FV. Let the current time be $t = 0$ and let the maturity date of the bond be $t = m$. Between the present and $t = m$, the firm operates, generating cash flows. We further assume that the firm is operated by agents of the shareholders for the benefit of the shareholders. Also, during this period, new information about the prospects of the firm becomes available. At any time, the value of the firm equals the present value of the firm's future cash flows. The firm value also equals the total value of its outstanding securities. At $t = 0$, the firm's value, V_0, is:

$$V_0 = S_0 + B_0 \qquad\qquad 8.1$$

where:

S_0 = entire value of all stocks outstanding at time zero
B_0 = entire value of all bonds outstanding at time zero

The value of the bonds equals the present value of the face value, discounted at the appropriate risky discount rate r' for m periods.

$$B_0 = FVe^{-r'm} \qquad\qquad 8.2$$

When the bond matures, the firm can either pay the indebtedness, FV, or default. If the firm defaults, the bondholders take over the firm to salvage whatever they can. If the firm has a value greater than its indebtedness, FV, the firm will pay the bondholders and the firm will then belong entirely to the stockholders. Thus, the stockholders' payoff at $t = m$, S_m, is either zero (if they default) or the value of the firm minus the debt to the bondholders ($V_m - FV$). In other words, the stock is just like a European call, with a payoff that equals:

$$S_m = \text{MAX}(0, V_m - FV) \qquad\qquad 8.3$$

Therefore, the stock is a call option on the firm with an exercise price equal to the debt obligation, FV. Figure 8.1 shows the position of the stockholders. If the firm value at expiration is less than or equal to FV, then the stockholders do not have enough to pay the bondholders. Accordingly, they default and receive nothing. If the firm value exceeds FV, the stockholders pay the bondholders and keep any excess value.

From our analysis of stock options, we know the call value must equal or exceed the stock price minus the present value of the exercise price. Applying that principle to our treatment of stock itself as an option, we have:

$$S_0 \geq V_0 - FVe^{-r't} \qquad\qquad 8.4$$

This formula emphasizes another principle of options pricing. We know that call prices increase for higher risk in the underlying good. In analyzing common stock as an option on the value of the firm, we see that increasing

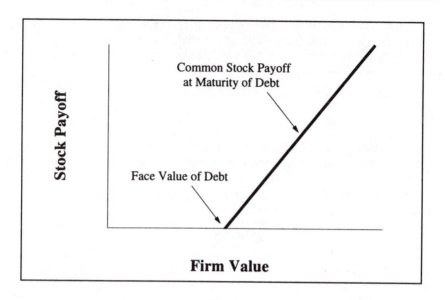

FIGURE 8.1 Common Stock Analyzed as a Call Option

the risk of the firm will make the stock more valuable. This is true even if the increasing risk does not increase the expected value of the firm at the expiration of the bond. The reason for this increase in value is the same that we saw for stock options. The stockholders have an incentive to increase risk. If the higher risk pays off, the stockholders keep all the benefits. If the risk does not pay off, the limited liability feature of stock protects the stockholders from losing more than their investment. There-fore, increasing risk gives a better chance for a very positive outcome for the stockholders, while the option protects against very negative out-comes. However, increasing the risk of the firm without increasing its expected value cannot increase the value of the firm as a whole. The increase in the value of the stock must come at the expense of the bond-holders. Increasing the risk of the firm without increasing the firm's ex-pected value transfers wealth from bondholders to stockholders. Bond-holders are aware of this incentive for the stockholders. As a result, bond covenants often prevent the borrower from increasing the risk of the firm.

The Options Analysis of Corporate Debt

Let us now examine the same simple firm from the perspective of the debtholder. The stockholders have promised to pay FV to the debtholders at $t = m$. However, the stockholders will pay only if the firm's value exceeds FV at the maturity of the debt. Otherwise, they will let the bond-holders have the firm. Therefore, the payoff for the bondholders at $t = m$, B_m, will be the lesser of the firm's value or FV. Figure 8.2 graphs the payoffs that the bondholders receive. As the figure shows, the bondholders receive the entire value of the firm if the firm value at the maturity of the debt is less than the debt obligation, FV. However, the bondholders never receive more than the promised payment of FV. Thus, the payoff to the bondholders, B_m, is the lesser of the firm's value, V_m, or FV.

$$B_m = \mathrm{MIN}(V_m, \mathrm{FV}) \qquad 8.5$$

We have already seen the payoff to the stockholders at $t = m$ and we know that the value of the bonds and stocks must equal the value of the firm. Therefore:

$$B_m = V_m - \mathrm{MAX}(0, V_m - \mathrm{FV}) \qquad 8.6$$

This equation shows that the bondholders have effectively purchased the entire firm and written a European call option to the stockholders. The call option is on the entire firm. The face value of the debt, FV, is

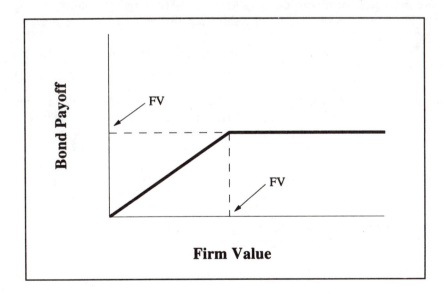

FIGURE 8.2 The Options Analysis of Corporate Debt

the exercise price. This conclusion exactly complements our analysis of the stock as a call option on the value of the firm.

A closer analysis of Figure 8.2 shows that it has the same payoff shape that we studied in Chapter 2. In essence, the bondholders' payoff consists of two embedded positions. The general shape matches that of a short position in a put. However, the entire position can never be worth less than zero. The bondholders effectively hold a short position in a put with an exercise price of FV, in addition to a long position in a risk-free bond paying FV. To see why this is so, assume that the firm's value at maturity exactly matches the obligation to the bondholders, V_m = FV. From Figure 8.2, we see that the bondholders receive FV for this terminal firm value. With V_m = FV, the put option the bondholders issued expires worthless.

Now consider any lower value for the firm at maturity. If the firm value is lower than FV, the stockholders exercise their put option, forcing the firm upon the bondholders. Now the bondholders receive their risk-free payment of FV, but they lose an amount equal to the shortfall in the firm's value below FV. In our notation, the bondholders receive FV. They also lose either zero, if the firm's value exceeds FV, or they lose FV − V_m, if the debt obligation exceeds the value of the firm:

$$B_m = FV - MAX(0, FV - V_m) \qquad 8.7$$

As this equation shows, the bondholders receive a payoff equal to a long position in a riskless bond and a short position in a put with an exercise price of FV.

Thus, we have seen that we can analyze the position of the bondholders in two ways:

1.   The bond consists of ownership of the entire firm with a short position in a call on the entire firm given to the shareholders. The exercise price of the call possessed by the shareholders is FV.
2.   The bond consists of a risk-free bond paying FV combined with a short position in a put option sold to the shareholders, which allows the shareholders to put the entire firm to the bondholders for an exercise price of FV.

From our exploration of put–call parity in Chapter 2, we know that the following relationship must hold:

$$S_t - c_t = Xe^{-r(T - t)} - p_t \qquad 8.8$$

We can apply put–call parity to our present situation by recalling that the value of the entire firm, V_o, plays the role of the stock and that the exercise price equals the promised payment to the bondholders, FV.

$$V_o - S_o = B_o \quad \text{or} \quad V_o - c_t = FVe^{-r(T-t)} - p_t \qquad 8.9$$

In Equation 8.9, notice that the promised payment on the bond, FV, is discounted at the risk-free rate of interest, r, not the risky rate of interest r'. This difference reflects the analysis of the risky bond as consisting of a risk-free bond with a promised payment of FV plus a short position in the put option on the entire firm. The difference in price between the risk-free and risky bond equals the short position in the put.

SENIOR AND SUBORDINATED DEBT

Many firms have two or more debt issues in their capital structure. Thus, we now consider a firm with three securities: stock, senior debt, and subordinated debt. Subordinated debt is a bond issue that receives payment only after the firm fully meets senior debt obligations. Let the two debt issues be pure discount bonds that both mature at $t = m$. The face values on the two obligations are FV_s for the senior debt and FV_j for the junior or subordinated debt. We want to analyze the subordinated debt in options terms.

The holders of the subordinated debt receive payment only after the firm fully meets the claims of the senior debtholders. Therefore, for any firm value V_m that is less than FV_s, the junior debtholders receive zero. If the firm value exceeds FV_s, the junior debtholders receive at least some payment. The subordinated debtholders receive full payment if the firm's value equals or exceeds the entire amount due on both debt issues, $V_m \geq FV_s + FV_j$. Figure 8.3 shows the payoffs for the senior and junior debt. The payoffs on the junior debt match a portfolio of a long call with a striking price of FV_s and a short call with a striking price of FV_j, as Figure 8.4 shows. The stockholders in this firm own a call on the value of the firm with a striking price equal to $FV_s + FV_j$. For the call option represented by the stock to come into the money, the value of the firm must exceed the total payoff of the two debt issues. Therefore, the payoff on the call in this situation is:

$$S_m = \text{MAX}[0, V_m - (FV_s + FV_j)]$$

As always, the value of the firm must equal the value of all outstanding securities. However, the different classes of securities offer different ways

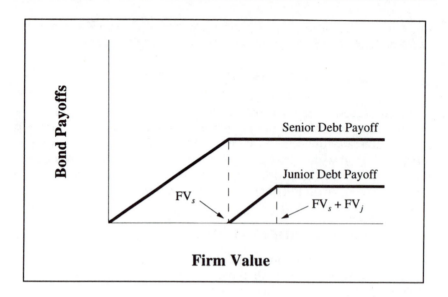

FIGURE 8.3   Payoffs on Junior and Senior Corporate Debt

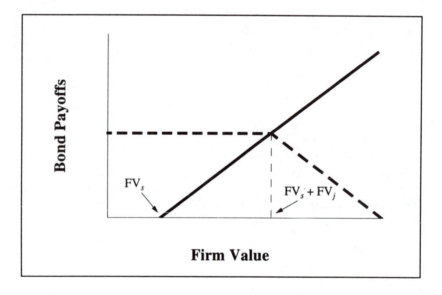

FIGURE 8.4   Junior Debt Analyzed as a Portfolio of Calls

to create various options and provide different divisions of the corporate pie when the bonds mature.

CALLABLE BONDS

The typical corporate bond is a callable bond. A **callable bond** is a bond that can be redeemed at the will of the issuer by the payment of a specified amount. Usually, the bond is not callable until a specified number of years after its issuance. Thereafter, the issuer may call the bond at any time. As an example, a firm might issue a bond today that is callable in five years (and thereafter), with a required payment equal to 110 percent of the face value of the bond. Typical call provisions allow this required payment to decline in subsequent years. In some cases, the bond is callable only on certain dates.

The issuer of the bond has an incentive to call the bond if the coupon rate exceeds the current market rate of interest. For example, if the callable bond were issued at 11 percent and current rates for similar debt are 6 percent, the issuer might wish to call the 11 percent bond and issue new debt at the prevailing market rate of 6 percent.

When it issues a callable bond, the firm itself retains a valuable option to require the bondholder to surrender the bond in return for the payment of a certain amount. Therefore, the call feature of a corporate bond means that the issuing firm has a call option on the outstanding bond. The exercise price of this call option is the call price that the firm must pay to call the bond.

For the bondholder, a callable bond is less desirable than a bond with no call feature. The bondholder knows that the issuer will exercise the call feature only when it benefits the issuing firm. In our example, the bondholder receiving an 11 percent coupon payment in a 6 percent interest rate environment certainly would prefer that the issuer not call the bond. Therefore, in accepting a callable bond, the bondholder realizes that he is implicitly buying a (noncallable) bond and selling a call option on the bond to the issuer. As we have seen, this call option held by the issuer has greater value when market rates of interest lie below the coupon rate on the bond.

The value of the noncallable bond varies inversely and smoothly with interest rates over the entire range of rates. By contrast, the value of a callable bond parallels the value of the noncallable bond for higher interest rates. For low interest rates, however, the value of the callable bond remains constant at a lower level.

To understand the difference in the values of callable and noncallable bonds, consider the following example of two similar bonds. One is noncallable while the other is callable on a single date in five years at a call price of $1,100.[2] We assume that both bonds have an initial maturity of 30 years and that both have an 8 percent coupon and a $1,000 face value. We further assume that the noncallable bond has an 8 percent yield at issuance, so it is priced at its face value of $1,000. The callable bond is identical in its promised coupon payments and maturity and differs from the noncallable bond only in its call feature. As we have seen, this means that the buyer of the callable bond grants the issuer a call option which has some value. Therefore, we know that the price of the callable bond at issuance must be less than the otherwise identical noncallable bond.

Figure 8.5 illustrates the values of the two bonds five years after issuance, when both bonds have 25 years remaining until maturity. If market rates of interest are 8 percent, the noncallable bond will still be worth $1,000. The callable bond will be priced below $1,000 because of the call feature. If interest rates are higher, at 10 percent for example, the price of the noncallable bond will be $817, and the price of the callable bond will still be somewhat lower. If interest rates are substantially lower than 8 percent, say 6 percent for example, the price of the noncallable bond will be $1,257. At this point we can see that there will be a sub-

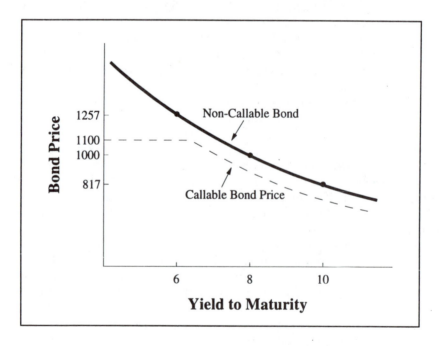

FIGURE 8.5   Callable versus Noncallable Bonds

stantial divergence between the price of the callable and noncallable bond. The call price for the bond of $1,100 is effectively the upper bound on the price of the callable bond, even in a low interest rate environment. Investors will not be willing to pay more than $1,100 for the callable bond, because they know it can be called away from them at that price.

The issuing firm holds a call option on the bond and a short position in the underlying bond. If interest rates fall, the value of bonds will rise in general. However, the callable bond is a single security, meaning that the bond and the call option on the bond are inextricably bound together. To capture the value of the call option, the issuer must exercise the call feature of the bond. This union of the call and the underlying bond in a single security helps to explain why the value of the callable bond cannot rise significantly above its call price. The resulting pricing is depicted in Figure 8.5. Summarizing, for prices at or below the call price on the callable bond, the two bonds will behave similarly. However, the callable bond will always be worth somewhat less than an otherwise similar bond due to the presence of the call feature. For higher prices on the noncallable bond, the price of the callable bond will be capped at or near the call price of the bond.

Figure 8.5 does not show the exact price of the callable bond, because it does not attempt to exactly price the call that is embedded in the callable bond. However, we know that the price of the embedded call will depend on the time until expiration, the prevailing interest rate, the price of the otherwise similar bond, the call price, and the volatility of the price of the otherwise similar bond.

CONVERTIBLE BONDS

Many corporate bonds are convertible into shares of the issuing firm. The holder of the bond has the option to convert the bond into shares under the terms specified in the bond indenture. For example, a firm might issue a $1,000 face value convertible bond with a 20-year maturity and a coupon rate of 9 percent. The bond could be converted into eight shares of stock by surrendering the bond.[3] We assume that a share of the issuing firm was worth $100 at the time of issuance. We can analyze this type of convertible bond as consisting of two elements: a regular bond with no conversion feature, plus a call option on eight shares of stock with the exercise price of the option being the value of the bond. The number of shares received for the bond upon conversion is the **conversion ratio.** Because the purchase of a convertible bond receives a call option on the shares of the issuing firm, the convertible bond sells for more than an otherwise similar nonconvertible bond. This means that the issuing firm can issue a convertible bond at a lower interest rate than an otherwise similar nonconvertible bond. However, the firm gives a call option to secure this lower interest rate.

At any time during its life, the bond must be worth at least its conversion value. In our example, we assume that the conversion ratio was eight shares, so the bond must be worth at least eight times the current share price. If this condition were not met, there would be an immediate arbitrage opportunity because a trader could buy the bond, exercise the conversion feature to secure the shares, and sell the shares for more than the price of the bond. Of course, the bond can sell for more than its conversion value, because the bond always has all of the features of a straight bond.

At the maturity of the bond, the bond will pay its face value, will be converted, or the firm will default. The firm will default if the face value exceeds the value of the firm. In the case of default, the owners of the convertible bond will take over the entire firm. Assuming the firm does not default, the convertible bond will be worth the maximum of the face value or the conversion ratio times the stock price.

In many instances, the bond indenture prohibits the issuing firm from paying a dividend during the life of the convertible bond. In this case, the bond will not be converted prior to its maturity date. This is clear by analogy to a call. Exercising a call or converting a convertible bond on a nondividend stock terminates the option in favor of its intrinsic value. As we saw for a call, the owner is better off selling the call and buying the stock in the open market. Similarly, the holder of a convertible bond on a nondividend stock will not exercise, because doing so discards the excess value of the call option over and above its intrinsic value.

Some convertible bonds are also callable. For convertible callable bonds, both the issuer and the bondholder hold an option associated with the bond. As we have seen, the issuer has a call option on the underlying bond, and the owner of a convertible bond has a call option on the firm's shares. Consider a convertible bond that could be profitably converted, and assume that the underlying shares pay no dividend. As we have just seen, the bondholder will not willingly convert prior to the maturity of the bond, because converting the bond discards the time value that is inherent in the option. However, the issuer would like the holder of the convertible to convert as soon as possible for the same reason. Therefore, the issuer of a convertible callable bond can force conversion by calling the bond. As soon as the convertible callable bond can be converted, the issuer should call the bond to force conversion. This is clear, because if it behooves the bondholder to delay conversion, it must benefit the issuer to force conversion. After all, the bond is an asset to the bondholder, but a liability to the issuer. Therefore, forcing conversion eliminates the time premium associated with the conversion option.

WARRANTS

A typical warrant allows the owner to surrender the warrant and pay a stated price for a share of common stock of the firm that issues the warrant. Usually, warrants are created with three to seven years to expiration. As such, a warrant is very much like a call option on the stock of the issuing firm. However, a call option has as its underlying instrument an existing share. By contrast, the exercise of a warrant requires the issuing firm to create a new share and deliver it to the exerciser of the warrant. Therefore, the exercise of a warrant involves a dilution of ownership because a new share is created. Warrants are often attached to bonds as a "sweetener" to make the bonds more salable. Often these warrants are detachable and can even trade in a separate market. However warrants are issued, they are valuable instruments with all of the features of a call option, except for the fact that they command a newly created share upon exercise rather than an existing share.

At the expiration date of the warrant, exercise would make sense only if the resulting share value from exercise exceeds the exercise price. Let V_B = the share price before exercise, X = the exercise price of the warrant, n = the number of shares outstanding before exercise, and q = the number of warrants. The value of the firm after exercise will be $nV_B + qX$, because the total exercise price on the warrants is qX, and the firm's value increases by the influx of cash from the exercise of the warrants. There will be $n(1 + q/n)$ shares outstanding after exercise. Therefore, the value of a share after exercise will be:

$$\frac{n V_B + qX}{n + q} \qquad 8.10$$

As an example, consider a firm with 100 outstanding shares priced at $48 per share, and assume that the shares pay no dividend. The firm has warrants for 10 shares outstanding with an exercise price on the warrants of $50. If the warrants are exercised, the firm will be worth $5,300, the present value of the firm plus the $500 exercise price of the warrants. The firm will then have 110 shares outstanding after it issues the 10 shares to meet the exercise of the warrants. Consequently, each share after exercise would be worth $48.18. With an exercise price of $50 and a postexercise share price of $48.18, exercise is not feasible. Thus, exercise will only be feasible if the stock price equals or exceeds the exercise price.

As with a call option, a warrant should not be exercised until expiration. The reasoning is the same; early exercise discards the time premium associated with the option. Instead of exercising the call or warrant, the owner should sell the call or warrant and purchase the underlying good.

The value of a European warrant equals the value of a parallel European call after adjustment for the dilution of ownership caused by the exercise of the warrant. If q warrants are exercised and n shares are outstanding before exercise, there will be $n(1 + q/n)$ shares outstanding after exercise. The European warrant gives title to one of those shares. Therefore, the value of a European warrant at time t, W_t, must be:

$$W_t = \frac{c_t}{1 + \dfrac{q}{n}}$$

In other words, the value of a European warrant equals the value of a European call option divided by one plus the proportion of shares created in response to the exercise of the warrant.

SUMMARY

In this chapter, we have explored how various corporate securities can be analyzed in terms of the options concepts developed throughout this book. We began by considering an extremely simple firm drawing its capital only from common stock and a single pure discount bond. For such a firm, we saw that the common stock can be treated as a call option on the entire firm. In this case, the call option has an exercise price equal to the payment promised to the bondholders and the expiration date for the option is the maturity of the bond.

The bond itself can be analyzed in options terms as well. We used put–call parity to show that the bond can be analyzed in two equivalent ways. First, the bond represents ownership of the entire firm coupled with a short position in a call on the entire firm given to the shareholders. The exercise price of the call possessed by the shareholders is the payment promised to the bondholders. As a second and equivalent analysis, the bond consists of a risk-free bond paying the face value of the bond combined with a short position in a put option sold to the shareholders, which allows the shareholders to put the entire firm to the bondholders for an exercise price of the face value of the bond.

We next considered a firm with stock, senior debt, and subordinated debt in its capital structure. The stock owners have essentially the same position as in the simplest case. They own a call on the entire firm and the exercise price of the call is the total set of payments promised to both the senior and subordinated debtholders. The subordinated debtholder essentially holds a long call on the firm with an exercise price equal to the payment promised to the senior bondholders coupled with a short call on the entire firm with an exercise price equal to the payment promised to the junior bondholders. If the shareholders decide not to exercise their call, it will be because the value of the firm is less than the exercise price that the stockholders face—the payments promised to the junior and senior debtholders. The junior debtholders can then claim the firm by exercising their call on the senior debtholders; they merely must pay the senior debtholders as promised. However, the junior debtholders have also issued a call, because the stockholders may call the firm away from them by making the promised payment.

Both callable and convertible bonds have options embedded in them. As we saw, a callable bond consists of a straight bond, but the issuer of the bond retains a call option on the bond. Thus, the issuer is long this call and the bondholder has sold the call to the issuer. This call gives the issuer of the bond the right to purchase the bond and avoid any further payments by paying the call price. In a bond convertible into common stock, the owner of the bond has a call option on the shares of the firm. The bondholder in this case can convert a bond into shares by surrendering the bond and paying the stipulated price to acquire the shares permitted by the bond covenant. In both the case of the callable bond and the convertible bond, the embedded options have value, and this value can be a considerable proportion of the total value of the bond.

Finally, we considered the pricing of warrants. We noted that a warrant is similar to a call option. However, a call option gives the holder the right to buy an existing share, while a warrant gives the holder the right to buy a newly issued share from the firm. Therefore, the exercise of the warrant involves a dilution of ownership in the firm, and a warrant is, therefore, slightly less valuable than an otherwise similar call option.

REVIEW QUESTIONS

1. Explain why common stock is itself like a call option. In the options analysis of common stock, what plays the role of the exercise price and what plays the role of the underlying stock?

2. Consider a firm that issues a pure discount bond that matures in one year and has a face value of $1,000,000. Analyze the payoffs that the bondholders will receive in options pricing terms, assuming the only other security in the firm is common stock.

3. Consider a firm with common stock and a pure discount bond as its financing. The total value of the firm is $1,000,000. There are 10,000 shares of common stock priced at $70 per share. The bond matures in ten years and has a total face value of $500,000. What is the interest rate on the bond, assuming annual compounding? Would the interest rate become higher or lower if the volatility of the firm's cash flows increases?

4. A firm has a capital structure consisting of common stock and a single bond. The managers of the firm are considering a major capital investment that will be financed from internally generated funds. The project can be initiated in two ways, one with a high fixed cost component and the other with a low fixed cost component. Although both technologies have the same expected value, the high fixed cost approach has the potential for greater payoffs. (If the product is successful, the high fixed cost approach gives much lower total costs for large production levels.) What does options theory suggest about the choice the managers should make? Explain.

5. In a firm with common stock, senior debt, and subordinated debt, assume that both debt instruments mature at the same time. What is the necessary condition on the value of the firm at maturity for each security holder to receive at least some payment? With two classes of debt, does options theory counsel managers to increase the riskiness of the firm's operations? Would there be any difference on this point between a firm with a single debt issue and two debt issues? Which bondholders would tend to be more risk averse as far as choosing a risk level for the firm's operations? Explain.

6. Consider a firm financed solely by common stock and a single callable bond issue. Assume that the bond is a pure discount bond. Is there any circumstance in which the firm should call the bond before the maturity date? Would such an exercise of the firm's call option discard the time premium? Explain.

7. Consider a firm financed only by common stock and a convertible bond issue. When should the bondholders exercise? Explain. If the common shares pay a dividend, could it make sense for the bondholders to exercise before the bond matures? Explain by relating your answer to our discussion of the exercise of American calls on dividend-paying stocks.

8. Warrants are often used to compensate top executives in firms. Often these warrants cannot be exercised until a distant expiration date. This form of compensation is used to align the manager's incentives with the maximization of the shareholders' wealth. Ex-

plain how the manager's receiving warrants might thwart the efforts to change his or her incentives.

NOTES

1. Of course the original Black–Scholes paper, "The Pricing of Options and Corporate Liabilities," *Journal of Political Economy*, 81, 1973, 637–659, already focused on the options characteristics of stocks and bonds.
2. Generally, bonds are not callable until their first call date, and they are then callable at any time thereafter.
3. Other features are possible. For example, some bonds can be converted to preferred stock. Some convertible bonds can be converted only by surrendering the bond and making a cash payment. Some convertible bonds can be converted only on certain dates. Further, some convertible securities are preferred stock that can be converted into common stock.

Answers to Review Questions

CHAPTER ONE: THE OPTIONS MARKET

1. Call and put options are the two fundamental kinds of exchange-traded options. They differ in the rights and privileges that ownership conveys. The owner of a call option has the right to buy the good that underlies the option at a specified price, with this right lasting until a stated expiration date. The put owner has the right to sell the good that underlies the option at a specified price with this right lasting until a stated expiration date. Thus, owning a call gives the right to buy and owning a put gives the right to sell. Correlatively, the seller of a call receives a payment and must sell the underlying good at the option of the call owner. The seller of a put receives a payment and must buy the underlying good at the option of the put owner.

2. To initiate a long call position, a trader buys a call option. At the time of purchase, the trader must pay the price of the option, which the seller of the call collects. Upon purchase, the owner of a call has the right to purchase the underlying good at the specified call price with that right lasting until the stated expiration date. The owner of a call has no obligations, once he or she pays the purchase price.

3. The owner of a call or put has already paid the purchase price. After buying the option, the owner has only rights and no obligations. The option owner may exercise the option, sell it, or allow it to expire worthless, but the option owner is not compelled to do anything.

4. Taking a short position in an option involves selling an option. Upon the sale, the seller receives a cash payment. This is the only benefit associated with selling an option. After receiving payment

for the option, the seller has only potential obligations, because the seller may be required to perform at the discretion of the option owner.

5. The short call position is obtained when a trader sells a call option. The seller of a call may be required to surrender the underlying good in exchange for the payment stated in the options contract. The short call position has a maximum benefit equal to the price that the seller received to enter the short call position. The short call position is most favorable when the price of the underlying good remains below the exercise price. Then the seller of the call retains the full price of the option as profit. The higher the stock price above the exercise price, the worse for the call seller.

    In a long put position, the trader buys a put option. Owning the put gives the trader the right to sell the underlying good at the stated exercise price until the option expires. The put purchaser profits when the price of the underlying good falls below the exercise price. Then the owner of the put can require the put seller to buy the underlying good at the exercise price. When the underlying good has a price above the exercise price, the long put trader cannot exercise and loses the entire purchase price of the option.

    In contrasting the short call and the long put positions, we note that the short call trader has a maximum profit equal to the original sales price, and the long put trader has a maximum loss equal to the original sales price. For the long put position, there is the chance of a virtually unlimited profit as the stock price falls to zero. For the short call position, there is the chance of a theoretically unlimited loss, as the stock price rises toward infinity.

6. The premium is the same as the option price and equals $5. The exercise price is the same as the striking price and equals $100.

7. At the time of trading, the short trader of a put or call receives a payment. This is the only benefit the short trader receives from trading. If the option expires worthless, then the option was not exercised and the short trader attains the maximum possible profit. In selling an option, the short trader exposes himself or herself to the risk that the purchaser will exercise. For accepting this risk, the seller has received the option premium. If the option expires worthless, the short trader has escaped that risk.

8. The clearinghouse guarantees the financial integrity of the market and oversees the performance of traders in the market. If there were no clearinghouse, each trader would have to be concerned with the financial integrity of his trading partner. Assuring that the opposite trading party will perform as promised is difficult and expensive.

With a clearinghouse, each trader has an assurance that the opposite side of his transaction will be fulfilled. The clearinghouse guarantees it.

9. A European option can be exercised only at expiration, while an American option can be exercised at any time prior to expiration. This difference implies that the American option must be at least as valuable as the European option.

10. The trader will be either long or short. If the trader is long, he or she can close the position by selling the exact same option. The option that will be sold must be on the same underlying good, have the same expiration, and the same striking price as the original option that is to be closed. If the trader were short initially, the trader would close the position by buying the identical option. In essence, the trader closes the position by trading to bring his or her net position back to zero. Again, making sure that all characteristics of the option match is an essential condition.

CHAPTER TWO: OPTIONS PAYOFFS AND OPTIONS STRATEGIES

1.

Profit/Loss for Call #1 for Various Stock Prices

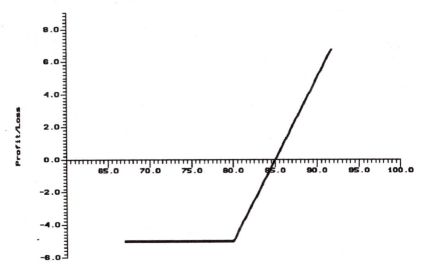

Stock Price
Press ESC to Return to Graphics Menu

2.   Profit/Loss for Put #1 for Various Stock Prices

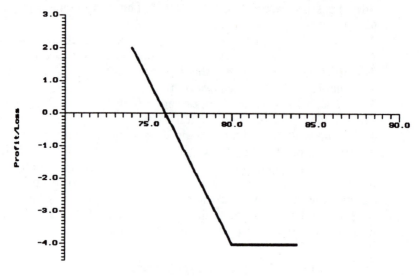

Press ESC to Return to Graphics Menu

3.   Profit/Loss for All Options for Various Stock Prices

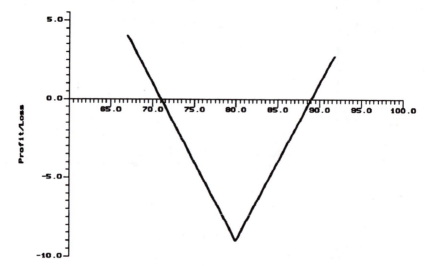

Press ESC to Return to Graphics Menu

With a stock price at $80 at expiration, neither the call nor the put can be exercised. Both expire worthless, giving a total loss of $9. The straddle breaks even (has a zero profit) if the stock price is either $71 or $89.

4. With these prices, an arbitrage opportunity exists because the call price does not equal the maximum of zero or the stock price minus the exercise price. To exploit this mispricing, one should buy the call and exercise it for a total out-of-pocket cost of $74. At the same time, the trader should sell the stock and deliver the stock just acquired through exercise for a $75 cash inflow. This produces a riskless profit without investment of $1. Because the option is at expiration, both the American and European options have the same right to exercise. Therefore, the American or European character of the option has no effect on the trading strategy.

5. At expiration, the put price must equal the maximum of zero or the exercise price minus the stock price to avoid arbitrage. Therefore, the put price should be $20 in this situation, but it trades for $22. This difference gives rise to an arbitrage opportunity, because the put is priced too high relative to its theoretical value. To exploit this, the trader should simply sell the put and receive $22. Now the option can be exercised against the trader or not. If it is not exercised, the put expires worthless, the obligation is complete, and the trader retains the $22 as total profit. However, the purchaser of the option may choose to exercise immediately. In this case, the seller of the put must buy the stock for the exercise price of $140. The trader then sells the stock for $120 in the market, giving a $20 loss on the exercise. But the put seller already received $22, so she still has a $2 profit. In summary, selling the put leads to a $22 profit if the put buyer foolishly fails to exercise. Alternatively, if the put buyer exercises, the put seller still has a $2 profit. This is an arbitrage opportunity, because selling the overpriced put gives a profit without investment in all circumstances.

6. As in the previous problem, these prices violate the no-arbitrage condition. Now, however, the put is underpriced relative to the other values. To conduct the arbitrage, the trader should buy the stock and buy and exercise the put. In this sequence of transactions, the trader pays $120 to acquire the stock, pays $18 to acquire the put, and receives $140 upon exercise of the put. These transactions yield a profit of $2 with no risk and no investment.

7.   Profit/Loss for All Options for Various Stock Prices

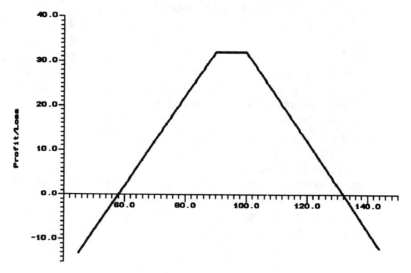

The worst outcomes occur when the stock price is very low or very high. First, the strangle loses $1 for each dollar the stock price falls below $58. With a zero stock price, the strangle loses $58. If the stock price is too high, the strangle also loses money. Because the stock could theoretically go to infinity, the potential loss on the strangle is unbounded. For stock prices of $58 or $132, the strangle gives exactly a zero profit.

8.

Profit/Loss for All Calls for Various Stock Prices

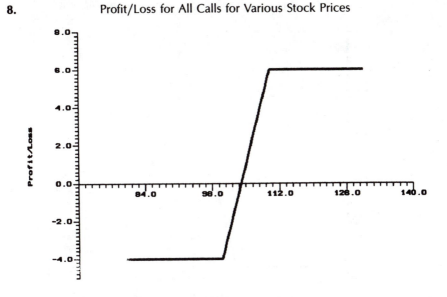

This position is a bull spread with calls, because it is designed to profit if the stock price rises. The entire position has a zero profit if the stock price is $104. At this point, the call with the $100 exercise price can be exercised for a $4 exercise profit. This $4 exercise value exactly offsets the price of the spread. The worst loss occurs when the stock price is $100 or below, because the option with the $100 exercise cannot be exercised, and the entire position is worthless. This gives a $4 loss. The best outcome occurs for any stock price of $110 or above and the total profit is $6.

9.   Value of All Calls for Various Stock Prices

Press ESC to Return to Graphics Menu

This is a long position in a butterfly spread. If the stock price is $90, the value of the spread is zero. For a $15 stock price, the spread is worth zero. The entire spread can be worth zero at expiration. This zero value occurs for any stock price of $30 or below and $40 or above.

10.   Value of Puts and Stocks for Various Stock Prices

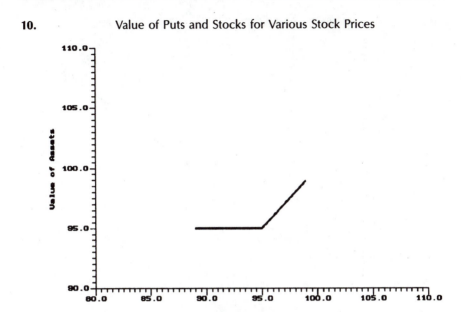

Press ESC to Return to Graphics Menu

The worst result is a portfolio value of $95. The purchase of the put for $3 gives a loss of $8. This worst outcome occurs for a terminal stock portfolio value of $95 or less. This combined position is an insured portfolio. The position insures against any terminal portfolio value less than $95 or any loss greater than $8.

11.

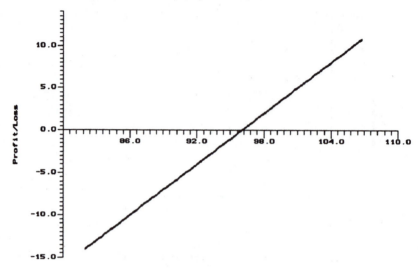

Profit/Loss for All Options for Various Stock Prices

No matter what stock price results, the options portfolio will have $1 less profit than the stock itself. For example, the options portfolio costs $1, but both options are worthless at a stock price of $95. Therefore, at a stock price of $95, the stock has a zero profit, and the options portfolio has a $1 loss. Further, the options portfolio will be worth exactly $95 less than the stock at every price. With a stock price of $80, the call is worthless and the put will be exercised against the option holder for an exercise loss of $15. Therefore, the options portfolio is worth −$15 for an $80 stock price. If the stock trades for $105, the options portfolio will be worth $10.

12. A portfolio consisting of one long call, one short put, and a riskless investment equal to the common exercise price of the two options gives exactly the same payoffs as a share of the underlying stock on the common expiration date. This put–call parity relationship requires that this portfolio of long call, short put, plus riskless investment should have the same price as the stock. With our data, the riskless bond must therefore cost $120 − $11 + $8 = $117. The riskless interest rate must be 2.53 percent.

13. As the previous answer already indicated, the described portfolio (long call, short put, plus long bond) must have the same value as the stock itself. This illustrates the put–call parity relationship.

14. These prices violate put–call parity. The long call, plus short put, plus riskless investment of the present value of the exercise price must together equal the stock price:

$$S = C - P + Xe^{-r(T - t)}$$

Instead, we have $50 ≥ $5 − $4 + $45 = $46. Therefore, the stock is overpriced relative to the duplicating right-hand-side portfolio. Accordingly, we transact as follows, with the cash flows being indicated in parentheses: Sell stock (+$50), buy call (−$5), sell put ($4), and buy the riskless bond (−$45). This gives a positive cash flow of $4 at the time of trading. To close our position, we collect $50 on the maturing bond. If the stock price is above $50, we exercise our call and use our $50 bond proceeds to acquire the stock, which we can then repay to close our short position. The put cannot be exercised against us, so we conclude the transaction with our original $4 profit. If the stock price is below $50, the put will be exercised against us. If so, we lose $50 − S on the exercise, paying our $50 bond proceeds to acquire the stock. Now with the stock in hand, we close our short position and the call expires worthless. As a result, we still have our $4 original cash inflow as profit. No matter what the stock price may be at expiration, our profit will be $4.

15. A synthetic call option consists of the following portfolio: long the stock, long the put, and short a risk–free bond paying the exercise price at the common maturity date of the call and put. Therefore, the following relationship must hold:

$$C = S + P - \frac{X}{(1 + r)^t}$$

Therefore, with the information given:

$$C = \$80 + \$2 - \$67.67 = \$14.43$$

16. Put–call parity implies:

$$S - \frac{X}{(1 + r)^{T-t}} = C - P$$

In this case, the stock and bond have the same price, so the left-hand side of the equation equals zero. For the right-hand side to equal zero, the call and put must have the same price as well. However, from the information given, we cannot determine what that price would be.

17. This position will profit for very low (say below $70) or very high (say above $85) stock prices at expiration. For prices in the range of $75 to $85, the position will lose. The exact breakeven points cannot be determined from the information given, however. In effect, the pair of strangles described is a short condor position.

18. From the information given, and applying put–call parity, we know:

$$S - \frac{X}{1 + r} = C - P = \$9$$

The stock price is $75 and must exceed the bond price by $9, so the price of the bond is $66. Thus, the present value of the $70 exercise price is $66, implying an interest rate of 6.06 percent.

19. The bull spread with puts and these exercise prices implies buying the put with $X = \$40$ and selling the put with $X = \$45$. To buy the bear spread implies buying a put with $X = \$50$ and selling a put with $X = \$45$. If the stock price at expiration is $53, all of the puts expire worthless. In making this trade, one has bought puts with $X = \$40$ and $X = \$50$, and sold two puts with $X = \$45$. This is equivalent to a long butterfly spread with puts.

20. The box spread gives a riskless payoff, so it is equivalent to a synthetic risk-free bond.

21. If the exercise price of a put is zero, there can be no payoff from the put so the price must be zero. In this circumstance, the call must be worth the stock price. With respect to bounds on the option prices, the call price can never exceed the stock price and the put price can never exceed the exercise price.

$$C = S + P - \frac{X}{(1 + r)^{T-t}}$$

22. The put price declines as the ratio S/X becomes large. The call option must increase in value. As we will see, the call must always be worth at least the stock price minus the present value of the exercise price.

CHAPTER THREE: BOUNDS ON OPTIONS PRICES

1. The highest price theoretically possible for a call option is to equal the value of the underlying stock. This happens only for a call option

that has a zero exercise price and an infinite time until expiration. With such a call, the option can be instantaneously and costlessly exchanged for the stock at any time. Therefore, the call must have at least the value of the stock itself. Yet it cannot be worth more than the stock, because the option merely gives access to the stock itself. As a consequence, the call must have the same price as the stock.

2. The maximum value of a put equals the potential inflow of the exercise price minus the associated outflow of the stock price. The maximum value for this quantity occurs when the stock price is zero. At that time, the value of the put will equal the exercise price. In this situation, the put gives immediate potential access to the exercise price because it is an American option.

3. As with the American put, the European put attains its maximum value when the stock price is zero. However, before expiration, the put cannot be exercised. Therefore, the maximum price for a European put is the present value of the exercise price, when the exercise price is discounted at the risk-free rate from expiration to the present. This discounting reflects the fact that the owner of a European put cannot exercise now and collect the exercise price. Instead, she must wait until the option expires.

4. The exercise value of a put option equals the exercise price (an inflow) minus the value of the stock at the time of exercise (an outflow). In our notation, this exercise value is $X - S$. For any put, the maximum value occurs when the stock is worthless, $S = 0$. The American and European puts have different maximum theoretical values because of the different rules governing early exercise. Because an American put can be exercised at any time, its maximum theoretical value equals the exercise price, X. If the stock price is zero at any time, an American put gives its owner immediate access to amount X through exercise. This is not true of a European put, which can be exercised only at expiration. If the option has time remaining until expiration and the stock is worthless, the European put holder must wait until expiration to exercise. With the stock worthless, the exercise will yield X to the European put holder. Because the exercise must wait until expiration, however, the put can be worth only the present value of the exercise price. Thus, the theoretical maximum value of a European put is $Xe^{-r(T-t)}$. In the special case of an option at expiration, $t = 0$, the maximum value for a European and an American put is X.

5. The call price varies inversely with the exercise price. The exercise price is a potential liability that the call owner faces, because the

call owner must pay the exercise price in order to exercise. The smaller this potential liability, other factors held constant, the greater will be the value of a call option.

6. A no-arbitrage condition places an upper bound on the value of Call 2. The price of Call 2 cannot exceed the price of the option with the higher exercise price plus the $5 difference in the two exercise prices. Thus, the upper bound for the value of Call 2 is $12. If Call 2 is priced above $12, say, at $13, the following arbitrage becomes available.

   Sell Call 2 for cash flow +$13 and buy Call 1 for cash flow −$7. This is a net cash inflow of +$6. If Call 2 is exercised against you, you can immediately exercise Call 1. This provides the stock to meet the exercise of Call 1 against you. On the double exercise you receive $95 and pay $100, for a net cash flow of −$5. However, you received $6 at the time of trading for a net profit of $1. This is the worst-case outcome.

   If Call 1 cannot be exercised, the profit is the full $6 original cash flow from the two trades. Also, if the stock price lies between $95 and $100 when Call 1 is exercised against you, it may be optimal to purchase the stock in the market rather than exercise Call 2 to secure the stock. For example, assume the stock trades for $98 when Call 1 is exercised against you. In this case, you buy the stock for $98 instead of exercising Call 2 and paying $100. Then your total cash flows are +$6 from the two trades, +$95 when Call 1 is exercised against you and −$98 from purchasing the stock to meet the exercise. Now your net arbitrage profit is $3. In summary, stock prices of $95 or below give a net profit of $6, because Call 1 cannot be exercised. Stock prices of $100 or above give a net profit of $1, because you will need to exercise Call 2 to meet the exercise of Call 1. Prices between $95 and $100 give a profit equal to +$6 +$95 − stock price at the time of exercise.

7. We know from the no arbitrage arguments that: $C \geq S - Xe^{-r(T-t)}$. In this case, we have $C = S - X$ exactly. Therefore, the interest rate must be zero.

8. We know from the no-arbitrage arguments that: $C \geq S - Xe^{-r(T-t)}$. Substituting the specified values gives $C \geq \$80 - \$70e^{-0.12(0.33)} = \$80 - \$67.28 = \$12.72$. Therefore, the call price must equal or exceed $12.72 to avoid arbitrage.

9. Here we have two calls that are identical except for their time to expiration. In this situation, the call with the longer time until expiration must have a price equal to or exceeding the price of the

shorter-lived option. These values violate this condition, so arbitrage is possible as follows.

Sell Call 2 and buy Call 1 for a net cash inflow of $1. If Call 2 is exercised at any time, the trader can exercise Call 1 and meet the exercise obligation for a net zero cash flow. This retains the $1 profit no matter what happens. It may also occur that the profit exceeds $1. For example, assume that Call 2 cannot be exercised in the first three months and expires worthless. This leaves the trader with the $1 initial cash inflow plus a call option with a three month life, so the trader has an arbitrage profit of at least $1, perhaps much more.

10. Exercising a call before expiration discards the time value of the option. If the underlying stock pays a dividend, it can be rational to discard the time value to capture the dividend. If there is no dividend, it will always be irrational to exercise a call, because the trader can always sell the call in the market instead. Exercising a call on a no-dividend stock discards the time value, while selling the option in the market retains it. Thus, only the presence of a dividend can justify early exercise. Even in this case, the dividend must be large enough to warrant the sacrifice of the time value.

11. Because the American option gives every benefit that the European option does, the price of the American option must be at least as great as that of the European option. The right of early exercise inherent in the American option can give extra value if a dividend payment is possible before the common expiration date. Thus, if there is no dividend to consider, the two prices will be the same. If a dividend is possible before expiration, the price of the American call may exceed that of the European call.

12. The minimum value of an American put must equal its value for immediate exercise, which is $X - S$. A lower price results in arbitrage. For example, assume $X = \$100$, $S = \$90$ and $P = \$8$. To exploit the arbitrage inherent in these prices, buy the put and exercise for a net cash outflow of $-\$98$. Sell the stock for $+\$100$ for an arbitrage profit of $2.

13. For a put, the exercise value is $X - S$. However, a European put can be exercised only at expiration. Therefore, the present value of the exercise value is $Xe^{-r(T-t)} - S$, and this is the minimum price of a European put. For example, consider $X = \$100$, $S = \$90$, $T - t = 0.5$ years, and $r = 0.10$. The no-arbitrage condition implies the put should be worth at least $5.13.

Assume that the put actually trades for $5. With these prices, an arbitrageur could trade as follows. Borrow $95 at 10 percent for six months and buy the stock and the put. This gives an initial net zero cash flow. At expiration, the profit depends upon the price of the stock. First, there will be a debt to pay of $99.87 in all cases. If the stock price is $100 or above, the put is worthless and the profit equals S − $99.87. Thus, the profit will be at least $0.13, possibly much more. For stock prices below $100, exercise of the put yields $100, which is enough to pay the debt of $99.87 and keep $0.13 profit.

14. The difference in minimum values for American and European puts stems from the restrictions on exercising a put. An American put offers the immediate access to the exercise value X if the put owner chooses to exercise. Because the European put cannot be exercised until expiration, the cash inflow associated with exercise must be discounted to $Xe^{-r(T-t)}$. The difference in minimum values equals the time value of the exercise price.

15. The value of an American put increases with the time until expiration. A longer-lived put offers every advantage that the shorter-lived put does. Therefore, a longer-lived put must be worth at least as much as the shorter-lived put. This implies that value increases with time until expiration. Violation of this condition leads to arbitrage.

16. For a European put, the value may or may not increase with time until expiration. Upon exercise the put holder receives X − S. If the European put holder cannot exercise immediately, the inflow represented by the exercise price is deferred. For this reason, the value of a European put can be lower the longer the time until expiration. However, having a longer term until expiration also adds value to a put, because it allows more time for something beneficial to happen to the stock price. Thus, the net effect of time until expiration depends on these two opposing forces. Under some circumstances, the value of a European put will increase as time until expiration increases, but it will not always do so.

17. For two European puts, the price differential cannot exceed the difference in the present value of the exercise prices. With our data, the difference cannot exceed ($110 − $100)$e^{-0.12(0.5)}$ = $9.42. If the price differential on the European puts exceeds $9.42, we have an arbitrage opportunity. To capture the arbitrage profit, we sell the relatively overpriced put with the exercise price of $110 and buy the put with the $100 exercise price. If the put we sold is exercised against us, we accept the stock and dispose of it by exercising the put we bought. This will always guarantee a profit. For example, assume that the put with X = $100 trades for $5 and the put with X = $110 sells for $15, giving a $10 differential. We sell the put

with $X = \$110$ and buy the put with $X = \$100$, for a net inflow of $10. We invest this until expiration, at which time it will be worth $\$10e^{0.12(0.5)} = \$10.62$. If the put we sold is exercised against us, we pay $110 and receive the stock. We can then exercise our put to dispose of the stock and receive $10. This gives a $10 loss on the double exercise. However, our maturing bond is worth $10.62, so we still have a profit of $.62.

For two American puts, the price differential cannot exceed the difference in the exercise prices. If it does, we conduct the same arbitrage. However, we do not have to worry about the discounted value of the differential, because the American puts carry the opportunity to exercise immediately and to gain access to the value of the mispricing at any time, not just at expiration.

18. For a call, the price increases with interest rates. The easiest way to see this is to consider the no-arbitrage condition: $C \geq S - Xe^{-r(T-t)}$. The higher the interest rate, the smaller will be the present value of the exercise price, a potential liability. With extremely high interest rates, the exercise price will have an insignificant present value and the call price will approach the stock price.

19. Put prices vary inversely with interest rates. This holds true for both American and European puts. For the put owner, the exercise price is a potential inflow. The present value of this inflow, and the market value of the put, increases as the interest rate falls. Therefore, put prices rise as interest rates fall.

20. Call prices rise as the riskiness of the underlying stock increases. A call option embodies insurance against extremely bad outcomes. Insurance is more valuable the greater the risk it insures against. Therefore, if the underlying stock is very risky, the insurance embedded in the call is more valuable. As a consequence, call prices vary directly with the risk of the underlying good.

21. From put–call parity, $S - Xe^{-r(T-t)} = C - P$. Therefore, the $C - P$ must equal:

$$\$50 - \$40e^{-0.5(0.1)} = \$11.95$$

We cannot determine what the two option prices are. Information about how the stock price might move is lacking.

22. From Question 21, we saw that the call price must exceed the put price by $11.95 according to put–call parity. Therefore, if the difference is only $7, there is an arbitrage opportunity, and the call price is cheap relative to the put. The long call/short put position is supposed to be worth the same as the long stock/short bond

position. But the long call/short put portfolio costs only $7, not the theoretically required $11.95. To perform the arbitrage we would buy the relatively underpriced portfolio and sell the relatively overpriced portfolio. Specifically we would: buy the call, sell the put, sell the stock, and buy the risk-free bond that pays the exercise price in six months. From these transactions we would have the following cash flows: from buying the call and selling the put $-$7$; from selling the stock $+$50$, and from buying the risk-free bond $-$38.05$, for a net cash flow of $4.95. This net cash flow exactly equals the pricing discrepancy.

At expiration, we can fulfill all of our obligations with no further cash flows. If the stock price is below the exercise price, the put we sold will be exercised against us and we must pay $40 and receive the stock. We will have the $40 from the maturing bond, and we use the stock that we receive to repay our short sale on the stock. If the stock price exceeds $40, we exercise our call and use the $40 proceeds to pay the exercise price. We then fulfill our short sale by returning the share.

CHAPTER FOUR: EUROPEAN OPTIONS PRICING

1. The binomial model is binomial because it allows for two possible stock price movements. The stock can either rise by a certain amount or fall by a certain amount. No other stock price movement is possible.

2. There is no chance. In every period, the stock price will either rise or fall. Therefore, in two adjacent periods, the stock price cannot be the same. From this period to the next, the stock price must necessarily rise or fall. However, the stock price can later return to its present price. This depends on the up and down factors for the change in the stock price.

3. Our data are:

$$C_u = \$2$$
$$C_d = \$0$$
$$US = \$132$$
$$DS = \$96$$
$$R = 1.06$$
$$B^* = (C_u D - C_d U)/[(U - D)R]$$
$$= [2(0.8) - 0(1.1)]/[(1.1 - 0.8)(1.06)] = \$5.03$$
$$N^* = (C_u - C_d)/(U - D)S = (2 - 0)/(1.1 - 0.8)120$$
$$= 0.0556$$

Therefore, $C = .0556(\$120) - \$5.03 = \$1.64$.

The probability of a stock price increase is:

$$(R - D)/(U - D) = (1.06 - 0.8)/(1.1 - 0.8) = 0.8667$$

4. Because $C = N*S - B*$, the portfolio of $C - N*S + B*$ should be a riskless portfolio.

5. Terminal stock prices in two periods are given as follows: $UUS = \$145.20$, $DDS = \$76.80$, and $UDS = DUS = \$105.60$. The probabilities of these different terminal stock prices are: $\pi_{uu} = (0.8667)(0.8667) = 0.7512$, $\pi_{ud} = (0.8667)(0.1333) = 0.1155$, $\pi_{du} = (0.1333)(0.8667) = 0.1155$, and $\pi_{dd} = (0.1333)(0.1333) = 0.0178$. The call price at expiration equals the terminal stock price minus the exercise price of \$100, or zero, whichever is larger. Therefore, we have $C_{uu} = \$15.20$, $C_{dd} = 0$, $C_{du} = C_{ud} = 0$.

   We have already found that the probability of an increase is 0.8667, so the probability of a down movement is 0.1333. Because the option pays off only with two increases, we need consider only that path. Thus, the value of the call is:

$$C = \pi_{uu}C_{uu}/R^2 = (0.7512)(\$15.20)/(1.06)^2 = \$10.16$$

6. From Question 3, we see that $US = \$132$. This is not enough to bring the call into the money. Therefore, we know that the call must expire worthless, so its current price is zero.

7. The call is worth \$6.12 and the put is worth \$3.04.

Three-Period Binomial Tree for a Stock and a Call

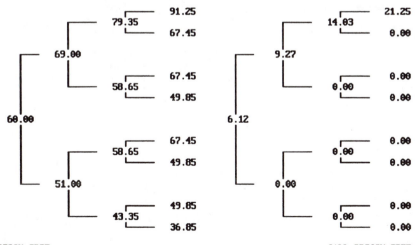

STOCK TREE   CALL OPTION TREE

Three-Period Binomial Tree for a Stock and a Put

STOCK TREE   **PUT OPTION TREE**

8. Substituting values for our problem, and realizing that the expected value of a drawing for a $N(0,1)$ distribution is zero, gives:

$$S_{t+1} - S_{-t} = \$55(0.15)(175/365) = \$3.96$$

Adding this amount to the initial stock price of $55 gives $58.96 as the expected stock price in 175 days.

9. $$d_1 = \frac{\ln\left[\dfrac{110}{105}\right] + [0.11 + 0.5(0.25)(0.25)]\left[\dfrac{43}{365}\right]}{0.25\sqrt{\dfrac{43}{365}}} = 0.7361$$

$$d_2 = d_1 - \sigma\sqrt{t} = 0.7361 - 0.25\sqrt{\frac{43}{365}} = 0.6503$$

$N(0.7361) = 0.769165$ and $N(0.6503) = 0.742251$. Therefore,

$$c = \$110(0.769165) - \$105e^{-0.11(43/365)}(0.742251) = \$7.6752.$$

For the put option with $X = \$140$:

$$d_1 = \frac{\ln\left[\dfrac{110}{140}\right] + [0.11 + 0.5(0.25)(0.25)]\left[\dfrac{43}{365}\right]}{0.25\sqrt{\dfrac{43}{365}}} = -2.6177$$

$$d_2 = d_1 - \sigma\sqrt{t} = -2.6177 - 0.25\sqrt{\frac{43}{365}} = -2.7035$$

The Black–Scholes put pricing model is:

$$p_t = Xe^{-r(T-t)} N(-d_2) - S_t N(-d_1)$$

$N(2.7035) = 0.996569$ and $N(2.6177) = 0.995574$. Therefore,

$$p_t = \$140e^{-0.11(43/365)}(0.996569) - \$110(0.995574) = \$28.21$$

10. $$d_1 = \frac{\ln\left[\dfrac{75}{70}\right] + [0.09 + 0.5(0.35)(0.35)]\left[\dfrac{150}{365}\right]}{0.35\sqrt{\dfrac{150}{365}}} = 0.5845$$

$$d_2 = d_1 - \sigma\sqrt{t} = 0.5845 - 0.35\sqrt{\frac{150}{365}} = 0.3601$$

$N(0.5845) = 0.720558$, $N(0.3601) = 0.640614$, $N(-0.5845) = 0.279442$, $N(-0.3601) = 0.359386$.

$$c_t = \$75(0.720558) - \$70\, e^{-0.09(150/365)}\,(0.640614)$$
$$= \$54.04 - \$43.21 = \$10.83$$
$$p_t = \$70e^{-0.09(150/365)}\,(0.359386) - \$75\,(0.279442)$$
$$= \$24.24 - \$20.96 = \$3.29$$

11. $$d_1^M = \frac{\ln\left[\dfrac{75}{70}\right] + [0.09 - 0.04 + 0.5(0.35)(0.35)]\left[\dfrac{150}{365}\right]}{0.35\sqrt{\dfrac{150}{365}}} = 0.5113$$

$$d_2^M = d_1^M - \sigma\sqrt{t} = 0.5113 - 0.35\sqrt{\frac{150}{365}} = 0.2869$$

$N(0.5113) = 0.695430$; $N(0.2869) = 0.304570$; $N(-0.5113) = 0.612906$; and $N(-0.2869) = 0.387094$.

$c_t^M = e^{-0.04(150/365)}\$75\,(0.695430) - \$70\,e^{-0.09(150/365)}\,(0.612906) = \$9.96$

$p_t^M = \$70\,e^{-0.09(150/365)}\,(0.387094) - \$75\,e^{-0.04(150/365)}\,(0.304570) = \$3.64$

12. From the text, we have:

$$P_{TB} = 1 - 0.01\left(\frac{B + A}{2}\right)\left(\frac{\text{Days Until Maturity}}{360}\right)$$

$$= 1 - 0.01\left(\frac{9.43 + 9.37}{2}\right)\left(\frac{173}{360}\right)$$

$$= 0.9548$$

Therefore, the price of the bill is 95.48 percent of par. To find the corresponding continuously compounded rate, we solve the following equation for r:

$$e^{r(T - t)} = 1/P_{TB}$$
$$e^{r(173/365)} = 1./0.9548$$
$$r = 0.0962$$

Thus, the continuously compounded rate on the bill is 9.62 percent.

13. Let P_t = the price on day t, $PR_t = P_t/P_{t-1}$, PR_μ = the mean daily logarithmic return, and σ = the standard deviation of the daily logarithmic return. Then,

P_t	PR_t	$\ln(PR_t)$	$[\ln PR_t - PR_\mu]^2$
47			
49	1.0426	0.0417	0.000454
46	0.9388	-0.0632	0.006989
45	0.9783	-0.0219	0.001789
51	1.1333	0.1251	0.010962

$$PR_\mu = (0.0417 - 0.0632 - 0.0219 + 0.1251)/4 = 0.0204$$

$$\text{VAR}(PR) = (1/3)(0.000454 + 0.006989 +$$
$$0.001789 + 0.010962) = 0.006731.$$

σ = the square root of $0.006731 = 0.082045$.
The annualized $\sigma = \sigma$ times the square root of $250 = 1.2972$.

14. $\sigma = 0.332383$. It is also possible to find this value by repeated application of the Black–Scholes formula. For example, with this option data, different trial values of σ give the following sequence of prices:

Call Price:	Trial Value of σ:	σ is:
$6.29	0.1	too low
9.84	0.5	too high
7.67	0.3	too low
8.72	0.4	too high
8.18	0.35	too high
7.98	0.33	too low
8.03	0.335	too high
8.01	0.333	too high
8.00	0.332	very close

15. Note that $0.5 (1.09) + 0.5 (0.91) = 1.0$, so the expected return on the stock is zero. The expected return on the stock must equal the risk-free rate in the risk-neutral setting of the binomial model. Therefore, these up and down factors imply a zero interest rate.

16. With no dividends, the call price is $27.54, and the put price is $3.67. With the known dividend adjustment, the call price is $25.14, and the put price is $4.23.

17. The call price is $5.80, and the put price is $6.38. $U = 1.0969$, and $D = 0.9116$.

$$\pi_U = \frac{e^{0.11\left(\frac{50}{365}\right)} - 0.9116}{1.0969 - 0.9116} = 0.5590$$

18. Recalling that these are European options, the call is worth $4.66, and the put is worth $7.14.

19. The call is worth $4.62, and the put is worth $7.16.

20. The apparent contradiction arises because the intrinsic value of the put is $75 - $65.59 = $9.41, which exceeds the put price of $8.84.

However, because this is a European put, it cannot be exercised to capture the intrinsic value prior to expiration. Thus, the European put price can be less than the intrinsic value.

21. One of the arbitrage conditions we have considered says that the call price must equal or exceed $S - X$. In this situation, $S - X = \$88.35 - \$75.00 = \$13.35$, which is greater than the call price of $12.94. Thus, it appears that an arbitrage opportunity exists. The apparent contradiction dissolves when we realize that the call price reflects the dividend that will occur before the option can be exercised.

CHAPTER 5: OPTIONS SENSITIVITIES AND OPTIONS HEDGING

1.
$$c = \$1.82$$
$$\text{DELTA} = 0.2735$$
$$\text{GAMMA} = 0.0279$$
$$\text{THETA} = -8.9173$$
$$\text{VEGA} = 9.9144$$
$$\text{RHO} = 3.5985$$

2.
$$p = \$10.79$$
$$\text{DELTA} = -0.7265$$
$$\text{GAMMA} = 0.0279$$
$$\text{THETA} = -4.7790$$
$$\text{VEGA} = 9.9144$$
$$\text{RHO} = -13.4083$$

3.   price $= c + p = \$12.61$
$$\text{DELTA} = 0.2735 - 0.7265 = -0.4530$$
$$\text{GAMMA} = 0.0279 + 0.0279 = 0.0558$$
$$\text{THETA} = -8.9173 - 4.47790 = -13.6963$$
$$\text{VEGA} = 9.9144 + 9.9144 = 19.8288$$
$$\text{RHO} = 3.5985 - 13.4083 = -9.8098$$

4. As we saw for this call, DELTA = 0.2735. The DELTA-neutral portfolio, given a short call component is 0.2735 shares − 1 call, costs:

$$0.2735 \ (\$60) - \$1.82 = \$14.59$$

If the stock price goes to $55, the call price is $0.77, and the portfolio will be worth:

$$0.2735 \ (\$55) - \$0.77 = \$14.27$$

With a stock price of $65, the call is worth $3.55, and the portfolio value is:

$$0.2735 \ (\$65) - \$3.55 = \$14.23$$

Notice that the portfolio values are lower for both stock prices of $55 and $65, reflecting the negative GAMMA of the portfolio.

5. The DELTA of the portfolio is $-1.0 = -0.2735 - 0.7265$. This is necessarily true, because the DELTA of the call is $N(d_1)$, the DELTA of the put is $N(-d_2)$, and $N(d_1) + N(d_2) = 1.0$. If a long share of stock is added to the portfolio, the DELTA will be zero, because the DELTA of a share is always 1.0.

6. The GAMMA of a share of stock is always zero. All other information in the question is irrelevant. The GAMMA of a share is always zero because the DELTA of a share is always 1.0. As GAMMA measures how DELTA changes, there is nothing to measure for a stock since the DELTA is always 1.0.

7. As observed in Problem 1, for Call A, $c = \$1.82$, DELTA $= 0.2735$, and THETA $= -8.9173$. For Call B, $c = \$11.64$, DELTA $= 0.8625$, and THETA $= -7.7191$. The long bull spread with calls consists of buying the call with the lower exercise price (Call B) and selling the call with the higher exercise price (Call A). The spread costs $11.64 - \$1.82 = \$9.82$. The DELTA of the spread equals DELTA$_B$ − DELTA$_A$ = $0.8625 - 0.2735 = 0.5890$. If the stock price is $60 at expiration, Call B will be worth $10, and Call A will expire worthless. If the stock price remains at $60, the value of the spread will have to move from $9.82 now to $10.00 at expiration, so the THETA for the spread must be positive. This can be confirmed by computing the two THETAs and noting: THETA$_A$ = -8.9173 and THETA$_B$ = -7.7191. For the spread, we buy Call B and sell Call A, giving a THETA for the spread of $-7.7191 - (-8.9173) = 1.1982$.

8. The presence of a continuous dividend makes d_1 smaller than it otherwise would be, because the continuous dividend rate, δ, is subtracted in the numerator of d_1. With a smaller d_1, $N(d_1)$ is also

smaller. But, $N(d_1)$ = DELTA for a call, so the DELTA of a call will be smaller with a dividend present. By the same reasoning, the DELTA of the put must increase.

Sensitivity	C2	P2
DELTA	0.5794	−0.4060
GAMMA	0.0182	0.0182
THETA	−10.3343	−5.5997
VEGA	26.93	26.93
RHO	23.9250	−23.4823

9.

Measure	Call C	Call D	Call E
Price	$11.40	$7.16	$4.60
DELTA	0.9416	0.8088	0.6018
GAMMA	0.0147	0.0343	0.0421

For a DELTA-neutral portfolio comprised of Calls C and D that is long one Call C, we must choose a position of Z shares of Call D to satisfy the following equation:

$$0.9416 + 0.8088\ Z = 0$$

Therefore, $Z = -1.1642$, and the portfolio consists of purchasing one Call C and selling 1.1642 units of Call D.

To form a portfolio of Calls C, D, and E that is long one Call C and that is also DELTA-neutral and GAMMA-neutral, the portfolio must meet both of the following conditions, where Y and Z are the number of Call Cs and Call Ds, respectively.

DELTA-neutrality: $0.9416 + 0.8088\ Y + 0.6018\ Z = 0$
GAMMA-neutrality: $0.0147 + 0.0343\ Y + 0.0421\ Z = 0$

Multiplying the second equation by $(0.8088/0.0343)$ gives:

$$0.3466 + 0.8088\ Y + 0.9927\ Z = 0$$

Subtracting this equation from the DELTA-neutrality equation gives:

$$0.5950 - 0.3909 \ Z = 0$$

Therefore, $Z = 1.5221$. Substituting this value of Z into the DELTA-neutrality equation gives:

$$0.8088 \ Y + 0.9416 + 0.6018 \ (1.5221) = 0$$

$Y = -2.2968$. Therefore, the DELTA-neutral and GAMMA-neutral portfolio consists of buying one unit of Call C, selling 2.2968 units of Call D, and buying 1.5221 units of Call E.

CHAPTER SIX: AMERICAN OPTIONS PRICING

1. An American option is just like a European option, except the American option carries the right of early exercise. Exercising a call before expiration discards the time value inherent in the option. The only offsetting benefit from early exercise arises from an attempt to capture a dividend. If there is no dividend, there is no incentive to early exercise, so the early exercise feature of an American call on a nondividend stock has no value.

2. The exercise value of a put is $X - S$. On a European put, this value cannot be captured until the expiration date. Therefore, before expiration the value of the European put will be a function of the present value of these exercise proceeds: $e^{-r(T-t)}(X - S)$. The American put gives immediate access at any time to the full proceeds, $X - S$, through exercise. In certain circumstances, notably on puts that are deep-in-the-money with time remaining until expiration, this differential in exercise conditions can give the American put extra value over the corresponding European put, even in the absence of dividends.

3. Early exercise of an American put provides the holder with an immediate cash inflow of $X - S$. These proceeds can earn a return from the date of exercise to the expiration date that is not available on a European put. However, early exercise discards the time value of the put. Therefore, the early exercise decision requires trading off the sacrificed time value against the interest that can be earned by investing the exercise value from the date of exercise to the expiration date of the put. For deep-in-the-money puts with time remaining until expiration, the potential interest gained can exceed the time value of the put that is sacrificed.

4. The key factor is an approaching dividend, and exercise of an American call should occur only at the moment before an ex-dividend

date. The dividend must be "large" relative to the share price, and the call will typically also be deep-in-the-money.

5. Dividends make early exercise of an American put less likely. Dividends decrease the stock price and increase the exercise value of the put. Thus, the holder of the American put has an incentive to delay exercising and wait for the dividend payments.

6. Dividends increase the likelihood of early exercise on an American call. In fact, if there are no dividends on the underlying stock, early exercise of an American call is irrational.

7. In pseudo-American call pricing, the analysis treats the stock price as the current stock price reduced by the present value of all dividends to occur before the option expires. It then considers potential exercise just prior to each ex-dividend date, by reducing the exercise price by the present value of all dividends to be paid, including the imminent dividend. (The dividends are a reduction from the exercise price because they represent a cash inflow if the option is exercised.) For each dividend date, the analysis values a European option using the Black–Scholes model. The pseudo–American price is the maximum of these European option prices. Implicitly, the pricing strategy assumes exercise on the date that gives the highest European option price.

8. First, notice that the second dividend is scheduled to be paid in 130 days, after the option expires. Therefore, the second dividend cannot affect the option price and it may be disregarded. To apply the pseudo-American model, we begin by subtracting the present value of the dividend from the stock price to form the adjusted stock price:

$$\text{Adjusted stock price} = \$140 - \$2\, e^{-0.10(40/365)} = \$138.02$$

For the single dividend date, we reduce the exercise price by the $2 of dividend so the adjusted exercise price is $148. Applying the Black–Scholes model with $S = \$138.02$, $E = \$148$, $T - t = 40$ days, gives a price of $4.05. Applying the Black–Scholes model with $S = \$138.02$, $E = \$150$, $T - t = 100$, gives a price of $8.29. The higher price, $8.29, is the pseudo-American option price.

9. Yes. Once we notice that the second dividend falls beyond the expiration date of the option, the exact American model fits exactly and gives a price of $8.28, almost the same as the pseudo-American price of $8.29.

10. The exact American model applies to call options on stocks with a single dividend occurring before the option expires. Early exercise

of an American call is optimal only at the ex-dividend date. At the ex–dividend date, the holder of an American call has a choice: exercise and own the stock or do not exercise and hold what is then equivalent to a European option that expires at the original expiration date of the American call. (The option that results from not exercising is equivalent to a European call because there are no more dividends occurring before expiration.) Thus, the exact American call model recognizes that the call embodies an option to own a European option at the dividend date. It also embodies the right to acquire the stock at the stated exercise price at the ex-dividend date.

11. The bivariate cumulative distribution considers the probability of two standardized normal variates having values equal to or below a certain threshold at the same time given a certain correlation between the two. Consider first a univariate standardized normal variate. The probability of its value being zero or less equals the chance that it is below its mean of zero, which is 50 percent. Considering two such variates, with a zero correlation between them, the probability that both have a value of zero or less equals $0.5 \times 0.5 = 0.25$. If the two variables had a correlation other than zero, this probability would be different.

12. The exact American model uses the cumulative bivariate standardized normal distribution, which considers the correlation between a pair of variates. The formula, for example, evaluates the probability of not exercising and the option finishing in the money, and of not exercising and the option finishing out of the money. If there were more dividends, the bivariate distribution would be inadequate to handle all of the possible combinations and higher multivariate normal distributions would have to be considered. For these, no solution has yet been found.

13. The critical stock price, S^*, is the stock price that makes the call owner indifferent regarding exercise at the ex-dividend date. If the option is not exercised at the ex-dividend date, the American call effectively becomes a European call and the value is simply given by the Black–Scholes model. If the owner exercises, he receives the stock price, plus the dividend, less the exercise price. Therefore, where D_1 is the dividend, the critical stock price makes the following equation hold:

$$S^* + D_1 - X = \text{European call}$$

14. Both models pertain to underlying goods with a continuous dividend rate.

15. The critical stock price is the stock price that makes the owner of an American call indifferent regarding exercise. If the stock price exceeds the critical stock price, the owner should exercise. Otherwise, the option should not be exercised.

16. If the stock price exceeds the critical stock price, the owner should exercise to capture the exercise proceeds. These can be invested to earn a return from the date of exercise to the expiration of the option. The critical stock price is the price at which the benefits of earning that interest just equal the costs of discarding the time value of the option. If the stock price exceeds the critical stock price, the potential interest proceeds are worth more than the time value of the option, and the option should be exercised.

17. $U = 1.1215; D = 0.8917; \pi_U = 0.5073$. The American call is worth $18.93, while the American put is worth $5.48. The American call should not be exercised at any time; there is no dividend. The put should be exercised if the stock price drops three straight times from $120.00 to $85.07. Then the exercisable proceeds would be $24.93, but the corresponding European put would be worth only $24.03. The asterisk in the options tree indicates a node at which exercise should occur.

Stock Price Lattice for Problem 17

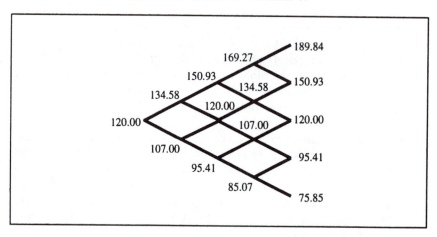

Call Price Lattice for Problem 17

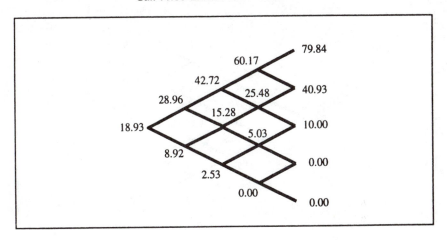

Put Price Lattice for Problem 17

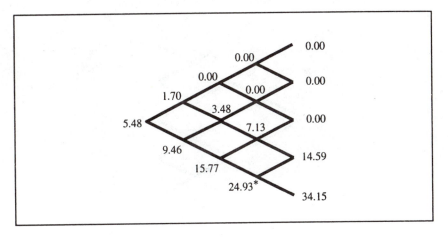

18. $U = 1.1215$; $D = 0.8917$; $\pi_U = 0.5073$. The call is worth $16.14, and the put is worth $6.28. The call should never be exercised. The put should be exercised if the stock price drops three straight times to $82.52. This gives exercisable proceeds of $27.48, compared to a computed value of $26.58. The asterisk in the options tree indicates a node at which exercise should occur.

Stock Price Lattice for Problem 18

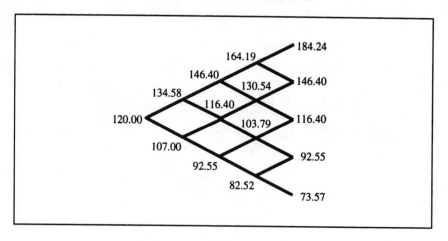

Call Price Lattice for Problem 18

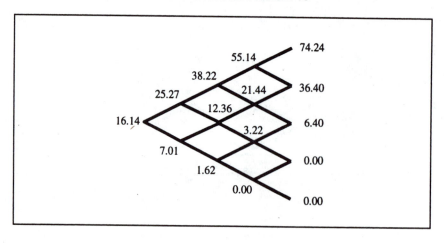

Put Price Lattice for Problem 18

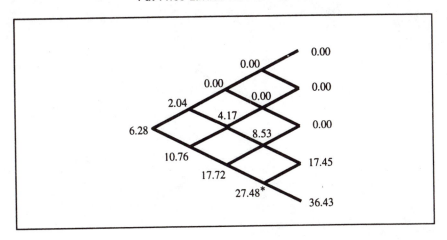

19. $U = 1.1215$; $D = 0.8917$; $\pi_U = 0.5073$. The call is worth $16.63, while the put is worth $6.14. The call should never be exercised. The put should be exercised if the stock price drops three straight times to $82.97. This gives exercisable proceeds of $27.03, which exceeds the computed value of $26.13. The asterisk in the options tree indicates a node at which exercise should occur.

Stock Price Lattice for Problem 19

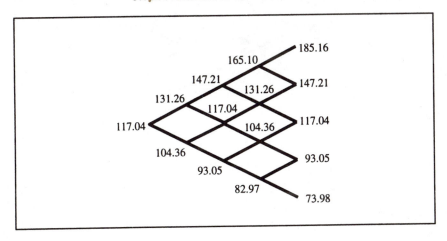

Adjusted Stock Price Lattice for Problem 19

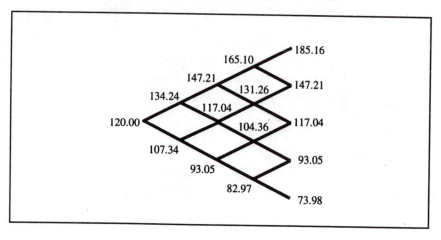

Call Price Lattice for Problem 19

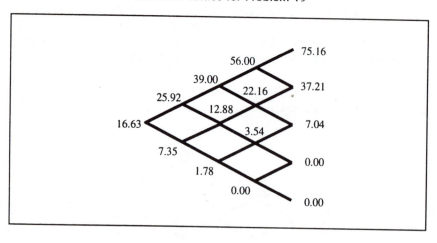

Put Price Lattice for Problem 19

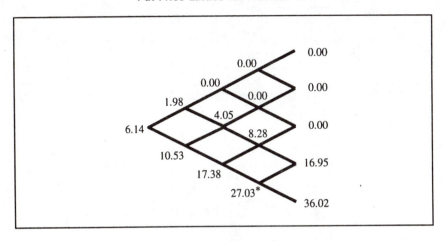

20. For the call, the critical price is $S^* = \$604.08$. For the put, the critical price is $S^{**} = \$103.88$. To verify that these critical prices are correct, we need to show that they satisfy the following two equations.

Call: $S^* - X = c_t(S^*, X, T - t) + \{1 - e^{-\delta(T - t)}N(d_1)\}(S^*/q_2)$

Put: $X - S^{**} = p_t(S^{**}, X, T - t) - [1 - e^{-\delta(T - t)}N(-d_1)](S^{**}/q_1)$

$$q_1 = \frac{1 - n - \sqrt{(n - 1)^2 + 4k}}{2}$$

$$q_2 = \frac{1 - n + \sqrt{(n - 1)^2 + 4k}}{2}$$

$$n = \frac{2(r - \delta)}{\sigma^2}, \quad k = \frac{2r}{\sigma^2(1 - e^{-r(T - t)})}$$

With these values:

$$n = 2(0.12 - 0.03)/(0.3 \times 0.3) = 2.00$$

$$k = (2 \times 0.12)/[0.3 \times 0.3(1 - 0.9425)] = 0.24/0.0052 = 46.4082$$

$$q_1 = \frac{1 - 2 - \sqrt{(2-1)^2 + 4(46.4082)}}{2} = -7.3307$$

$$q_2 = \frac{1 - 2 + \sqrt{(2-1)^2 + 4(46.4082)}}{2} = 6.3307$$

For the call, evaluating d_1 at the critical price for the call, $604.08, gives $d_1 = 35.4167$:

$$d_1 = \frac{\ln\left(\dfrac{604.08}{130}\right) + [0.12 - 0.03 + 0.5(0.3)(0.3)]\left(\dfrac{180}{365}\right)}{0.3\sqrt{\dfrac{180}{365}}} = 35.4167$$

For the put, evaluating d_1 at the critical price for the put, $103.88, gives $d_1 = -0.7487$:

$$d_1 = \frac{\ln\left(\dfrac{103.88}{130}\right) + [0.12 - 0.03 + 0.5(0.3)(0.3)]\left(\dfrac{180}{365}\right)}{0.3\sqrt{\dfrac{180}{365}}} = -0.7487$$

For the call, $N(d_1) = N(35.4167) = 1.0000$, while for the put, $N(-d_1) = N(-27.0603) = 0.772981$. The prices of the corresponding European call and put, each evaluated at its critical price, are $472.68 and $22.74, respectively.

With these values, we now verify that the specified critical prices are correct. For the call:

$$604.08 - 130.00 = 474.08 = 472.68 + (0.0147)(604.08/6.3307)$$

For the put:

$$130.00 - 103.88 = 26.12 = 22.74 - (0.2384)(103.88/-7.3307)$$

21. Something is amiss. The critical price for a call must lie above the exercise price, while the critical price for a put must lie below the exercise price. Therefore, $90 might be the critical price for the put, but it cannot be the critical price for the call.

CHAPTER SEVEN: OPTIONS ON STOCK INDEXES, FOREIGN CURRENCY, AND FUTURES

1. For a stock, dividends represent a leakage of value from the asset. If dividends were not paid, the stock price would continue to grow at a higher rate, compounding the value of the dividends. The same is true for a currency. The interest rate paid by a currency represents a leakage of value from the currency. Therefore, dividends from common stock and interest payments from a currency can be treated in the same way for options pricing purposes.

2. For pricing options on futures, the important consideration is that the futures price follow the cost-of-carry relationship very closely. This adherence to the cost-of-carry model is much more important than the exact amount of the cost-of-carry. The options pricing model for futures does not work well if there is not an adherence to the cost-of-carry model. Thus, it is mainly a matter of convenience that we assume the cost-of-carry to equal the risk-free rate. In the real world, this assumption performs very well for financial futures, but it performs less well for futures on agricultural goods.

3. The text considers three types of dividend payments: constant proportional payments, occasional payments equal to a percentage of the asset value, and occasional payments of a fixed dollar amount. In every case, the presence of the dividend requires an adjustment in the stock price lattice. In essence, the nodes in the stock price lattice must be decreased by the present value of the dividends that will occur from the time represented by that node until the expiration of the option. Dividends occurring after the expiration date of the option play no role and may be disregarded. Once the stock price lattice has been adjusted to reflect the dividends, the corresponding lattice for the put or call can be worked through in the normal way to price the option correctly.

4. If the two have an identical price, it means that the early exercise feature of the American option has no value. Any difference in the prices will stem from the value associated with the early exercise privilege.

5.
$$U = e^{0.4\sqrt{1}} = 1.4918; \quad D = \frac{1}{U} = 0.6703$$

$$\pi_U = \frac{e^{(0.10 - 0.10)1} - 0.6703}{1.4918 - 0.6703} = 0.4013$$

The expected price movement is:

$$0.4013\ (1.4918) + 0.5987\ (0.6703) = 1.00$$

Thus, the futures price is not expected to change over the next year. In general, this will be true for futures. The futures price already impounds the expected price change in the asset between the current date and the expiration of the futures contract.

6. The prices in the following table show that the American call and put have no exercise potential. The difference between the Merton and Whaley model put prices, on the one hand, and the binomial model put prices, on the other, are due to the very few periods being employed.

	Merton Model	European Binomial	Whaley Model	American Binomial
Call	0.5104	0.5097	0.5104	0.5097
Put	0.0008	0	0.0008	0

7.
$$U = e^{0.2\sqrt{\frac{60}{365}}} = 1.0845; \quad D = \frac{1}{1.0845} = 0.9221$$

$$\pi_U = \frac{1.0116 - 0.9221}{1.0845 - 0.9221} = 0.5510$$

As the following price lattices show, the European and American calls are worth $19.19. The European put is worth $27.67, and the American put is worth $30.21.

Stock Price Lattice for Problem 7

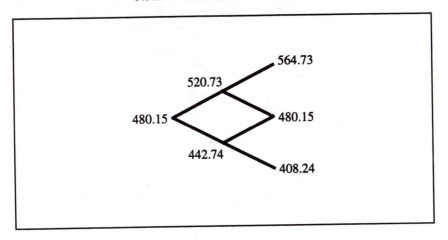

Adjusted Stock Price Lattice for Problem 7

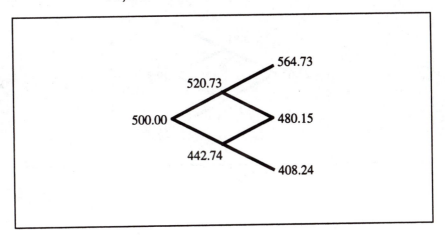

Call Price Lattice for Problem 7

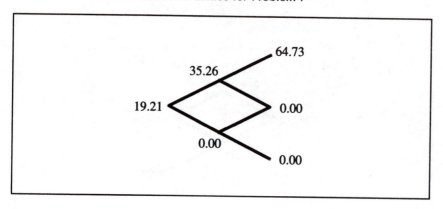

European Put Price Lattice for Problem 7

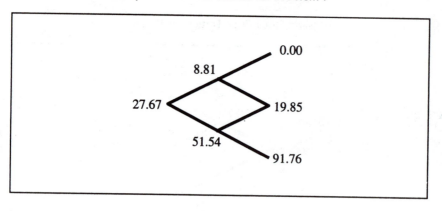

American Put Price Lattice for Problem 7

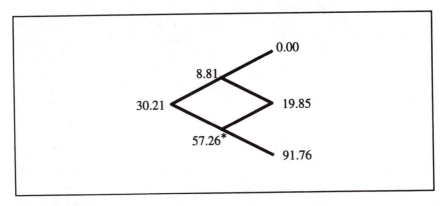

8. With $X = \$0.90$, the call is worth \$0.0640, and the put is worth \$0.1338. With $X = \$1.00$, the call is worth \$0.0392, and the put is worth \$0.2014. Comparing the ratio of the options prices to the ratio of exercise prices shows that the call is more sensitive to a change in the exercise price than is the put. A change of about 10 percent in the exercise price causes about a 63 percent change in the call price, but only about a 51 percent change in the put price.

CHAPTER EIGHT: THE OPTIONS APPROACH
TO CORPORATE SECURITIES

1. Common stock is like a call option on the entire firm. To see how this can be the case, consider a firm with a single bond issue outstanding and assume that the bond is a pure discount bond. When the bond matures, the common stockholders have a choice: They can pay the bondholders the promised payment or they can surrender the firm to the bondholders. If the firm is worth more than the amount due to the bondholders, the stock owners will pay the bondholders and keep the excess. If the firm is worth less than the amount due to the bondholders, the stock owners will abandon the firm to the bond owners.

In this situation, the amount due to the bond owners plays the role of the exercise price. The maturity date of the bond is the expiration date of the call option represented by the common stock. The common stock is like a call option. At expiration, the stock owners can exercise their call option by paying the claim of the bondholders (the exercise price). Upon exercising, the stockholders receive the underlying asset (the entire firm).

2. When the bond matures, the stock owners decide whether to pay the bonds or surrender the firm to the bond holders in lieu of payment. If the value of the firm exceeds the amount owed to the bond owners, $1,000,000, the bond holders receive full payment and the stock owners retain the excess. If the firm's value is less than the promised payment, the stock owners abandon the firm and the bondholders receive a payment equal to the value of the entire firm. However, by hypothesis, this is less than the promised payment of $1,000,000. This pattern of payment is like the payments on a short put position with an exercise price that equals the face value of the bond. However, a short position in a put can give a payoff at expiration that is negative. This is not true of a bond. The worst payoff for the bond is zero. Therefore, the payoff has the same pattern as a short position in a put with an exercise price that equals the face value of the bond plus a long position in a riskless bond.

3. The $1,000,000 value of the firm equals the sum of the stock and bond values. As the outstanding stock is worth $700,000, the bonds must be worth $300,000. Therefore, the interest rate is 5.24 percent. If the volatility of the firm's cash flows increases, the total value of the firm will not change. However, because the common stock can be analyzed as a call option on the firm, the value of the common stock must increase. This means that the value of the bonds must decrease. If the bond value decreases, its yield must increase. This makes sense, because the bonds should be worth less if the firm's cash flows become more risky.

4. Assuming that the managers perform in the interest of their shareholders, they must make the decision that increases the value of the stock. As the stock represents a call option on the total firm value, the managers should prefer the higher operating leverage/higher operating risk strategy.

5. For the senior debtholders to receive some payment, the value of the firm must exceed zero. For the subordinated debtholders to receive some payment, the value of the firm must exceed the total owed to the senior debtholders. For the common stockholders to receive any payment, the value of the firm must exceed the amount owed on both classes of debt. If the managers perform in the interest of the stockholders, the mere presence of two classes of debt does not suggest a change in operating policy. The stockholders get paid only after all the bondholders are paid, so it does not matter to the stockholders how the debt is split up, but only how much the total amount of debt payments is. Given that the junior debtholders have already purchased the junior debt, they are (by revealed preference)

more risk tolerant than the holders of the senior debt. However, increasing operating risk transfers wealth away from bondholders to stockholders. Thus, the junior debtholders would probably prefer a low-risk operating strategy if funds would be certain to sufficiently cover their holdings. However, consider an operating policy that would only generate enough cash to pay the senior debtholders. In this situation, it is clear that the junior debtholders would prefer a more risky operating policy that might give sufficient payoffs to repay their obligations.

6. The stockholders should wait until the maturity date. The stockholders' situation here is analogous to a call on a nondividend stock. Early payment of the bond discards the time premium inherent in the option they hold.

7. If the common stock pays no dividend, the bondholders should not exercise until the last possible date. However, if the stock pays a sufficiently large dividend, it might pay the bondholders to convert earlier. The bondholder holds a call option on the firm's shares. If those shares pay dividends, then they are leaking value. The bondholders must decide whether it is worthwhile to discard the time premium in favor of securing the dividend. This is exactly analogous to the problem faced by the holder of an American call option on a dividend paying stock.

8. If a manager holds warrants, and the value of these warrants is large relative to other forms of compensation, the manager will focus on maximizing the value of the firm at the expiration date of the warrants. This incentive might be incompatible with making decisions that will increase the value of the firm at other dates. For example, if markets are not perfect, then the value of the shares might not fully reflect a good decision to make a large capital budgeting outlay. Therefore, the manager might forgo the investment in order to enhance the share price on the critical date for the manager.

Appendix

Cumulative Distribution Function for the Standard Normal Random Variable

	.00	.01	.02	.03	.04	.05	.06	.07	.08	.09
0.0	.5000	.5040	.5080	.5120	.5160	.5199	.5239	.5279	.5319	.5359
0.1	.5398	.5438	.5478	.5517	.5557	.5596	.5636	.5675	.5714	.5753
0.2	.5793	.5832	.5871	.5910	.5948	.5987	.6026	.6064	.6103	.6141
0.3	.6179	.6217	.6255	.6293	.6331	.6368	.6406	.6443	.6480	.6517
0.4	.6554	.6591	.6628	.6664	.6700	.6736	.6772	.6808	.6844	.6879
0.5	.6915	.6950	.6985	.7019	.7054	.7088	.7123	.7157	.7190	.7224
0.6	.7257	.7291	.7324	.7357	.7389	.7422	.7454	.7486	.7517	.7549
0.7	.7580	.7611	.7642	.7673	.7704	.7734	.7764	.7794	.7823	.7852
0.8	.7881	.7910	.7939	.7967	.7995	.8023	.8051	.8078	.8106	.8133
0.9	.8159	.8186	.8212	.8238	.8264	.8289	.8315	.8340	.8365	.8389
1.0	.8413	.8438	.8461	.8485	.8508	.8531	.8554	.8577	.8599	.8621
1.1	.8643	.8665	.8686	.8708	.8729	.8749	.8770	.8790	.8810	.8830
1.2	.8849	.8869	.8888	.8907	.8925	.8944	.8962	.8980	.8997	.9015
1.3	.9032	.9049	.9066	.9082	.9099	.9115	.9131	.9147	.9162	.9177
1.4	.9192	.9207	.9222	.9236	.9251	.9265	.9279	.9292	.9306	.9319
1.5	.9332	.9345	.9357	.9370	.9382	.9394	.9406	.9418	.9429	.9441
1.6	.9452	.9463	.9474	.9484	.9495	.9505	.9515	.9525	.9535	.9545
1.7	.9554	.9564	.9573	.9582	.9591	.9599	.9608	.9616	.9625	.9633
1.8	.9641	.9649	.9656	.9664	.9671	.9678	.9686	.9693	.9699	.9706
1.9	.9713	.9719	.9726	.9732	.9738	.9744	.9750	.9756	.9761	.9767
2.0	.9772	.9778	.9783	.9788	.9793	.9798	.9803	.9808	.9812	.9817
2.1	.9821	.9826	.9830	.9834	.9838	.9842	.9846	.9850	.9854	.9857
2.2	.9861	.9864	.9868	.9871	.9875	.9878	.9881	.9884	.9887	.9890
2.3	.9893	.9896	.9898	.9901	.9904	.9906	.9909	.9911	.9913	.9916
2.4	.9918	.9920	.9922	.9925	.9927	.9929	.9931	.9932	.9934	.9936
2.5	.9938	.9940	.9941	.9943	.9945	.9946	.9948	.9949	.9951	.9952
2.6	.9953	.9955	.9956	.9957	.9959	.9960	.9961	.9962	.9963	.9964
2.7	.9965	.9966	.9967	.9968	.9969	.9970	.9971	.9972	.9973	.9974
2.8	.9974	.9975	.9976	.9977	.9977	.9978	.9979	.9979	.9980	.9981
2.9	.9981	.9982	.9982	.9983	.9984	.9984	.9985	.9985	.9986	.9986
3.0	.9987	.9987	.9987	.9988	.9988	.9989	.9989	.9989	.9990	.9990
3.1	.9990	.9991	.9991	.9991	.9992	.9992	.9992	.9992	.9993	.9993
3.2	.9993	.9993	.9994	.9994	.9994	.9994	.9994	.9995	.9995	.9995
3.3	.9995	.9995	.9995	.9996	.9996	.9996	.9996	.9996	.9996	.9997
3.4	.9997	.9997	.9997	.9997	.9997	.9997	.9997	.9997	.9997	.9998

Index